Translational Bioinformatics
in Healthcare and Medicine

ADVANCES IN UBIQUITOUS SENSING APPLICATIONS FOR HEALTHCARE 13

Translational Bioinformatics in Healthcare and Medicine

Volume 13

Edited by

Khalid Raza
Assistant Professor, Department of Computer Science,
Jamia Millia Islamia (Central University), India

Nilanjan Dey
Associate Professor, JIS University, Kolkata, India

Series Editors

Nilanjan Dey

Amira S. Ashour

Simon James Fong

ACADEMIC PRESS
An imprint of Elsevier

ELSEVIER

Academic Press is an imprint of Elsevier
125 London Wall, London EC2Y 5AS, United Kingdom
525 B Street, Suite 1650, San Diego, CA 92101, United States
50 Hampshire Street, 5th Floor, Cambridge, MA 02139, United States
The Boulevard, Langford Lane, Kidlington, Oxford OX5 1GB, United Kingdom

Notices

Knowledge and best practice in this field are constantly changing. As new research and experience broaden our understanding, changes in research methods, professional practices, or medical treatment may become necessary.

Practitioners and researchers must always rely on their own experience and knowledge in evaluating and using any information, methods, compounds, or experiments described herein. In using such information or methods they should be mindful of their own safety and the safety of others, including parties for whom they have a professional responsibility.

To the fullest extent of the law, neither the Publisher, nor the authors, contributors, or editors, assume any liability for any injury and/or damage to persons or property as a matter of products liability, negligence or otherwise, or from any use or operation of any methods, products, instructions, or ideas contained in the material herein.

Library of Congress Cataloging-in-Publication Data
A catalog record for this book is available from the Library of Congress

British Library Cataloguing-in-Publication Data
A catalogue record for this book is available from the British Library

ISBN: 978-0-323-89824-9

For information on all Academic Press publications visit our website at
https://www.elsevier.com/books-and-journals

Publisher: Stacy Masucci
Senior Acquisitions Editor: Rafael E. Teixeira
Senior Editorial Project Manager: Susan Ikeda
Production Project Manager: Niranjan Bhaskaran
Cover Designer: Matthew Limbert

Typeset by TNQ Technologies

Jamia Millia Islamia (Central University), New Delhi (India), completed 100 years on October 29, 2020. On the occasion of the centenary celebration, *this volume is dedicated to all the founders, forefathers, teachers, researchers, students, staff, and other stakeholders of Jamia Millia Islamia for their selfless and valuable contributions*.

Contents

5. A review of a hybrid IoT-NG-PON system for translational bio-informatics in healthcare

Meet Kumari, Reecha Sharma and Anu Sheetal

6. IoT applications in translational bioinformatics

Rejaul Karim Barbhuiya and Naeem Ahmad

7. Blockchain technology in healthcare: making digital healthcare reliable, more accurate, and revolutionary

Md Tauseef Alam and Khalid Raza

8. Integrity promised: leveraging blockchain technology for medical image sharing

S. Sridevi, S. Vishnuvardhan, B. Vinoth Kumar, G.R. Karpagam and P. Sivakumar

9. From molecules to patients: the clinical applications of biological databases and electronic health records

Ayyagari Ramlal, Shaban Ahmad, Laxman Kumar, Fatima Nazish Khan and Rubina Chongtham

10. Translational bioinformatics methods for drug discovery and drug repurposing

Salim Ahmad, Sahar Qazi and Khalid Raza

Contributors

Kayode I. Adenuga, Faculty of Enterprise, Creative and Professional Studies, Farnborough College of Technology, Hampshire, United Kingdom

Nadia Ahmad, Department of Biotechnology and Bioinformatics, Jaypee University of Information Technology, Waknaghat, Himachal Pradesh, India

Salim Ahmad, Department of Computer Science, Jamia Millia Islamia, New Delhi, Delhi, India

Naeem Ahmad, Department of Computer Applications, Madanapalle Institute of Technology and Science, Madanapalle, Andhra Pradesh, India

Shaban Ahmad, Department of Computer Science, Jamia Millia Islamia, New Delhi, Delhi, India

Sarra Akermi, Annotations Analytics Pvt Ltd., Gurgaon, Haryana, India

Afroj Alam, Department of Computer Application, Integral University, Lucknow, Uttar Pradesh, India

Md Tauseef Alam, Department of Computer Science, Jamia Millia Islamia, New Delhi, Delhi, India

Rangel Arthur, Faculty of Technology (FT), State University of Campinas (UNICAMP), Limeira, São Paulo, Brazil

Rejaul Karim Barbhuiya, National Council of Educational Research and Training, New Delhi, Delhi, India

Anam Beg, Department of Computer Science, Jamia Millia Islamia, New Delhi, Delhi, India

Rubina Chongtham, Department of Botany, Deshbandhu College, University of Delhi, New Delhi, Delhi, India

Mohinikanti Das, Department of Botany, College of Basic Science & Humanities, Orissa University of Agriculture and Technology, Bhubaneswar, Odisha, India

Rutumbara Dash, School of Life Sciences, Sambalpur University, Burla, Odisha, India

Reinaldo Padilha França, School of Electrical Engineering and Computing (FEEC), State University of Campinas (UNICAMP), Campinas, São Paulo, Brazil

Ekta Gandotra, Department of Computer Science & Engineering and Information Technology (CSE & IT), Jaypee University of Information Technology, Waknaghat, Himachal Pradesh, India

E.J. Garba, Computer Science Department, Modibbo Adama University of Technology, Yola, Adamawa State, Nigeria

A.B. Garko, Computer Science Department Federal University Dutse, Jigawa State, Nigeria

Rajesh Kumar Gazara, Laboratório de Química e Função de Proteínas e Peptídeos, Centro de Biociências e Biotecnologia, Universidade Estadual do Norte Fluminense Darcy Ribeiro, Campos dos Goytacazes, Rio de Janeiro, Brazil

Arabinda Ghosh, Department of Botany, Guwahati University, Assam, Guwahati, India

Yuzo Iano, School of Electrical Engineering and Computing (FEEC), State University of Campinas (UNICAMP), Campinas, São Paulo, Brazil

Nor Syahidatul Nadiah Ismail, Faculty of Computing, Universiti Malaysia Pahang, Pekan, Pahang, Malaysia

Sunil Jayant, Annotations Analytics Pvt Ltd., Gurgaon, Haryana, India

Surabhi Johari, School of Biosciences Institute of Management Studies Ghaziabad (University Courses), Uttar Pradesh, India

G.R. Karpagam, PSG College of Technology, Coimbatore, Tamil Nadu, India

Fatima Nazish Khan, Department of Computer Science, Jamia Millia Islamia, New Delhi, Delhi, India

Laxman Kumar, Department of Botany, Jamia Hamdard, New Delhi, Delhi, India

Narendra Kumar, Department of Biotechnology and Bioinformatics, Jaypee University of Information Technology, Waknaghat, Himachal Pradesh, India

Meet Kumari, Department of Electronics and Communication Engineering, Punjabi University, Patiala, Punjab, India

Aina Umairah Mazlan, Faculty of Computing, Universiti Malaysia Pahang, Pekan, Pahang, Malaysia

Piyus Mohanty, Department of Biotechnology and Bioinformatics, Jaypee University of Information Technology, Waknaghat, Himachal Pradesh, India

Ana Carolina Borges Monteiro, School of Electrical Engineering and Computing (FEEC), State University of Campinas (UNICAMP), Campinas, São Paulo, Brazil

L.J. Muhammad, Mathematics and Computer Science Department, Federal University of Kashere, Gombe State, Nigeria

N.D. Oye, Computer Science Department, Modibbo Adama University of Technology, Yola, Adamawa State, Nigeria

Manasa Kumar Panda, School of Life Sciences, Sambalpur University, Burla, Odisha, India; Environment & Sustainability Department, CSIR- IMMT, Bhubaneswar, Odisha, India

Rafat Parveen, Department of Computer Science, Jamia Millia Islamia, New Delhi, Delhi, India

Sahar Qazi, Department of Computer Science, Jamia Millia Islamia, New Delhi, Delhi, India

Ayyagari Ramlal, Department of Botany, University of Delhi, New Delhi, Delhi, India

Ismail Rashid, Computer Science Faculty, Bakhtar University, Kabul, Afghanistan

Khalid Raza, Department of Computer Science, Jamia Millia Islamia, New Delhi, Delhi, India

Muhammad Akmal Remli, Institute for Artificial Intelligence and Big Data, Universiti Malaysia Kelantan, Kota Bharu, Kelantan, Malaysia; Data Science Department, Universiti Malaysia Kelantan, Kota Bharu, Kelantan, Malaysia

Noor Azida Sahabudin, Faculty of Computing, Universiti Malaysia Pahang, Pekan, Pahang, Malaysia

Abhishek Sahu, School of Life Sciences, Sambalpur University, Burla, Odisha, India

Reecha Sharma, Department of Electronics and Communication Engineering, Punjabi University, Patiala, Punjab, India

Ashwani Sharma, Computational Centre, Rennes, France

Anu Sheetal, Department of Electronics and Communication Engineering, Guru Nanak Dev University, Gurdaspur, Punjab, India

Yengkhom Disco Singh, Department of Post Harvest Technology, College of Horticulture and Forestry, Central Agricultural University, Pasighat, Arunachal Pradesh, India

Subrata Sinha, Centre for Biotechnology and Bioinformatics Dibrugarh University, Assam, Dibrugarh, India

P. Sivakumar, PSG College of Technology, Coimbatore, Tamil Nadu, India

S. Sridevi, PSG College of Technology, Coimbatore, Tamil Nadu, India

Sandhya Verma, Shri Vaishnav Institute of Science, Shri Vaishnav Vidyapeeth Vishwavidyalaya, Indore, Madhya Pradesh, India

B. Vinoth Kumar, PSG College of Technology, Coimbatore, Tamil Nadu, India

S. Vishnuvardhan, PSG College of Technology, Coimbatore, Tamil Nadu, India

G.M. Wajiga, Computer Science Department, Modibbo Adama University of Technology, Yola, Adamawa State, Nigeria

About the Editors

Khalid Raza is an assistant professor at the Department of Computer Science, Jamia Millia Islamia (Central University), New Delhi. Dr. Raza has been honored with "ICCR Chair Visiting Professor" by the Indian Council for Cultural Relation (ICCR), Ministry of Foreign Affairs, Government of India, and deputed at the faculty of Computer and Information Sciences, Ain Shams University, Cairo, Egypt. He has over 10 years of teaching and research experience in the field of translational bioinformatics and computational intelligence applications in healthcare. He has contributed over 70 research articles in reputed journals and edited books. He has authored and edited books with reputed publishers. He has reviewed over 150 research articles for reputed journals and conferences in the last 5 years. Dr. Raza has delivered several keynote addresses, invited talks, public lectures, and seminars in national and international conferences, workshops, and chaired technical sessions at various conferences. He has served as the technical program committee member of several international conferences and workshops. He has also executed two Indian government-funded research projects. Dr. Raza is a member of several professional bodies. His research interests include translational bioinformatics, computational intelligence methods, and applications in bioinformatics and health-informatics.

Nilanjan Dey is an associate professor, Department of Computer Science and Engineering, JIS University, Kolkata, India. He is a visiting fellow of the University of Reading, UK. He was an honorary visiting scientist at Global Biomedical Technologies, Inc., CA, USA (2012−15). He was awarded his PhD from Jadavpur University in 2015. He has authored and edited more than 70 books with Elsevier, Wiley, CRC Press, and Springer, and published more than 300 papers. He is the editor in chief of the International Journal of Ambient Computing and Intelligence, IGI Global, associated editor of IEEE Access, and International Journal of Information Technology, Springer. He is the series co-editor of Springer Tracts in Nature-Inspired Computing, Springer, series co-editor of Advances in Ubiquitous Sensing Applications for Healthcare, Elsevier, and series editor of Computational Intelligence in Engineering Problem Solving and Intelligent Signal Processing and Data Analysis, CRC. His main research interests include medical imaging, machine learning, computer-aided diagnosis, data mining, etc. He is the Indian ambassador of the International Federation for Information Processing, Young ICT Group, and senior member of IEEE.

Preface

Modern biologic experiments, including high-throughput measurement techniques such as next-generation sequencing and microarray technologies, have generated massive amounts of biologic data, giving rise to various biologic databases. These databases are valuable resources and tools for various stakeholders including but not limited to biologists, clinicians, bioinformaticians, and healthcare professionals. Translational bioinformatics is an emerging field of studies that involves the development of storage, analytics, and sophisticated computational methods to transform voluminous biomedical data into proactive, predictive, preventative, and participatory healthcare. The final product of translation bioinformatics is newly discovered knowledge that can be disseminated to a variety of fields including healthcare and medicine. Further, in the era of interdisciplinary and multidisciplinary sciences, such as bio-informatics, chemo-informatics, health-informatics, viro-informatics, drug-informatics, and so on, it is difficult for the target audience to find a single resource covering various aspects of informatics related to healthcare and medicine.

Translational Bioinformatics in Healthcare and Medicine, part of the Advances in Ubiquitous Sensing Application for Healthcare series, offers a detailed overview of translational bioinformatics, translational medicine in healthcare, precision medicine and personalized treatment, IoT and blockchain applications in healthcare, clinical applications of biologic databases and electronic health records, translational bioinformatics in drug discovery, drug repurposing and cancer research, viro-informatics and viral disease databases, machine learning applications in translational bioinformatics, and real-case applications of translational bioinformatics in healthcare and medicine.

This edited volume contains 18 chapters that bring together various aspects of translational bioinformatics in healthcare and medicine and bundle them as a unique resource of knowledge. Each chapter is reviewed by the editorial board for its originality, correctness, technical strength, presentation quality, interest to readers, and relevance to the theme of the book. It is not only a valuable resource for health educators, clinicians, and healthcare professionals but also graduate students of biology, biostatistics, biomedical sciences, bioinformatics, and interdisciplinary sciences.

Khalid Raza
Nilanjan Dey
(Editors)

Acknowledgments

The editors and contributors are very thankful to all the anonymous reviewers for their valuable expert comments and suggestions on the chapters. Special thanks go to the series editors, editorial project manager, publication and production manager, and other editorial staff members of Elsevier for their necessary support despite the ongoing COVID-19 pandemic.

Chapter 1

Translational bioinformatics in healthcare: past, present, and future

Sahar Qazi and Khalid Raza*

Department of Computer Science, Jamia Millia Islamia, New Delhi, Delhi, India

*Corresponding author: E-mail: kraza@jmi.ac.in

Chapter outline

1. Introduction

Bioinformatics is a multidisciplinary field of science that encapsulates biology, chemistry, physics, statistics, and computer science as base domains to solve complex biologic phenomenon. Bioinformatics is one of the magnanimously growing scientific fields that are very flexible. Thus, Nancy Lorenzi has defined bioinformatics as an "*amoeba — without any definite shape or size.*" The main purpose of bioinformatics is to store, analyze, and retrieve essential information about organisms that can in turn help understand the dynamics of such organisms. The term "*bioinformatics*" was coined by Paulien Hogeweg and Ben Hesper in 1970 (Hogeweg, 1978). Howbeit, the study of bioinformatics was initiated in the early 1950s by the leading pioneer and founder of bioinformatics as a subject, Margaret Oakley Dayhoff, also known as the "*mother and father of bioinformatics.*" Dayhoff worked in the application of mathematics and computational methods to the fields and applied them to biochemistry-based problems. She dexterously worked toward developing databases that stored vital information about the proteins and nucleic acids and also developed various tools for analysis (Hunt, 1983). *Point/Percent Accepted Mutations* (PAM) is one such substitution matrix devised by her to identify single (point) amino acid displacement in the primary structure or protein sequences accepted by the natural selection process. This matrix was meant to reduce the size of the data files describing the amino acid sequences (Pevsner, 2009). Bioinformatics has changed its definition since the 1950s to the 1970s through 2000s. Today, bioinformatics is much more than a simple analysis of proteins and nucleic acid sequences.

The basis of bioinformatics lies in the data provided and generated. The human body is made up of cells whose processing unit is DNA (deoxyribonucleic acid), which provides essential information about organisms and also aids in predicting the risk of diseases in the future. Previously, biologic sequence data was retrieved by doing traditional methods of sequencing, namely Sanger's sequencing, developed in the 1950s where Fredrick Sanger first sequenced insulin protein. However, since it was a tedious process to compare multiple sequences manually, Dayhoff developed the first protein sequence database and published her books about the same (Eck and Dayhoff, 1966). Current sequencing technologies, including Next Generation Sequencing (NGS) (Raza and Ahmad, 2019) and Nanopore Sequencing (Raza and Qazi, 2019), have generated a large amount of data. Another pioneer in bioinformatics origin was Elvin A. Kabat, who executed biologic sequence analysis in the 1970s along with his colleague Tai Te Wu, wherein they sequenced a variety of antibody sequences (Johnson and Wu, 2000). Over the past decades, we have grown in data magnanimously, which is now called *"big data,"* encapsulating the genome, transcriptome, proteome, metabolome, interactome, and others, some which are now organized into databases and analyzed for various purposes in healthcare management, personalized medicine (PM), finding drug targets, and drug discovery. The preliminary aims of bioinformatics are to develop an understanding of biologic phenomenon, disease mechanism, and develop hypotheses for treatment and therapeutics. The defining aspect of bioinformatics is its special focus on developing and employing computational tools to achieve this aim. For instance, many computationally intensive algorithms and techniques have been devised, namely, pattern identification, data mining, machine learning/deep learning (ML/DL), fuzzy logic, artificial intelligence (AI), etc. It entails the development of humongous databases and repositories, as well as algorithms, which can help to better our biologic tenets and to solve practical problems that arise due to the expanding data, its management, and analysis.

Major research domains of bioinformatics include *genomic/proteomic sequence analysis* (Wani and Raza, 2019a), *drug design* and *discovery* (Khatoon et al., 2019; Sahu et al., 2020a, b; Rai et al., 2020; Karwasra et al., 2020), *structural predictions* and *analysis*, *expression studies* (Raza, 2014, 2016a), and *interactome analysis* and *genome-wide association studies* (GWAS) (Raza, 2016b, 2019; Raza and Alam, 2016; Wani and Raza, 2019b, 2019c, 2021), leading to its transformation into *translational bioinformatics* that encapsulates an umbrella-wide range of subbranches such as genomics, proteomics, metabolomics, nutritionomics, evolutionary analysis, bioengineering, disease prediction, healthcare management, pharmacogenomics, drug discovery and designing, systems biology, cheminformatics, immunoinformatics, epigenformatics, network biology (Raza and Parveen, 2013a, b; Raza, 2017), mathematical model development (Kumar et al., 2019), model simulations, development of computational software and tools, and so on. With the advent and growth of computational sciences and their deployment in biologic sciences, translational bioinformatics has achieved a greater momentum in advancing in decoding critical diseases such as cancer and is a rapidly evolving field of bioinformatics that mainly focuses on health informatics to formulate knowledge and develop medical tools that can be deployed by researchers, medical practitioners, and the public to engage in person-centric healthcare management by employing computational systems to predict, diagnose, prognose, and manage diseases (Butte, 2008).

2. Origin of translational bioinformatics: a big leap

Translational bioinformatics (TBI) came in the limelight with the fulfilment of the Human Genome Project (HGP) (https://www.genome.gov/), a 13-year-long international project during 1990—2003 whose purpose was to discover the DNA sequence of the entire human genome. This field is still young and evolving compared to its ancestor bioinformatics. Google trends showcased that the use of the term *"bioinformatics"* has reduced drastically since the 1990s (Ouzounis, 2012). In its initial days, TBI was thought of as only concerned with data organization, accessibility, and analyzing medical data (Lesko, 2012), employed much as a secondary support system that had the potential to amalgamate biomedical information with decision-making processes. It was also thought that TBI was simply for ontology purposes searching the huge data stores. However, TBI has accomplished tremendous growth in integrating biomedical data with higher-order algorithms to link data, structures, and functions in networks (Ouzounis, 2012). With this, TBI achieved a successful appreciation and wide acceptance from the medical fraternity, researchers, and the general public. To see the leap in the trend line of both bioinformatics and TBI, we retrieved the number of publications published from the 1950s to 2020 based on the query term "bioinformatics" and between the 1980s and 2020 based on the query term "translational bioinformatics," searched in all fields from PubMed biomedical literature repository, which is plotted as a bar graph (Fig. 1.1). It is evident, though TBI grew to prominence in the early 2000s, that it has gained a lot of attention from researchers and medical consultants.

When the first draft of the HGP was accomplished in the 2000s, TBI grew magnanimously and acted as an overpass between bioinformatics and health informatics (Sarkar et al., 2011), paving a way for the concept of PMs and point of care (PoC) to become a reality. Fig. 1.2 represents the role of TBI as a traverse between bioinformatics and health informatics. Gene expression profiling, data mining for analysis of trends in healthcare, and pan-population-based data mining have been significant in providing insights into the healthcare sector and are significant contributions of TBI to date. Such data retrieved by TBI techniques have been used to extract knowledge about ancestral pedigree, identification of genomic composition, disease risk prediction by whole genome sequencing, drug discovery leading to the development of person-centric medicine, and data sharing in pharmacogenomics. These successful achievements have gained TBI public trust and interest along with investments of various governments and corporatations in the training and learning of TBI techniques that can help professionals get expertise in the field (Ouzounis, 2012).

Year-wise publications in PubMed

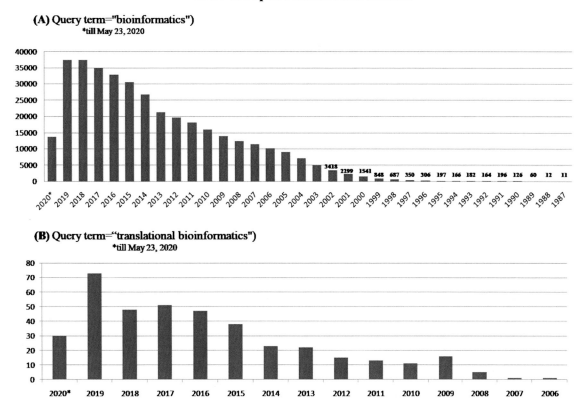

(A) Query term="bioinformatics")
*till May 23, 2020

(B) Query term="translational bioinformatics")
*till May 23, 2020

FIGURE 1.1   Year-wise number of publications in PubMed with the query term (A) "bioinformatics" and (B) "translational bioinformatics" searched in all fields.

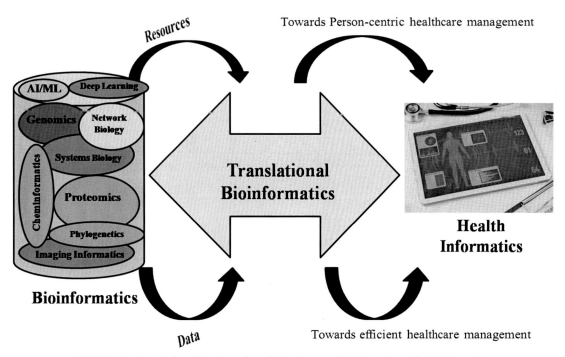

FIGURE 1.2   Translational bioinformatics: a bridge between bioinformatics and health informatics.

The *American Medical Informatics Association* (AMIA) defined translational bioinformatics as *"the generation of storage, analytic, and predictive methods to enhance the transfiguration of big biological data into person-centric healthcare system,"* which refers to its potential to develop methods that can utilize humongous data for promoting an efficient healthcare platform as its main crux is to employ informatics techniques to combine biologic units such as genes/proteins/small molecules to clinical units such as diseases/drugs or vice versa to depict a broader picture of the biomedical healthcare platform (Tenenbaum, 2016).

3. Scope and applications

With the advancement and expansion of translational bioinformatics, especially in healthcare, its scope and applications have been employed in myriad domains, namely, *"omics-based analysis,"* drug designing and discovery, *network biology, expression analysis, epigenetics, immunology, cheminformatics, big data analytics in healthcare, PMs,* and so on. Fig. 1.3 is a representation of the main scope and applications of TBI. Fig. 1.3 also highlights how bioinformatics shares a major chunk of applications in TBI for improving biomedical system platforms. Each of these theoretical and technologic advances necessitates an expansion of combined growth in the methods and techniques used for investigation and interpretation of the results. Such types of humongous data when turned into new information provide novel knowledge about treating diseases and how to prevent them. All in all, these applications when combined together provide insight into how to improve the current healthcare infrastructure and management (Li, 2015).

3.1 Pharmacogenomics

Bioinformatics is a vigorous scientific field that has beautifully transformed into translational bioinformatics and has discerned its value in decoding the contemporary genomic and proteomic aspects of various complex diseases. The preliminary force behind TBI is its nature of exploration and discovery. TBI has been beneficial in improvising the well-known clinical pharmacology research domains of pharmacogenomics and pharmacovigilance with the easy accessibility to gigantic data sources for research in pharmacology (Li, 2015). Data sources encapsulate observational data such as electronic health records (EHRs) and drug compound knowledge that can be easily retrieved from various databases, namely, DrugBank, PubMed, PharmGKB, ChEMBL, ZINC, etc. Using data from such sources helps pharmacology to link databases and extract essential information and annotations (Altman, 2012). For instance, the observational medical

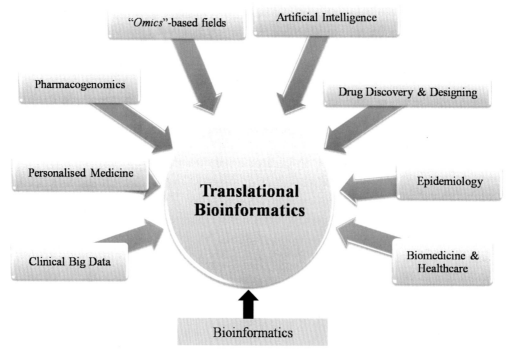

FIGURE 1.3 Scope and applications of translational bioinformatics.

outcomes partnership (OMOP) linked the databases by employing normalizing diagnoses, prognoses, and drug database information via a common data model across all its OMOP databases. Also, the platform provides classification and annotated information about the nature of drugs, clinical investigations, information about adverse drug reactions, and diagnoses (Stang et al., 2010). Pharmacokinetic (PK) and pharmacodynamic (PD) analyses are vital for pharmacologic research. Studies revolving on PK and PD have suggested essential model settings, parameters, and in vitro design for connecting the ontology of adverse events, viz., a biomedical ontology in the domain of adverse events developed by He et al. (2014) to the OMOP linking the PK to adverse drug effect (Wu et al., 2013).

3.2 Omics-based fields

Genomics: Genomics is one of the widely studied and researched domains of the *"omics"*-based fields that deals with the understanding of the functional effect of genetic alterations. Variations such as single nucleotide variants (SNVs), single nucleotide polymorphisms (SNPs), copy number variations (CNVs), etc., define the common types of alterations that occur in the human body leading to genetic disorders. Researchers and medical physicians have a great interest in such genomic variations, so many researchers have come up with various databases and genomic annotation tools for analyzing such genomic data. The HUGO Gene Nomenclature Committee (HGNC) (https://www.genenames.org/) approves the names of genes and also provides wide information about them. Capriotti et al. (2012) highlight the databases and tools for analyzing human genetic variation such as determining stability upon mutations and their impact at the genomic level. Nonetheless, there are a few loopholes that restrict their use in a clinical scenario, such as (A) standard examination of functional variation, (B) integration to easily accessible resources for retrieving annotated genetic variations, and (C) scoring of multiple variations along with the development of user-friendly tools in the healthcare context. Such restrictions must be met to develop a platform for accurate disease-specific examinations to determine the risk of disease development and its spread because of alterations in the genome (Capriotti et al., 2012). Simon and Roychowdhary (2013) provided insights to the challenges of amalgamating basic genomic research in cancer genomic research aiding in identifying cancer subtypes and molecular drugs that were effective. The clinical trial design of cancer patients was easily developed by employing NGS techniques as it has the power to give a moment to development of diagnostics for FDA-approved drugs, helping to validate the therapeutic and efficacy of the drug (Simon and Roychowdhary, 2013; Rai et al., 2020).

Proteomics: Proteomics not only provides information about the protein expression but also explains how protein molecules are produced, their localization, and also about their interacting partners. The Human Proteome Organization (HUPO) (https://www.hupo.org/) organized an international initiative, namely, *the Human Proteome Project* (HPP), that has gained wide acceptance and appreciation globally and aims to develop an extensive map of all the proteins that are present in the human body, to help in understanding disease diagnoses and provide person-centric treatment. This project has been categorized into two different chunks elucidating (A) *chromosome-based HPP* (C-HPP) and (B) *biology/disease HPP* (B/D-HPP) (Paik et al., 2012) wherein the C-HPP characterizes proteins, especially the posttranslational modifications, by the 23 pairs of chromosomes present in the cells, whereas B/D/HPP gives information about proteins involved in diseases. The C-HPP combines data retrieved from cell biology, molecular biochemistry, *"omics"*-fields, molecular biology, bioinformatics, clinical data, epigenetics, etc. (Paik et al., 2012; Hühmer et al., 2013; Díez et al., 2015). Generally, protein characterization is executed by mass-spectrometry and immunological assays, namely, enzyme-linked immunosorbent assays (ELISAs) or western blots. Howbeit, these techniques are not feasible for producing enormous data henceforth, so microarrays have replaced them over time, as their main advantage is their multiparallel nature and being able to characterize thousands of proteins in a single run by deploying a small amount of input biologic sample (Sutandy et al., 2013; Dasilva et al., 2013; Raza, 2014). This technique has also aided magnanimously in generating novel and useful data for clinical settings.

Clinical big data: Enormous growth of clinical data requires knowledge-based platforms wherein large-scale integration and multiparallel clinical datasets can be analyzed simultaneously. A broad spectrum of knowledge-based platforms for helping clinical decision support has been developed to impart knowledge for defining and tailoring suitable diagnosis and prognosis of various diseases (Payne, 2012). The implementation of knowledge demesne in biomedicine is deployed from a medical decision support system to epidemiologic surveillance of data. Clinical big data eventually help researchers and developers to develop knowledge base systems to generate awareness and predict future events and interrelationships between and across phases. One such knowledge base is *"The Electronic Medical Records and Genomics"* (eMERGE) repository, which is a simple medical system inclusive of biobank and genotyping data that aids in high-throughput phenotyping of patients using EHRs and relies mainly on data normalization and synchronization with both the clinical and genomic references (Chute et al., 2013; Regan and Payne, 2015). Furthermore, cloud computing has also paved a way in data integration, management, and analysis as it allows one to access humongous processing power, storage, and data analysis in real time. A couple examples of cloud computing in TBI for healthcare data analysis are *CloudBLAST*, a cloud-based program for sequence similarity analysis, and *MapReduce*, which is an analysis of large-scale medical imaging. *HealthVault* is another platform useful for EHR sharing and its integration systems (Chen et al., 2013).

Epidemiology: The National Cancer Institute (NCI) Epidemiology and Genomics Research Program (EGRP) (https://epi.grants.cancer.gov/) is one of the latest platforms that promotes research in humans to cancer biology, its development and progression. Also, it covers how these studies can be translated for the betterment of public healthcare. Data is growing as each day passes, so there is a need to create translational epidemiologic discoveries that can be used for improving current healthcare management. The EGRP is one such platform that provides cancer-related data and aids in identifying novel findings. The main *"drivers"* of such a translational platform include (a) collaboration between various scientific fields, (b) employing novel technologies, (c) multilevel and parallel analysis, and (d) a knowledge base system (Lam et al., 2013).

Artificial intelligence: AI has gained momentum for the past few decades and has been adopted by the medical fraternity in developing and shaping the current healthcare infrastructure and facilities. AI in medicine (AIM) has been categorized into two main groups: *virtual* and *physical*. The virtual aspect of AIM deals with the EHRs and artificial neural network-based decision support for treatment of diseases, while the physical aspect aims at developing and employing robots for various medical supports from performing surgeries to being prostheses for handicapped people (Amisha et al., 2019). The basis of the functionality of AIM is how computers grasp the art of learning, understanding, forming associations, and thus, developing a specific treatment approach for patients. One of the practical examples of AIM is the use of *smart biosensors* as a tool for people to manage and maintain their healthcare at homes without going to any healthcare center (Qazi and Raza, 2020). Biosensors have helped in achieving PoC treatment with easy usage at home. Another major practical success of AIM in promoting translational healthcare is the use of *virtual reality* for many psychiatric diseases, namely, autism spectrum disease, and it has become a beneficial platform for healthcare (Qazi and Raza, 2019). Furthermore, for people who reside in remote areas where there is hardly any scope to manage healthcare, *tele-based healthcare* has paved a way for such people to keep a constant check on their healthcare regimen with a user- and a pocket-friendly experience (Qazi et al., 2019). All such advances have made a gigantic change in the perspective of healthcare in just a few years. AIM has played a major role in translating tailor-made diagnosis to specific person-centric healthcare routine.

Biomedicine and healthcare: The biomedical and healthcare data is retrieved from various databases and repositories, namely, biobanks, biorepositories, clinical trial registries, patient portals, EHRs, electronic medical records, etc., which are data taken from clinical research or clinical trials. These databases and repositories have been developed to store and maintain patient data during the occurrence of a disease or for the selection of criteria for the person to participate in a clinical trial (Shameer et al., 2016). Howbeit, *Apple ResearchKit* (http://www.apple.com/researchkit/) and *Google Fit* (https://www.google.com/fit/) are mainly application development frameworks that help to gather and store data easily. Apple ResearchKit stores individual data by interacting on myriad complexities of the individual who is embedded with sensors, while ResearchKit develops applications that can combine data on a single platform. For instance, the accelerometer in an iPhone tracks steps walked by a person, or heart rate sensing can check fluctuations in heart rate. Researchers are adopting such applications to develop applications that are pocket friendly and can easily store patient data and can use the data for selecting individuals who can participate as volunteers for clinical trials, thus improving the regulation of the current healthcare system (Berwick et al., 2008; Shah and Tenenbaum, 2012; Eisenstein, 2015).

Personalized medicine: PM is a novel domain of research that aims at developing a person-centric treatment strategy for individuals rather than tailor-made ones. It has been able to help patients receive an early diagnosis, risk predictions for serious diseases, and have improved healthcare at lower costs. It promises *"the right drug of the right dosage to the right person at the right time,"* and it has proven to be better at treating severe diseases (Qazi, 2017). For pharmaceutical industries, PM helps to develop and manufacture low-cost, effective medications that have the least side effects for disease, wherein traditional medications have completely failed. As far as hospitals and health clinics are concerned, PM provides ethical, legal, and regulatory constructs along with healthcare management. Also, it helps consultants with decision-making during the diagnosis and prognosis of patients. The PM has achieved global acceptance and appreciation of researchers, medical consultants, healthcare staff, patients, and the public and is one of the leading domains of healthcare today (Bush et al., 2019). It has helped shape the medical healthcare platform for the better and is one of the pioneers in translational healthcare.

Drug discovery and designing: Therapeutic strategies lead to the late development of a drug when the treatment result is predictable and not effective, which raises a concern toward novel approaches for drug identification and designing that take an individual's genomic composition and environmental factors into account. With the rise and expansion of translational bioinformatics in the pharmaceutical industry, such an apex challenge has been curbed down, and effective techniques for the discovery and development of drugs have been generated that are useful for creating a *personalized platform* in healthcare management. The only lack today in this field of research is the lack of professionals who are well versed with biomedical and bioinformatics practicalities (Readhead and Dudley, 2013). With such developments in drug designing and development, it is feasible to construct person-centric, multiparallel, large-scale disease network models by amalgamating gene expression, genotypic and phenotypic data, and clinical trial data. This can, in turn, be used to determine the "*key drivers*" that may represent new therapeutic biomarkers or drug targets directly linked to the progression of a disease (Sahu et al., 2020a).

Table 1.1 represents a summary of large-scale TBI-based projects and repositories that have paved a way for making translational healthcare systems a reality. All these initiatives have allowed TBI to flourish in the medical healthcare system and create a more personalized healthcare regimen.

4. Limitations with biologic data: ethical challenges

With the flourishing TBI in healthcare, there is an evident bias, particularly observed in patients with their genomic composition. Patients are worried about their privacy of clinical data as it is very sensitive and highly confidential, shared only between the patients and their consultants. When screening a patient, not only the patients, but the relatives of that patient also are asked for their clinical history. This usually leads to the prediction of risks of various diseases, which makes an individual uncomfortable, and they are asked for a genetic examination for further assessment. Since genetic profiling is still not common and is not affordable by everyone, it creates havoc in people, leading to misleading assumptions about the privacy of their data (Pascovici et al., 2018).

Medical data collection is not as easy as it is surrounded by risk and privacy issues. All the registered court cases highlight the fact that genetic data of an individual reflect the need to protect the individual's ethical, legal, and social implication (ELSI) rights. There are many such authorized committees that assure that there are no violations or misuses with the patient's genetic profile data for any other purpose other than diagnosis, treatment, or research. The researchers/medical consultants must first pass the congressional passage of the *Genetic Information Nondiscrimination Act* (GINA) and only then proceed with their analysis on the private genetic data. GINA first came into existence on May 21, 2008, wherein it became the legal standard for the gathering, employment, and sharing of genetic information for the use of treatment that must be abided by all healthcare professionals. GINA describes the genetic data as (a) genetic examination that will be undergone by the patient, (b) genetic examination of relatives accompanying the patient, (c) the presence of any genetic disease in the family pedigree, (d) the format must also state a declaration for participating in clinical trials for the patient or the family member, and (e) genetic information about a fetus carried by a pregnant woman must be legally dealt by an individual or a family member by deploying assisted reproductive technology that must also be protected. Moreover, GINA also highlights the importance of genetic counseling and education to patients and their accompanying relatives (Pascovici et al., 2018). GINA has allowed a nonbiased way of ensuring ethical, legal, and social issues that usually arise by the genetic profiling and assessment raised by people. This severely affects TBI applications in healthcare as people lack awareness about the necessity of sharing their data for the development of personalized healthcare systems. Hence, there is a need to educate people and gain their trust in this novel research field that holds the potential to alter traditional methods of health management.

5. The road ahead: future prospects

TBI is still a novice when it comes to its predecessor bioinformatics in terms of research relevance; however, it gained a lot of momentum after the fulfilment of the Human Genome Project. The future is very bright for TBI as many novel sub-branches are coming together for developing a personalized platform for healthcare management that is user and pocket friendly, specific, sensitive toward people, and abides by the ELSI regulations. It holds the potential to evolve traditional domains of biomedical sciences for an improved and better management of healthcare infrastructure and regulation. The future scopes of TBI in healthcare mentioned are as follows:

(a) One of the essential scopes of TBI would be to help in prognostic marker identification research for many psychiatric disorders. To date, many prognostic indicators have been cataloged for many diseases mainly in cardiology and cancers, namely, prostate cancer, nonsmall cell lung cancer, etc. Nonetheless, treatment is a challenge still. Specific biomarkers would help in better diagnosis and classification of neurologic disorders such as *major depressive disorder*, *bi-polar disorder*, and *manic episodes* (Insel and Cuthbert, 2015; Qazi, 2017), thus leading to personalized healthcare in psychiatry as well.

TABLE 1.1 Summarized TBI-based projects and repositories employed in the healthcare.

S. no.	TBI-based projects	Descriptions	URL
1.	The eMERGE Consortium	An NIH-funded project that is a consortium amalgamating DNA domains with electronic health records (EHRs) for large-scale genetic research aiding in developing a person-centric healthcare system	https://emerge.mc.vanderbilt.edu
2.	China Kadoorie Biobank	A Chinese biobank aiming to provide genetic and environmental factors engaged in severe diseases	http://www.ckbiobank.org/site/
3.	MURDOCK Study	A repository that reclassifies diseases based on molecular biomarkers	http://www.murdock-study.com
4.	UK Biobank	A UK-based biobank providing proper diagnosis, prognosis and treatment options for various diseases	http://www.ukbiobank.ac.uk
5.	Million Veteran Program	A program funded by the US Veterans Affairs to collaborate with veterans to analyze how genes affect the health of an individual	http://www.research.va.gov/mvp/veterans.cfm
6.	Personal Genome Project	A project responsible for sharing genomic, environmental, and related human data to emphasize on "personalized" healthcare. It is based at Harvard University	http://www.personalgenomes.org/
7.	The Human Proteome Project (HUPO)	A project maintained and run by the Human Proteome Organization that aims to entail all the experimentally known proteins that are produced in the human body at one platform	https://www.hupo.org/human-proteome-project
8.	Framingham Heart Study	An ongoing heart and lung study that was initiated in 1948 in Framingham, Massachusetts	https://www.framinghamheartstudy.org/
9.	Google Baseline	A platform collecting clinical data to categorize whether a person is "healthy" or "looks healthy"	https://www.projectbaseline.com/
10.	National Biobank of Korea	A Korean-based biobank that provides annotated biologic specimens for developing a person-centric system	http://www.nih.go.kr/NIH/eng/contents/NihEngContentView.jsp?cid=17881
11.	US Precision Medicine Cohort	A US-based project aiming to improve healthcare, diagnosis, and treatment approaches, paving a way for personalized medicines (PM)	http://www.nih.gov/precision-medicineinitiative-cohort-program
12.	The Human Genome Project (HUGO)	The Human Genome Project was an international scientific research project (1990–2003) that provided the genomic composition of a human along with its functionalities, paving a way for translational bioinformatics (TBI)	https://gohugo.io/contribute/
13.	The Epidemiology and Genomics Research Program (EGRP)	An NCI-funded project that is one of the latest platforms to promote research in humans to cancer biology, its development, and progression	https://epi.grants.cancer.gov/
14.	Apple's ResearchKit	ResearchKit is an open-source tool initiated by Apple permitting researchers and developers to generate powerful applications for medical research helpful for managing healthcare on fingertips	http://researchkit.org/

(b) Another scope is to train professionals so they can recognize and address significant issues in myriad aspects of translational research. As genetic profiling is also becoming a new trend, there is also a need for genetic counselors who can aid in developing awareness about genetic examinations and profiling in the public. There is a need to collaborate on a much larger level to allow multiinterdisciplinary research to *reduce redundant research, enhance the significance of the research, and allow progress in translational healthcare management and maintenance* along with the *development of privacy policies* (Tenenbaum et al., 2014; Tenenbaum, 2016).

(c) There is a requirement for practical understanding, exploring, and adoption of medical data for fulfilling ELSI rights. TBI must ensure patients and their family members that their data will not be misused or employed for any kind of nefarious research but only for a significant contribution in the society (Tenenbaum, 2016). It may take time for gaining trust and acceptance, but once assured, TBI will not look back in the field of the biomedical healthcare system.

(d) Furthermore, with advancements in computational intelligence, TBI has converged many technologies such as nanopore sequencing (Raza and Qazi, 2019), smart biosensors (Qazi and Raza, 2020), the internet of living things (IoLT), cloud and fog computing, and AI for expanding the relevance and expertise of TBI in the healthcare sector. It is being reiterated here that the growth of AIM in healthcare has allowed better and easier healthcare monitoring by deploying biosensors that can rectify diseases, keep a check on current disease tracking, and can also predict the risk of getting a disease in the future. A nanopore sequencer, for instance, MinION, is a small-sized massively parallel sequencer that can be connected to our mobile devices for regulating bodily changes. This highlights the potential of IoLT and is now ubiquitously available in homes, hospitals, schools, offices, etc. IoLT has made healthcare of the fingertips now, which showcases the difference in the perception of the traditional healthcare scenario. Previously, it was a mere dream to retrieve, store, and manage genomic data on the internet. However, people are now monitoring their healthcare and storing their private data on the cloud (Raza and Qazi, 2019). All this is because of rapid expansion of TBI in the healthcare system that has eventually paved a way for person-centric health management to come into the forefront. TBI is the future of healthcare and PM.

6. Conclusions

This chapter systematically introduces the fundamental concepts of bioinformatics and TBI. The term *"bioinformatics"* was coined in 1970, but "translational bioinformatics" is relatively new, which started flourishing after the Human Genome Project in 2006. The field of TBI is still young and evolving compared to its ancestor bioinformatics. Initially, it was thought of as only concerned with data organization, accessibility, and analyzing medical data, employed as a secondary support system that had the potential to amalgamate biomedical information with decision-making processes. However, TBI has covered a tremendous milestone in integrating biomedical data with higher-order algorithms to link data, structures, and functions in networks. Hence, TBI achieved a successful appreciation and wide acceptance from the medical fraternity and researchers. TBI acted as an overpass between bioinformatics and health informatics, paving a way for the concept of PMs and PoC.

This chapter also presented the advancement and expansion of TBI and its applications in healthcare, including *omics-based analysis, drug designing and discovery, network biology, expression analysis, epigenetics, immunology, cheminformatics, big data analytics in healthcare, PMs,* and so on. These applications in combination provide insight as to how to improve the current healthcare infrastructure and management. Some of its scope and applications have been discussed in pharmacogenomics, omics-based fields, proteomics, clinical big data, epidemiology, AI, biomedicine and healthcare, PM, drug discovery, and designing. With the flourishing application of TBI in healthcare, there are ethical challenges related to biologic data. Patients are worried about their privacy of clinical data. When screening a patient, not only the patient's but also their relative's clinical history is asked. This usually leads to the prediction of risks to various diseases, which makes an individual uncomfortable. The chapter highlights some of the ethical issues and how to protect them.

The last section of the chapter highlights the prospects of TBI. Novel subbranches of bioinformatics and TBI are emerging to develop a personalized platform for U-healthcare management that should be patient and pocket friendly, specific, sensitive toward people, and abide by the ELSI regulations. It holds the potential to evolve traditional domains of biomedical sciences for improved and better management of U-healthcare infrastructure and regulation. However, there is still a need to develop a standard for private medical data sharing, practical understanding, exploring, and adoption of medical data for fulfilling ELSI rights.

List of abbreviation

AIM Artificial intelligence in medicine
AMIA American Medical Informatics Association
CNV Copy number variation
EGRP Epidemiology and Genomics Research Program
EHRs Electronic health records
ELISA Enzyme-linked immunosorbent assay
ELSI Ethical, legal, and social implications
eMERGE The Electronic Medical Records and Genomics
GINA Genetic Information Nondiscrimination Act
GWAS Genome-Wide Association Studies
HGNC HUGO Gene Nomenclature Committee
HGP Human Genome Project
HPP Human Proteome Project
HUPO Human Proteome Organization
IoLT Internet of living things
NCI National Cancer Institute
NGS Next generation sequencing
OMOP Observational Medical Outcomes Partnership
PAM Percent accepted mutations
PD Pharmacodynamic
PK Pharmacokinetic
PM Personalized medicine
PoC Point of care
SNPs Single nucleotide polymorphisms
SNVs Single nucleotide variants
TBI Translational bioinformatics

Acknowledgments

Sahar Qazi is supported by DST-INSPIRE fellowship provided by the Department of Science and Technology, Government of India.

References

Altman, R.B., 2012. Translational bioinformatics: linking the molecular world to the clinical world. Clin. Pharmacol. Ther. 91, 994–1000.

Amisha, Malik, P., et al., 2019. Overview of artificial intelligence in medicine. J. Fam. Med. Prim. Care 8 (7), 2328.

Berwick, D.M., Nolan, T.W., Whittington, J., 2008. The triple aim: care, health, and cost. Health Aff. 27, 759–769.

Bush, W.S., Cooke Bailey, J.N., et al., 2019. Bridging the gaps in personalized medicine value assessment: a review of the need for outcome metrics across stakeholders and scientific disciplines. Public Health Genomics 22 (1–2), 16–24.

Butte, A.J., 2008. Translational bioinformatics: coming of age. J. Am. Med. Inf. Assoc. 15 (6), 709–714.

Capriotti, E., Nehrt, N.L., et al., 2012. Bioinformatics for personal genome interpretation. Briefings Bioinf. 13 (4), 495–512.

Chen, J., Qian, F., et al., 2013. Translational biomedical informatics in the cloud: present and future. BioMed Res. Int. 2013, 658925.

Chute, C.G., Ullman-Cullere, M., et al., 2013. Some experiences and opportunities for big data in translational research. Genet. Med. 15 (10), 802–809.

Dasilva, N., Díez, P., et al., 2013. Proteinmicroarrays: technological aspects, applications, and intellectual property. Recent Pat. Biotechnol. 7 (2), 142–152.

Díez, P., Droste, C., et al., 2015. Integration of proteomics and transcriptomics data sets for the analysis of a Lymphoma B-cell line in the context of the chromosome-centric human proteome project. J. Proteome Res. 14 (9), 3530–3540.

Eck, R.V., Dayhoff, M.O., 1966. Evolution of the structure of ferredoxin based on living relics of primitive amino Acid sequences. Science 152 (3720), 363–366.

Eisenstein, M., 2015. GSK collaborates with Apple on ResearchKit. Nat. Biotechnol. 33, 1013–1014.

He, Y., Sarntivijai, S., et al., 2014. OAE: the ontology of adverse events. J. Biomed. Semant. 5, 29.

Hogeweg, P., 1978. Simulating the growth of cellular forms. Simulation 31 (3), 90–96.

Hunt, L.T., 1983. Margaret O. Dayhoff 1925–1983. DNA Cell Biol. 2 (2), 97–98.

Hühmer, A.F.R., Paulus, A., et al., 2013. The chromosome-centric human proteome project: a call to action. J. Proteome Res. 12 (1), 28–32.

Insel, T.R., Cuthbert, B.N., 2015. Medicine. Brain disorders? Precisely. Science 348, 499–500.

Johnson, G., Wu, T.T., 2000. Kabat Database and its applications: 30 years after the first variability plot. Nucleic Acids Res. 28 (1), 214–218.

Karwasra, R., Fatihi, S., Raza, K., Singh, S., Khanna, K., Sharma, N., Sharma, S., Sharma, D., Varma, S., 2020. Filgrastim loading in PLGA and SLN nanoparticulate system: a bioinformatics approach. Drug Dev. Ind. Pharm. 46 (8), 1354–1361. https://doi.org/10.1080/03639045.2020.1788071.

Khatoon, N., Alam, H., Khan, A., Raza, K., Sardar, M., 2019. Ampicillin silver nanoformulations against multidrug resistant bacteria. Sci. Rep. 9, 6848. https://doi.org/10.1038/s41598-019-43309-0.

Kumar, S., Ahmad, S., Siddiqi, M.I., Raza, K., 2019. Mathematical model for plant-insect interaction with dynamic response to PAD4-BIK1 interaction and effect of BIK1 inhibition. Biosystems 175, 11–23. https://doi.org/10.1016/j.biosystems.2018.11.005.

Lam, T.K., Spitz, M., et al., 2013. "Drivers" of translational cancer epidemiology in the 21st century: needs and opportunities. Cancer Epidemiol. Biomarkers Prev. 22 (2), 181–188.

Lesko, L.J., 2012. Drug research and translational bioinformatics. Clin. Pharmacol. Ther. 91 (6), 960–962.

Li, L., 2015. The potential of translational bioinformatics approaches for pharmacology research. Br. J. Clin. Pharmacol. 80 (4), 862–867.

Ouzounis, C.A., 2012. Rise and demise of bioinformatics? Promise and progress. PLoS Comput. Biol. 8 (4), 1–5.

Paik, Y.-K., Jeong, S.-K., et al., 2012. The Chromosome-Centric Human Proteome Project for cataloging proteins encoded in the genome. Nat. Biotechnol. 30 (3), 221–223.

Pascovici, D., Wu, J.X., et al., 2018. Clinically relevant post-translational modification analyses—maturing workflows and bioinformatics tools. Int. J. Mol. Sci. 20 (1), 16.

Payne, P.R.O., 2012. Chapter 1: biomedical knowledge integration. PLoS Comput. Biol. 8 (12), e1002826.

Pevsner, J., 2009. Pairwise Sequence Alignment. Bioinformatics and Functional Genomics, second ed. Wiley-Blackwell, ISBN 978-0-470-08585-1, pp. 58–68.

Qazi, S., Tanveer, K., et al., 2019. From telediagnosis to teletreatment. In: Telemedicine Technologies, pp. 153–169.

Qazi, S., Raza, K., 2019. Towards a VIREAL platform: virtual reality in cognitive and behavioural training for autistic individuals. In: Advanced Computational Intelligence Techniques for Virtual Reality in Healthcare, pp. 25–47.

Qazi, S., 2017. Personalized medicines in psychiatry: promises and challenges. J. Appl. Comput. 2 (2), 50–55.

Qazi, S., Raza, K., 2020. Smart biosensors for an efficient point of care (PoC) health management. In: Smart Biosensors in Medical Care, pp. 65–85.

Rai, A., Qazi, S., Raza, K., 2020. In silico analysis and comparative molecular docking study of FDA approved drugs with Transforming Growth Factor Beta receptors in Oral Submucous Fibrosis. Indian J. Otolaryngol. Head Neck Surg. https://doi.org/10.1007/s12070-020-02014-5. Springer.

Raza, K., 2014. Clustering analysis of cancerous microarray data. J. Chem. Pharmaceut. Res. 6 (9), 488–493.

Raza, K., 2016a. Analysis of microarray data using artificial intelligence based techniques. In: Handbook of Research on Computational Intelligence Applications in Bioinformatics. IGI Global, USA, pp. 216–239. https://doi.org/10.4018/978-1-5225-0427-6.ch011.

Raza, K., 2016b. Reconstruction, topological and gene ontology enrichment analysis of cancerous gene regulatory network modules. Curr. Bioinf. 11 (2), 243–258. https://doi.org/10.2174/1574893611666160115212806.

Raza, K., 2017. Protein features identification for machine learning-based prediction of protein-protein interactions. In: Proc. of Communications in Computer and Information Science, vol. 750. Springer, pp. 305–317. https://doi.org/10.1007/978-981-10-6544-6_28.

Raza, K., 2019. Fuzzy logic based approaches for gene regulatory network inference. Artif. Intell. Med. 97, 189–203. https://doi.org/10.1016/j.artmed.2018.12.004.

Raza, K., Parveen, R., 2013a. Soft computing approach for modeling genetic regulatory networks. Adv. Intell. Syst. Comput. 178, 1–11. https://doi.org/10.1007/978-3-642-31600-5_1.

Raza, K., Parveen, R., 2013b. Reconstruction of gene regulatory network of colon cancer using information theoretic approach. In: Proc. of 4th International Conference (CONFLUENCE-2013): The Next Generation Information Technology Summit 2013, pp. 461–466. https://doi.org/10.1049/cp.2013.2357.

Raza, K., Qazi, S., 2019. Nanopore sequencing technology and Internet of living things: a big hope for U-healthcare. Sens. Health Monit. 5, 95–116.

Raza, K., Ahmad, S., 2019. Recent advancement in next-generation sequencing techniques and its computational analysis. Int. J. Bioinf. Res. Appl. Indersci. 15 (3), 191–220.

Raza, K., Alam, M., 2016. Recurrent neural network based hybrid model for reconstructing gene regulatory network. Comput. Biol. Chem. 64, 322–334. https://doi.org/10.1016/j.compbiolchem.2016.08.002.

Readhead, B., Dudley, J., 2013. Translational bioinformatics approaches to drug development. Adv. Wound Care 2 (9), 470–489.

Regan, K., Payne, P.R.O., 2015. From molecules to patients: the clinical applications of translational bioinformatics. Yearbook Med. Inf. 24 (01), 164–169.

Sahu, A., Pradhan, D., Raza, K., Qazi, S., Jain, A.K., Verma, S., 2020a. In silico library design, screening and MD simulation of COX-2 inhibitors for anticancer activity. In: Proc. of 12th International Conference on Bioinformatics and Computational Biology (BICOB-2020), San Francisco, USA, March 23–25, 2020. EPiC Series in Computing, vol. 70, pp. 21–32. https://doi.org/10.29007/z2wx.

Sahu, A., Qazi, S., Raza, K., Varma, S., 2020b. COVID-19: hard road to find integrated computational drug repurposing pipeline. In: Computational Intelligence for COVID-19: Surveillance, Prevention, Prediction and Diagnosis, Studies in Computational Intelligence (SCI), vol. 923. Springer, pp. 295–309. https://doi.org/10.1007/978-981-15-8534-0_15.

Shah, N.H., Tenenbaum, J.D., 2012. The coming age of data-driven medicine: translational bioinformatics' next frontier. J. Am. Med. Inf. Assoc. 19, e2–4.

Sarkar, I.N., Butte, A.J., et al., 2011. Translational bioinformatics: linking knowledge across biological and clinical realms. J. Am. Med. Inf. Assoc. 18 (4), 345–357.

Shameer, K., Badgeley, M.A., et al., 2016. Translational bioinformatics in the era of real-time biomedical, health care and wellness data streams. Briefings Bioinf. 18 (1), 105–124.

Simon, R., Roychowdhury, S., 2013. Implementing personalized cancer genomics in clinical trials. Nat. Rev. Drug Discov. 12 (5), 358–369.

Stang, P.E., Ryan, P.B., et al., 2010. Advancing the science for active surveillance: rationale and design for the Observational Medical Outcomes Partnership. Ann. Intern. Med. 153, 600–606.

Sutandy, F.X.R., Qian, J., et al., 2013. Overview of protein microarrays. Curr. Protoc. Protein Sci. Chapter 27. Unit 27.1.

Tenenbaum, J.D., Sansone, S.A., Haendel, M., 2014. A sea of standards for omics data: sink or swim? J. Am. Med. Inf. Assoc. 21, 200–203.

Tenenbaum, J.D., 2016. Translational bioinformatics: past, present, and future. Genomics, Proteomics Bioinf. 14 (1), 31–41.

Wani, N., Raza, K., 2019a. Raw sequence to target gene prediction: an integrated inference pipeline for ChIP-seq and RNA-seq datasets. In: Malik, H., Srivastava, S., Sood, Y., Ahmad, A. (Eds.), Applications of Artificial Intelligence Techniques in Engineering, Advances in Intelligent Systems and Computing, vol. 697. Springer, pp. 557–568.

Wani, N., Raza, K., 2019b. iMTF-GRN: integrative matrix tri-factorization for inference of gene regulatory networks. IEEE Access 7, 126154–126163. https://doi.org/10.1109/ACCESS.2019.2936794.

Wani, N., Raza, K., 2019c. Integrative approaches to reconstruct regulatory networks from multi-omics data: a review of state-of-the-art methods. Comput. Biol. Chem. 83, 107120. https://doi.org/10.1016/j.compbiolchem.2019.107120.

Wani, N., Raza, K., 2021. MKL-GRNI: A parallel multiple kernel learning approach for supervised inference of large-scale gene regulatory networks. PeerJ Comput. Sci. 7, e363. https://doi.org/10.7717/peerj-cs.363.

Wu, H.Y., Karnik, S., et al., 2013. An integrated pharmacokinetics ontology and corpus for text mining. BMC Bioinf. 14, 35.

Chapter 2

The fundamentals and potential of translational medicine in healthcare

Ana Carolina Borges Monteiro[1,*], Reinaldo Padilha França[1], Rangel Arthur[2] and Yuzo Iano[1]

[1]*School of Electrical Engineering and Computing (FEEC), State University of Campinas (UNICAMP), Campinas, São Paulo, Brazil;* [2]*Faculty of Technology (FT), State University of Campinas (UNICAMP), Limeira, São Paulo, Brazil*

Corresponding authors: E-mail: monteiro@decom.fee.unicamp.br, padilha@decom.fee.unicamp.br

Chapter outline

1. Introduction

In a sense, translational research consists of research that ranges from basic science to the practical application of the knowledge generated by basic research. In the case of medicine, serious translational medicine, therefore, is one that encompasses everything from the concept of research in a medical clinic to its application in the clinical setting or surgical clinic. It is a new paradigm to accelerate the download of knowledge generated on the bench for medical practice. It involves the set of knowledge developed in biomedical laboratories, associated with the same resources used by other sciences, in search of improving health services (Birmingham, 2002).

In particular, it applies its application in medicine, when, for example, research on a specific protein present in the cell membrane channel has a process of investigation until its culmination with the development of a medication for specific degenerative disease therapy. In traditional research, the task is currently divided into two tight groups: one for basic (or laboratory) research and the other for clinical research, where, in most cases, no articulation between the two permeates, with a permanent gap between these two types of research (Rubio et al., 2010).

Often, the knowledge produced by basic research is not well used for practical purposes, or at its best, its use occurs in a very slow and not very promising way. With the advent of translational medicine, there is a continuity of the researcher's work with the articulation between the laboratory (where the discoveries of basic science are developed) and the clinic (where practical applications are made) (Fig. 2.1) (Birmingham, 2002; Rubio et al., 2010).

But translational medicine in a broader sense can also comprise the translation of the most varied types of medical knowledge into clinical practice. Also, it deals with how to use the new medical knowledge that is emerging to improve medical practice. Thus, translational medicine aims to streamline the transfer of knowledge produced on the bench for

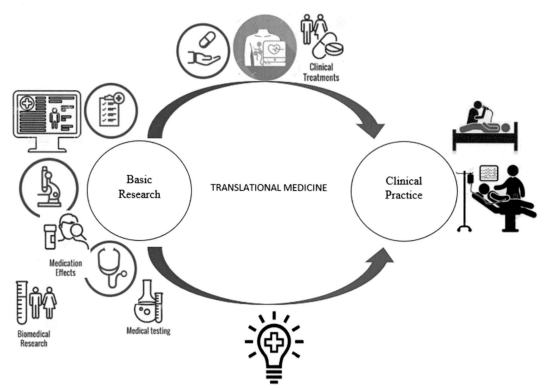

FIGURE 2.1 Basic science to practice clinic.

application in clinical research and public health. It is the idea of establishing the connection between the creation and application of knowledge, integrating researchers from the basic and clinical areas to better assist the population (Mankoff et al., 2004).

Therefore, this chapter has the mission and objective of providing an updated review and overview of translational medicine, addressing its evolution and fundamental concepts, showing its relationship as well as approaching its success, with a concise bibliographic background, categorizing and synthesizing the potential of the technique.

2. Translational medicine concepts from a brief historical perspective

Medicine is a field of knowledge that is based on science. However, the problems faced by users and professionals in the public health system are known. Many of them are related to the existence of a large gap between the development of research in universities and medical practice in hospitals and health centers, and there are also diverse economic and political factors to be faced to change this reality. With that, the recent emergence is translational medicine that has foundations and guidelines to solve this context (Mittra and Milne, 2013).

The meaning of the term comes from research and scientific investigation. It is the result of translational research, which is research that ranges from basic science to the practical application of the knowledge generated by basic research. In the case of medicine, translational medicine is, therefore, that which would cover everything from the concept generated in a basic medical investigation to its application in a clinical setting or surgical practice (Littman et al., 2007).

Translational medicine is a new paradigm that emerged to accelerate the transfer of knowledge generated on the bench to medical practice, involving clinical research, to produce benefits for the community as a whole. It is to move from theory to practice. It involves the set of knowledge conceived in biomedical laboratories, associated with that produced by other sciences, in search of improving health services (Littman et al., 2007; Adithan, 2017).

Translational medicine, more similar to the one we see today, started around the 1980s and 1990s when American pharmaceutical industries, through the analysis of cellular mechanisms of diseases, developed a new strategy for the creation of new drugs. It had its landmark in translational medicine from the Institute of Medicine of the Academy (Macaluso et al., 2019).

For an illustrative context, the normal path of science is where basic researchers, who live in the laboratory and on the bench, discover the news regarding the cellular, subcellular, and molecular environment. Consequently, it comes to carry out tests with these findings in animals and later in humans, and develop drugs or diagnostic tests for diseases. Finally, this knowledge is used by specialized clinicians who try these new drugs on human beings, and it is only after this phase that it is possible to say that the knowledge was, after all, applied. Finally, it is only possible to affirm success after being applied to a large number of people, concerning medicines (Burke and Grizzle, 2017).

Concerning translational medicine, the objective is to encourage the formation of multidisciplinary teams and create a culture of approximation of the basic area with the clinical area and, mainly, to make sure that what resulted from basic research and which was seen as useful in clinical research reaches the patient (Burke and Grizzle, 2017; Gallagher and LeRoith, 2016).

3. Translational medicine from a practical perspective

Translational medicine, in a broader sense, can also comprise the translation of the most varied types of medical knowledge to clinical practice, with the challenge of also taking this knowledge produced at the university to public health (Gallagher and LeRoith, 2016).

That is the virtuous circle of the development of a new therapy and how it could be improved with the participation of the industry. In this long path, which usually lasts for years, the research groups that worked around the theme were distinct and, not infrequently, without immediate communication between them. This forms the basic science group, the animal experimentation group, and, finally, the clinical research group. Until success, that is, the final result, a lot of time was spent. And so, it is confirmed that there is a time lag between the discoveries made by basic science and their use in applied science, between the initial experimental results and their conversion into new diagnostic tests, devices, and medicines used in health (Wei et al., 2017).

To elucidate this context, it is possible to highlight the example of the discovery of inhibitors of angiotensin-converting enzyme, which are drugs used in the treatment of arterial hypertension. Its cycle lasted 10 years of basic research until arriving at the medicine and, finally, the hands of the patients. Thus, translational medicine involves basic science, ranging from clarifying the mechanisms of diseases to the development of new drugs, their application, the dissemination of this knowledge, and new protocols that will benefit patients and the whole of society (Ahmad et al., 2017).

Another illustrative scenario is the question of research and development, ranging from genetic analysis to molecular studies on the most varied and specific topics. However, the central question is how these projects will influence clinical practice. That point is pure translational medicine since it is about how to use this new medical and biomedical knowledge that appears to also improve medical practice, and thus result in the production of benefits for the community as a whole (Agarwal et al., 2017).

Similarly, through the results of the genetic sequencing of the coronavirus, it is possible to identify the regions responsible for its attachment to human tissues as well as the receptors for drugs. Such results from molecular biology directly impact the development of prophylactic practices, drug testing, and the development of DNA-based vaccines (Liu, 2019).

In this sense, research aimed at obtaining biomarkers of the therapeutic evolution of patients should be created to find out if a patient responds better or worse to a given treatment. In the same way, funding must be provided for hospitals to create an infrastructure capable of carrying out this related clinical research. And in the same vein, universities also create their centers. Generating greater interdisciplinarity is obtained, reaching one of the goals of translational medicine, which is to transform what is seen in clinical research into measures for public health. Nowadays, the speed with which the research is done on the bench and the knowledge reaches the application has fundamentally changed. The university itself takes the knowledge to the industry, or the industry will get it (Burke and Grizzle, 2017; Bravo-Merodio et al., 2019).

Another historical illustrative scenario of the translation of knowledge for use in the medical field is very old and what is being conceptualized today by translational medicine. It is the possibility to mention the achievements of Louis Pasteur in microbiology that influenced the antiseptic techniques that continue today. Since the world context of the time was different, among its basic discoveries and respective applications, there was almost no time lag. Pasteur laid the foundations for modern microbiology, while influencing agriculture (research on fermentation) and preventive medicine (vaccines). Another case is that of Jenner, who coincidentally practiced a kind of translational medicine when discovering and using vaccination (Watts, 2016).

The study of medicine must become transdisciplinary, developing a partnership with chemistry concerning new therapies; with physics, aiming at the creation of new equipment; with mathematics, depending on statistics; with informatics through computational capacity in modern times; with engineering due to the possibility of creating equipment; and with other disciplines that can contribute to innovation in clinical approaches and the improvement of medicine (Martins, 2019).

The purpose of translational medicine is, therefore, to accelerate this long road. Representing a recent movement of the international medical community, it aims at structuring interdisciplinary and multidisciplinary medical research groups, in which naturally there is a collaboration between researchers in the basic area and those who work in the professional, clinical, surgical, or epidemiological areas, all with a focus on the development of new technologies applied to health (Chen et al., 2012).

4. Translational medicine as part of an evolution of modern medicine

Translational medicine is part of an evolution of medicine, in search of a more effective fulfillment of its objectives of the bench and the clinic, and it is the best way to achieve the reengineering of the health system because it reconciles the demands of doctors, researchers, managers, and patients, with the main goal of shortening the time spent between the production of new knowledge and this becoming a new product, be it a diagnosis or a new therapeutic form. However, effectively, researchers who will dedicate themselves to translational medicine must receive specific training to learn how to work as true interdisciplinary teams, in which processes are much more complex as well as dynamic (Cai, 2014).

Also, from a human and adaptive point of view, for a basic researcher, there will be the challenge of needing to understand how the discovery will follow a trajectory until its final practical use, and they should be able to pass on to the clinical colleague or surgeon very clear and objective information of the concept of their discovery. The same is for the clinician or surgeon of the "other end," where there will also be the challenge of being permanently updated with the specific basic part of medicine that allows one to understand the language of the colleague working at the base (Wehling, 2008).

Translational medicine involves doctors, clinical professionals, researchers, and professionals from other areas in health care. It is an evolution of the form previously practiced, in a procedural way, based on evidence, but developing the research in a less specialized way or in a more comprehensive way. For this, it will be necessary to overcome the challenge of public implementation, which is variant and dependent on the unique context of each country, to serve the entire population, applying its advantages in each country's unified health system (Mittra and Milne, 2013).

In the same way that specialization and super-specialization generate the requirement of the specialist who masters knowledge that is not exclusive to his area, showing that general knowledge, in any area, but especially in the medical area, is indispensable as a basis for research, in any specialty, generating valorization of the synthesis in development and the collaboration. The current challenges of translational medicine bring together a greater number of engaged professionals, the increase in investments in the area, the establishment of a network of partnerships, and more accurate information exchanges. To overcome them, it will be necessary to create strategies to obtain resources within the regular forms of support (Edelman and FitzGerald, 2019).

The full development of proteomics, genomics, use of stem cells for therapeutic purposes, reproductive medicine, regenerative medicine, neuroscience applied to medicine, and other areas of great technologic complexity will only be achieved through the incorporation and practice of the concept of translational medicine (Soldner and Jaenisch, 2018).

A good environment for the proper practice of translational medicine should provide researchers with a comprehensive, complete, and sophisticated infrastructure; the problem under study must be known to the team in minimal detail, including at the molecular level; she must be prepared to carry out these studies in humans with refinements of complexity and scientific precision, based on the knowledge that leaves "from the bench at the bedside" that can be transferred in an effective and useful process to medical practice (Barile et al., 2017).

This means the demonstration that the two ends of the area, ranging from basic science and medicine, unite their largest institutions to consolidate translational medicine. In the same way, unclear clinical problems should be a challenge for clinicians or surgeons to integrate with basic science teams to seek the appropriate solution through research, which should be following inter- and multidisciplinary guidelines (Jiang and Cui, 2017).

The objectives of translational medicine justify the efforts of the two scientific academies to increase knowledge about the area and the commitment to obtain more involvement in increasing the capacity for health research, stimulating the development of innovative approaches, accelerating knowledge transfer, and in the formation of a new generation of the interdisciplinary researcher. Ideally, one should break the limit of the biomedical area and actively seek new knowledge and collaborations in engineering, physics, chemistry, economics, and many other fields of knowledge, aiming at practical application for the benefit of the patient (Yoon et al., 2018).

Translational medicine aims to streamline the transfer of knowledge produced on the bench for application in clinical research and public health in terms of research and most hospitals, including university students, that must have an adequate structure for the practice of translational medicine, concerning the geographic proximity between the "bench" and the "bed," which is far from ideal today. In other words, the idea is to establish the connection between the creation and application of knowledge, integrating researchers from the basic and clinical areas to better assist the population (Barile et al., 2017; Suchkov et al., 2018).

5. Translational research

Translational research is conceptualized as being all research that has its beginning in basic science and its conclusion in the practical application of learned knowledge. It seeks to promote interdisciplinary research and accelerate the bidirectional exchange between basic and clinical science to move basic laboratory research findings to applied environments involving patients and populations (Krueger et al., 2019).

This area integrates with greater emphasis the biologic/biomedical areas, clinical and reference research, collective health, and the development and production of health supplies, aiming to develop critical and transversal knowledge to seek solutions to combat the diseases in question, support services, protocols, and clinical trials, products for the diagnosis, prevention or treatment, and studies on how, where, and when to best apply them (Crabu, 2018).

Translational research appears to try to break this vacuum and bring the researcher closer to the fields of practice. Although relatively recent, the notion of "transferring search results" is not. In particular, it has its application in medicine, when, in the research on a certain protein present in a cell membrane channel, the process is continued until its culmination with the development of a medication for the therapy of a certain degenerative disease, for example (Smith et al., 2017).

This study is fundamentally essential to improve human health, aiming at the need to translate new knowledge, mechanisms, and techniques generated by the advance in basic research to offer new possibilities for the prevention, diagnosis, and treatment of diseases. As long as the focus is on the importance of academic and interdisciplinary "translation" of research to promote quality patient care (Burbelo et al., 2010).

In traditional research, one must take into account aspects related to scientific research, technologic development, clinical research, the industrial production process, the world of regulation, the commercialization of products, and, not least, the health systems themselves. And the task is currently divided into two tight groups: one for basic or laboratory research, and the other for clinical research, where in general, in most cases, no articulation is permeated between the two, with a permanent gap between these two types (Hörig et al., 2005).

And so, it was incorporating more and more stages in the knowledge chain, overflowing with aspects inherent to research and development, even encompassing production processes and even the incorporation of new products and processes in healthcare practices. The idea is to speed up the translation of laboratory treatment findings to the reality of patients, engaging local communities in research, as well as to train a new generation of translational researchers and clinicians (Ruttenberg et al., 2007).

For this reason, the knowledge produced by basic research is often not well used for practical purposes, or at best, it is used very slowly and with little promise. In this sense, an aspect very much focused on by researchers is the importance of interdisciplinary work for the development of studies that can not only solve the health problems of patients and communities, but also influence the formulation of health policies consistent with the needs of the population (Ruttenberg et al., 2007; Woods and Magyary, 2010).

6. Translational research concepts from a brief historical perspective

With the advent of translational research, it is possible to observe the continuity of the researcher's work with the articulation between the laboratory, where the discoveries of basic science are developed, and the clinic, where practical applications are made (Woods and Magyary, 2010).

In 2007, researchers from the Center for Disease Control and Prevention (CDC) proposed the existence of four phases within the scope of translational research, which consisted of phase T1 with the translation of basic research to a candidate application in health; in phase T2, the research would evaluate the value of the application for health practice leading to the development of evidence-based guidelines; in phase T3 the research would try to move these guidelines to health practice, through delivery and dissemination/diffusion; and finally, in phase T4, the translation would seek to assess the real outcomes of the application in the practice of healthcare (Cha and Koo, 2016).

The feedback path from the clinic to the laboratory also favors the advancement of the conquest and improvement of basic science since this type of itinerary from the laboratory to the clinic defines the essence of translational research in its purpose of translating the basic discoveries of the laboratory into practical applications for the clinic with efficiency, effectiveness, and agility (Plebani, 2008).

The clinical results also tend to return to the laboratory, in feedback, contributing significantly to the improvement of that therapeutic strategy, completing the itinerary of return from the clinic to the laboratory. Translational research aims to fill this gap between the basic science researcher and the clinician in their fields of practice (Lippi et al., 2007).

From a historical point of view, translational research expands to other aspects of health practices that are not directly related to research (T1 and T2); however, over time, translational medicine (T3 and T4) arises when thematic and interaction with commerce, ethics, and law are accepted in the translational field, and the need for a translational science was presented. Thus, translational research spread intensely and rapidly to the entire planet as a result of the effort to promote health research, related to biomedical, epidemiological, and clinical aspects, which was projected globally in the massive presence of scientific work and cooperation in most countries (Cha and Koo, 2016).

In this sense, translational science is the research that begins in basic science and concludes in the practical application of learned knowledge; what translational research has as its central object is to promote, finance, and encourage the development of intervention research, i.e., to stimulate research that provokes changes in care practice, in the management of important health problems. And the greatest contribution of translational medicine to scientific culture is the production of this alignment in the field of health research and, in particular, in biomedicine. In this sense, a focus is needed for the entire wide range of scientific research in health, concerning the biomedical, clinical, technologic, and epidemiological scope to prioritize the most promising lines, following the guidelines of translational research that focuses on basic research inspired by use (Banerjee, 2016).

7. Bioinformatics in healthcare

In the last decades, there has been considerable evolution in technologies for the study, analysis, and understanding of issues relevant to biologic sciences, boosting the tools for research in several related sectors. One of these sectors is bioinformatics, a great multidisciplinary science. Bioinformatics is a multidisciplinary science that arose from the need to understand biologic functions and more specific genes. Software engineering, mathematics, physics, chemistry, statistics, computer science, and molecular biology are some areas of knowledge related to it (Baxevanis et al., 2020).

It is a branch of science, based on in silico experimentation, that aims at grouping, interpreting, and elucidating biologic events through the organization and understanding of data and information based on the use of tools from biology, computing, mathematics, and related areas. Bioinformatics is the use of computational and mathematical techniques related to chemical, physical, and biologic knowledge to process your information about genes, proteins, enzymes as well as cell simulation, sequence alignment, the grouping of homologous proteins, the assembly of trees phylogenetic, and others (Lesk, 2019).

Bioinformatics builds computational models of the molecules that make up living beings. And that involves any molecule, from the DNA molecules in our cells, our proteins to the water that exists in our body. In these models of molecules, we can describe each atom, and how it binds to other atoms, forming one (or even millions of) complete molecule (s) (Chen et al., 2017; Pucker et al., 2019).

It is a scientific field that advances more and more, due to the growth of large databases of genes, molecules, and proteins. From this, we better understand biology using computational techniques, such as programming. Through modeling seeking to discover new drugs and innovative treatments to combat various diseases, it is possible, for example, to predict the possible variations of a particular protein so that its entry into a cell is better understood, improving its efficiency in fighting bacteria (Hadfield, 2017).

Informatics in "bio" informatics consists of the computational part, going from the management of basic information with their respective databases, through the processing of them through various algorithms and comparing them with the data generated by the researchers for, finally, simulation/modeling of systems to be carried out to better elucidate their operation. From a scientific point of view, bioinformatics was developed to analyze biologic data in a short period through the isolation of pathogens and host characteristics. Such achievements are acquired by the development of software that can find specific substances to process accurate information (Mercado, 2019).

From a computational point of view, the medical/biologic data can be treated in the same way as any other, where the results and conclusions of its analysis are strongly dependent on the experimental methodology by which they were obtained. Since although computational, statistical, and mathematical methods are necessary to organize and process this data, they must also be analyzed through the biologic lens, taking into account the particularities of living systems. This is necessary for choosing the best data analysis approach and for facilitating dialogue with biologic and health professionals (Shukla, 2017).

From the development point of view, the new diagnostic methodologies also have bioinformatics tools for processing, integrating, and analyzing all the information, making it possible to also compare the data generated in the laboratory with the various existing databases. In this way, it also speeds up the analysis and release of the patient's result, making it more efficient. The functioning of the system is monitored in production, that is, in the laboratory routine, following the platform's security protocols, the need for data backup, the volume of that data, and the integration with third-party systems, among other functions (Bhardwaj et al., 2019).

8. Bioinformatics from an applicable molecular point of view

The possible processes for its application start from the acquisition of biologic data, through storage, processing, distribution, analysis, and interpretation. Bioinformatics had its conceptual framework in the 1970s driven by the high growth in the number of amino acid sequences and the need for a more efficient analysis of them. The techniques used to learn the machines used in bioinformatics are artificial neural networks, support vector machines, decision trees, genetic algorithms, watershed transform, Hough transform, digital image processing, clustering algorithms, and hidden Markov chains, among many more. Since this science is responsible for storing and relating biologic data, with the aid of computational methods and mathematical algorithms, it recognizes patterns that would probably be impossible to analyze without such help (Ibrahim et al., 2018; Monteiro et al., 2017, 2018a,b, 2019a,b, 2020a,b; Borges Monteiro et al., 2019).

Technologic advances in both hardware and software, as well as access to the internet, also allowed the advancement of this science to be possible and is still constantly updated today. The high amount of data available has made storage more organized and universal, facilitating the exchange of information and quick access to data. Simultaneously as in the ease of access to the internet, it was the main factor that allowed the advancement of the science that unites computing and biology. The great demand for available data, where, currently, this information is deposited in several databases that are structured in a way directed to the structure, functionality, and/or interaction between biomolecules or segmented by a logical organization, made it possible for storage to make it more universal and organized, facilitating the exchange of information and speeding up access to data, which is constantly updated (Wang et al., 2016; Monteiro et al., 2018, 2019).

Bioinformatics is a tool that, through the use of software, can be applied in the search and allows the analysis of innumerable genetic information, mainly tumors, clinical trials, as well as drug targets. The target can cover a range of biologic entities, which include understanding the different functions of proteins, which are obtained through genes through (somatic) sequencing, reaching genomics, making this data able to generate the genetic profile tumor as if it were a genetic signature of the tumor (Wang et al., 2016; Monteiro et al., 2018, 2019).

In other words, a drug target acts mainly on cancer cells, which avoids acting on most healthy cells, resulting in fewer side effects. The target needs to be druggable, which makes them selective targets for the design of new drugs, that is, reducing the impact of drugs on humans and having a better biologic response, being measurable both in vitro and in vivo. Thus, this genetic data allows the search for target treatments, characterizing protein structures, where there is a compatible molecular alteration, DNA, and RNA, with a specific drug (Wang et al., 2016; Monteiro et al., 2018, 2019).

For this, using bioinformatics methods, this information based on sequences and molecular structures is analyzed and explored to infer the essential identification of genes, the development of a drug target against a given pathogen, and the probability of minimizing the chance of that pathogen developing a drug resistance. Thus, bioinformatics is an essential science for target-based drug discovery against certain pathogens (Wang et al., 2016; Monteiro et al., 2018, 2019).

This is the biologic question that is based on the analysis of the genome/DNA, which is transcribed in RNA, and which will later be translated into proteins. Consequently, it leads to the development of molecular chains, giving rise to cells. Each of these categories has highly relevant components within the field of bioinformatics, such as understanding the formation of proteins, being able to perform the alignment of the amino acid sequence that generated its synthesis, and then, it is possible to use a database to find patterns and similarities (Monteiro, 2019).

The relevance of these models, as well as a large part of the studies for the practical life of society, seeks to understand the origin of diseases. And, based on this information, bioinformatics is also used in the search for new drugs. For some decades, most drugs have used bioinformatics methods during their development. It is also possible to use bioinformatics to find genes with a high degree of similarity between different species and, subsequently, generate a more accurate definition of their degree of kinship (genomic taxonomy).

9. Bioinformatics from an applicable perspective

Currently, these data are deposited in several databases that follow a logical or structured organization aimed at the structure, functionality, and/or interaction between biomolecules. To predict structures and results, to study and simulate cell metabolism, to study three-dimensional structures of molecules, to build evolutionary trees, to analyze biologic images and signals, and even to unravel the biologic function of a specific DNA sequence are some activities that bioinformatics allows (Mercado, 2019; Shukla, 2017).

The main applications of bioinformatics can be seen in the storage, analysis, and processing of biologic sequences (large-scale proteins and DNA/RNA); extraction of information for useful knowledge from biologic sequences (data mining), handling and organization of biologic databases; identification of genes/annotation of genomes related to the prediction of the structure and function of biomolecules; simulation of biologic processes and modeling of biologic processes; modeling of metabolic and regulatory processes of cellular tissues, organisms, and at the cellular level modeling and alignment of sequences and structures; solving complex optimization problems; grouping of genes by their expression; and inference of phylogenetic trees and pattern identification (Lesk, 2019; Chen et al., 2017).

The area of activity of bioinformatics is broad, taking into account hospitals, clinical analysis laboratories, the pharmaceutical industry, and public and private research centers. It is fundamental in the analysis process within the sequencing process due to the high volume of data generated by next-generation sequencing technologies, which allows for a new approach to large-scale sequencing (HGS, high throughput sequencing), providing direct sequencing and parallel flow of millions and billions of DNA molecules, considerably increasing the scale and resolution of analyses. It is able to offer a variety of information about a given genome or metagenome, from its structural characteristics to later analyses that allow inferring their functionality. Such factors make bioinformatics an indispensable process for the biotechnologic advance applied to several areas (Pucker et al., 2019; Hadfield, 2017; Mercado, 2019).

Bioinformatics is a multidisciplinary area that develops and implements several computational technologies to study biomedical subjects and issues. It is the use of computers to amplify knowledge about the blocks of life, from the simple atoms that form the genes to living beings. The volume of data describing complex biologic phenomena will never stop growing since there is an integrated demand for technologic development in information science and data modeling. The growth potential of the field of precision and translational medicine, focused on genomic knowledge applied to clinical decisions, is enormous, and this interaction is the key for health systems worldwide to exploit its full potential (Baxevanis et al., 2020; Shukla, 2017).

10. Smart healthcare

The need to better analyze the cost-benefit ratio for the adoption of different technologies is precisely why so-called smart healthcare is gaining more and more importance. These intelligent systems help to preserve doctors' current workflow, allowing them to interact with patients in a normal and natural way, while reducing the time spent on administrative and nondirect healthcare tasks, a critical concern for many doctors (França et al., 2019; França et al., 2020).

Smart healthcare can basically be defined as the appropriate treatment offered to the right patient at the right time and place. It involves technology to accurately diagnose, treat, and deliver care; keep patients well informed and involved in their health care; effectively use information and communication between all parts of the health ecosystem, in an integrated manner; allow new health models to expand access and deliver healthcare more cost-effectively; and increase efficiency and reduce waste (Fig. 2.2) (Khan et al., 2017).

It also considers virtual assistants allow doctors to navigate through the clinical documentation process in a transparent manner using natural and interactive dialogue. Using this technology, it is possible to capture and analyze patient data, automatically filling in the patient's medical record and asking the doctor to provide more details when necessary. Virtual assistants help manage these tasks, reserving the doctor's time for patient care. This allows doctors to focus their attention on the individual needs of their patients, rather than a computer screen, which helps to humanize the interaction and facilitates a deeper and more natural dialogue. This natural dialogue also allows patients to make additional comments or correct any inaccuracies in their own records, resulting in more accurate and complete clinical documentation, which helps to ensure that the patient receives adequate and quality treatment at the point of care (Tian et al., 2019).

An illustrative scenario is a fact that part of inpatient services is migrating to nontraditional care environments, such as home care and outpatient clinics. However, the challenge is to overcome the logistics in coordinating members of the healthcare supply chain who often work in different locations such as hospitals, medical clinics, doctor's offices, and diagnostic laboratories, among others. Besides, patients may reside in a city or certain cases even in a country far from their caregivers. Or, there is the fact that the patient's journey in some cases takes him from doctor to doctor, sometimes going through the public system or different private operators. In this context comes virtual assistants who can assist in coordinating patient care among multiple caregivers, providing immediate access to all details of the patient's history, regardless of where the patient was last seen. This allows doctors and caregivers who refer them to offer patients safe and effective treatment, even in the most complex environments (Gupta et al., 2016).

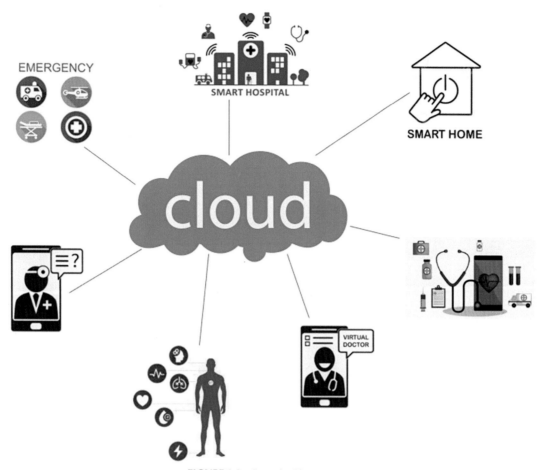

FIGURE 2.2 Smart healthcare concept.

11. Smart healthcare from a technologic interpretation

These technologies also have the ability to address recurring issues, such as medication adherence and patient adherence. As health records are often stored in different formats and systems, it is difficult to track this patient's health history, making it easier for many doctors and health managers to have better process management. In certain situations, it becomes increasingly difficult to coordinate consultations and procedures, share test results, and involve patients in their treatment plans without the aid of technology. By reinventing the way doctors and patients interact with technology, it dramatically changes the overall health experience, with the power to understand natural dialogue and process huge amounts of data using artificial intelligence. One way is to use technology to implement and coordinate preventive medicine programs, thus generating more quality of life for its beneficiaries and lower costs (Baker et al., 2017).

Emerging technologies will be combined with clinical knowledge in the field of healthcare, which will result in reducing costs and increasing their value, since smart healthcare is a strategic bet, due to the increasing weight of medical expenses in population and the increased need for well-being. The interactions of these factors and information technology for the analysis of their effects on health are close to the paradigm of the digital transformation of health through 4P medicine, corresponding to the "predictive, preventive, personalized, and participatory" that increasingly becomes practical and real. Over the years, the world has witnessed great advances in biomedical and bioinformatics informatics. Biomedical informatics is an emerging field of health that aims to translate laboratory observation into clinical practice. Smart medical care has also developed rapidly with ubiquitous sensor and communication technologies (Alonso et al., 2019).

Also related are the biologic elements essential to human health, which play an important role in a variety of diseases and disorders. Through translational research, bioinformatics focuses on experimental verification and computer-aided diagnosis by providing a medical procedure that assists doctors in the interpretation of exams, such as employing medical images. The occurrence and progression of certain diseases are strongly associated with a combination of genetic, lifestyle, and environmental factors. And understanding the interaction between genetic and nongenetic components provides deep insights into the pathogenesis of the disease and promotes personalized strategies for healthcare for people. This is what is brought up through the bioinformatics present in smart healthcare. What is related in its broad definition is that bioinformatics involves the application of information and communication technology in the analysis of any area of biology (Bouchard, 2017).

Emerging and multidisciplinary research paradigms have fundamentally transformed biomedical science and the provision of clinical care, along with translational science fundamentally aimed at the right treatment for the right patient, at the right time. Increasing amounts of information about a patient can be efficiently collected, analyzed, and retrieved, increasingly making it possible to direct medical treatment and preventive care to the individual (Khan et al., 2017).

In light of the exponential growth of biomedical data, methodologies are needed to transform data into knowledge. This is closely linked to the conduct of clinical and translational research projects, which are by their nature complex and generally computationally intensive due to various types of information needs that occur simultaneously. At each step, from conceptualization of the project to design and implementation, a variety of data and knowledge resources are consumed or produced. Making sure of the promise of knowledge-driven medical assistance, it is necessary to capitalize on the advances in translational computing (Thompson, 2020).

12. Discussion

A doctor has access to a patient's digital medical record, with all his history of diagnoses, treatments, outcomes, tests performed, and genetic data, in addition to physical activity data, heart rate, weight, and eating habits, all of which are still visualized in trend charts, so it is still a distant reality.

As knowledge of basic science can be brought to the patient, the results of these interactions remain long-term, causing a multiplier effect on knowledge. Related is translational science that seeks to dilute the watertight separations between basic science and applied science by access to the vast disease bank available in institutions.

The fusion of technology and bioinformatics and biology follows the guidelines of translational science through the digitization and processing of large masses of genetic data, from DNA, in search of variants associated with genetic diseases or certain phenotypes, which are expressed or observable in our human body. Or as well, there are other aspects related to human biologic data, making is possible to notice that an era is reached in which the understanding, in particular, of a patient's genome, or part of it, is fundamental to the practice of medicine in several specialties.

In the same way that the use of a patient's genetic data and other medical records can assist in the diagnosis or treatment of a specific disorder, this individualized analysis requires the joint participation of biology and computing through bioinformatics.

Responsibility for the health, the use of these data, first for the patient's own individual management, through the monitoring of the physical condition, acting in prevention, and a change of habits and behaviors is a major objective in achieving a healthy and quality life. Second, by providing this holistic view to a clinical doctor or geneticist, he will be able to look at all of a patient's health components at the same time to make better informed diagnosis and treatment decisions. Still considering the current technologic context, it represents a new era of patient empowerment, which is becoming increasingly involved in treatment decisions, whether home diagnostics and higher added value services.

Basic science is needed, but when working to understand a biologic system, it always has a degree of applicability. A disease bank, especially tumors from a specific hospital or educational institution, is fundamental for translational research because it is a direct link to the clinical part. Because it is very well organized, it allows the verification of the relevant test of scientific questions. It is possible to search for answers in real cases and correlate the data with the clinical history of the patients, which is widely recorded.

On the other hand, we can act in another way to achieve this scenario, unlocking the value of healthcare data, since, in general, these data reside in information silos. This concerns translational medicine, which is a branch of medical research that seeks to directly connect scientific research to the treatment of patients.

Translational medicine aims to streamline the transfer of knowledge produced on the bench for application in clinical research and public health. The idea is to establish the connection between the creation and application of knowledge, integrating researchers from the basic and clinical areas to better assist the population. In this context, through technology, data presents two main challenges: volume and variety. The internet of things (IoT), sensors and mobile technology, additional diagnostic information from connected medical devices, information from patient-reported results (ePRO), which results reported by the patient are collected by electronic methods, whether from smartphones or medical-grade wearables, contribute to a large amount of data that can be collected and interpreted.

In this sense, the objective of translational medicine is to stimulate the formation of multidisciplinary teams and to create a culture of approximation of the basic area with the clinical area and, mainly, to make what resulted from basic research and was seen as useful in the research clinic reach the patient. It is the challenge of taking the knowledge produced at the university to public health.

Bioinformatics deals with an enormous amount of data and integrates computational analytical tools, results obtained by laboratory procedures, and state-of-the-art genetic sequencing equipment, in addition to a network of scientists from all corners of the planet interconnected by the internet. It is through this technology and with this variety of data, considering the types of data available concerning patient demographics, pathology, and results of laboratory tests, radiology, radiation treatments, medications, treatments, posttherapy care, notes, and documents of the caregiver, operational, financial, and information about plans, insurance, and characteristics of the provider. Still, one must consider larger sources of data that are images and complete genomic information. Per patient, thousands of fields and data files can be collected and mapped on our timeline, all describing our health status.

The application of technology through bioinformatics with the bias of translational medicine must be done responsibly. Particular cases such as DNA sequencing cannot be seen as a genetic horoscope, but a powerful tool that implies ethical issues. If not done well, it can be a stigma for the rest of the patient's life and their family as well. Health data is structured or unstructured. Electronic medical records systems usually support structured data, but an abundance of data used to treat diseases such as cancer is still unstructured. What is implied to implement successful analysis, unstructured data must be analyzed and transformed into structured data.

From the point of view of translational cancer research, and following the objectives of translational medicine through bioinformatics, in general, the analysis and interpretation of these types of data are complex. These teams, formed by a specialized multidisciplinary team with an academic background in the areas of biologic and exact sciences, composed of computational biology and bioinformatics, focus on the application of existing analytical and computational approaches and on the development of new methods to deepen the understanding about the cancer biology and perfect future therapies.

This amount of data and all its qualities are difficult to understand, which is why advanced technologies, a real-time processing platform, and a suite of healthcare applications are a necessity. These three components are the basis of smart healthcare, which is 21st-century modeling that helps to provide results and provide healthier quality for patients and health professionals.

Using smart technologies such as artificial intelligence, machine learning (ML), IoT resources, and real-time analysis achieves operational and clinical excellence in care delivery. The efforts of these teams are focused on the application of modern technologic techniques, such as ML, seeking to explore complex data to produce models for the classification and prediction of patients with high or low risk of response.

The objective is to transform what is seen in clinical research, through biologic or computational technology, into measures for public health. It represents one of the goals of translational medicine.

Through collaboration and sharing of care practices and clinical indicators, we can promote process improvement, implement innovative teaching activities, and leverage translational, clinical, and quality of life research activities.

Clinical and translational research studies are encouraged by collaboration. Some clinical studies can be carried out in partnership and include patients from cooperating institutions, which catalyzes the analytical power of the data. In this way, translational studies will also be stimulated among scientists, exchanging samples, molecules, among other resources, and further qualifying collaborative research.

Thus, they generate structural benefits from the point of view of hospitals concerning greater patient satisfaction, less variation in clinical practice, less risk of readmission, capacity for resources and productivity metrics, better adherence to medication, effective sharing of resources between providers, optimization of the revenue cycle, better risk management at the point of care for high-cost disease cohorts, and alternative revenue resources monetizing insights from evidence data in the real world as a service, among other aspects.

Benefits from the patient's point of view include higher quality of patient care due to continuous integrated care, better patient treatment due to specialization, precision medicine, better disease prevention among patients, better personalized and individualized patient care, among other aspects.

13. Conclusions

Translational medicine is a form of medicine that begins in basic science and results in the practical application of knowledge, bringing academic institutions closer to the organization. It is an interdisciplinary domain of the biomedical area, sustained by three main pillars related to bench, bed, and community. Its objective is to match resources, disciplines, knowledge, and techniques within these pillars promoting improvements in diagnosis, prevention, and therapies. It is a discipline within the scope of biomedical research targeting public health concerning the community and the health of individuals. Translational research penetrates all specialties considering their particularity and individuality as a promising evolution of evidence-based medicine and with the aim of getting closer and closer to personalized medicine.

By translating scientific findings into diagnostic procedures, policies, tools, education, and therapies, the rapid growth that translational medicine has achieved is by assessing its ability to accelerate discoveries. Translational medicine is a promising domain of medical research seeking a direct connection of scientific research to the treatment of patients, enabling clinically significant research, which is fundamental concern for the practice of evidence-based medicine. Translational research also grants for the faster progress of therapeutic potentials, bringing the concept of interdisciplinarity in its basic concept, decreasing the time between the identification of the drug target and clinically expressive and considerable therapeutic options.

Basic research is essentially necessary concerning granting the best understanding of conditions concerning normal perspective versus disease status. However, it is not properly translating that particular knowledge into specific and useable clinical applications. Translational research is fruitful in the aspect related to the progress of science employed to the development of new diagnostic drugs, drug targets, and tests, in the same sense as intervention techniques related to the context of patients signed in understanding the development and progression of a certain disease, as it allows a greater approximation between the knowledge generated and its application for the individual or society. It has evolved over time, ceasing to be a field linked to clinical research, with perspectives that were mainly focused on the development of new health technologies. The principal objective of translational research is related to compose, assimilate, and aggregate advances in biotechnology, with clinical trials, stimulating research from the bench to the bed, including the production of basic, clinical, and translational science studies.

The scope of translational research comprises clinical demands, studies, health management, public health, policies, and economics. It is paramount in the progress of contemporary biomedical science, and its influence follows ethical-social, political-economic, and educational-scientific approaches. Translational research also involves collaboration between all users of knowledge, which tend to progress through the reorganization of academic teams following a translational way, merging assets of different natures within the individual pillars to significantly enhance and refine the global health system.

Through translational science, it is clear to note the need to do basic science, as it is worked with a focus on understanding a biologic system, and this always has a degree of applicability, so it is fundamental for translational research because it is a direct link with the clinical part, since it is allowed to reduce the distance between the research developed and the needs of a health system.

Bioinformatics is an area of science that integrates mathematics, computational technology, and molecular biology, and it has a very broad meaning, which as science uses methodologic techniques from computer science, or more generally, from the exact sciences, to solve problems in biology. It is dependent on computational resources because it works with research areas based on a large volume of data generation, and this volume of data has increased exponentially over the years. It requires interpretation of results, and it is necessary to have processing capacity to interpret the data, analyze, and understand how a given biologic process works, or analyze certain biologic materials.

The technology provides a more detailed analysis, especially of tumors, cells, and blood molecules to map cellular characteristics of patients being treated. Technology expands the human view of what happens, in detail, with thousands of cells or with just one cell. It is possible to analyze both cells obtained from the blood and the biopsy of a given tumor.

14. Future trends

Translational biotechnology is explained and elucidated from that used in medicine "from the bench at the bedside," which aims to highlight science oriented by the scientific method concerning the use of biotechnology linked to innovation. Biotechnology as a science has been employed in multiple forms, allowing the rapid progress of knowledge related to the inclusion of technology in the treatment of diseases through the academic environment (Wang et al., 2020).

It is related to the existence of the need to analyze the applicability of biotechnologic products to the reality of medicine in public health, as well as the guarantee of social and economic relevance related to the advancement of knowledge and application of results, especially concerning the solution of priority problems of health. And this lack of innovation in the system interrupts the translational research process (Morrison, 2016).

Scientific research comes from a great source of material that is still little used, and one of the pillars of biotechnology is the scientific production produced in universities, research centers, and science and technology institutions. And with biotechnology, partner companies create cooperation networks in search of the complementary of specific assets to establish a translational development model, which enables a technologic catch-up of the sector, to reduce the gap, and to structure technologic development platforms and manufacturing that allow the generation of a portfolio of products with high added value (Moo-Young, 2019).

From a historical point of view, it has been employed for the development of gene and cell therapy, vaccines, and development, the manipulation, and use of embryonic stem cells. Thus, the results generated by biotechnology are eventually transformed into commercial products, having a solid correlation with the concept of innovation, instead of innovating, meaning-making a product available for consumption, resulting in actions applicable to the improvement of the population's living conditions. Biotechnology has favored the evidenced discovery of new bioactive molecules (Coordinators, 2017).

The spectrum of translational science describes each stage of research, which is focused on research involving people, including clinical trials, and research in partnership with the community, the science of implementation and dissemination, from the biologic basis of diseases following interventions impacting the health of the community as a whole in the same sense that improves the health of individuals. Each phase of the translational research spectrum is based on basic research, where the term translational describes the process of transforming observations in the clinic, laboratory, hospitals, and community into interventions, ranging from therapeutics and diagnostics to medical procedures extending behavioral changes. In this sense, translational science in the area focused on understanding touches the scientific and operational principles underlying investigation in each stage of the translation process (Moo-Young, 2019; Coordinators, 2017).

Patient-oriented research is a specific type of translational clinical research, playing an essential role in several types of clinical translation research, which include mechanistic, therapeutic, and observational studies, as well as clinical trials. Here, the patient is the center and core of the investigation, requiring greater interaction concerning contact, treatment, and dialogue with the patient to test the research hypotheses and carry out the studies regarding disease mechanisms, therapy or interventions in diseases, clinical trials, and studies for the development of new technology related to the health of a person or a group of people (Field et al., 2019).

The Undiagnosed Diseases Network (UDN) improves and accelerates the diagnosis of rare and undiagnosed conditions and was made for academic medical centers, hospitals, and institutions. The UDN is an expansion of a multidisciplinary model that developed based on the Department of Biomedical Informatics at Harvard Medical School and aims to bring together clinical and research specialists from several countries to solve the most challenging medical mysteries using advanced technologies, the largest being dedicated exclusively to research. The UDN's goal is to support translational clinical research with a focus on improving care and outcomes for people with rare diseases (Ramoni et al., 2017; Farooqi et al., 2019; Qazi et al., 2019).

References

Adithan, C., 2017. Principles of translational science in medicine: from bench to bedside. Indian J. Med. Res. 145 (3), 408.

Agarwal, A., Cho, C.L., Majzoub, A., Esteves, S.C., 2017. The society for translational medicine: clinical practice guidelines for sperm DNA fragmentation testing in male infertility. Transl. Androl. Urol. 6 (Suppl. 4), S720.

Ahmad, I., Yanuar, A., Mulia, K., Mun'im, A., 2017. Review of angiotensin-converting enzyme inhibitory assay: rapid method in drug discovery of herbal plants. Phcog. Rev. 11 (21), 1.

Alonso, S.G., de la Torre Díez, I., Zapiraín, B.G., 2019. Predictive, personalized, preventive and participatory (4P) medicine applied to telemedicine and eHealth in the literature. J. Med. Syst. 43 (5), 140.

Baker, S.B., Xiang, W., Atkinson, I., 2017. Internet of things for smart healthcare: technologies, challenges, and opportunities. IEEE Access 5, 26521–26544.

Banerjee, E.R., 2016. Perspectives in Translational Research in Life Sciences and Biomedicine. Springer, Singapore, pp. 1–10.

Barile, S., Polese, F., Saviano, M., Carrubbo, L., 2017. Service innovation in translational medicine. In: Innovating in Practice. Springer, Cham, pp. 417–438.

Baxevanis, A.D., Bader, G.D., Wishart, D.S. (Eds.), 2020. Bioinformatics. John Wiley & Sons.

Bhardwaj, K.K., Banyal, S., Sharma, D.K., 2019. Artificial intelligence based diagnostics, therapeutics and applications in biomedical engineering and bioinformatics. In: Internet of Things in Biomedical Engineering. Academic Press, pp. 161–187.

Birmingham, K., 2002. What Is Translational Research?.

Borges Monteiro, A.C., Iano, Y., França, R.P., Arthur, R., 2019. Medical-laboratory algorithm WTH-MO for segmentation of digital images of blood cells: a new methodology for making hemograms. Int. J. Simulat. Syst. Sci. Technol. 20.

Bouchard, B. (Ed.), 2017. Smart Technologies in Healthcare. CRC Press.

Bravo-Merodio, L., Williams, J.A., Gkoutos, G.V., Acharjee, A., 2019. Omics biomarker identification pipeline for translational medicine. J. Transl. Med. 17 (1), 155.

Burbelo, P.D., Ching, K.H., Han, B.L., Klimavicz, C.M., Iadarola, M.J., 2010. Synthetic biology for translational research. Am. J. Tourism Res. 2 (4), 381.

Burke, H.B., Grizzle, W.E., 2017. Clinical validation of molecular biomarkers in translational medicine. In: Biomarkers in Cancer Screening and Early Detection, vol. 3.

Cai, W. (Ed.), 2014. Engineering in Translational Medicine. Springer, Berlin, Germany.

Cha, Y.J., Koo, J.S., 2016. Next-generation sequencing in thyroid cancer. J. Transl. Med. 14 (1), 322.

Chen, F.M., Zhao, Y.M., Jin, Y., Shi, S., 2012. Prospects for translational regenerative medicine. Biotechnol. Adv. 30 (3), 658−672.

Chen, C., Huang, H., Wu, C.H., 2017. Protein bioinformatics databases and resources. In: Protein Bioinformatics. Humana Press, New York, NY, pp. 3−39.

Coordinators, N.R., 2017. Database resources of the national center for biotechnology information. Nucleic Acids Res. 45 (Database issue), D12.

Crabu, S., 2018. Rethinking biomedicine in the age of translational research: organisational, professional, and epistemic encounters. Sociol. Compass 12 (10), e12623.

Edelman, E.R., FitzGerald, G.A., 2019. A Decade of Science Translational Medicine.

Farooqi, M.R., Iqbal, N., Singh, N.K., et al., 2019. Wireless Sensor Networks towards convenient infrastructure in health care industry: a systematic study. In: Sensors for Health Monitoring, vol. 5. Elsevier, pp. 31−46. https://doi.org/10.1016/B978-0-12-819361-7.00002-6.

Field, T.S., Dizonno, V., Park, S.S., Hill, M.D., 2019. Patient-Oriented Research Can be Meaningful for Clinicians and Trialists in Addition to Patients.

França, R.P., Iano, Y., Monteiro, A.C.B., Arthur, R., Estrela, V.V., Assumpção, S.L.D.L., Razmjooy, N., 2019. Potential Proposal to Improvement of the Data Transmission in Healthcare Systems.

França, R.P., Iano, Y., Monteiro, A.C.B., Arthur, R., 2020. Potential proposal to improve data transmission in healthcare systems. In: Deep Learning Techniques for Biomedical and Health Informatics. Academic Press, pp. 267−283.

Gallagher, E.J., LeRoith, D., 2016. 1 principles of translational medicine and applications to thyroid cancer investigation. In: Thyroid Cancer: From Emergent Biotechnologies to Clinical Practice Guidelines, vol. 1.

Gupta, P., Agrawal, D., Chhabra, J., Dhir, P.K., 2016. IoT based smart healthcare kit. In: 2016 International Conference on Computational Techniques in Information and Communication Technologies (ICCTICT). IEEE, pp. 237−242.

Hadfield, J., 2017. Overview of next generation sequencing technologies (and bioinformatics) in cancer. J. Pathol. 243, S7.

Hörig, H., Marincola, E., Marincola, F.M., 2005. Obstacles and opportunities in translational research. Nat. Med. 11 (7), 705−708.

Ibrahim, B., McMahon, D.P., Hufsky, F., Beer, M., Deng, L., Le Mercier, P., Marz, M., 2018. A new era of virus bioinformatics. Virus Res. 251, 86−90.

Jiang, H., Cui, Y.H., 2017. The operating obstacles and solving strategy of translational medicine in China. Int. J. Inf. Educ. Technol. 7 (9), 650.

Khan, S.U., Zomaya, A.Y., Abbas, A. (Eds.), 2017. Handbook of Large-Scale Distributed Computing in Smart Healthcare. Springer, New York.

Krueger, A.K., Hendriks, B., Gauch, S., 2019. The Multiple Meanings of Translational Research in Medical Research.

Lesk, A., 2019. Introduction to Bioinformatics. Oxford university press.

Lippi, G., Plebani, M., Guidi, G.C., 2007. The paradox in translational medicine. Clin. Chem. 53 (8), 1553.

Littman, B.H., Di Mario, L., Plebani, M., Marincola, F.M., 2007. What's next in translational medicine? Clin. Sci. 112 (4), 217−227.

Liu, W., 2019. Journal of Translational Medicine Advances in Translational Genomics and Genetics Era.

Macaluso, M., Krams, M., Savitz, J., Drevets, W.C., Preskorn, S.H., 2019. New approaches in translational medicine for phase I clinical trials of CNS drugs. In: Handbook of Behavioral Neuroscience, vol. 29. Elsevier, pp. 81−91.

Mankoff, S.P., Brander, C., Ferrone, S., Marincola, F.M., 2004. Lost in translation: obstacles to translational medicine. J. Transl. Med. 2 (1), 14.

Martins, P.N., 2019. Transdisciplinary innovation in health care: an essay. Science 4 (2), 169−171.

Mercado, L., 2019. Exploring Bioinformatics. Scientific e-Resources.

Mittra, J., Milne, C., 2013a. Introduction to translational medicine. In: Translational Medicine: The Future of Therapy, pp. 3−16.

Mittra, J., Milne, C.P. (Eds.), 2013b. Translational Medicine: The Future of Therapy?. CRC Press.

Monteiro, A.C.B., Iano, Y., França, R.P., 2017. An improved and fast methodology for automatic detecting and counting of red and white blood cells using watershed transform. In: VIII Simpósio de Instrumentação e Imagens Médicas (SIIM)/VII Simpósio de Processamento de Sinais da UNICAMP.

Monteiro, A.C.B., Iano, Y., França, R.P., Arthur, R., Estrela, V.V., October 2018a. A comparative study between methodologies based on the Hough transform and watershed transform on the blood cell count. In: Brazilian Technology Symposium. Springer, Cham, pp. 65−78.

Monteiro, A.C.B., Iano, Y., França, R.P., Arthur, R., October 2018b. Methodology of high accuracy, sensitivity and specificity in the counts of erythrocytes and leukocytes in blood smear images. In: Brazilian Technology Symposium. Springer, Cham, pp. 79−90.

Monteiro, A.C.B., Iano, Y., França, R.P., 2019a. Detecting and counting of blood cells using watershed transform: an improved methodology. In: Proceedings of the 3rd Brazilian Technology Symposium, p. 301.

Monteiro, A.C.B., Iano, Y., França, R.P., Razmjooy, N., 2019b. WT-MO algorithm: automated hematological software based on the watershed transform for blood cell count. In: Applications of Image Processing and Soft Computing Systems in Agriculture. IGI Global, pp. 39−79.

Monteiro, A.C.B., Iano, Y., França, R.P., Arthur, R., 2020a. Development of a laboratory medical algorithm for simultaneous detection and counting of erythrocytes and leukocytes in digital images of a blood smear. In: Deep Learning Techniques for Biomedical and Health Informatics. Academic Press, pp. 165−186.

Monteiro, A.C.B., Iano, Y., França, R.P., Arthur, R., 2020b. Applied medical informatics in the detection and counting of erythrocytes and leukocytes through an image segmentation algorithm. Set Int. J. Broadcast Eng. 5, 7.

Monteiro, A.C.B., 2019. Proposta de uma metodologia de segmentação de imagens para detecção e contagem de hemácias e leucócitos através do algoritmo WT-MO.

Moo-Young, M., 2019. Comprehensive Biotechnology. Elsevier.

Morrison, B.W., 2016. Biotechnology and translational medicine. Clin. Transl. Sci. 9 (3), 125.

Plebani, M., 2008. The changing scenario in laboratory medicine and the role of laboratory professionals in translational medicine. Clin. Chim. Acta 393 (1), 23−26.

Pucker, B., Schilbert, H.M., Schumacher, S.F., 2019. Integrating molecular biology and bioinformatics education. J. Integr. Bioinf. 16 (3).

Qazi, S., Tanveer, K., El-bahnasy, K., Raza, K., 2019. From telediagnosis to teletreatment: the role of computational biology and bioinformatics in tele-based healthcare. In: Telemedicine Technologies. Elsevier, pp. 153−169. https://doi.org/10.1016/B978-0-12-816948-3.00010-6.

Ramoni, R.B., Mulvihill, J.J., Adams, D.R., Allard, P., Ashley, E.A., Bernstein, J.A., Shashi, V., 2017. The undiagnosed diseases network: accelerating discovery about health and disease. Am. J. Hum. Genet. 100 (2), 185−192.

Rubio, D.M., Schoenbaum, E.E., Lee, L.S., Schteingart, D.E., Marantz, P.R., Anderson, K.E., Esposito, K., 2010. Defining translational research: implications for training. Acad. Med. 85 (3), 470.

Ruttenberg, A., Clark, T., Bug, W., Samwald, M., Bodenreider, O., Chen, H., Kinoshita, J., 2007. Advancing translational research with the semantic web. BMC Bioinf. 8 (S3), S2.

Shukla, N., 2017. Bioinformatics in environmental bioremediation-a review. Int. J. Sci. Res. Sci. Eng. Technol. 3, 195−205.

Smith, C., Baveja, R., Grieb, T., Mashour, G.A., 2017. Toward a science of translational science. J. Clin. Transl. Sci. 1 (4), 253−255.

Soldner, F., Jaenisch, R., 2018. Stem cells, genome editing, and the path to translational medicine. Cell 175 (3), 615−632.

Suchkov, S., Notkins, A., Marshall, T., 2018. Personalized & translational medicine as a tandem of the new philosophy, updated mentality and technological platforms. Meta Gene 17, S1−S2.

Thompson, D., 2020. Biomedical big data in patient-centered healthcare services and personalized clinical care. Am. J. Med. Res. 7 (1), 34−40.

Tian, S., Yang, W., Le Grange, J.M., Wang, P., Huang, W., Ye, Z., 2019. Smart healthcare: making medical care more intelligent. Glob. Health J. 3 (3), 62−65. https://doi.org/10.1016/j.glohj.2019.07.001.

Wang, X., Baumgartner, C., Shields, D.C., Deng, H.W., Beckmann, J.S. (Eds.), 2016. Application of Clinical Bioinformatics, vol. 11. Springer, Netherlands.

Wang, T., Liang, C., An, Y., Xiao, S., Xu, H., Zheng, M., Nie, L., 2020. Engineering the translational machinery for biotechnology applications. Mol. Biotechnol. 1−9.

Watts, S., 2016. A mini-review on technique of milk pasteurization. J. Pharmacogn. Phytochem. 5 (5), 99.

Wehling, M., 2008. Translational medicine: science or wishful thinking? J. Transl. Med. 6 (1), 31.

Wei, D.Q., Ma, Y., Cho, W.C., Xu, Q., Zhou, F. (Eds.), 2017. Translational Bioinformatics and its Application. Springer.

Woods, N.F., Magyary, D.L., 2010. Translational research: why nursing's interdisciplinary collaboration is essential. Res. Theor. Nurs. Pract. 24 (1), 9−24.

Yoon, H.B., Do Joon Park, J.S.S., Ahn, C., 2018. Developing a core competency model for translational medicine curriculum. Korean J. Med. Educ. 30 (3), 243.

Chapter 3

Next-generation sequencing: an expedition from workstation to clinical applications

Sandhya Verma[1,b,*] and Rajesh Kumar Gazara[2,a,b,*]

[1]*Shri Vaishnav Institute of Science, Shri Vaishnav Vidyapeeth Vishwavidyalaya, Indore, Madhya Pradesh, India; [2]Laboratório de Química e Função de Proteínas e Peptídeos, Centro de Biociências e Biotecnologia, Universidade Estadual do Norte Fluminense Darcy Ribeiro, Campos dos Goytacazes, Rio de Janeiro, Brazil*

Corresponding authors: E-mail: raj.gzra@gmail.com, sandhya.nipgr@gmail.com

Chapter outline

1. Introduction

Next-generation sequencing (NGS) technologies are new sequencing methods for DNA and RNA sequencing (Goodwin et al., 2016). Researchers are using NGS in basic, applied, and clinical research. In 1970, the first DNA sequencing called Sanger sequencing or original DNA sequencing was developed by Frederick Sanger et al. (1977). Sanger DNA sequencing allowed the analysis of single genes or parts thereof. For three decades, Sanger sequencing was extensively used by the biologists. Later, the emergence of NGS occurred that has opened new possibilities and challenges to biologists and clinicians in the field of genomes exploration and clinical diagnosis (Goodwin et al., 2016; Müllauer, 2017; Raza and Ahmad, 2019). NGS has several advantages over Sanger sequencing. NGS can provide the massive parallel and high-throughput data from multiple samples per run at significantly reduced cost in comparison to Sanger (Goodwin et al., 2016). Moreover, NGS provides more accurate and reliable sequencing data than Sanger DNA sequencing. The human genome was sequenced in almost 13 years using Sanger sequencing at a cost greater than one million dollars (Naidoo et al.,

---

a. Present address: Department of Biotechnology, Indian Institute of Technology Roorkee, Roorkee, India; Department of Electrical Engineering, Indian Institute of Technology Roorkee, Roorkee, India.
b. Equal contribution.

2011), whereas now, it is possible to sequence the human genome within a week at the cost of 100 US dollars (https:// www.genome.gov/about-genomics/fact-sheets/Sequencing-Human-Genome-cost). Due to these advantages, NGS has become a powerful and valuable tool for research and clinical applications. Improvements in NGS technologies and bioinformatics pipelines have created opportunities for researchers to perform whole genome and transcriptome sequencing (of tissues, cells, and organisms) (Jabeen et al., 2018), methylation sequencing, whole exome sequencing (Kulski et al., 2014; Verma et al., 2016; Gazara et al., 2019), and chromatin immunoprecipitation followed by sequencing (ChIP-seq) (Schmidt et al., 2010; Wani and Raza, 2019) and their subsequent in-depth analyses. Moreover, data generated through sequencing technologies also motivate researchers to perform in-depth gene family analysis that could help us to understand the evolutionary history of gene families (Gazara et al., 2018; Nizam et al., 2014). NGS technologies have also been extensively used in rare variant identification using whole genome resequencing and discovery of epigenetic markers related to diseases (Xuan et al., 2013). However, there are some challenges that are needed to be overcome for NGS applications in clinics.

2. Evolution of NGS technologies

To date, one after another, first to third generations of sequencing technologies have evolved. First-generation sequencing (FGS) or Sanger sequencing is also known as dideoxynucleotide method or sequencing by synthesis method. It is based on the principle of DNA chain termination. This method generates long (1.9–84 Kb) and high-quality (99.999% accuracy) sequencing reads (https://www.hindawi.com/journals/bmri/2012/251364/tab1/). Though this method takes much time and cost to generate a DNA sequence, it is a gold standard for small-scale sequencing projects (Totomoch-Serra et al., 2017).

To reduce the sequencing cost and time and to increase accuracy of sequencing, Sanger was replaced by next-generation sequencing or second-generation sequencing (SGS) technologies. The basic features of SGS technologies are as follows: (1) generate millions of reads in one run, (2) much faster in comparison to Sanger, (3) much lower sequencing cost in contrast to Sanger, and (4) no need of electrophoresis to detect output. Moreover, SGS sequencing approach can be broadly categorized into (1) sequencing by ligation and (2) sequencing by synthesis (SBS) (Goodwin et al., 2016). The main steps of the SGS or high-throughput sequencing technologies are sample preparation, DNA fragmentation, library preparation, sequencing, and data analysis. Roche/454 (2005), Illumina/Solexa (2006), ABI/SOLiD (2007), and Ion Torrent (2010) are SGS platforms. Two of these sequencing technologies, the Illumina platforms and Ion Torrent sequencers (Life Technologies), are widely used in biomedical laboratories (Di Resta et al., 2018).

Both Illumina sequencing platform and Ion Torrent are based on SBS approach. Illumina platform can generate "single-end" as well as "paired-end" reads, whereas Ion Torrent can generate only single-end reads. The major limitation of Illumina is relatively short reads, which leads to misassembled and fragmented genome along with hundreds of contigs. In addition, using Illumina short reads, identification and characterization of large structural variations (SVs) that are linked to many diseases (Weischenfeldt et al., 2013) become very challenging tasks. The limitation of Ion Torrent technology is inaccurate quantification of long homopolymeric repeats of the system (Merriman et al., 2012).

Although SGS technologies are able to generate a huge amount of data within a short period of time compared to FGS, these technologies need PCR amplification step, which is a long processing step. Also, assemblies of complex genomes with repetitive regions longer than reads generated by SGS remains a challenge. To overcome the disadvantages of SGS, scientists developed third-generation sequencing (TGS), which is capable of generating long reads at low sequencing cost, and it is faster than SGS because it does direct sequencing of a single DNA molecule without DNA fragmentation and PCR amplification. This is also known as long read sequencing because it generates reads longer than several kilobases. Single-molecule sequencing (SMS) and sequencing in real time are two specific features of TGS technologies. The two most widely used TGS technologies are Single-Molecule Real-Time (SMRT) sequencing by Pacific Biosciences and Nanopore sequencing by Oxford Nanopore (ONT) (Eid et al., 2009; Jain et al., 2015). The ONT released the first sequencer called MinION, a pocket-sized device. It is the only portable and real-time device that generates long reads. These features led it to use in various researches including studies of Ebola and Zika virus (Faria et al., 2016; Quick at al., 2016). Afterward, a new sequencing platform emerged known as PromethION, a standalone benchtop instrument, which is bigger than MinION. Both are useful for high-throughput and high sample number analyses (Kchouk et al., 2017). The emergence of TGS technologies is revolutionizing the genomics field as they open great opportunities to explore genomes at high resolution. Table 3.1 depicts the features of FGS to TGS technologies (Jain et al., 2017; Korlach, 2013; Kulski, 2016; Kchouk et al., 2017; https://www.hindawi.com/journals/bmri/2012/251364/tab1/).

The evolution of NGS technologies and development of bioinformatics tools/software have built our knowledge to translate the multiomics data into clinical applications. The NGS technologies are envisaged at five "omics" levels:

TABLE 3.1 Comparisons between FGS, SGS, and TGS sequencers.

	FGS	SGS		TGS		
	Sanger[a]/3730xl[b]	Illumina[a]/HiSeq[b]	Ion Torrent[a]/Ion Proton[b]	PacBio[a]/Sequel II[b]	ONT[a]/PromethION[b]	ONT[a]/MinION mk[b]
Accuracy	99.999%	99.9%	>99%	85%—89%	Up to 85%	Up to 85%
Read length	400—900 bp	150 bp	200 bp	20 kbp	9846	9545
Sequencing approach	Dideoxy terminator	Reversible terminators	Proton detection	Real-time SMS	Real-time SMS	Real-time SMS
Read type	SE	SE, PE	SE	SE	1D, 2D	1D, 2D
Data generated per run	0.69—2.1 mb	1.5 Tb	10 Gb	~100 Gb	7.6 Tb	50 Gb
Error type	NA	Mismatch	Indel	Indel	NA	Indel/Mismatch
Year	2002	2012	2012	2018	2016	2015
Applications	Small genomic regions, sequencing of variable regions, validating results from NGS, HLA typing, genotyping of microsatellite markers	Human WGS, WES, RNA-seq, methylation-seq	Genome sequencing, drug resistance testing, microbial characterization and targeted sequencing in cancer studies	WGS, targeted sequencing, RNA sequencing, epigenetic characterization	WGS, variants analysis, targeted sequencing, RNA sequencing, metagenomics, and epigenetics	WGS, Variants analysis, target sequencing, RNA sequencing, metagenomics, and epigenetics

[a]Sequencing technology.
[b]Instrument name, bp, base pair; FGS, first-generation sequencing; Gb, gigabyte; kbp, kilobase pair; Mb, megabyte; NA, not available; SGS, second-generation sequencing; tb, terabyte; TGS, third-generation sequencing.

genomics, epigenomics, transcriptomics, proteomics, and metabolomics. These levels are well interconnected with the processes of transcription, translation, and protein modifications (Gibney and Nolan, 2010).

2.1 Multiomics data

2.1.1 Genomics

Clinical applications of genomic data have increased after decrease in the cost of sequencing. In the genomic field, various mutations (such as SNPs, CNVs, and indels) are detected using whole exome sequencing (WES), whole genome sequencing (WGS), and targeted sequencing (TS). WGS can detect these mutations in noncoding and coding parts of genome, whereas WES is capable of discovering these mutations only in protein coding regions. Also, it has been shown that these mutations are linked to diseases. For example, SNPs in the *VCAM-1* and *ARFGEF2* genes cause sickle cell anemia (Dworkis et al., 2011), and frame shift mutation in the *CTFR* gene is associated with cystic fibrosis (White et al., 1990). Moreover, mutation V600E in *BRAF* gene gives rise to a disease called papillary craniopharyngioma, a rare type of brain tumor (Brastianos et al., 2014). TS find mutations only in specific parts of genome only if prior information is available for a disease. TS has been applied usually for diagnosis of Mendelian disorders (Sun et al., 2018).

2.1.2 Epigenomics

Study of epigenetic modifications is called epigenomics. Epigenetic modifications are reversible in nature without a change in DNA sequence. These are chemical modifications that affect gene expression and regulation in normal development and disease conditions. The impacts of epigenetic modifications in various diseases (i.e., cancer, autoimmune, and metabolic) have been studied. DNA methylation and histone modification are two of the most characterized epigenetic modifications. Different sequencing technologies, such as bisulphate sequencing, ChIP-seq, DNase seq, FAIRE seq, and Hi-C are being used to detect modifications in genetic material. For example, Rackham et al. identified the role of methylated *Ifitm3* gene in development of glomerulonephritis, a kidney disease, using whole genome base bisulphate sequencing (Rackham et al., 2017). Several studies have used ChIP-seq to identify changes in histone modifications, transcription factors, and other DNA-binding proteins linked with diseases such as H3K4me3 in neurodevelopmental disease (Shulha et al., 2012), H3K27ac in Crohn disease (Farh et al., 2015) and *LMO1* in neuroblastoma tumorigenesis (Oldridge et al., 2015).

2.1.3 Transcriptomics

Transcriptomics is the study of the transcriptome, a set of total RNAs present in a cell including mRNA (majorly studied form of RNAs), rRNA, tRNA, and other noncoding RNAs (i.e., microRNA). Different kinds of tissues, cellular conditions, and environmental factors make transcriptome dynamic in nature. Potential applications of transcriptome study are gene expression quantification at specific tissue or developmental stage, identification of differentially expressed genes, detection of variable splice events (such as exon skipping, exon truncation, and exon elongation), and discovery of novel transcripts and chimeric gene fusion. Previously, it has been shown that Mendelian disorders are caused by abnormal splicing events (Scotti and Swanson, 2016). Using whole blood transcriptome, identification of insufficient low expression of *RARS2* has been shown. The *RARS2* gene is connected with global developmental delay, seizures, microcephaly, hypotonia, and progressive scoliosis (Fresard et al., 2018). Moreover, recent studies have shown prediction of the breast cancer biomarkers using RNA-seq (Brueffer et al., 2018). Furthermore, metastasis-linked microRNAs in lung adeno-carcinoma have been identified using microRNA sequencing (Daugaard et al., 2017). Overall, transcriptomic approach is essential in clinical routine including disease diagnosis, prognosis, and therapeutic selection.

2.1.4 Proteomics

Proteomics is the study of the proteome, which is the entire set of proteins in a cell at a particular time. Like the transcriptome, the proteome is also dynamic in nature. Proteomics studies are dependent on a source from where proteins can be obtained because proteins cannot be amplified like DNA. Proteomics has two-fold application in clinical routine. First, it unravels the information streaming through the protein networks that gets perturbed either to cause or to reflect the consequence of disease in the microenvironment of the host tissue. This information is monitored during therapy to analyze the change in patterns. Secondly, clinical proteomics is utilized to develop biomarker profiling skills for early detection of diseases and their effective treatment (Kumar et al., 2017). Integration of the proteome with the genome is called proteogenome, and its study called proteogenomics. Recent studies have identified cancer-related single amino acid variants using a proteogenomics approach (Tan et al., 2017).

2.1.5 Metabolomics

In the last decade, remarkable progress has been observed in clinical applications of the most recent member of the omics family, i.e., metabolomics. The study of metabolites is known as metabolomics. Metabolites are small molecules (such as amino acids, lipids, peptides, nucleic acids, carbohydrates, vitamins, and minerals) that are intermediate products of biochemical processes that take place in living organisms. The development in this field is by virtue of improvement in mass spectrometry (Zhang et al., 2020) and molecular imaging technologies, such as positron emission tomography and magnetic resonance spectroscopic imaging (Spratlin et al., 2009). The aim of metabolomics is to detect the concentration or level of metabolites that could become potential biomarkers in the clinical diagnosis and prediction of disease. Using the knowledge of metabolomics in the field of biomedicine, researchers have discovered a number of markers for diseases such as risk for pancreatic cancer (Mayers et al., 2014), type 2 diabetes (Rhee et al., 2011), and memory impairment (Mapstone et al., 2014). A range of metabolites (from 40,153 to 114,100) have been reported in the human metabolome; among those, 3105 to 5498 metabolites are associated with diseases (Wishart et al., 2018).

3. Computation power and data analysis

NGS is extremely versatile. Data generated through sequencing and analysis is of a huge amount (around hundreds of gigabytes to terabytes). To analyze the massive amount of data, many different tools and pipelines have been developed, which are typically functional in the Linux environment. Storing and analyzing the massive data requires high-performance computing, including processing power, high memory (RAM), and big data storage hardware. Specifically, computing power and storage capacity depend on the size, number of samples, and type of analysis.

One of the major needs of NGS experiments is data analysis. The NGS sequencers generate a large amount of data that cannot be interpreted without bioinformatic analysis. Sequencers provide raw reads in FASTQ format or the native raw file formats (such as SFF, HDF5, bam, and SOLID), depending on sequencing platforms. Scientists submit raw reads generated from NGS platforms in the public repositories before publication. The most widely used public repositories are Gene Expression Omnibus (https://www.ncbi.nlm.nih.gov/geo/), Sequence Read Archive (https://www.ncbi.nlm.nih.gov/sra), and European Nucleotide Archive (https://www.ebi.ac.uk/ena). The initial, general, and important step of bioinformatic analysis, which is applied to data generated from sequencing platforms, is preprocessing of raw reads, also known as quality check (QC). The QC is required to correct the sequencing errors and is performed by removing adapters that remain during the sample preparation and few first bases with low quality (quality score ≥ 20). Downstream analysis varies according to the aim and type of the generated data. There are various pipelines available for downstream analysis for NGS, depending on data and biologic queries, for example, variant analysis (insertion, deletion, and SNPs) related to disease (Kumar et al., 2012), improvement in previously predicted genes, and finding differentially expressed genes that could be used as biomarkers for clinical research (Conesa et al., 2016). Fig. 3.1 represents an NGS data analysis pipeline with its clinical applications.

4. Clinical applications of NGS

Since NGS technologies are able to interrogate targets on a huge scale, the list of applications of NGS based assays is expanding generously. The application ranges from academics, basic research, pharmaceutical research, and biomedical research to clinical decision-making tests. The genetic data obtained by NGS assists clinical practices by precisely identifying biomarkers of disease, discovering congenital disorders, and identifying such genetic factors that can guide to predict responses to therapies. In the biomedical field, to assess disease progression and to predict treatment response or patient survival, the genes and proteins from the patient's tissue sample are characterized as biomarkers with the help of NGS. In the upcoming sections, we will take into account the common clinical applications of NGS technology.

4.1 Oncology

One of the greatest concerns for human society is the effective treatment of cancer. An in-depth understanding of the pathogenesis of cancer is mandatory to develop new therapies. However, getting the picture of this extremely complex and heterogeneous group of diseases is quite challenging. Cancer is typically genetic and epigenetic changes that occur in a single or a group of cells resulting in clonal expansion and uncontrolled growth. The genomic alterations such as point mutations, insertions, deletions, copy number alterations, and SVs induce cancer, and these genomic alterations can either be somatic or inheritable. Therefore, NGS-based analyses of cancer cells and structures provide endless opportunities to

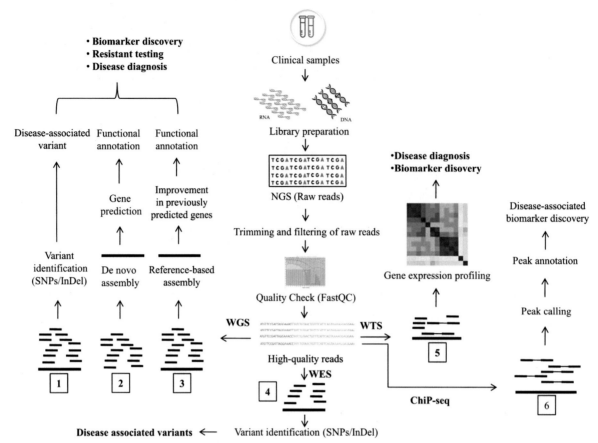

FIGURE 3.1 NGS data analysis pipeline with its clinical applications. Abbreviations: *WES*, whole exome sequencing; *WGS*, whole genome sequencing; *WTS*, whole transcriptome sequencing. Numbers 1 to 6 used in figure are as follows: (1) WGS reads alignment on reference genome, (2) *de novo* genome assembly, (3) reference-based genome assembly, (4) WES reads mapping on reference genome, (5) RNA-seq reads mapping on reference genome, and (6) ChiP-seq reads mapping on reference genome.

understand pathogenesis, diagnosis, management, disease treatment, and development of personalized treatment strategies. The larger WGS and WES are employed for cancer research, while targeted NGS panels provide backing in cancer patient management. The advanced sequencing platforms such as MinION and PromethION are now used for WGS of various types of cancer like lung cancer (Sakamoto et al., 2019), central nervous system tumors (Patel et al., 2018), etc., to obtain much longer reads. On the other hand, a targeted NGS panel represents a group of gene mutations with potential clinical significance that is interrogated using NGS assays for a particular type of cancer. With the help of genomic data and WES, various novel mutations associated with melanoma (Hodis et al., 2012; Kunz et al., 2013) and breast cancer (Gottlieb et al., 2013) were identified. The first New York State Department of Health (NYSDOH)−approved WES-based test known as EXaCT-1 (Exome Cancer Test) came into existence in 2015 (Rennert et al., 2016). However, since the exome is much larger than a targeted panel, the sequencing by EXaCT-1 and other WES assays has substantially lower read depth, due to which sensitivity for variant calling is lower than the result of targeted gene panels. Instead, clinically relevant genomic features such as tumor mutational burden (Chalmers et al., 2017), loss of heterozygosity (Swisher et al., 2017), and microsatellite instability status (Vanderwalde et al., 2018) are precisely assessed by targeted panels.

In recent years, clinical NGS has experienced a rapid upsurge with more than 250 academic and commercial Clinical Laboratory Improvement Amendments (CLIA)−certified laboratories that offer NGS-based testing of oncology bio-specimens (Wadapurkar and Vyas, 2018). The majority of clinical laboratories widely use targeted gene panels for investigations by employing two totally distinctive approaches. Within the first approach, the targeted gene panel is centered solely on the genes related to a selected cancer type, for example, *BRCA1* and *BRCA2* genes associated with breast and ovarian cancer. In this context, MinION led to successful identification of a 200-kb target region including the 80-kb *BRCA1* gene body and its flanking regions from primary human peripheral blood cells (Gabrieli et al., 2018). The second approach may be focused on one or a few histologies highly associated with clinically actionable mutations, but also include several hundred pan-cancer genes such as Memorial Sloan Kettering Cancer Center's 468-gene IMPACT test or Foundation Medicine's 359-gene FoundationOne test to enhance the diagnostic yields (Karlovich and Williams, 2019). Furthermore, identification of cancer-related genes has additionally driven advancement of molecularly targeted therapies like trastuzumab that is one of the first therapies specifically targeted to *HER2+* breast cancers. Similarly, when WGS was used in a patient with acute myeloid leukemia, an unknown insertional fusion was found generating a classic bcr3 PML-RARA fusion gene, which led to an immediate change in the patient's treatment schedule (Welch et al., 2011). Additionally, to monitor improvement in a patient's health and inspect for any signs of relapse, clinicians can design patient-specific probes using the patient's blood serum DNA (Samuel and Hudson, 2013).

The NGS-based tests are also useful in establishing new molecular disease classifications in terms of cancer-driving mutations and drug sensitivity (instead of the tissue of origin) that might be helpful in clinical decision-making and patient care. Additionally, pharmacogenomic tests have recently gained popularity, in which the mutational status of selected genes is determined in the patients, so the molecularly targeted treatment can be given along with determining susceptibility to drug toxicity, assessment of prognosis, and prediction of resistance, and the study of mosaicism. Another potential use for NGS in oncology is related to "last resort" patients, i.e., patients who have consumed all possible options to identify putative cancer-related genes that could act as druggable targets. NGS can identify potential druggable targets and possibly find an off-label drug or appropriate clinical trials. More recently, investigation of circulating tumor DNA (ctDNA) testing (Vendrell et al., 2017), cell-free DNA in prenatal genetic testing (Ordulu et al., 2016), human leukocyte antigen (HLA) typing (Weimer et al., 2016), microbial analysis (Yohe and Thyagarajan, 2017), RNA sequencing and expression, and methylation have emerged as the clinical applications of NGS in oncology. The testing of ctDNA, often referred to as "liquid biopsy," is minimally invasive and allows real-time assessment of the tumor molecular model. The ctDNA testing overcomes the limitations of convectional tumor biopsy in terms of acquisition of the sample, analysis of the material, clinical complications, and the cost involved. However, the relatively low sensitivity of liquid biopsies in early stage of tumors is the prime limitation. Of late, MinION has been used for microbiome sequencing of colorectal cancers to investigate the role of gut microbiome in the development and progression of colorectal cancer (Taylor et al., 2020). In the case of HLA genotyping, MinION provides accuracy along with the cost-effective and scalable genotyping with minor shortcomings (Lang et al., 2018). The RNA sequencing data has also emerged to complement DNA in the clinical management of cancer patients. This is achieved by the identification of fusion events using an RNA template. Therapeutically actionable RNA fusions have been identified in multiple carcinoma types (Mertens et al., 2015). The advantage of RNA over DNA is the overexpression of several fusion driver events in cancer that may eventually be more readily identified using RNA as a template.

4.2 Hematologic disorders

Remarkable progress in NGS applications for both benign and malignant hematology has been accomplished. Approaches such as WES, gene targeted panel, and long amplicon-based NGS have been used to diagnose hematologic diseases ranging from various red cell disorders, bleeding disorders, and primary immune deficiency disorders. Targeted exome sequencing has already been applied for diagnosis of clinical syndromes such as Fanconi anemia (FA), neuro-acanthocytosis (NA) syndromes, and Diamond-Blackfan anemia (DBA). Exome sequencing in FA patients has identified a number of mutations in FA-associated genes, many of which were novel (Schuster et al., 2013). In addition, a new gene in FA genes i.e., a truncating mutation of the *XRCC2,* was discovered in a male child by exome sequencing (Shamseldin et al., 2012). In NA syndromes, each family lineage has unique mutations making the mutation detection difficult. Also, many NA genes are quite large, making traditional Sanger sequencing unmanageable. The use of exome sequencing assisted in identifying compound heterozygous mutations of the *VPS13A* gene in two NA patients that allowed precise genetic diagnosis (Walker et al., 2012). Similarly, targeted WES has been used to study ribosomal proteins genes in DBA patients, identifying mutations in 15 out of 17 patients (Gerrard et al., 2013).

Genome-wide association studies (GWAS) have been shown to identify the causal genes in given loci for hematologic traits by recognizing the rare variants in genes (Galarneau et al., 2010). By investigating variations in the candidate genes near loci associated with fetal hemoglobin (HbF) level using GWAS, it was found that rare variants in *MYB* were associated with HbF levels. Likewise, WES was performed on 761 African Americans, and then newly identified variants were analyzed into a larger sample of 13,000 African Americans for association studies with traits for hemoglobin, hematocrit, white blood cell count, and platelet count (Auer et al., 2012). It resulted in the discovery of an association between coding variants in MPL and higher platelet count, CD36 and lower platelet counts, LCT and higher white blood cell count, and α-globin gene variants with lower hemoglobin. This was the first time when imputation of low-frequency missense variants identified by WES onto GWAS data was demonstrated as a powerful approach to examine complex and genetically heterogeneous traits in population-based studies (Auer et al., 2012).

A major cause of blood group polymorphism is single nucleotide variations in the coding region of blood group antigens. These days, genotyping has become superior to serologic typing of blood group antigens in terms of avoiding the false negatives of weak antigen expression. NGS is particularly advantageous for genes with several variants, such as *RHD* or *RHCE* (Dezan et al., 2017). However, NGS is more suitable for donor typing in contrast to patient typing for the reason that an optimal number of samples can be collected and processed steadily, and a large number of blood group alleles can be tested for each donor simultaneously by NGS (Fürst et al., 2020). In cases where patients with blood group antibodies need to be transfused, a well-typed inventory is very helpful for blood banks (Meny et al., 2013). Even very rare phenotypes, e.g., Vel negative, Lan negative, or In(b−) phenotypes, can easily be screened by including additional primers in the panel. Furthermore, an amplicon-based approach using Illumina short-read technology was successfully employed to develop a high-throughput blood group donor typing protocol (Fichou et al., 2014).

In the past few years, nanopore sequencing has provided a wide range of opportunities in blood diseases. To evaluate the mutational status of single or multiple genes involved in a specific disease, ONT has been widely used. For instance, in chronic lymphocytic leukemia (CLL) patients, *TP53* gene analysis by ONT can be performed even from one single amplicon, resulting in long reads throughout the gene. And if more than one variant is identified, their phasing is conveniently established (Minervini et al., 2020). In addition to this, long reads performances make AML molecular evaluation easier. Long-read sequencing applied to transcriptome analysis is very effective in Philadelphia chromosome (Ph)-like acute lymphoblastic leukemia in terms of gene/isoform expression analysis and fusion transcripts detection (Tasian et al., 2017).

4.3 Cardiology

Nowadays, it is possible to perform WGS and WES for the detection of variations in patients with rare genetic diseases as well as complex disorders such as common cardiovascular diseases (CVDs). The variant identification helps in establishing a risk profile for the pathology process of diseases. NGS has clinical applications in both Mendelian disorders of the cardiovascular system and complex genetic CVDs. Mendelian disorders in cardiovascular medicine include hypertrophic and familial dilated cardiomyopathies, familial hypercholesterolemia, and channelopathies, whereas most common CVDs include stroke and coronary artery disease (CAD). It has been found that mutations in almost 30 different genes are responsible for the inherited forms of cardiomyopathies. Therefore, it becomes highly important to conduct specific genetic tests in patients with cardiomyopathies. To thoroughly identify the variants in the genes implicated in cardiomyopathies, a targeted resequencing by combining long-range PCR and NGS has been proposed (Dames et al., 2010). In a much larger study including 223 cardiomyopathy patients, massive parallel resequencing on Illumina GAIIx was performed to analyze coding, intronic, and regulatory regions of 41 cardiovascular genes (Lopes et al., 2013). A total of 152 potentially causative variants in sarcomeric or associated genes, out of which 89 were novel, were identified. The discovery of a truncating mutation in the *TTN* gene as a main cause of dilated cardiomyopathies is another remarkable example of utilization of NGS disclosing the genetic context of cardiomyopathies (Herman et al., 2012). Earlier, the analysis of *TTN* gene by traditional Sanger sequencing was problematic owing to its large size (363 exons). Similarly, an NGS approach with a panel of several cardiomyopathy- and arrhythmia-associated genes was successfully used to reveal the scale of genetic causes in patients with cardiomyopathies (Kostareva et al., 2016).

Genetic testings are gradually revolutionizing the process of disease management in the case of channelopathies due to the exclusive role of NGS techniques in detecting causative mutations for frequently fatal conditions and screening of family members presently at risk (Bai et al., 2009). Another application of comprehensive genetic testing is the determination of the cause of sudden cardiac death. Genetic testing of *KCNQ1*, *KCNH2*, *SCN5A*, and *RYR2* genes in samples procured after death revealed that ion channelopathies are the cause of almost 35% of sudden arrhythmic death syndrome (Semsarian and Hamilton, 2012). In 2017, for the first time a targeted multigene NGS custom panel of 13 long QT syndrome-associated genes was established with the help of Ion PGM platform, and the system was validated for further routine use in clinical genetic diagnosis of long QT syndrome and other genetic diseases (Chae et al., 2017). Similarly, in case of familial hypercholesterolemia, a comprehensive detection approach including targeted NGS, testing for variations in copy number, and counts of polygenic trait can aid in diagnosing most patients (Trégouët et al., 2009). However, in the case of congenital heart diseases (CHDs), genetic testing was not possible until the dramatic improvement in pediatric cardiology and surgical interventions in recent years that led to a significant increase in the survival rate of CHD patients. The first application of NGS in CHD was exome sequencing on DNA samples of two cousins of a large family with pleiotropic CHD, where a novel *MYH6* mutation was identified as a genetic cause of CHD (Arrington et al., 2012). Later on, several NGS-based studies were performed on a larger number on individuals, and several new CHD-associated genes were identified with numerous disease-causing variants (Al Turki et al., 2014). Other major causes of mortality and morbidity are CAD and stroke. GWAS has been performed using an array of technologies to millions of SNPs in independent haplotype blocks in large cases (Schunkert et al., 2011). But GWAS only provides population-attributable risks information and is not of much help for CAD individuals. In contrast to this, the NGS results can be employed to the affected individual directly. Furthermore, NGS acts as an unbiased approach in that it allows the identification of both rare and common variants.

Gene expression survey by RNA-seq is an effective method in cardiovascular research. There are several reports that suggest the significant role of miRNAs as biomarkers in CADs (Chini, 2015). With the help of NGS, the identification of novel miRNAs and elucidation of molecular mechanisms of miRNA involvement in cardiovascular disease have become feasible. In addition to this, epigenetic biomarkers that include DNA methylation, histone modifications, and RNA-based mechanisms have recently emerged as promising biomarkers for CVDs. In the same way, metabolomics has great potential in identifying new pathophysiologic pathways, preventing primary and secondary CVDs, detecting therapeutic targets, as well as assisting in improved risk-stratification and personalized cardiovascular medicine.

4.4 Clinical microbiology

In clinical microbiology, NGS technologies have been useful for an array of applications such as identifying outbreak origins, tracking transmissions, investigating epidemic dynamics, determining etiologic agents of disease, antibiotic resistance, and discovering novel human pathogens. NGS is broadly applicable to almost every pathogen like viruses, bacteria, fungi, parasites, animal vectors, and human hosts. The key applications of NGS in clinical microbiology include (1) WGS, (2) targeted NGS, and (3) metagenomics NGS. So far, the most widespread application of WGS in clinical microbiology is immediate identification, typing, and antimicrobial susceptibility prediction for microbial pathogens. The remarkable use of WGS in public health epidemiology is the identification and tracking of outbreaks. For instance, with the help of WGS, CTX-M-15−producing *Klebsiella pneumonia* clone and colistin-resistant carbapenemase-producing *K. pneumoniae* isolate was detected, and their transmission was monitored, which facilitated in adopting preventive measures to inhibit the further spread of these multidrug-resistant organisms (Zhou et al., 2015). Recently, ONT was employed to predict phenotypic aspartate aminotransferase results within 14 h of isolation of carbapenem-resistant *K. pneumonia* clinical isolates (Tamma et al., 2019). Additionally, MinION was found very efficient for WGS of bacterial organisms for pathogen detection in mixed samples (Tyler et al., 2018). Similarly, WGS of various strains of novel coronavirus is being carried out currently across the globe, which will help scientists to understand the functionality of genes involved in the growth, development, and maintenance of an organism. Also, more importantly, the origin of this virus could be understood from the sequence data. WGS also provides vital information about pathogen virulence and the detection of novel mechanisms of resistance. Using WGS, virulence genes such as *spa* and PVL toxins in *Staphylococcus aureus* were identified (Leopold et al., 2014). Similarly, novel synonymous mutations in *Rv3792* in *Mycobacterium tuberculosis* that resulted in elevated ethambutol minimum inhibitory concentration were discovered (Safi et al., 2013). Furthermore, WGS of HIV has been found to increase the sensitivity for the detection of low-frequency, drug-resistant mutations in HIV-1 (Tzou et al., 2018).

Targeted NGS involves enrichment of microbial sequences of interest before sequencing using methods like amplicon sequencing, probe hybridization, and CRISPR-Cas9. The advantage of targeted NGS over metagenomics is that it amplifies microbial sequences present in minimal numbers within highly cellular samples. Targeted NGS is mainly used to detect pathogens and antibiotic resistance genes in patient samples. Larger multiplex panel assays have also been developed for both viral (VirCapSeq-VERT) and bacterial (BacCapSeq) detection in blood and tissue samples (Briese et al., 2015; Allicock et al., 2018). In addition, TS employing amplicon sequencing was found to be highly sensitive for detecting cytomegalovirus resistance in clinical samples, particularly for minor variants (Sahoo et al., 2013). Another application of NGS in clinical microbiology is metagenomics NGS, which is a pan-nucleic acid detection method directly from patient samples. Its main benefit is that it provides unbiased sampling that facilitates comprehensive recognition of known as well as unanticipated pathogens or maybe the discovery of new microorganisms, resistance markers, virulence factors, and host biomarkers associated with different disease states (Chiu, 2013). It can also be coupled to DNA- or RNA-based methods to detect intact microbes from cell-free DNA. The primers designed from conserved internal transcribed spacer sequences and 16S rRNA can be used with metagenomics NGS for universal fungal and bacterial detection (Cummings et al., 2016). Furthermore, the supplementary genomic information to trace evolutionary lineage, identify different strains, and drug resistance prediction is made accessible by metagenomics NGS (Gu et al., 2019). For instance, strain typing of Zika virus was carried out in blood linked acquisition in an endemic area due to a subsequent secondary, nonsexual transmission case (Swaminathan et al., 2016).

4.5 Prenatal diagnosis

With the advancement of NGS technologies and the discovery of fetal cell-free DNA (cfDNA) in maternal plasma, there has been a revolution in the field of prenatal diagnosis. The development of highly sensitive screening tests for fetal aneuploidies has led to the progress in two main areas: (1) noninvasive prenatal diagnosis (NIPD) for monogenic disorders and (2) fetal exome sequencing. Earlier, NIPD was commonly used for most generic aneuploidies such as trisomy 21, 13, and 18, but now a number of diseases can be detected prenatally by NIPD. In addition, NIPD provides a safe, accurate, and definitive diagnosis of single gene disorders during early gestation. With the help of NGS technologies, panels of mutations can be used for NIPD in a single test. For instance, a panel testing for NIPD of skeletal dysplasias caused by numerous different mutations in the *FGFR3* gene was performed with superior accuracy using NGS, and 29 potentially causative mutations were screened (Chitty et al., 2015). This NGS panel-based approach is also used for paternal exclusion in autosomal recessive disorders such as cystic fibrosis (Hill et al., 2015) and β-thalassaemia (Xiong et al., 2015). The scope of NIPD is further extended by NGS for X-linked disorders and autosomal recessive conditions where parents carry the same mutation, by implying relative mutation dosage that determines the relative proportions of mutant versus wild-type alleles (Lun et al., 2008). Another approach to successfully reach genetic diagnoses is fetal WES, which provides much broader prenatal diagnostic ability, offering better diagnoses and prognostic information for fetuses with abnormalities detected on prenatal ultrasound. Prenatal WES can provide diagnostic yields between 6% and 80% in fetuses with undiagnosed sonographic abnormalities and normal karyotype/microarray (Best et al., 2018). The greatest speed of diagnosis is achieved by WES of fetus, mother, and father in parallel.

Prenatal WES also facilitates the discovery of novel candidate genes. For instance, *KIF* was discovered as a cause of two multiple malformation disorders, i.e., fetal hydrolethalus and acrocallosal syndromes (Putoux et al., 2011). Other novel candidate genes identified include *WDR60* causing short-rib polydactyly syndrome (McInerney-Leo et al., 2013), *KIF14* related to complex brain and genitourinary malformations (Filges et al., 2014), and *MKL2* associated with extreme microcephaly (Ramos et al., 2014). Since prenatal WES is performed in abnormal fetuses, "developmentalome," i.e., genes critical to human development, might be identified. An alternative to WES is a targeted molecular panel, particularly when the structural abnormality has a well-characterized phenotype (Rasmussen et al., 2018). A targeted panel is more cost-effective with faster turn-around time and more accessible in routine clinical care. In a few prenatal cases, WGS is applied to show proof of principle, but it is not used in clinical routine since it is difficult to interpret intronic or regulatory regions of the genome. However, WGS is effective in identifying copy number variants, other structural variants, and expansions of short tandem repeats with higher sensitivity than WES. Lately, the development of fetal cfDNA analysis using transcriptome and methylome sequencing offered clinical benefits for monitoring other pregnancy-related pathologies such as preeclampsia and intrauterine growth restriction. Single-cell RNA-seq can be applied to the placenta for characterizing placental cell types and defining cell type-specific gene signatures (Tsang et al., 2017). By combining this information with datasets derived from cell-free RNA in maternal plasma, noninvasive monitoring of the cellular dynamics of the placenta could be achieved, reflecting the potential of NGS technologies and bioinformatics.

4.6 Clinical epigenetics

Clinical epigenetics is employed for patient management in oncology, neurologic and infectious diseases, and immune system disorders. Epigenetics provides a molecular bridge for the gap between the genome and environmental signals confronted during intrauterine or postnatal development. Epigenetic modifications are considered indispensable candidates in the biomarker field since they represent an association of molecular markers with lifestyle and environment, and also, epigenetic marks are highly stable, especially DNA methylation. In general, DNA-based biomarkers are more stable than RNA-based biomarkers, while epigenetic biomarkers are seemingly the intermediate ones. Epigenetic modifications such as DNA methylation, histone modifications, the transcriptome, RNA−protein interactions, and DNA−protein interactions like RNA Pol II binding are now widely analyzed using NGS. Other epigenetic modifications for which NGS methods have been developed include several aspects of chromatin organization such as DNA accessibility and long-range interactions (Handoko et al., 2011). The accurate quantification of DNA methylation at single base pair resolution in the entire genome is possible only with whole genome shotgun bisulfite sequencing methods like BS- and MethylC-seq. DNA methylation is heritable, and the human genome has 80% of cytosines in CpG dinucleotides chemically modified at their fifth carbon atom with a methyl group, associated with transcriptional silencing or transcriptional activation (Fig. 3.2). Cancer exhibits a characteristic of inconsistent deregulation of CpG methylation patterns that result in genome instability, along with regional gains of CpG methylation leading to silencing of particular tumor suppressor genes (Berdasco and Esteller, 2010). Therefore, various NGS-based assays have been developed for cancer diagnosis. The most common test

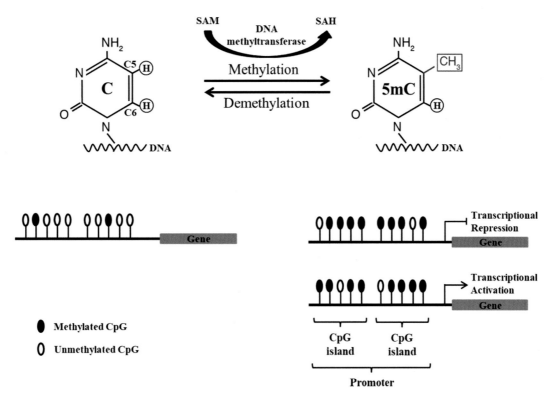

FIGURE 3.2 DNA methylation/demethylation. During methylation, chemical modification of cytosines in CpG dinucleotides of the promoter regions takes place by the addition of methyl group at the fifth carbon atom of cytosines. This results in significant transcriptional silencing or transcriptional activation of genes. Generally, DNA methylation results in transcriptional repression, but in a few instances, it is also involved in transcriptional activation. *5 mC*, 5-methylcytosine; *C*, cytosine; *SAH*, S-adenosyl homocysteine; *SAM*, S-adenosyl methionine.

that uses epigenetic-based biomarkers is for the screening of early colorectal cancer. There are other FDA-approved tests that detect gain of CpG methylation at specific gene promoters. Similarly, a methylation panel of the twist family bHLH transcription factor 1 (*TWIST1*), one cut homeobox 2 (*ONECUT2*), and orthodenticle homeobox 1 (*OTX1*) genes combined with additional mutation analysis is used for estimating the risk of bladder cancer in patients diagnosed with hematuria (van Kessel et al., 2016).

Other than CpG methylation, histone-based biomarkers also play a vital role in early tumorigenesis (Yuen and Knoepfler, 2013). Histone modifications detected in circulating cell-free nucleosomes in blood can be correlated with the cell type of origin and, thus, can be utilized as a potential biomarker (Snyder et al., 2016). A technique called MNase-seq has been developed to map nucleosome occupancy where micrococcal nuclease (MNase) is used for digestion of the chromatin, followed by high-throughput sequencing (Bell et al., 2011). However, due to a biased preference of MNase toward AT-rich regions and lack of single base pair resolution data, other MNase-independent techniques have been developed (Brogaard et al., 2012). NGS technologies have contributed a lot in the field of epigenome-targeted therapies. In the past years, there has been a considerable increase in the number of small-molecule inhibitors that target the cancer epigenome (Ganesan, 2016). DNA methyltransferase inhibitors (DNMTi) were the first FDA-approved epidrugs that consisted of the nucleoside analogs and had a large-scale effect on the methylome (Jones et al., 2016). They result in acute genome-wide demethylation of repetitive elements, as well as loss of methylation of specific tumor suppressor genes (Esteller et al., 2000) and restored normalization of cell growth in patients with hematologic malignancies. Other approved broad reprogrammers belong to the histone deacetylase inhibitors (HDACi) class that brings about a decrease in global histone acetylation. A combination of DNMTi and HDACi to obtain viable chromatin modulation, and stable reactivation of silenced genes has been explored for the treatment of hematologic malignancies.

4.7 Precision medicine

Over the years, the precision medicine model has replaced the conventional medicine model in diagnosis, which has made more precise disease diagnosis and subsequent individual treatment possible. Precision medicine utilizes genetic, environmental, and behavioral features of an individual for providing custom-tailored strategies in response to a disease. The advancements in molecular knowledge and NGS technologies have led to the rapid evolution of precision medicine in cancer, rare diseases, neurodegeneration, diabetes, and cardiovascular pathologies, among others. Various studies have demonstrated the application of NGS in the identification of clinically actionable mutations in cancer patients. For instance, an international data-sharing consortium named Genomics Evidence Neoplasia Information Exchange (GENIE) assessed an actionable rate of 30% among various cancers (AACR Project GENIE Consortium, 2017). This means that out of all the tumors sequenced in the GENIE, 30% comprised a mutation that could be targeted by an existing targeted therapy. Utilizing sequencing data for matching patients to a treatment based on their tumor mutations showed overall improved response rate, time to treatment failure, and survival compared to the patients who were not given sequencing-matched therapy (Tsimberidou et al., 2012). Similarly, numerous studies found a significant improvement in progression free survival (Schwaederle et al., 2016), overall survival (Aisner et al., 2016), and tumor response (Stockley et al., 2016) in patients receiving therapy matched to their DNA mutations, copy number variations, or mRNA levels compared to patients with non-matched therapy. A solely precision medicine approach could be seen where tumor-driving mutations were targeted using PD-1 blockade treatment effective across 12 different tumor types (Le et al., 2017), and this resulted in the launch of the first mutation-based FDA-approved drug named pembrolizumab.

The NGS-based diagnostic assays have evolved from hotspot panels to WGS approach. In addition, metabolomics also provides valuable information for the diagnosis and prognosis of patients as well as for predicting pharmacologic responses to specific interventions. Drug treatment often results in the occurrence of specific metabolic signatures, providing crucial information from pathways targeted or affected by drug therapy, thus allowing better decision-making for therapy to be used. A nuclear magnetic resonance—based metabolomics study was performed for examining serum metabolomic profiles of early stage, untreated CLL patients, and the observed distinct metabolic reprogramming highlighted the effectiveness of metabolomics as a noninvasive tool for discriminating different CLL molecular subgroups (MacIntyre et al., 2010). In the case of pancreatic ductal adenocarcinoma (PDAC), a lack of effective pretreatment evaluation methods to choose an optimal therapeutic strategy for an individual patient seems to be responsible for poor outcomes. A metabolomics approach could identify three highly distinct metabolic subtypes in PDAC distinguished by different proliferative capacities that aided in the clinical assessment of a variety of metabolic inhibitors such as monocarboxylate transporter 1 (MCT1) and glutaminase inhibitors to be used for precision therapy (Daemen et al., 2015). Similarly, a metabolomics approach overcomes the need for repeated biopsies and subsequent histopathology for breast cancer diagnosis and subtype classification. Use of ultraperformance liquid chromatography-quadrupole time of flight mass spectrometry and gas chromatography-quadrupole mass spectrometry offers a noninvasive, rapid, and sensitive analysis (Murtaza et al., 2013). A remarkable example of the metabolomics potential to identify disease-specific molecular fingerprints is the molecular characterization of gliomas (Zhao et al., 2016). Furthermore, metabolomics provides a much more comprehensive assessment of disease progression and therapy response. In recent years, the investigation of metabolic reprogramming in different neoplastic processes following drug administration has become the main focus of many studies.

4.8 Neurology and psychiatry

NGS methods enable the rare molecular diagnoses in neurodegenerative diseases such as schizophrenia, epilepsy, Parkinson disease (PD), Alzheimer disease (AD), bipolar disorder, etc., facilitating proper therapeutic regimens. The causes and factors responsible for the onset and effect of neurologic conditions on human well-being can be understood by interdisciplinary approaches including genomics-based analyses such as NGS, GWAS, and GCTA. Currently, the targeted gene panels are the most effective choice for many neurodegenerative diseases. The most remarkable example of WGS technology was the detection of a coded mutation in a rare Charcot-Marie-tooth neurodegenerative disease (Pang et al., 2017), followed by premature epilepsy, and sensory and motor neuropathy with microcephaly (Martin et al., 2014; Gonzaga-Jauregui et al., 2013). Usually, mutations in coding sequences that affect the development of a known disease-gene are easily interpretable. However, in cases like microcephaly syndrome, a relatively high prevalence of noncoding mutations are found that are not detected by WES, thus making WGS an effective approach for a full evaluation of undiagnosed neurologic diseases. WES is found to be more efficient when people with clinical neurologic symptoms also show a higher diagnostic value than non-neurologic cases (Farwell et al., 2015). However, the association between genotype and phenotype is not well known in many neurodegenerative diseases. In such cases, the creation of targeted gene panels is a suitable method for molecular detection. For instance, detection by the NGS comprehensive panel is almost three times higher than single gene testing for heterogeneous genetic disorders such as limb-girdle muscular dystrophies and congenital muscular dystrophies (Ankala et al., 2015).

AD is a progressive neurologic disease for which the existing clinical drugs for treatment are not satisfactory, as they only improve symptoms but do not cure it. Thus, further studies are required for effective therapeutic strategies for AD.

NGS provides rapid and cost-effective sequencing strategies to sequence a complete genome, facilitating detection in the shortest time possible (Van Giau and Au, 2019). Almost 50 non-synonymous variants in late-onset AD risk factor genes have been identified by NGS, which highlights the role of mutations in the pathogenesis of AD. In PD that can be diagnosed with a neurologic examination, 13 loci and 9 genes are involved (Lesage and Brice, 2009). Still, no laboratory could clearly define this neurologic disease. Therefore, NGS can be used to determine the effect of genes on PD to discover genes associated with the disease. Similarly, in epilepsy, NGS was used to categorize 977 genes related to epilepsy (Wang et al., 2017). WGS and WES approaches have identified mosaic mutations in several genes related to different forms of epilepsy (Halvorsen et al., 2015; Campostrini et al., 2018). The targeted gene panel study of 36−265 epilepsy genes showed a diagnostic efficiency of 10%−50% (Oates et al., 2018). Such mosaic diagnostic problems may lead to the underreporting of genetic disorders.

5. Challenges and limitations

Although NGS technology has been gaining momentum for usage in clinical backdrops, the challenges and controversies continue to persist. Today, a diverse range of molecular diagnostic tests utilize NGS technology such as WGS, WES, transcriptomics, epigenetics, metabolomics profiling, targeted panel tests, cell-free DNA for NIPD, etc. Since the application of NGS technology in diagnostics is still in the nascent stage, the major challenges faced are an accurate determination of targeted genes, identification of a suitable NGS method for NGS panel, and proper validation of NGS-based assays performed (Qin, 2019). The other challenges include the decision-making process of requisitioning the tests as to when and whom to order. In addition, interpretation and comunication of the test results to the patient and family needs to cautiously handled (Jamuar and Tan, 2015). Thus, understanding the application, potential, challenges, and limitations of different approaches is indispensable to figure out the most appropriate approach suitable for a particular case.

The challenging factors also include adequate coverage and 100% genome sequencing for diagnostics. Even the best of the platforms (Illumina) could sequence 51 out of 56 clinically significant genes with adequate coverage (Dewey et al., 2015). Thus, complete gene coverage is indispensable for improvement in the diagnostic yield of genetic testing. This task could be best addressed with a massively parallel sequencing approach. Also, genome-based diagnostics are not able to sequence the whole genome (8% genome not sequenced). Complete genome sequencing is quintessential to reveal epigenetic changes. The availability of samples or the small sample size is another major limitation. The biology of several diseases like cancer itself makes the analysis complicated due to a limited amount of DNA, tumor−normal tissue comparisons, intratumor clonal heterogeneity, and poor quality of formalin-fixed paraffin-embedded (FFPE) samples. However, few of these problems can be overcome by NGS since it can be performed on a range of tumor samples including FFPE samples and is relevant to small specimens, fine-needle aspiration samples, circulating tumor cells, and circulating free DNA in plasma. In reproductive health, NGS diagnostics are used for prenatal, newborn, and preimplantation screening. At present, the majority of users of NGS testing are women who are at high risk of carrying babies with chromosomal abnormalities. The future market potential will have a major impact of whether or not NGS-based screening will be embraced by the average-risk patient population. To facilitate this, the insurance providers and alternate payers will have to understand and identify the sheer clinical benefit of screening this section of people. Similarly, NGS has a strong potential future market in cardiovascular and neurologic disorders. This is due to amalgamation of identification of genetic changes associated with the risk of disease onset or progression and clinical research.

Despite the proven worth of NGS technologies in cancer research, their application in clinical and routine laboratory practices is still in its early stages. There are two main reasons for the limited use of NGS technologies in clinical backdrops. The first problem is reimbursement. Insurance providers are strictly focused on only those clinical tests that provide information directly influencing the patient's care; otherwise the test will not be reimbursed. The second problem is related to regulatory issues. The knowledge of individual genetic characteristics is required by personalized medicine to customize targeted therapy. More often than not, personalized treatment requires the knowledge of the whole exome and transcriptome. However, there is still no FDA-approved NGS-based diagnostic test available to be used. Therefore, consistent improvement in sequencing technologies and analysis algorithms are required to bridge the gap between NGS advancements and their clinical applications.

6. Ethical aspect

The ability to obtain personal genome-wide sequence data raises many ethical issues, which must be addressed during counseling before and after the test. Counseling must include a discussion of the test modality, the clinical and health implications of a molecular diagnosis (or lack thereof), and the concept of secondary findings. Sometimes, the role of parental samples in test interpretation, kinship, and the likelihood of finding nonparentage may raise ethical issues. Therefore, in the view of ensuring the privacy of clinical data and protection against misuse, numerous regulations have been established. This includes the federal Health Insurance Portability and Accountability Act privacy rule, Patient Safety and Quality Improvement Act (US), the European Union General Data Protection Regulation, Data Protection Act (UK), IT Act and IT (Amendment) Act (India), and Personal Information Protection and Electronic Documents Act (Canada) to name a few. These laws provide protection for individually identifiable health information. It allows the healthcare providers to give choice to patients about disclosure of their health information for key purposes such as treatment, payment, and healthcare operations. Moreover, the patient data available at electronic medical records are also governed by the governing bodies such as institutional review boards and individual institution-specific guidelines (Nass et al., 2009). Therefore, on the basis of regulatory access restrictions, the clinical data can be categorized as fully identified clinical data, privacy law-limited clinical data, deidentified clinical data, and synthetic data. However, strong measures are required to make sure that such laws are practiced diligently by healthcare providers. Greater use of encryption and multiple layers of security should be implemented to reduce the risk of data theft. The development of genuine privacy-enhancing techniques should be encouraged by governing bodies to ensure minimal collection of personally identifiable data. Apart from the data privacy issues, in some clinical scenarios, confronting insurance inferences, authorization, and checking prices may well be applicable. Since these problems are complicated, they are usually taken care of in clinical genetics settings, and formal written consent is mostly suggested prior to testing.

7. Future directions

The advancement in NGS technologies and their decreasing cost have created a new path for clinicians to diagnose, predict, and make a prognosis-specific feature in each patient. There are many technical, analytical, and ethical challenges that need further processing. For example, the use of NGS in the clinical market will depend on its cost, which needs to be lowered further, so it can reach common people. Apart from the cost, bioinformaticians need to be thoroughly trained to handle big data in terms of analysis, sharing, storage, and security. In addition to this, clinicians must be skilled to understand the patterns of diseases and clinical diagnosis along with genetic testing. Furthermore, hardware and software (NGS data analysis tools) must be developed faster as NGS technologies. Looking at the current developments in NGS, its medical uses, and the relevant progress, the future seems to have universal medical software systems that will not only strengthen the translational medicine paradigm but will also provide customized toolboxes for different stages of diagnosis and therapy. Nevertheless, such systems cannot replace or diminish the role of a physician. The NGS-based diagnostics are instrumental tools to provide overall support to a physician. Therefore, it is very important to develop and maintain a physician user-friendly interface of database structure and cloud processing. If NGS-based tools are complex, education programs at medical institutions should be organized with the help of genome medicine professionals. All the future clinical applications of NGS technology mainly depends on the improvement and elaboration of regulated guidelines for both "wet" laboratory procedures and bioinformatics analyses. By overcoming these challenges, looking to future, NGS technologies would become a standard investigation tool in diagnosis and therapeutic interventions by translating NGS results into clinical use.

References

AACR Project GENIE Consortium, 2017. AACR project GENIE: powering precision medicine through an international consortium. Canc. Discov. 7 (8), 818−831.

Aisner, D., Sholl, L.M., Berry, L.D., Haura, E.B., Ramalingam, S.S., Glisson, B.S., et al., 2016. Effect of expanded genomic testing in lung adenocarcinoma (LUCA) on survival benefit: the lung cancer mutation consortium II (LCMC II) experience. J. Clin. Oncol. 34, 11510-11510.

Al Turki, S., Manickaraj, A.K., Mercer, C.L., Gerety, S.S., Hitz, M.P., Lindsay, S., et al., 2014. Rare variants in NR2F2 cause congenital heart defects in humans. Am. J. Hum. Genet. 94 (4), 574−585.

Allicock, O.M., Guo, C., Uhlemann, A.C., Whittier, S., Chauhan, L.V., Garcia, J., et al., 2018. BacCapSeq: a platform for diagnosis and characterization of bacterial infections. mBio 9 (5).

Ankala, A., da Silva, C., Gualandi, F., Ferlini, A., Bean, L.J., Collins, C., et al., 2015. A comprehensive genomic approach for neuromuscular diseases gives a high diagnostic yield. Ann. Neurol. 77 (2), 206−214.

Arrington, C.B., Bleyl, S.B., Matsunami, N., Bonnell, G.D., Otterud, B.E., Nielsen, D.C., et al., 2012. Exome analysis of a family with pleiotropic congenital heart disease. Circ. Cardiovasc. Genet. 5 (2), 175−182.

Auer, P.L., Johnsen, J.M., Johnson, A.D., Logsdon, B.A., Lange, L.A., Nalls, M.A., et al., 2012. Imputation of exome sequence variants into population-based samples and blood-cell-trait-associated loci in African Americans: NHLBI GO exome sequencing project. Am. J. Hum. Genet. 91 (5), 794−808.

Bai, R., Napolitano, C., Bloise, R., Monteforte, N., Priori, S.G., 2009. Yield of genetic screening in inherited cardiac channelopathies: how to prioritize access to genetic testing. Circ. Arrhythm. & Electrophysiol. 2 (1), 6–15.

Bell, O., Tiwari, V.K., Thomä, N.H., Schübeler, D., 2011. Determinants and dynamics of genome accessibility. Nat. Rev. Genet. 12 (8), 554–564.

Berdasco, M., Esteller, M., 2010. Aberrant epigenetic landscape in cancer: how cellular identity goes awry. Dev. Cell 19 (5), 698–711.

Best, S., Wou, K., Vora, N., Van der Veyver, I.B., Wapner, R., Chitty, L.S., 2018. Promises, pitfalls and practicalities of prenatal whole exome sequencing. Prenat. Diagn. 38 (1), 10–19.

Brastianos, P.K., Taylor-Weiner, A., Manley, P.E., Jones, R.T., Dias-Santagata, D., Thorner, A.R., et al., 2014. Exome sequencing identifies BRAF mutations in papillary craniopharyngiomas. Nat. Genet. 46 (2), 161.

Briese, T., Kapoor, A., Mishra, N., Jain, K., Kumar, A., Jabado, O.J., Lipkin, W.I., 2015. Virome capture sequencing enables sensitive viral diagnosis and comprehensive virome analysis. mBio 6 (5) e01491-15.

Brogaard, K., Xi, L., Wang, J.P., Widom, J., 2012. A map of nucleosome positions in yeast at base-pair resolution. Nature 486 (7404), 496–501.

Brueffer, C., Vallon-Christersson, J., Grabau, D., Ehinger, A., Häkkinen, J., Hegardt, C., et al., 2018. Clinical value of RNA sequencing–based classifiers for prediction of the five conventional breast cancer biomarkers: a report from the population-based multicenter Sweden cancerome analysis network–breast initiative. JCO Precis. Oncol. 2, 1–18.

Campostrini, G., DiFrancesco, J.C., Castellotti, B., Milanesi, R., Gnecchi-Ruscone, T., Bonzanni, M., et al., 2018. A loss-of-function HCN4 mutation associated with familial benign myoclonic epilepsy in infancy causes increased neuronal excitability. Front. Mol. Neurosci. 11, 269.

Chae, H., Kim, J., Lee, G.D., Jang, W., Park, J., Jekarl, D.W., et al., 2017. Considerations when using next-generation sequencing for genetic diagnosis of long-QT syndrome in the clinical testing laboratory. Clin. Chim. Acta 464, 128–135.

Chalmers, Z.R., Connelly, C.F., Fabrizio, D., Gay, L., Ali, S.M., Ennis, R., et al., 2017. Analysis of 100,000 human cancer genomes reveals the landscape of tumor mutational burden. Genome Med. 9 (1), 1–14.

Chini, V.P., 2015. Micro-RNAs and next generation sequencing: new perspectives in heart failure. Clin. Chim. Acta 443, 114–119.

Chitty, L.S., Mason, S., Barrett, A.N., McKay, F., Lench, N., Daley, R., Jenkins, L.A., 2015. Non-invasive prenatal diagnosis of achondroplasia and thanatophoric dysplasia: next-generation sequencing allows for a safer, more accurate, and comprehensive approach. Prenat. Diagn. 35 (7), 656–662.

Chiu, C.Y., 2013. Viral pathogen discovery. Curr. Opin. Microbiol. 16 (4), 468–478.

Conesa, A., Madrigal, P., Tarazona, S., Gomez-Cabrero, D., Cervera, A., McPherson, A., et al., 2016. A survey of best practices for RNA-seq data analysis. Genome Biol. 17 (1), 13.

Cummings, L.A., Kurosawa, K., Hoogestraat, D.R., SenGupta, D.J., Candra, F., Doyle, M., et al., 2016. Clinical next generation sequencing outperforms standard microbiological culture for characterizing polymicrobial samples. Clin. Chem. 62 (11), 1465–1473.

Daemen, A., Peterson, D., Sahu, N., McCord, R., Du, X., Liu, B., et al., 2015. Metabolite profiling stratifies pancreatic ductal adenocarcinomas into subtypes with distinct sensitivities to metabolic inhibitors. Proc. Natl. Acad. Sci. U. S. A. 112 (32), E4410–E4417.

Dames, S., Durtschi, J., Geiersbach, K., Stephens, J., Voelkerding, K.V., 2010. Comparison of the illumina genome analyzer and roche 454 GS FLX for resequencing of hypertrophic cardiomyopathy-associated genes. J. Biomol. Tech. 21 (2), 73–80.

Daugaard, I., Venø, M.T., Yan, Y., Kjeldsen, T.E., Lamy, P., Hager, H., et al., 2017. Small RNA sequencing reveals metastasis-related microRNAs in lung adenocarcinoma. Oncotarget 8 (16), 27047.

Dewey, F.E., Grove, M.E., Pan, C., Goldstein, B.A., Bernstein, J.A., Chaib, H., et al., 2015. Clinical interpretation and implications of whole-genome sequencing. J. Am. Med. Assoc. 311 (10), 1035–1045.

Dezan, M.R., Ribeiro, I.H., Oliveira, V.B., Vieira, J.B., Gomes, F.C., Franco, L.A., et al., 2017. RHD and RHCE genotyping by next-generation sequencing is an effective strategy to identify molecular variants within sickle cell disease patients. Blood Cell Mol. Dis. 65, 8–15.

Di Resta, C., Galbiati, S., Carrera, P., Ferrari, M., 2018. Next-generation sequencing approach for the diagnosis of human diseases: open challenges and new opportunities. EJIFCC 29 (1), 4.

Dworkis, D.A., Klings, E.S., Solovieff, N., Li, G., Milton, J.N., Hartley, S.W., et al., 2011. Severe sickle cell anemia is associated with increased plasma levels of TNF-R1 and VCAM-1. Am. J. Hematol. 86 (2), 220.

Eid, J., Fehr, A., Gray, J., Luong, K., Lyle, J., Otto, G., et al., 2009. Real-time DNA sequencing from single polymerase molecules. Science 323 (5910), 133–138.

Esteller, M., Garcia-Foncillas, J., Andion, E., Goodman, S.N., Hidalgo, O.F., Vanaclocha, V., et al., 2000. Inactivation of the DNA-repair gene MGMT and the clinical response of gliomas to alkylating agents. N. Engl. J. Med. 343 (19), 1350–1354.

Farh, K.K.H., Marson, A., Zhu, J., Kleinewietfeld, M., Housley, W.J., Beik, S., et al., 2015. Genetic and epigenetic fine mapping of causal autoimmune disease variants. Nature 518 (7539), 337–343.

Faria, N.R., Sabino, E.C., Nunes, M.R., Alcantara, L.C.J., Loman, N.J., Pybus, O.G., 2016. Mobile real-time surveillance of Zika virus in Brazil. Genome Med. 8 (1), 97.

Farwell, K.D., Shahmirzadi, L., El-Khechen, D., Powis, Z., Chao, E.C., Davis, B.T., et al., 2015. Enhanced utility of family-centered diagnostic exome sequencing with inheritance model–based analysis: results from 500 unselected families with undiagnosed genetic conditions. Genet. Med. 17 (7), 578–586.

Fichou, Y., Audrézet, M.P., Guéguen, P., Le Maréchal, C., Férec, C., 2014. Next-generation sequencing is a credible strategy for blood group genotyping. Br. J. Haematol. 167 (4), 554–562.

Filges, I., Nosova, E., Bruder, E., Tercanli, S., Townsend, K., Gibson, W.T., et al., 2014. Exome sequencing identifies mutations in KIF14 as a novel cause of an autosomal recessive lethal fetal ciliopathy phenotype. Clin. Genet. 86 (3), 220–228.

Fresard, L., Smail, C., Smith, K.S., Ferraro, N.M., Teran, N.A., Kernohan, K.D., et al., 2018. Identification of Rare-Disease Genes in Diverse Undiagnosed Cases Using Whole Blood Transcriptome Sequencing and Large Control Cohorts. BioRxiv, p. 408492.

Fürst, D., Tsamadou, C., Neuchel, C., Schrezenmeier, H., Mytilineos, J., Weinstock, C., 2020. Next-generation sequencing technologies in blood group typing. Transfus. Med. Hemother. 47 (1), 4–13.

Gabrieli, T., Sharim, H., Fridman, D., Arbib, N., Michaeli, Y., Ebenstein, Y., 2018. Selective nanopore sequencing of human BRCA1 by Cas9-assisted targeting of chromosome segments (CATCH). Nucleic Acids Res. 46 (14) e87-e87.

Galarneau, G., Palmer, C.D., Sankaran, V.G., Orkin, S.H., Hirschhorn, J.N., Lettre, G., 2010. Fine-mapping at three loci known to affect fetal hemoglobin levels explains additional genetic variation. Nat. Genet. 42 (12), 1049–1051.

Ganesan, A., 2016. Multitarget drugs: an epigenetic epiphany. ChemMedChem 11 (12), 1227–1241.

Gazara, R.K., de Oliveira, E.A., Rodrigues, B.C., da Fonseca, R.N., Oliveira, A.E.A., Venancio, T.M., 2019. Transcriptional landscape of soybean (Glycine max) embryonic axes during germination in the presence of paclobutrazol, a gibberellin biosynthesis inhibitor. Sci. Rep. 9 (1), 1–12.

Gazara, R.K., Moharana, K.C., Bellieny-Rabelo, D., Venancio, T.M., 2018. Expansion and diversification of the gibberellin receptor GIBBERELLIN INSENSITIVE DWARF1 (GID1) family in land plants. Plant Mol. Biol. 97 (4–5), 435–449.

Gerrard, G., Valgañón, M., Foong, H.E., Kasperaviciute, D., Iskander, D., Game, L., et al., 2013. Target enrichment and high-throughput sequencing of 80 ribosomal protein genes to identify mutations associated with Diamond-Blackfan anaemia. Br. J. Haematol. 162 (4), 530–536.

Gibney, E.R., Nolan, C.M., 2010. Epigenetics and gene expression. Heredity 105 (1), 4–13.

Gonzaga-Jauregui, C., Lotze, T., Jamal, L., Penney, S., Campbell, I.M., Pehlivan, D., et al., 2013. Mutations in VRK1 associated with complex motor and sensory axonal neuropathy plus microcephaly. JAMA Neurol. 70 (12), 1491–1498.

Goodwin, S., McPherson, J.D., McCombie, W.R., 2016. Coming of age: ten years of next-generation sequencing technologies. Nat. Rev. Genet. 17 (6), 333.

Gottlieb, B., Alvarado, C., Wang, C., Gharizadeh, B., Babrzadeh, F., Richards, B., et al., 2013. Making sense of intratumor genetic heterogeneity: altered frequency of androgen receptor CAG repeat length variants in breast cancer tissues. Hum. Mutat. 34 (4), 610–618.

Gu, W., Miller, S., Chiu, C.Y., 2019. Clinical metagenomic next-generation sequencing for pathogen detection. Annu. Rev. Pathol. 14, 319–338.

Halvorsen, M., Petrovski, S., Shellhaas, R., Tang, Y., Crandall, L., Goldstein, D., Devinsky, O., 2015. Mosaic mutations in early-onset genetic diseases. Genet. Med. 18 (7), 746–749.

Handoko, L., Xu, H., Li, G., Ngan, C.Y., Chew, E., Schnapp, M., et al., 2011. CTCF-mediated functional chromatin interactome in pluripotent cells. Nat. Genet. 43 (7), 630–638.

Herman, D.S., Lam, L., Taylor, M.R., Wang, L., Teekakirikul, P., Christodoulou, D., et al., 2012. Truncations of titin causing dilated cardiomyopathy. N. Engl. J. Med. 366 (7), 619–628.

Hill, M., Twiss, P., Verhoef, T.I., Drury, S., McKay, F., Mason, S., et al., 2015. Non-invasive prenatal diagnosis for cystic fibrosis: detection of paternal mutations, exploration of patient preferences and cost analysis. Prenat. Diagn. 35 (10), 950–958.

Hodis, E., Watson, I.R., Kryukov, G.V., Arold, S.T., Imielinski, M., Theurillat, J.P., et al., 2012. A landscape of driver mutations in melanoma. Cell 150 (2), 251–263.

Jabeen, A., Ahmad, N., Raza, K., 2018. Machine learning-based state-of-the-art methods for the classification of RNA-seq data. In: Classification in BioApps. Springer, Cham, pp. 133–172.

Jain, M., Fiddes, I.T., Miga, K.H., Olsen, H.E., Paten, B., Akeson, M., 2015. Improved data analysis for the MinION nanopore sequencer. Nat. Methods 12 (4), 351–356.

Jain, M., Tyson, J.R., Loose, M., Ip, C.L., Eccles, D.A., O'Grady, J., et al., 2017. MinION analysis and reference consortium: phase 2 data release and analysis of R9. 0 chemistry. F1000Res. 6.

Jamuar, S.S., Tan, E.C., 2015. Clinical application of next-generation sequencing for Mendelian diseases. Hum. Genom. 9, 10.

Jones, P.A., Issa, J.P.J., Baylin, S., 2016. Targeting the cancer epigenome for therapy. Nat. Rev. Genet. 17 (10), 630–641.

Karlovich, C.A., Williams, P.M., 2019. Clinical applications of next-generation sequencing in precision oncology. Canc. J. 25 (4), 264–271.

Kchouk, M., Gibrat, J.F., Elloumi, M., 2017. Generations of sequencing technologies: from first to next generation. Biol. Med. 9 (3).

Korlach, J., 2013. Understanding Accuracy in SMRT® Sequencing. Pacific Biosciences, pp. 1–9.

Kostareva, A., Kiselev, A., Gudkova, A., Frishman, G., Ruepp, A., Frishman, D., et al., 2016. Genetic spectrum of idiopathic restrictive cardiomyopathy uncovered by next-generation sequencing. PLoS One 11 (9), e0163362.

Kulski, J.K., 2016. Next-generation sequencing—an overview of the history, tools, and "Omic" applications. In: Next Generation Sequencing—Advances, Applications and Challenges, pp. 3–60.

Kulski, J.K., Suzuki, S., Ozaki, Y., Mitsunaga, S., Inoko, H., Shiina, T., 2014. In phase HLA genotyping by next generation sequencing-a comparison between two massively parallel sequencing bench-top systems, the Roche GS Junior and ion torrent PGM. In: HLA and Associated Important Diseases. Intech, Croatia, pp. 141–181.

Kumar, S., Banks, T.W., Cloutier, S., 2012. SNP discovery through next-generation sequencing and its applications. Int. J. Plant Genom. 2012.

Kumar, S., Gaur, V., Khurana, S., Bose, S., Kiran, M., Kiran, M., 2017. Proteomics tools—an update. Clin. Oncol. 2, 1358.

Kunz, M., Dannemann, M., Kelso, J., 2013. High-throughput sequencing of the melanoma genome. Exp. Dermatol. 22, 10–17.

Lang, K., Surendranath, V., Quenzel, P., Schofl, G., Schmidt, A.H., Lange, V., 2018. Full-length HLA class I genotyping with the MinION nanopore sequencer. Methods Mol. Biol. 1802, 155–162.

Le, D.T., Durham, J.N., Smith, K.N., Wang, H., Bartlett, B.R., Aulakh, L.K., et al., 2017. Mismatch repair deficiency predicts response of solid tumors to PD-1 blockade. Science 357 (6349), 409–413.

Leopold, S.R., Goering, R.V., Witten, A., Harmsen, D., Mellmann, A., 2014. Bacterial whole-genome sequencing revisited: portable, scalable, and standardized analysis for typing and detection of virulence and antibiotic resistance genes. J. Clin. Microbiol. 52 (7), 2365–2370.

Lesage, S., Brice, A., 2009. Parkinson's disease: from monogenic forms to genetic susceptibility factors. Hum. Mol. Genet. 18 (R1), R48–R59.

Lopes, L.R., Zekavati, A., Syrris, P., Hubank, M., Giambartolomei, C., Dalageorgou, C., et al., 2013. Genetic complexity in hypertrophic cardiomyopathy revealed by high-throughput sequencing. J. Med. Genet. 50 (4), 228–239.

Lun, F.M., Tsui, N.B., Chan, K.A., Leung, T.Y., Lau, T.K., Charoenkwan, P., et al., 2008. Noninvasive prenatal diagnosis of monogenic diseases by digital size selection and relative mutation dosage on DNA in maternal plasma. Proc. Natl. Acad. Sci. U. S. A. 105 (50), 19920–19925.

MacIntyre, D.A., Jimenez, B., Lewintre, E.J., Martín, C.R., Schäfer, H., Ballesteros, C.G., et al., 2010. Serum metabolome analysis by 1 H-NMR reveals differences between chronic lymphocytic leukaemia molecular subgroups. Leukemia 24 (4), 788–797.

Mapstone, M., Cheema, A.K., Fiandaca, M.S., Zhong, X., Mhyre, T.R., MacArthur, L.H., et al., 2014. Plasma phospholipids identify antecedent memory impairment in older adults. Nat. Med. 20 (4), 415.

Martin, H.C., Kim, G.E., Pagnamenta, A.T., Murakami, Y., Carvill, G.L., Meyer, E., et al., 2014. Clinical whole-genome sequencing in severe early-onset epilepsy reveals new genes and improves molecular diagnosis. Hum. Mol. Genet. 23 (12), 3200–3211.

Mayers, J.R., Wu, C., Clish, C.B., Kraft, P., Torrence, M.E., Fiske, B.P., et al., 2014. Elevation of circulating branched-chain amino acids is an early event in human pancreatic adenocarcinoma development. Nat. Med. 20 (10), 1193.

McInerney-Leo, A.M., Schmidts, M., Cortés, C.R., Leo, P.J., Gener, B., Courtney, A.D., et al., 2013. Short-rib polydactyly and Jeune syndromes are caused by mutations in WDR60. Am. J. Hum. Genet. 93 (3), 515–523.

Meny, G.M., Flickinger, C., Marcucci, C., 2013. The American rare donor program. J. Crit. Care 28 (1), 110-e9–18.

Merriman, B., R&D Team, I.T., Rothberg, J.M., 2012. Progress in ion torrent semiconductor chip based sequencing. Electrophoresis 33 (23), 3397–3417.

Mertens, F., Johansson, B., Fioretos, T., Mitelman, F., 2015. The emerging complexity of gene fusions in cancer. Nat. Rev. Canc. 15 (6), 371–381.

Minervini, C.F., Cumbo, C., Orsini, P., Anelli, L., Zagaria, A., Specchia, G., Albano, F., 2020. Nanopore sequencing in blood diseases: a wide range of opportunities. Front. Genet. 11, 76.

Müllauer, L., 2017. Next generation sequencing: clinical applications in solid tumours. Memo-Mag. Eur. Med. Oncol. 10 (4), 244–247.

Murtaza, M., Dawson, S.J., Tsui, D.W., Gale, D., Forshew, T., Piskorz, A.M., et al., 2013. Non-invasive analysis of acquired resistance to cancer therapy by sequencing of plasma DNA. Nature 497 (7447), 108–112.

Naidoo, N., Pawitan, Y., Soong, R., Cooper, D.N., Ku, C.S., 2011. Human genetics and genomics a decade after the release of the draft sequence of the human genome. Hum. Genom. 5 (6), 577.

Nass, S.J., Levit, L.A., Gostin, L.O., 2009. The value and importance of health information privacy. In: Beyond the HIPAA Privacy Rule: Enhancing Privacy, Improving Health through Research. National Academies Press (US).

Nizam, S., Verma, S., Borah, N.N., Gazara, R.K., Verma, P.K., 2014. Comprehensive genome-wide analysis reveals different classes of enigmatic old yellow enzyme in fungi. Sci. Rep. 4, 4013.

Oates, S., Tang, S., Rosch, R., Lear, R., Hughes, E.F., Williams, R.E., et al., 2018. Incorporating epilepsy genetics into clinical practice: a 360 evaluation. NPJ Genom. Med. 3 (1), 1–11.

Oldridge, D.A., Wood, A.C., Weichert-Leahey, N., Crimmins, I., Sussman, R., Winter, C., et al., 2015. Genetic predisposition to neuroblastoma mediated by a LMO1 super-enhancer polymorphism. Nature 528 (7582), 418–421.

Ordulu, Z., Kammin, T., Brand, H., Pillalamarri, V., Redin, C.E., Collins, R.L., et al., 2016. Structural chromosomal rearrangements require nucleotide-level resolution: lessons from next-generation sequencing in prenatal diagnosis. Am. J. Hum. Genet. 99 (5), 1015–1033.

Pang, S.Y.Y., Teo, K.C., Hsu, J.S., Chang, R.S.K., Li, M., Sham, P.C., Ho, S.L., 2017. The role of gene variants in the pathogenesis of neurodegenerative disorders as revealed by next generation sequencing studies: a review. Transl. Neurodegener. 6 (1), 27.

Patel, A., Belykh, E., Miller, E.J., George, L.L., Martirosyan, N.L., Byvaltsev, V.A., Preul, M.C., 2018. MinION rapid sequencing: review of potential applications in neurosurgery. Surg. Neurol. Int. 9, 157.

Putoux, A., Thomas, S., Coene, K.L., Davis, E.E., Alanay, Y., Ogur, G., et al., 2011. KIF7 mutations cause fetal hydrolethalus and acrocallosal syndromes. Nat. Genet. 43 (6), 601–606.

Qin, D., 2019. Next-generation sequencing and its clinical application. Canc. Biol. & Med. 16 (1), 4–10.

Quick, J., Loman, N.J., Duraffour, S., Simpson, J.T., Severi, E., Cowley, L., et al., 2016. Real-time, portable genome sequencing for Ebola surveillance. Nature 530 (7589), 228–232.

Rackham, O.J., Langley, S.R., Oates, T., Vradi, E., Harmston, N., Srivastava, P.K., et al., 2017. A Bayesian approach for analysis of whole-genome bisulfite sequencing data identifies disease-associated changes in DNA methylation. Genetics 205 (4), 1443–1458.

Ramos, E.I., Bien-Willner, G.A., Li, J., Hughes, A.E., Giacalone, J., Chasnoff, S., et al., 2014. Genetic variation in MKL2 and decreased downstream PCTAIRE1 expression in extreme, fatal primary human microcephaly. Clin. Genet. 85 (5), 423–432.

Rasmussen, M., Sunde, L., Nielsen, M.L., Ramsing, M., Petersen, A., Hjortshøj, T.D., et al., 2018. Targeted gene sequencing and whole-exome sequencing in autopsied fetuses with prenatally diagnosed kidney anomalies. Clin. Genet. 93 (4), 860–869.

Raza, K., Ahmad, S., 2019. Recent advancement in next-generation sequencing techniques and its computational analysis. Int. J. Bioinf. Res. Appl. 15 (3), 191–220.

Rennert, H., Eng, K., Zhang, T., Tan, A., Xiang, J., Romanel, A., et al., February 2016. Development and validation of a whole-exome sequencing test for simultaneous detection of point mutations, indels and copy-number alterations for precision cancer care. NPJ Genom. Med. 1, 1–11.

Rhee, E.P., Cheng, S., Larson, M.G., Walford, G.A., Lewis, G.D., McCabe, E., et al., 2011. Lipid profiling identifies a triacylglycerol signature of insulin resistance and improves diabetes prediction in humans. J. Clin. Invest. 121 (4), 1402–1411.

Safi, H., Lingaraju, S., Amin, A., Kim, S., Jones, M., Holmes, M., et al., 2013. Evolution of high-level ethambutol-resistant tuberculosis through interacting mutations in decaprenylphosphoryl-β-D-arabinose biosynthetic and utilization pathway genes. Nat. Genet. 45 (10), 1190–1197.

Sahoo, M.K., Lefterova, M.I., Yamamoto, F., Waggoner, J.J., Chou, S., Holmes, S.P., et al., 2013. Detection of cytomegalovirus drug resistance mutations by next-generation sequencing. J. Clin. Microbiol. 51 (11), 3700–3710.

Sakamoto, Y., Xu, L., Seki, M., Yokoyama, T.T., Kasahara, M., Kashima, Y., et al., 2019. Long Read Sequencing Reveals a Novel Class of Structural Aberrations in Cancers: Identification and Characterization of Cancerous Local Amplifications. bioRxiv, 620047.

Samuel, N., Hudson, T.J., 2013. Translating genomics to the clinic: implications of cancer heterogeneity. Clin. Chem. 59 (1), 127–137.

Sanger, F., Nicklen, S., Coulson, A.R., 1977. DNA sequencing with chain-terminating inhibitors. Proc. Natl. Acad. Sci. U. S. A. 74 (12), 5463–5467.

Schmidt, D., Wilson, M.D., Ballester, B., Schwalie, P.C., Brown, G.D., Marshall, A., et al., 2010. Five-vertebrate ChIP-seq reveals the evolutionary dynamics of transcription factor binding. Science 328 (5981), 1036–1040. https://doi.org/10.1126/science.1186176.

Schunkert, H., König, I.R., Kathiresan, S., Reilly, M.P., Assimes, T.L., Holm, H., et al., 2011. Large-scale association analysis identifies 13 new susceptibility loci for coronary artery disease. Nat. Genet. 43 (4), 333–338.

Schuster, B., Knies, K., Stoepker, C., Velleuer, E., Friedl, R., Gottwald-Mühlhauser, B., et al., 2013. Whole exome sequencing reveals uncommon mutations in the recently identified Fanconi anemia gene SLX4/FANCP. Hum. Mutat. 34 (1), 93–96.

Schwaederle, M., Parker, B.A., Schwab, R.B., Daniels, G.A., Piccioni, D.E., Kesari, S., et al., 2016. Precision oncology: the UC San Diego moores cancer center predict experience. Mol. Canc. Therapeut. 15 (4), 743–752.

Scotti, M.M., Swanson, M.S., 2016. RNA mis-splicing in disease. Nat. Rev. Genet. 17 (1), 19.

Semsarian, C., Hamilton, R.M., 2012. Key role of the molecular autopsy in sudden unexpected death. Heart Rhythm 9 (1), 145–150.

Shamseldin, H.E., Elfaki, M., Alkuraya, F.S., 2012. Exome sequencing reveals a novel Fanconi group defined by XRCC2 mutation. J. Med. Genet. 49 (3), 184–186.

Shulha, H.P., Cheung, I., Whittle, C., Wang, J., Virgil, D., Lin, C.L., et al., 2012. Epigenetic signatures of autism: trimethylated H3K4 landscapes in prefrontal neurons. Arch. Gen. Psychiatr. 69 (3), 314–324.

Snyder, M.W., Kircher, M., Hill, A.J., Daza, R.M., Shendure, J., 2016. Cell-free DNA comprises an in vivo nucleosome footprint that informs its tissues-of-origin. Cell 164 (1–2), 57–68.

Spratlin, J.L., Serkova, N.J., Eckhardt, S.G., 2009. Clinical applications of metabolomics in oncology: a review. Clin. Canc. Res. 15 (2), 431–440.

Stockley, T.L., Oza, A.M., Berman, H.K., Leighl, N.B., Knox, J.J., Shepherd, F.A., et al., 2016. Molecular profiling of advanced solid tumors and patient outcomes with genotype-matched clinical trials: the Princess Margaret IMPACT/COMPACT trial. Genome Med. 8 (1), 109.

Sun, Y., Man, J., Wan, Y., Pan, G., Du, L., Li, L., et al., 2018. Targeted next-generation sequencing as a comprehensive test for Mendelian diseases: a cohort diagnostic study. Sci. Rep. 8 (1), 1–9.

Swaminathan, S., Schlaberg, R., Lewis, J., Hanson, K.E., Couturier, M.R., 2016. Fatal Zika virus infection with secondary nonsexual transmission. N. Engl. J. Med. 375 (19), 1907–1909.

Swisher, E.M., Lin, K.K., Oza, A.M., Scott, C.L., Giordano, H., Sun, J., et al., 2017. Rucaparib in relapsed, platinum-sensitive high-grade ovarian carcinoma (ARIEL2 Part 1): an international, multicentre, open-label, phase 2 trial. Lancet Oncol. 18 (1), 75–87.

Tamma, P.D., Fan, Y., Bergman, Y., Pertea, G., Kazmi, A.Q., Lewis, S., et al., 2019. Applying rapid whole-genome sequencing to predict phenotypic antimicrobial susceptibility testing results among carbapenem-resistant *Klebsiella pneumoniae* clinical isolates. Antimicrob. Agents Chemother. 63 (1) e01923-18.

Tan, Z., Nie, S., McDermott, S.P., Wicha, M.S., Lubman, D.M., 2017. Single amino acid variant profiles of subpopulations in the MCF-7 breast cancer cell line. J. Proteome Res. 16 (2), 842–851.

Tasian, S.K., Loh, M.L., Hunger, S.P., 2017. Philadelphia chromosome–like acute lymphoblastic leukemia. Blood J. Amer. Soc. Hematol. 130 (19), 2064–2072.

Taylor, W.S., Pearson, J., Miller, A., Schmeier, S., Frizelle, F.A., Purcell, R.V., 2020. MinION Sequencing of colorectal cancer tumour microbiomes—a comparison with amplicon-based and RNA-Sequencing. PLoS One 15 (5), e0233170.

Totomoch-Serra, A., Marquez, M.F., Cervantes-Barragán, D.E., 2017. Sanger sequencing as a first-line approach for molecular diagnosis of Andersen-Tawil syndrome. F1000Res. 6.

Trégouët, D.A., König, I.R., Erdmann, J., Munteanu, A., Braund, P.S., Hall, A.S., et al., 2009. Genome-wide haplotype association study identifies the SLC22A3-LPAL2-LPA gene cluster as a risk locus for coronary artery disease. Nat. Genet. 41 (3), 283–285.

Tsang, J.C., Vong, J.S., Ji, L., Poon, L.C., Jiang, P., Lui, K.O., et al., 2017. Integrative single-cell and cell-free plasma RNA transcriptomics elucidates placental cellular dynamics. Proc. Natl. Acad. Sci. U. S. A. 114 (37), E7786–E7795.

Tsimberidou, A.M., Iskander, N.G., Hong, D.S., Wheler, J.J., Falchook, G.S., Fu, S., et al., 2012. Personalized medicine in a phase I clinical trials program: the MD Anderson cancer center initiative. Clin. Canc. Res. 18 (22), 6373–6383.

Tyler, A.D., Mataseje, L., Urfano, C.J., Schmidt, L., Antonation, K.S., Mulvey, M.R., Corbett, C.R., 2018. Evaluation of Oxford Nanopore's MinION sequencing device for microbial whole genome sequencing applications. Sci. Rep. 8 (1), 1–12.

Tzou, P.L., Ariyaratne, P., Varghese, V., Lee, C., Rakhmanaliev, E., Villy, C., et al., 2018. Comparison of an in vitro diagnostic next-generation sequencing assay with Sanger sequencing for HIV-1 genotypic resistance testing. J. Clin. Microbiol. 56 (6), e00105–e00118.

van Kessel, K.E., Van Neste, L., Lurkin, I., Zwarthoff, E.C., Van Criekinge, W., 2016. Evaluation of an epigenetic profile for the detection of bladder cancer in patients with hematuria. J. Urol. 195 (3), 601–607.

Vanderwalde, A., Spetzler, D., Xiao, N., Gatalica, Z., Marshall, J., 2018. Microsatellite instability status determined by next-generation sequencing and compared with PD-L1 and tumor mutational burden in 11,348 patients. Canc. Med. 7 (3), 746–756.

Van Giau, V., An, S.S.A., 2019. Epitope mapping immunoassay analysis of the interaction between β-amyloid and fibrinogen. Int. J. Mol. Sci. 20 (3), 496.

Vendrell, J.A., Mau-Them, F.T., Béganton, B., Godreuil, S., Coopman, P., Solassol, J., 2017. Circulating cell free tumor DNA detection as a routine tool for lung cancer patient management. Int. J. Mol. Sci. 18 (2).

Verma, S., Gazara, R.K., Nizam, S., Parween, S., Chattopadhyay, D., Verma, P.K., 2016. Draft genome sequencing and secretome analysis of fungal phytopathogen *Ascochyta rabiei* provides insight into the necrotrophic effector repertoire. Sci. Rep. 6 (1), 1−14.

Wadapurkar, R.M., Vyas, R., 2018. Computational analysis of next generation sequencing data and its applications in clinical oncology. Inform. Med. Unlocked 11, 75−82.

Walker, R.H., Schulz, V.P., Tikhonova, I.R., Mahajan, M.C., Mane, S., Arroyo Muniz, M., Gallagher, P.G., 2012. Genetic diagnosis of neuro-acanthocytosis disorders using exome sequencing. Mov. Disord. 27 (4), 539−543.

Wang, J., Lin, Z.J., Liu, L., Xu, H.Q., Shi, Y.W., Yi, Y.H., et al., 2017. Epilepsy-associated genes. Seizure 44, 11−20.

Wani, N., Raza, K., 2019. Raw sequence to target gene prediction: an integrated inference pipeline for ChIP-seq and RNA-seq datasets. In: Applications of Artificial Intelligence Techniques in Engineering. Springer, Singapore, pp. 557−568.

Weimer, E.T., Montgomery, M., Petraroia, R., Crawford, J., Schmitz, J.L., 2016. Performance characteristics and validation of next-generation sequencing for human leucocyte antigen typing. J. Mol. Diagn. 18 (5), 668−675.

Weischenfeldt, J., Symmons, O., Spitz, F., Korbel, J.O., 2013. Phenotypic impact of genomic structural variation: insights from and for human disease. Nat. Rev. Genet. 14 (2), 125−138.

Welch, J.S., Westervelt, P., Ding, L., Larson, D.E., Klco, J.M., Kulkarni, S., et al., 2011. Use of whole-genome sequencing to diagnose a cryptic fusion oncogene. JAMA J. Amer. Med. Assoc. 305 (15), 1577−1584.

White, M.B., Amos, J., Hsu, J.M., Gerrard, B., Finn, P., Dean, M., 1990. A frame-shift mutation in the cystic fibrosis gene. Nature 344 (6267), 665−667.

Wishart, D.S., Feunang, Y.D., Marcu, A., Guo, A.C., Liang, K., Vázquez-Fresno, R., et al., 2018. HMDB 4.0: the human metabolome database for 2018. Nucleic Acids Res. 46 (D1), D608−D617.

Xiong, L., Barrett, A.N., Hua, R., Tan, T.Z., Ho, S.S.Y., Chan, J.K., et al., 2015. Non-invasive prenatal diagnostic testing for β-thalassaemia using cell-free fetal DNA and next generation sequencing. Prenat. Diagn. 35 (3), 258−265.

Xuan, J., Yu, Y., Qing, T., Guo, L., Shi, L., 2013. Next-generation sequencing in the clinic: promises and challenges. Canc. Lett. 340 (2), 284−295.

Yohe, S., Thyagarajan, B., 2017. Review of clinical next-generation sequencing. Arch. Pathol. Lab Med. 141 (11), 1544−1557.

Yuen, B.T., Knoepfler, P.S., 2013. Histone H3. 3 mutations: a variant path to cancer. Canc. Cell 24 (5), 567−574.

Zhang, X.W., Li, Q.H., Xu, Z. Di, Dou, J.J., 2020. Mass spectrometry-based metabolomics in health and medical science: a systematic review. RSC Adv. 10 (6), 3092−3104.

Zhao, H., Heimberger, A.B., Lu, Z., Wu, X., Hodges, T.R., Song, R., Shen, J., 2016. Metabolomics profiling in plasma samples from glioma patients correlates with tumor phenotypes. Oncotarget 7 (15), 20486−20495.

Zhou, K., Lokate, M., Deurenberg, R.H., Arends, J., Foe, L.T., Grundmann, H., et al., 2015. Characterization of a CTX-M-15 producing *Klebsiella pneumoniae* outbreak strain assigned to a novel sequence type (1427). Front. Microbiol. 6, 1250.

Chapter 4

Genomics in clinical care through precision medicine and personalized treatments

Rutumbara Dash[1], Abhishek Sahu[1], Manasa Kumar Panda[1,2,*], Mohinikanti Das[3] and Yengkhom Disco Singh[4]

[1]*School of Life Sciences, Sambalpur University, Burla, Odisha, India;* [2]*Environment & Sustainability Department, CSIR- IMMT, Bhubaneswar, Odisha, India;* [3]*Department of Botany, College of Basic Science & Humanities, Orissa University of Agriculture and Technology, Bhubaneswar, Odisha, India;* [4]*Department of Post Harvest Technology, College of Horticulture and Forestry, Central Agricultural University, Pasighat, Arunachal Pradesh, India*

*Corresponding author: E-mail: mkp.immt@gmail.com

Chapter outline

1. Introduction to genomics

Deciphering organisms' genetic architectures has contributed to a revolution in the field of medicine. Sequencing the organism's complete set of genomes of large samples of the population and identification of potential variations could provide significant insight into the potent role of DNA variants, and their association to phenotypic abnormality has become a tremendous challenge. This will also explore the organism's vulnerability to different diseases and explain how medicine can be personalized for better prevention, diagnosis, and treatment only made possible because of genomics (Bilkety et al., 2019). It can be said that genomics has opened a new chapter toward the progress of personalized treatment based on the genetic makeup of an organism. This is a remarkable achievement that enables us to identify the underlying causes of a disease and simultaneously tackle them even after onset of the disease (Bilkety et al., 2019). This is of increasing importance in the current health scenario where the disease burden has become a prominent problem with the rise of different noncommunicable diseases like diabetes, cancer, and cardiovascular diseases. Genomics has transformed our current understanding of disease and enables us to deliver care in a way specific for a personalized approach. Sequencing the genome, identification of mutations specific to a person, and establishment of a specific genotype–phenotype relationship could elucidate the cause, risk factors, and stage of the disease as well as side effects to a particular medication. Remarkable progress has been made over the past decades in understanding the human genome, proteome, and chemical complexity governing gene behavior (Fiore and Goodman, 2016).

Translational Bioinformatics in Healthcare and Medicine. https://doi.org/10.1016/B978-0-323-89824-9.00004-5

Inception of the Human Genome Project (HGP) in 1989 by the National Institute of Health (NIH) was an evolution for exploring the chemical blueprint of life contributing to the field of genomics. Scientists have deciphered a link between the structural characterization of genes with respect to human illness, treatment efficacy, and adverse consequences. Integration of the DNA sequencing data into electronic health records (EHRs) predominantly affects healthcare through more effective and accurate target treatments and therapy. This connectivity has enhanced the research dimension into clinical care with providing timely information to patients' physicians and medical researchers. Telemedicine is a new approach of treatment that can bring precision medicine technologies used by genomic researchers for many genomic practices (Qazi et al., 2019). More recently, scientists have identified genes that in turn will determine the potential severity, risk factors, and outcome to a particular disease. For example the mutation in breast cancer genes *BRCA1* and *BRCA2* make one more susceptible to breast cancer with higher risk, whereas the mutation in *HER2* poses a greater risk of reoccurrence (Feng et al., 2018). This potential novel approach has contributed to the emergence of another field, pharmacogenomics, which provides potential benefits for a safer and more effective drug therapy.

2. Technologic approach to genomics

Several gold standard technologic approaches have contributed to the milestone of genomics, including DNA sequencing that includes high-throughput DNA sequencing technology like next generation sequencing (NGS), clinical exome sequencing (CES), or whole exome sequencing (WES), whole transcriptomic sequencing (WTS), and single cell sequencing. Although the DNA sequencing was cost effective at merely a thousand dollars, lessening the cost has allowed a mainstay in the clinical context (Biesecker et al., 2009; Conley et al., 2013). Due to its increasing reading length, decreased cost, increasing demands for targeted resequencing, and rapid sequencing in the existing platform, it has emerged as a leading transcriptomic technology (Tang et al., 2009). Further refinement in the field of DNA sequencing has added for implications in therapeutic intervention. These include CES, WTS, and WES. CES has become the powerful tool so far as the diagnosis of rare genetic disorders is considered. The single cell–based method has also been a choice since 2013 for genomic study. However, recent microfluidics platforms offer utmost single cell DNA analysis and throughput facilitating the detection of genomic variability across the cell populations. In this context, artificial intelligence can be used to find suitable molecules that can inhibit breast cancer enzymes and other such diseases using molecular dockings and molecular dynamics simulations (Sahu et al., 2020).

2.1 Genomics: implications in healthcare and precision medicine

Identification and assessment of a patient's exact symptoms by gathering more data to prescribe a better prognosis in terms of clinical intervention is highly crucial. The ability of genomics in clinical decision-making has allowed it to improve the practice of medicine. Understanding the patient's genetic makeup is highly crucial for providing optimal care for several diseases. Sequencing the specific potent known and unknown variants, panel-based gene sequencing, sequencing of the exome, and their possible clinical correlation are highly crucial for clinicians. Accordingly, precision medicine involves an emerging approach for disease treatment and prevention, taking into account human genetic, environmental, and behavioral variation for each person (AL-Dewik and Qoronfleh, 2019).The approach not only allows both researchers and doctors prediction of accurate diagnosis but also understanding of the disease pathogenesis and prevention. Although the HGP is inherent to the field of precision medicine, the field dates back to the early medical discoveries that supported the use of therapies that are specialized for a patient's oriented characteristics (Ramaswami et al., 2018). The remarkable discoveries and scientific breakthrough of eminent scientists like Phoebus Levene, Erwin Chargaff, James D. Watson, Francis H. C. Crick, Frederick Sanger, and Karl Landsteiner allowed researchers for the first time in history to interconnect disease and health with a wide range of genetic and epigenetic context. Technologic advancement has helped healthcare professionals not only to develop the novel diagnostic approach, but also suitable treatment for several patients. Advancement in technical scenario, molecular genetics, and genomics today is discerned as a thriving part of the clinical diagnostic services. More importantly, this approach has resulted in the development of several targeted pharmacotherapeutic agents to optimize patient benefits with less cost and lower side effects. Some of the broadest areas of precision medicine include biomarker-specific therapy, gene editing, genetic therapy approach, pharmacogenomics, and a noncommunicable disease approach (Ramaswami et al., 2018).

These days, artificial intelligence (AI) method or computer assisted drug design is popularly used for design and preparation of medicine. It is a wide field dealing with different schemes, patterns, designs, and application of scientific systems for evaluation, knowledge, and elucidation of information (Mason, 2007). Compared to traditional practices, AI does not believe in complex physical and chemical theories rather than concentrating on biomedical information and transformable science. It comprises some usual principles such as strategy retrogression, naïve Bayesian categories, linear regression, neural network, and so on (Lavecchia and Di Giovanni, 2013). There are so many noteworthy approaches that have been created by applying figure identifications in pathology, radiology, and ophthalmology that provide more appropriate results than humans in the process of drug discovery and diagnosis (Williams et al., 2018). AI includes certain procedures for the production of medicines such as drug invention, medicine designing issues, and AI models. The medicine invention involves some major steps like identification of drug targets, hit detection, and hit to lead optimization, which are further followed by different drug designs. The selective identification of drugs in the series conducted with the convolutional neural network (CNN) and FD/DCA protein folding and protein−protein interactions (Weinshilboum and Wang, 2017) was predicted (Weinshilboum and Wang, 2017). Medicine repurposing, effective screening, and recording of ongoing activity are executed in the hit innovation step with the help of support vector machine (SVM), CNN, and network pathology (Liew et al., 2009). At last the hit to lead optimization involves QSAR, de novo drug designing, and ADME/T properties evaluation, which are carried out by traditional machine learning, deep neural network (DNN), deep learning, CNN, variational autoencoder, and multineural network (Gómez-Bombarelli et al., 2018). Therefore, the AI method is convoluted in the province of pharmaceutical designing and contributes a peculiar center in the deep learning process for the innovation of new medicines. It also consists of various molecular techniques, data learning transformation, cross-affirmation, and proficiency in deep neural networks (Zhong et al., 2018). There are so many noteworthy approaches that have been created by applying figure identifications in pathology, radiology, and ophthalmology that provide more appropriate results than humans in the process of drug discovery and diagnosis in skin cancer and diabetic retinopathy (Williams et al., 2018).

3. Biomarker-specific therapy

Biomarkers are mostly reliable in predicting several diseases like cardiovascular diseases, cancers, and heart disease. Although hereditary forms of ovary cancer have been elucidated previously in certain ethnic groups, like Ashkenazi Jewish populations, it still necessitates a panel biomarker approach in diseases like cancers (Antoniou et al., 2003). The presence of a specific biomarker rather than the tumor location provides a novel approach for therapeutic intervention. For example, approval of pembrolizumab (Keytruda) agent marked for the first solid cancer therapy used as a specific biomarker than the location of tumor. Similar findings have been observed by the previous study where trastuzumab-dskt (Ogivri) was used to target both stomach and breast tumors overexpressing *HER2* gene with low cost. Recently, it was observed that *BRCA1* and *BRCA2* mutations are highly crucial in determining the phenotypical severity and onset of breast and ovary cancer (Antoniou et al., 2003; Chen and Parmigiani, 2007).

4. High-risk assessment in the population

In evaluating pathophysiology and personalized monitoring, the detection and assessment of high-risk conditions play a significant role for patients of differing symptom severity. Sparing families and individuals that are not impacted becomes quite valuable by inadequate regular testing or scanning that could be associated by damage. The prediction regarding the health or possibility of disease like cardiovascular disease, hyperlipidemia, or cardiac arrhythmias in a person can be detected by genetic screening of his family (Hobbs et al., 1992; Nherera et al., 2011).

5. Pharmacogenomics

Understanding the genetic variants associated with the biologic effects of the drug in addressing the serious outcome of drugs at an individual level is highly important. Pharmacogenomics is the science of representing the interaction of drug response and adverse drug reaction at the individual level with respect to a particular disease. Merging of genomics and pharmacology would be highly ideal to develop effective and safe medications for tailoring medicine. The field encompasses two prominent areas: one is pharmacokinetics and another is pharmacodynamics. The former entails the amount of drug required to reach the target cells, in addition to the adsorption, distribution, metabolism, and excretion, whereas pharmacodynamics displays the behavior of different cellular systems like nerve cells, intestinal cells, stomach cells, etc., to respond to the drug in terms of receptors, ion channels, enzyme components, and immunologic response (Weinshilboum and Wang, 2017; Abubakar and Bentley, 2018). DNA sequencing technology has allowed identification of several gene single nucleotide polymorphisms (SNPs) like KRAS, KIT, EGFR, CYP2D6, CYP450 3A4/3A5, Factor II, Factor V Leiden, and MTHFR, allowing one to design and target the specific molecular target of a biochemical pathway of a particular patient with personalized therapy with less side effect of the drug (AL-Dewik and Qoronfleh, 2019). Furthermore, there is classification of special genetic variants with different metabolic pathways into their slow, intermediate, normal, and ultrafast metabolizing forms as suitable for each drug and patient groups into poor metabolizers, intermediate metabolizer, extensive metabolizers, and ultrarapid metabolizers (Pilotto et al., 2011; Ahmed et al., 2016).

6. Gene therapy

Personalized medicine has enabled significant advancement in the field of gene and cell-based therapy at an individual level. NGS and the advent of CRISPER technology have put a tremendous challenge to allow doctors better screening and therapeutic efficacy. In 2017, the US Food and Drug Administration (FDA) approved the first chimeric antigen receptor T cell (CAR-T) therapy for Kymriah (tisagenlecleucel) developed by the Swiss pharmaceutical company Novartis and researchers from the University of Pennsylvania. Kymriah indicates high therapeutic efficacy for the treatment of pediatric acute lymphoblastic leukemia (June et al., 2015; Boyiadzis et al., 2018).

Actually, genome editing automations such as ZFN, CRISPR-Cas9, and TALENs have been established to reliably split the dual-stranded DNA of the genome to obtain one-stranded RNA, contributing to improvements in effective gene targeting (Gurumurthy et al., 2019). Significant progress has made toward development of induced pluripotent stem cells (iPS) for stem cell modeling of diseases with patient-specific human embryonic stem cells (Hamazaki et al., 2017). Currently, researchers are implementing modeling of retinal diseases using patient-specific iPS cells; autologous transplantation of differentiated retinal cells that undergo gene correction at the iPS cell stage via gene editing tools (e.g., CRISPR/Cas9, TALENS, and ZFNs); and autologous transplantation of patient-specific iPS-derived retinal cells treated with gene therapy. Voretigene neparvovec (Luxturna) for retinal dystrophy was observed to be the first genetic therapy ever approved by the FDA used to treat the inherited disease. In 2016, another two orphan drugs were approved by the FDA for genetic neuromuscular disease, representing a major breakthrough in treatment of rare diseases, whereas eteplirsen (Exondys 51) for Duchenne muscular dystrophy and nusinersen (Spinraza) were approved for early fatal spinal muscular atrophy. Challenges to the utility of the personalized medicine approaches developed in the perspective of better clinical efficacy have shown to be improved for rare diseases like hemophilia B, cystic fibrosis, and chronic myeloid leukemia.

7. Infectious and chronic disease

The personalized medicine approach has shown a major role in improvement of disease processes and diagnosis of several infectious and chronic diseases. Personalized medicine has helped to understand better the nature and resistant strain responsible for several communicable diseases like influenza, Ebola, and AIDS (Ramaswami et al., 2018). Whole genome sequencing in the field of microbiology has contributed to the identification of potent phenotype, therapeutic strategy, and genetic relatedness in outbreaks. For instance, targeted whole genome sequencing approach was a gold standard to decipher the geographic distribution of the extensively drug-resistant tuberculosis (XDR-TB) (Shau et al., 2020).

Integration of electronic capture of medical records and advancement in the field of pharmacogenomics provides a unique framework for individual diagnostics and therapeutic approach for several diseases. This started with cancer to other chronic diseases like diabetes, neurodegenerative diseases, inflammatory diseases, and autoimmune diseases, which were initially associated with high mortality and observed to be a major burden both in the patients in childhood as well as adults. However, the onset of precision medicine has opened a new horizon in better diagnosis and therapeutic intervention. Precision medicine has shown to play a major role in tackling some rare inflammatory brain diseases like infectious meningitis, encephalitis, vasculitis, and T cell-mediated inflammatory brain diseases. Previous evidence by Obermeier et al. (2016) indicates development of a tool that enables physicians to classify patients consistently and accurately at the right time. These interventions could be further extended by adding the biomarker and omics (genomics, proteomics, transcriptomics, cytomics) approach could expand the dimension of personalized medicine. Clinical genomics and proteomics could act together with precision medicine for the treatment strategy of several diseases like mood disorder, autism, and related neurodegenerative disorders (Twilt, 2016). Significant improvement in the technology has shed light on the diagnostic and therapeutic regimen of different diseases like several types of cancers. Cell free nucleic acids like mRNA and microRNA are potential indicators and biomarkers for several abnormal clinic physiologic conditions like cardiovascular, metabolic, and fetal disorders (Nagy, 2019). Colloids with magnetic nanoparticles and high gradient magnetic separators have currently attracted the attention in quantifying and detecting the circulating tumor cells in patient biofluids and have enabled determination of exact clinical status of different cancer patients (Chen et al., 2019). Assessing the biochemical signature of the genomic deletions of both nuclear and mitochondrial DNA has contributed to the early prediction of severity and outcome of the disease, thus creating a streamline pathway for treatment possibility of several disorders like breast, colon, stomach, liver, and kidney cancers.

8. Genome sequencing and translational bioinformatics approach to genomics and precision medicine

Advent of the HGP has always proven to play an inherent role in deciphering the transparent picture and molecular blueprint of life. Understanding the functional consequence of associated genomic alterations has always been challenging and has contributed a new direction in the field of genomics and precision medicine. The HGP has transformed molecular biology into a new direction starting from deciphering the clear picture of the genome to diagnosis of different human disorders. Discovery of NGS added another chapter replacing the traditional Sanger sequencing approach with high sensitivity and low cost. To know about therapeutics ability of the molecules, thousands to millions of molecules may sequenced through NGS (Raza and Ahmad, 2019). NGS technologies were used by Shendure's Group in September 2009 to diagnose hereditary diseases. The WES approach was used to detect the first recessive condition (Miller syndrome) (Koboldt et al., 2013; Chong et al., 2015). Mgene map statistics, which display the number of genes with mutations attributable to phenotype, exceeded 3162 before February 27, 2014, according to the online Mendelian inheritance in men (OMIM).

NGS reduced the prices of scientific diagnosis and hospital services from $100 million in 2001 to $1000 in 2014. Common NGS systems, such as the Illumina sequencer, are used mainly for DNA sequence, RNA sequence, and bisulfite series. Emerged sequences have produced alternative short readings from the platforms that contribute to analyze the organisms, genomes, transcriptomes, and methylomes and help in the diagnosis and prognosis classification. Further, NGS pipeline consisting ChIP sequencing and RNA sequencing can target different genes which can regulate transcription factors to give better understanding of a disease (Wani and Raza, 2019). A number of promising approaches and evidence include several individual cell sequencing approaches such as pacBio RS and MinION nanopore sequencer, out of this, Oxford Nanopore Technologies MinION sequencer take the lead role in identification and characterization of viruses, antibiotic resistance genes in *Salmonella enteric*, S*erovar typhoid* and the transmission pattern of Ebola viruses. These approaches has become promising and powerful means of evaluating patients and the pathogens (Gardy et al., 2015). Along with that, the nanopore-based detection technology is very helpful in examining DNA−protein and protein−protein interaction and also analyzing ions and different drugs (Raza and Qazi, 2019). Ebola virus is a single-stranded RNA genome of size 19 kb in which surface glycoproteins and seven other proteins are encrypted. Some techniques such as ELISA and nRT-PCR are broadly accustomed in the treatment of Ebola virus disease (Khan et al., 2017).

The single nucleotide variants, copy number variations (CNV), and single exon changes can be detected by the tremendous potential of whole genome sequencing, WES, and genomic hybridization (CGH) approach (Tan et al., 2014; Retterer et al., 2015). Among the overhead approaches, the BEADCHIP mode shows more deflection due to prescreening of SNPs and greater percentage of ancestry informative markers (AIMs), whereas the WES approach does not display any unfairness and is convenient for sequencing the genome (Maróti et al., 2018). Furthermore, detection of variants across genic, untranslated regions, and noncoding regions with at least twenty times coverage provided more sensitivity by the Illumina platforms (Clark et al., 2011). In addition to this, RNA sequencing and DNA methylation analysis give further depth to gene quantification, differential gene expression analysis, and distinct clinical outcome of some distinct disease phenotypes. DNA methylation analysis using PCR-based methods, HpaII tiny fragment enriching the whole genome bisulfite-based sequences, reduced representation bisulfite sequencing, and targeted methylation sequencing provided for quantification and detection of regions with CpG, promoter regions, analysis of more patient samples, patient risk stratification, clinical profiling, and detection of several somatic mutations (Pan et al., 2012).

Per different clinical advises, i.e., the International Group of Experts of the Consortium for Clinic Pharmacogenetics Implementation (CPIC) record, current research to offer physicians advice on genotype drug treatment, was established as support for the pharmacogenetics evaluation in many patients. Around 35 medicinal products have been identified in this context, including warfarin, clopidogrel, simvastatins, thiopurines, tamoxifens, and retroviral agents (Gulilat et al., 2019).

9. Translational bioinformatics approach

Drawing a conclusive remark for interpretation and of data pertaining to patient disease phenotype by manual method is a very difficult task. For example, molecular modeling analysis of different mutations could elucidate the pathogenic nature of these mutations for appropriate diagnosis and therapeutic approach. Despite the relative ease of sequencing process, postsequencing computational and bioinformatics data analyses approaches are quintessential for interpretation of NGS data and biology of pharmacokinetic gene targets. Results of large genome sequencing projects have contributed a diverse amount of data that must be stored and analyzed for efficient health services and precision medicine. Data sequence analysis is a multilevel process in which sequence readings start to align with the genome, i.e., STAR, BSMAP, or BSmapper, for DNA reads, for RNA sequencing data, and is extremely significant. Different methods such as SnpEff, Oncotator, DNA and RNA sequence data analyses have allowed the study of several sample types utilizing the intratumor heterogeneity sensitive PyClone, the iCluster, and Cytoscape (McKenna et al., 2010; Shen et al., 2009).

A new window for the analysis of the NGS data used to create an algorithm, the utilization of the bases of quality, the allowances for gaps during alignment, and the quality threshold was opened by the discovery of short-read sequencing mapping tools, such as Bowtie2, BWA, SOAP2, SOAP2, and mrs-FAST/mrFAST (Li et al., 2008). In last few years, significant success has been achieved in bioinformatics analysis and medical interpretation of data where, for a small number of samples, the data are annotated into the form of variant caller format (VCF) file or VCF annotator and analyzed by tools like Cassandra, Anntools, ANNOVAR, Variant tools, Galaxy, Mercury, etc., whereas for analysis of large-scale samples workflow management systems are needed (Gonzalez-Garay, 2014). The majority of seminal findings have shed light on the perspective computational modeling of biomarkers and put emphasis on some of the algorithm or modules, for example, survival related gene network module, which was developed to assess the deep learning—based risk assessment in lung cancer, biologic pathway networking approach like Gene Rank algorithm for identification of reliable disease-associated pathways, SimRank and density-based clustering recommender model for miRNA diseases association prediction, dynamical network biomarkers, and early warning index approach for detection of predisease state of an individual sample (Cai et al., 2018). Furthermore, phylogenetic-based characterization of tumor development and impact of drugs on gene expression profiles on patients and cell lines modeling have been made easy by binary differential evolution algorithm and pressure-enabled drug delivery (PEDD) model (Cai et al., 2018) (Fig. 4.1).

10. Current challenges and solutions

The last few decades have led a considerable advancement in the fields of genomics and precision medicine together with data science that have contributed to the development of large-scale genomics datasets. The tremendous progress since the onset of the HGP has shed light on the genetic basis of health and disease. Currently, several efforts and initiatives are in progress for successful implementation on national and global levels. Advancement in gold standard technology and innovative research tools has added profound knowledge to help both clinicians and researchers to influence patient care by assessment of genomic variants. However, keeping the scenario in mind, genomics and precision medicine as a whole have

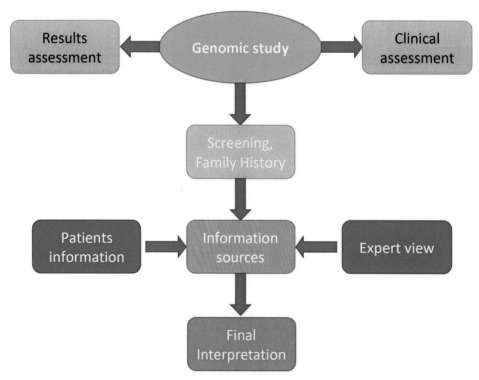

FIGURE 4.1 Genomics strategies to manage the enormous clinical data leading to an effective healthcare management.

experienced tremendous challenges in the last few decades. Molecular technologic advancements in the areas of genomic variation interpretation, as well as medical and technical aspects, which facilitated the production of laser-focused drugs and the ability to predict human personal risk factors, have been employed, including in the areas of metabolomics (metabolites), transcriptomics (RNAs), proteomics (proteins), and epigenomics. Continuous health and illness evaluation with varying conditions of disease states using body fluids will probably be key to metabolomics as well as sequencing of circulating microRNA and cell-free DNA. Existing AI developments have expanded the dimension of precision medicine, with access to broad data storage and integration of health records on a cloud-scale machine learning basis (Syrjala, 2018). The development of multiomic and genotype-phenotype data through generalized genome association studies and literary mining has allowed health professionals in the area of cancer genomics to provide personalized AI treatment (Li et al., 2018; Szymczak et al., 2009; Telenti et al., 2018). The subsequent generation sequencing and integrative analysis give a more comprehensive description of the biologic cycle that contributes to better comparisons of the single-layer research with DNA sequencing, RNA sequencing, proteomic, epigenomic, or microbiome evidence (Wang and Wheeler, 2014; Manzoni et al., 2018). In the United Kingdom, the goal of 100,000 genomes was reached, with 85,000 patients with several rare diseases and cancer, sequencing 100,000 whole genomes (Peplow, 2016).

Although the rapid availability of the technologic approach and genomic trend is expected to continue, it needs a set of confounding factors like quality evidence, data sharing and infrastructure need, incorporation of genomic and other clinical data into clinical care and research, diagnosis, drug discovery, economics of precision medicine, participant engagement, and trust. The generation of quality evidence is critically important in new patterns of risk sharing and evidence development among technology developers, healthcare systems, and payers. Precision medicine implementation will require access to broad, detailed, and highly integrated patient data (Bruen et al., 2016).

The need to include genomic and molecular data in clinical information is immense in adequate education, data systems, coverage and reimbursement, health system processes, and health policies. Researchers from around the world worked extensively in clinical and functional translation of cystic fibrosis transmembrane conductance regulator (CFTR) in a CFTR2 research project to identify the gene and benign lesions that allow more extensive treatment for cystic fibrosis patients and to distribute extensive patient data (Martiniano et al., 2016). Germline Mutant Alleles (ENIGMA) has a large collaborative research team to share data on genes *BRCA1* and *BRCA2* that predispose patients to breast and ovarian cancers (Spurdle et al., 2012).

Currently, patient-facing infrastructure and portals have been set up that have enabled accessibility to genetic data and participation in research. Another challenge is the patients must be aware or informed regarding the risks and benefits of the consent for treatment as well as research. For this, several groups have developed various consent tools. For example, the Global Alliance for Genomics and Health framework has contributed to data sharing in clinical care settings. The Genetics Partnership Enabling Forum for Connecting Others Respectfully allows people to track common privacy and access habits with a broad degree of accuracy for their well-being and genomic details. During genetic testing or sequencing, an expert in clinical context is important. Therefore, a skilled person with several tools must be employed for better improvement in standardization and assessment processes. For this approach, the ClinGen program was set up, which works in coordination with Cinvar to provide a better and efficient knowledge sharing network for extrapolation of gene—disease relationship (Rehm et al., 2018).

Case repositories like biobanks have been developed for collection and analysis of the case data. Repositories like European Bioinformatics Institute, The Cancer Genome Atlas, and the International Cancer Genome Consortium have developed through direct patient involvement and through a series of nonprofit academic and commercial activities. A variety of information services and networking platforms have been built for patient data access to clinical awareness including Genome Explorers, Exome Variant Repository, Exome Aggregation Community, OMIM, and the Human Gene Mutation Site. A better understanding of the genetic foundations of rare diseases and somatic cancer may lead to tangible success in understanding the nature of other common diseases, which is achieved through extensive, wide-ranging genome studies (Wu et al., 2019).

Nevertheless, open data sharing resources for minimization of cost of conducting research, addressing the HER stored patient data for continuous healthcare systems, and an improved foundational infrastructure for innovation and therapeutic development are crucial requirements for the expression of precision medicine to come into reality. The current knowledge about the clinical context of several pathogenic and chronic diseases is growing. With the establishment of The National Human Genome Research Institute (NHGRI) precision medicine program, the clinical center has provided unprecedented opportunities culminating into a better therapeutic approach and diagnostic for patients. In addition, in 2015, US President Barack Obama announced "All of Us" as the precision medicine program where participants will share the information generated over 10 years of sequencing, personal information, and EHR and digital medical technology. Although remarkable advancement has been done in genomics and precision medicine in countries like Australia, England, and the

United States, in developing countries like India the approach is still yet to be hit and under an early adoption stage. Due to the presence of consanguineous marriage, a large fraction of certain tribal population genetic disorders like sickle cell anemia and thalassemia is highly prevalent. Nevertheless, significant advancement in the field of pharmacogenomics in the recent past will definitely contribute to a remarkable progression in genomics and precision medicine.

11. Conclusion

Over the past few decades, a genomics and precision medicine approach has contributed to the development of understanding and prevention of several diseases like diabetes and cancers as well as genetic disorders. To eliminate unnecessary diagnostic tests and treatments, the field has created a most efficient treatment plan for each individual patient. There is no doubt, genomics and precision medicine is a novel approach that considers both genetic and epigenetic makeup of an organism, for disease treatment and prevention. However, translation of the patient clinical data into a multipronged scientific, clinical, and policy agenda must be implemented. Significant progress and development of an innovative, responsive, and well-connected gold standard high-throughput technology approach has enhanced the potential to revolutionize medicine and public health worldwide.

12. Future perspectives

Genomics with other omics technologies and knowledge is in the forefront of transforming healthcare into decision-making for therapeutic intervention. Responsible decision-making is an immense requirement for the escalating cost of healthcare for proper testing of precision medicine on a large scale for better patient outcome. Storage and sharing of big data, integration of genomic data into health records, and translational bioinformatics approach educational resources require a framework for evaluation of validity and clinical utility. Establishment of an infrastructure that will support the continuous learning healthcare system necessitates a collaborative approach of researchers, clinicians, and patients. In addition to this the field must put an emphasis on several directions like understanding of new clinical pathways, implementation of programs like genetic counseling psychological support, availability of reproductive health measures like prenatal diagnosis, equal access to all patients for given amenities and benefits of clinical trials, and awareness of all the professionals, which is an immense requirement to make it a reality at the global level.

References

Abubakar, A., Bentley, O., 2018. Precision medicine and pharmacogenomics in community and primary care settings. Pharm. Today 24 (2), 55—68.

Ahmed, S., Zhou, Z., Zhou, J., Chen, S.Q., 2016. Pharmacogenomics of drug metabolizing enzymes and transporters: relevance to precision medicine. Genomics Proteomics Bioinformatics 14 (5), 298—313.

AL-Dewik, N.I., Qoronfleh, M.W., 2019. Genomics and precision medicine: molecular diagnostics innovations shaping the future of healthcare in Qatar. Adv. Public Health 2019, 1—11.

Antoniou, A., Pharoah, P.D., Narod, S., Risch, H.A., Eyfjord, J.E., Hopper, J.L., et al., 2003. Average risks of breast and ovarian cancer associated with BRCA1 or BRCA2 mutations detected in case series unselected for family history: a combined analysis of 22 studies. Am. J. Hum. Genet. 72 (5), 1117—1130.

Biesecker, L.G., Mullikin, J.C., Facio, F.M., Turner, C., Cherukuri, P.F., Blakesley, R.W., Green, E.D., et al., 2009. The ClinSeq project: piloting large-scale genome sequencing for research in genomic medicine. Genome Res. 19 (9), 1665—1674.

Bilkey, G.A., Burns, B.L., Coles, E.P., Mahede, T., Baynam, G., Nowak, K.J., 2019. Optimizing precision medicine for public health. Front. Public Health 7, 42.

Boyiadzis, M.M., Dhodapkar, M.V., Brentjens, R.J., Kochenderfer, J.N., Neelapu, S.S., Maus, M.V., et al., 2018. Chimeric antigen receptor (CAR) T therapies for the treatment of hematologic malignancies: clinical perspective and significance. J. Immunother. Cancer 6 (1), 1—12.

Bruen, B.K., Docteur, E., Lopert, R., Cohen, J., DiMasi, J., Dor, A., et al., 2016. The Impact of Reimbursement Policies and Practices on Healthcare Technology Innovation. U.S. Department of Health and Human Services, Office of the Assistant Secretary for Planning and Evaluation.

Chen, S., Parmigiani, G., 2007. Meta-analysis of BRCA1 and BRCA2 penetrance. J. Clin. Oncol. 25 (11), 1329.

Cai, Y., Huang, T., Yang, J., 2018. Applications of bioinformatics and systems biology in precision medicine and immunooncology. BioMed Res. Int. 2018, 1427978.

Chen, J., Chen, L., Du, S., Wu, J., Quan, M., Yin, H., et al., 2019. High sensitive detection of circulating tumor cell by multimarker lipid magnetic nanoparticles and clinical verifications. J. Nanobiotechnol. 17 (1), 1—12.

Chong, J.X., Buckingham, K.J., Jhangiani, S.N., Boehm, C., Sobreira, N., Smith, J.D., et al., 2015. The genetic basis of mendelian phenotypes: discoveries, challenges, and opportunities. Am. J. Hum. Genet. 97, 199—215.

Clark, M.J., Chen, R., Lam, H.Y., Karczewski, K.J., Chen, R., Euskirchen, G., et al., 2011. Performance comparison of exome DNA sequencing technologies. Nat. Biotechnol. 29 (10), 908—914.

Conley, Y.P., Biesecker, L.G., Gonsalves, S., Merkle, C.J., Kirk, M., Aouizerat, B.E., 2013. Current and emerging technology approaches in genomics. J. Nurs. Scholarsh. 45 (1), 5−14.

Feng, Y., Spezia, M., Huang, S., Yuan, C., Zeng, Z., Zhang, L., et al., 2018. Breast cancer development and progression: risk factors, cancer stem cells, signaling pathways, genomics, and molecular pathogenesis. Genes Dis. 5 (2), 77−106.

Fiore, R.N., Goodman, K.W., 2016. Precision medicine ethics: selected issues and developments in next-generation sequencing, clinical oncology, and ethics. Curr. Opin. Oncol. 28 (1), 83−87.

Gardy, J., Loman, N.J., Rambaut, A., 2015. Real-time digital pathogen surveillance—the time is now. Genome Biol. 16 (1), 155.

Gómez-Bombarelli, R., Wei, J.N., Duvenaud, D., Hernández-Lobato, J.M., Sánchez Lengeling, B., Sheberla, D., Aguilera-Iparraguirre, J., Hirzel, T.D., Adams, R.P., Aspuru-Guzik, A., 2018. Automatic chemical design using a data-driven continuous representation of molecules. ACS Cent. Sci. 4, 268−276.

Gonzalez-Garay, M.L., 2014. The road from next-generation sequencing to personalized medicine. Pers. Med. 11 (5), 523−544.

Gulilat, M., Lamb, T., Teft, W.A., Wang, J., Dron, J.S., Robinson, J.F., et al., 2019. Targeted next generation sequencing as a tool for precision medicine. BMC Med. Genomics 12 (1), 81.

Gurumurthy, C.B., O'Brien, A.R., Quadros, R.M., Adams, J., Alcaide, P., Ayabe, S., Ballard, J., Batra, S.K., Beauchamp, M.C., Becker, K.A., Bernas, G., 2019. Reproducibility of CRISPR-Cas9 methods for generation of conditional mouse alleles: a multi-center evaluation. Genome Biol. 20 (1), 1−14.

Hamazaki, T., El Rouby, N., Fredette, N.C., Santostefano, K.E., Terada, N., 2017. Concise review: induced pluripotent stem cell research in the era of precision medicine. Stem Cell. 35 (3), 545−550.

Hobbs, H.H., Brown, M.S., Goldstein, J.L., 1992. Molecular genetics of the LDL receptor gene in familial hypercholesterolemia. Hum. Mutat. 1 (6), 445−466.

June, C.H., Riddell, S.R., Schumacher, T.N., 2015. Adoptive cellular therapy: a race to the finish line. Sci. Transl. Med. 7 (280), 280ps7.

Khan, F.N., Qazi, S., Tanveer, K., Raza, K., 2017. A review on the antagonist Ebola: a prophylactic approach. Biomed. Pharmacother. 96, 1513−1526.

Koboldt, D.C., Steinberg, K.M., Larson, D.E., Wilson, R.K., Mardis, E.R., 2013. The next-generation sequencing revolution and its impact on genomics. Cell 155, 27−38.

Lavecchia, A., Di Giovanni, C., 2013. Virtual screening strategies in drug discovery: a critical review. Curr. Med. Chem. 20 (23), 2839−2860.

Li, H., Ruan, J., Durbin, R., 2008. Mapping short DNA sequencing reads and calling variants using mapping quality scores. Genome Res. 18 (11), 1851−1858.

Li, Y., Shi, W., Wasserman, W.W., 2018. Genome-wide prediction of cis-regulatory regions using supervised deep learning methods. BMC Bioinf. 19 (1), 1−14.

Liew, C.Y., Ma, X.H., Liu, X., Yap, C.W., 2009. SVM model for virtual screening of Lck inhibitors. J. Chem. Inf. Model. 49, 877.

Manzoni, C., Kia, D.A., Vandrovcova, J., Hardy, J., Wood, N.W., Lewis, P.A., Ferrari, R., 2018. Genome, transcriptome and proteome: the rise of omics data and their integration in biomedical sciences. Briefings Bioinf. 19 (2), 286−302.

Maróti, Z., Boldogkői, Z., Tombácz, D., Snyder, M., Kalmár, T., 2018. Evaluation of whole exome sequencing as an alternative to Bead Chip and whole genome sequencing in human population genetic analysis. BMC Genomics 19 (1), 1−13.

Martiniano, S.L., Sagel, S.D., Zemanick, E.T., 2016. Cystic fibrosis: a model system for precision medicine. Curr. Opin. Pediatr. 28 (3), 312.

Mason, J.S., 2007. Introduction to the Volume and Overview of Computer-Assisted Drug Design in the Drug Discovery Process.

McKenna, A., Hanna, M., Banks, E., Sivachenko, A., Cibulskis, K., Kernytsky, A., et al., 2010. The genome analysis toolkit: a mapreduce framework for analyzing next-generation DNA sequencing data. Genome Res. 20, 1297−1303.

Nagy, B., 2019. Cell-free nucleic acids in prenatal diagnosis and pregnancy-associated diseases. EJIFCC 30 (2), 215.

Nherera, L., Marks, D., Minhas, R., Thorogood, M., Humphries, S.E., 2011. Probabilistic cost-effectiveness analysis of cascade screening for familial hypercholesterolaemia using alternative diagnostic and identification strategies. Heart 97 (14), 1175−1181.

Obermeier, P., Muehlhans, S., Hoppe, C., Karsch, K., Tief, F., Seeber, L., et al., 2016. Enabling precision medicine with digital case classification at the point-of-care. EBioMedicine 4, 191−196.

Pan, H., Chen, L., Dogra, S., Ling Teh, A., Hao Tan, J., Lim, Y.I., et al., 2012. Measuring the methylome in clinical samples: improved processing of the infinium human Methylation450 BeadChip array. Epigenetics 7 (10), 1173−1187.

Peplow, M., 2016. The 100,000 genomes project. Br. Med. J. 353, i1757.

Pilotto, A., Panza, F., Seripa, D., 2011. Pharmacogenetics in geriatric medicine: challenges and opportunities for clinical practice. Curr. Drug Metabol. 12 (7), 621−634.

Qazi, S., Tanveer, K., ElBahnasy, K., Raza, K., 2019. From telediagnosis to teletreatment: the role of computational biology and bioinformatics in tele-based healthcare. In: Telemedicine Technologies. Academic Press, pp. 153−169.

Ramaswami, R., Bayer, R., Galea, S., 2018. Precision medicine from a public health perspective. Annu. Rev. Publ. Health 39, 153−168.

Raza, K., Ahmad, S., 2019. Recent advancement in next-generation sequencing techniques and its computational analysis. Int. J. Bioinf. Res. Appl. 15 (3), 191−220.

Raza, K., Qazi, S., 2019. Nanopore sequencing technology and Internet of living things: a big hope for U-healthcare. In: Sensors for Health Monitoring. Academic Press, pp. 95−116.

Rehm, H.L., Berg, J.S., Plon, S.E., 2018. ClinGen and ClinVar—enabling genomics in precision medicine. Hum. Mutat. 39 (11), 1473−1475.

Retterer, K., Scuffins, J., Schmidt, D., Lewis, R., Pineda-Alvarez, D., Stafford, A., et al., 2015. Assessing copy number from exome sequencing and exome array CGH based on CNV spectrum in a large clinical cohort. Genet. Med. 17 (8), 623−629.

Sahu, A., Pradhan, D., Raza, K., Qazi, S., Jain, A.K., Verma, S., March 2020. In silico library design, screening and MD simulation of COX-2 inhibitors for anticancer activity. In: Proceedings of the 12th International Conference, vol. 70, pp. 21−32.

Shen, R., Olshen, A.B., Ladanyi, M., 2009. Integrative clustering of multiple genomic data types using a joint latent variable model with application to breast and lung cancer subtype analysis. Bioinformatics 25 (22), 2906−2912.

Spurdle, A.B., Healey, S., Devereau, A., Hogervorst, F.B., Monteiro, A.N., Nathanson, K.L., et al., 2012. ENIGMA—evidence-based network for the interpretation of germline mutant alleles: an international initiative to evaluate risk and clinical significance associated with sequence variation in BRCA1 and BRCA2 genes. Hum. Mutat. 33 (1), 2−7.

Syrjala, K.L., 2018. Opportunities for improving oncology care. Lancet Oncol. 19 (4), 449.

Szymczak, S., Biernacka, J.M., Cordell, H.J., González-Recio, O., König, I.R., Zhang, H., Sun, Y.V., 2009. Machine learning in genome-wide association studies. Genet. Epidemiol. 33 (S1), S51−S57.

Tan, R., Wang, Y., Kleinstein, S.E., Liu, Y., Zhu, X., Guo, H., et al., 2014. An evaluation of copy number variation detection tools from whole-exome sequencing data. Hum. Mutat. 35 (7), 899−907.

Tang, F., Barbacioru, C., Wang, Y., Nordman, E., Lee, C., Xu, N., et al., 2009. mRNA-Seq whole-transcriptome analysis of a single cell. Nat. Methods 6 (5), 377−382.

Telenti, A., Lippert, C., Chang, P.C., DePristo, M., 2018. Deep learning of genomic variation and regulatory network data. Hum. Mol. Genet. 27 (Supplement_R1), R63−R71.

Twilt, M., 2016. Precision Medicine: the new era in medicine. EBioMedicine 4, 24−25.

Wang, L., Wheeler, D.A., 2014. Genomic sequencing for cancer diagnosis and therapy. Annu. Rev. Med. 65, 33−48.

Wani, N., Raza, K., 2019. Raw sequence to target gene prediction: an integrated inference pipeline for ChIP-seq and RNA-seq datasets. In: Applications of Artificial Intelligence Techniques in Engineering. Springer, Singapore, pp. 557−568.

Weinshilboum, R.M., Wang, L., November 2017. Pharmacogenomics: precision medicine and drug response. Mayo Clin. Proc. 92 (11), 1711−1722.

Williams, A.M., Liu, Y., Regner, K.R., Jotterand, F., Liu, P., Liang, M., 2018. Artificial intelligence, physiological genomics, and precision medicine. Physiol. Genom. 50 (4), 237−243.

Wu, Y., Byrne, E.M., Zheng, Z., Kemper, K.E., Yengo, L., Mallett, A.J., et al., 2019. Genome-wide association study of medication-use and associated disease in the UK Biobank. Nat. Commun. 10 (1), 1−10.

Zhong, F., Xing, J., Li, X., Liu, X., Fu, Z., Xiong, Z., et al., 2018. Artificial intelligence in drug design. Sci. China Life Sci. 61 (10), 1191−1204.

Chapter 5

A review of a hybrid IoT-NG-PON system for translational bioinformatics in healthcare

Meet Kumari[1,*], Reecha Sharma[1] and Anu Sheetal[2]

[1]*Department of Electronics and Communication Engineering, Punjabi University, Patiala, Punjab, India;* [2]*Department of Electronics and Communication Engineering, Guru Nanak Dev University, Gurdaspur, Punjab, India*

Corresponding author: E-mail: meetkumari08@yahoo.in

Chapter outline

1. Introduction

Healthcare has extensively been growing information intensive. The emergence of genomic data and patient care remarkably accelerates the amount and complexity of clinical data. Bioinformatics is a multidisciplinary field aiming at the computational and statistical application methodologies to handle and interpret biologic information. Translational bioinformatics (TBI) has emerged as a significant component in medical research in the precision medicine era. TBI is a young discipline in healthcare and is defined as the evolution of storage, analytic, and critical approaches to optimize the growing vast biomedical genomic data transformation into predictive, proactive, participatory, and preventive healthcare. An unmatched amount of data is produced in bioinformatics through genomics, healthcare, as well as biomedical research regularly (Fenstermacher, 2005). Such data consists of genome sequences, clinical reports, gene expression profiles, medical images, biomedical literature reports, and sensor data. European Bioinformatics Institute sustained approximately 75 petabytes of proteins, genes, and small molecule data in December 2015. With this speed, it is imagined that 25,000 petabytes of information will be produced by 2020 in the medical domain (Nagaraj et al., 2018).

Bioinformatics involves handling, interpreting, and analyzing data from biologic structures and sequences, and it has extended sophisticated technology that continues to keep the miniaturization and automation of modern instruments that carry large-scale biomedical information. The development in technology has ultimately led to an exponential rise in the protein sequence and deoxyribonucleic acid (DNA) database (Manrai and Kohane, 2017). The three primary publicly present databases that provide as central repositories for protein sequence and DNA data are GenBank, DNA Databank, and European Molecular Biology Laboratory, and each year the data is continuously growing (Sethi and Theodos, 2009).

As medicine and biology move from computer-based to bench-based and models science, they replace particular experiments. Advanced biomedical research needs an overlap of clinical and genomic research. The assimilation of data at the cellular, organ, molecular, personal, and tissue levels will not only improve the collective research agenda, but also lead to the technologies and innovative tools development for improved care of patients. The goal of TBI is to use computational techniques and tools for large biologic database analysis and fully comprehend problem mechanisms by understanding the proteomics and genetics and associating with the medical data (Sethi and Theodos, 2009).

Moreover, optical technologies have performed well and will perform in the future a significant role in the internet of things (IoT) evolution and several applications in designs for smart world applications. There are various examples of utilizing optical equipment and systems in smart world infrastructures for measuring chemical and physical quantities like imaging sensors, temperature sensors, strain sensors, force sensors, acceleration sensors, tilt sensors, rotation sensors, vibration sensors, velocity sensors, fluorescence sensors, luminescence sensors, absorbance sensors, refractive index sensors, and humidity sensors. Other examples of optical systems are optical positioning network and passive optical network (PON). It is noticeable that optical systems are related to the optical device and network layers. Therefore, switching technologies and optical networks will keep performing the main role in providing a high-performance, ubiquitous, and feasible IoT transport network, and PON networks provide higher energy efficiency compared to radio transmission as well as copper wires for 5G networks (Aleksic, 2019).

The latest optical fiber access networks already provide information rate to 10 Gbps utilizing point-to-point as well as point-to-multipoint network topologies. PONs are broadly deployed as they inherently bear topologies such as tree and 1:256 split ratios. The summarized current and proceeding standards for PONs are described in the next sections. These proceeding standards next-generation PONs (NG-PONs) are regarded to be bracing technologies for 5G networks in the future (Aleksic, 2019).

In this book chapter, a hybrid IoT-NG-PON system for TBI in healthcare has been presented and reviewed. In this chapter, the system design is illustrated in Section 2. The comprehensive literature review and information about IoT-NG-PON system for TBI are discussed in Section 2 and 3 respectively. Sections 4 and 5 present the potential applications and open challenges, respectively. Finally, the conclusion and future scope are illustrated in Section 6.

2. Literature review

The comprehensive literature review of bioinformatics application is presented as follows.

Al Kawam, A. et al. (2018) reviewed the basics of bioinformatics integration including storage, genomic data generation, clinical data, and representation utilization. Here, the bioinformatics challenges are divided into seven intertwined integration series features covering the informatics, communication, management, and knowledge areas. For each feature, the latest research directions, challenges, and possible resolutions have been provided in detail. It is presented that it leads to reducing the gap between the various genomic applications areas, which are predominantly used in clinical adoption and research settings. Shameer, K. et al. (2017) discussed several health monitoring types of equipment, their application in personalized prognosis, diagnostics, wellness intervention, clinical intervention, and ability to apprehend the specific health state. They also presented the numerous TBI approaches, resources, and tools along with examples to merge patient-generated information with existing personal health records, electronic medical records, as well as clinical data repositories. Also, Qian, F. et al. (2018) reviewed the computational method's application to review cholangiocarcinoma spanned from the knowledge-based and biologic-based pattern recognition of data for biologic level and clinical translation systems. Again, various future challenges and opportunities about novel model developing, knowledge base building supporting system infrastructure for prognosis, diagnosis, and cholangiocarcinoma treatment have also been presented. Tsai, E.A. et al. (2016) reported and developed a clinical process in both diseased and healthy individuals for whole-genome sequencing. In this, a bioinformatics strategy to effectively deliver genomic data and process for clinical interpretation has been described. Here is also presented the data handling from the final variant list to FASTQ for the clinical review final report. Again, Parihar, J. et al. (2019) also described the healthcare integrated assessment using bioinformatics for the enhancement of the healthcare system to provide integrated and enhanced healthcare analytics and informatics. Like this, Qin, Z.S. (2017) presented the recent bioinformatics research developments that have been extensively considered a primary advancement of precision medicine stakeholder. This reviewed work covers the wide variety of topics that are extensively classified into algorithms, informatics method development, and statistical method development for TBI. Tenenbaum, J.D. (2016) reported a new era, i.e., TBI in data-driven medical care, along with the latest information technology, infrastructure, culture, and policy to meet some of the technologic advances. It is described that TBI approaches continue to make a difference in the patients' lives. In addition, Stefani, L. and Galanti, G. (2017) surveyed the latest progress in TBI analysis of discovered parameters' utilization, especially comparative genomics and function and metabolism of various important matters. The individual elements and various large-scale systematics based on diseases studies like case-control studies and genome-wide association studies have been discussed. Besides this, bionomics development and its latest applications in healthcare have also been introduced. Min, S. et al. (2017) presented the deep learning technique in bioinformatics along with recent examples of the latest research to supply a comprehensive and useful perspective. Here, both deep learning architecture and bioinformatics domains have been categorized to present the short descriptions of each. Moreover, practical and theoretical issues along with research direction for future deep learning bioinformatics models have also been presented. Also, Nagaraj, K. et al. (2018) reported the impact of big data in bio-informatics along with highlighted concepts of architectural platforms to handle data analytics, big data definition, and applications of analytical approaches toward complex issues in bioinformatics. The prospects and challenges of bio-informatics with big data analytics and the summary of various data analytical approaches for computer scientists and bioinformatics researchers have also been discussed. Further, Sethi, P. and Theodos, K. (2009) explored the ethical and computational challenges that emerged from the healthcare informatics and bioinformatics intersection. They also discussed the latest electronic health record (EHR) situation along with its abilities to collect genetic and clinic data, the Genetic Information Non-discrimination Act, and the synergy acquired from efforts of healthcare disciplines, genomics, and clinical disciplines to improve healthcare scenarios (Sethi and Theodos, 2009). Farooqi, R. M. et al. (2019) presented several aspects of healthcare schemes and a wireless sensor network (WSN) architecture platform to support healthcare information transmission and storage. They reported a deep insight into medical, supervision of chronic disease, and WSN applications in the medical care industry and location monitoring of patients. But it requires improvement in some areas such as the WSN communication network. Also, Raza, K. and Qazi, S. (2019) presented a review on nanopore sequencing technology, its U-healthcare application, internet of living things (IoLT) concepts, and the convergence of IoLT concepts with nanopore technology for healthcare applications. It has been presented that this technology can be utilized in recent sequencers and to create miniaturized versions that operate within an IoT network. This brings a new era in the area of cloud computation, big data analytics, and IoT in field of sequencing as well as in U-healthcare application. Furthermore, Al-Shammari et al., 2019 presented the energy efficient facilities utilizing mixed integer linear programming embedding framework in an IoT network. It is reported that this IoT network provides a smart road paradigm for several energy efficient applications assisted by a wireless communication and PON for a smart city. Here, a service-oriented architecture (SOA) paradigm has been utilized in a framework to provide the basic services as well as complex services that are exploited by application layers. The results show that it minimizes power consumption by reforming the computing nodes selection and traffic distribution to fulfill the service requirements. This network can be helpful in an energy efficient bioinformatics network.

The latest developments in bioinformatics consist of acquiring big data, deep learning, and other technologies. But the hybrid IoT-PON has not been presented yet in hospitals. Thus, this book chapter provides the review design of a hybrid IoT-NG-PON for healthcare applications.

3. Transitional bioinformatics

TBI is the evolution of analytic, storage, and expositive techniques to reform the encouraging voluminous biomedical as well as genomic data transformation into predictive, proactive, participatory, and preventive healthcare (Tenenbaum, 2016).

TBI, a comparatively young field, has become a prime discipline in the generation of precision and personalized medicine. The advancement in healthcare methods and schemes has unfolded a new domain of feasible observations. The microscope permitted doctor's invention and researchers to do an investigation at the biologic level. The arrival of the imaging technologies such as magnetic resonance, X-ray, and other technologies empowered tissue and organ visualization not at all before possible. Each of such advanced technologies necessitates an associated advancement in the methods as well as tools utilized to interpret and analyze the results. With the enhancing generally used technologies, for example, ribonucleic acid (RNA) and DNA sequencing, large-throughput metabolomics and proteomics, and DNA microarrays, comes the requirement for new methods to transfer these novel kinds of data given into the latest information as well as latest knowledge. This latest knowledge then provides insights concerning actions to treat and prevent disease (Tenenbaum, 2016).

TBI is a multidisciplinary domain that matured with the Human Genome Project initialization. It was proposed to evolve as a novel field recently. An IoT-driven system is the novel pattern for translational medicine. Medical and biologic data are specified with dynamics, diversity, interconnection, and association. However, the medical data analysis is cross-disciplinary, which requires field information from primary clinical medicine to life science. Again, the various informatics skills like computational programming, statistical inference, database building, and mathematics simulation along with developing a complex model are needed. Thus, this domain is now facing lots of new problems in the research field (Qian et al., 2018).

3.1 IoT-NG-PON system

With the outbreak of the IoT and exponential improvement in the demand for high data rate streaming applications, access networks must be extended to provide high speed and high flexibility, to large numbers of users (Sethi and Theodos, 2009). Data traffic is increasing at a high rate, and lots of users are accessing data online and use large mobile bandwidth-intensive services. Hence, today's mobility and large bandwidth are two main needs for future networks to support novel and real-time mobile bandwidth-intensive networks (Al-Azez et al., 2016). Such networks place considerable importance on the optical parts of access networks, and the required high flexibility and high capacity along with low latency provided by PONs. It allows an IoTs system to enable 5G developments by offering an optical front haul and backhaul wireless network (Browning et al., 2017; Obite et al., 2018).

The life-quality enhancing IoT environments like smart homes, healthcare premises, industries, and offices need high-capacity, safe, low-interference transmission among the various automation devices. All these essential needs can be satisfied by optical wireless communication that utilizes the optical spectrum encompassing visible, infrared (IR), and ultraviolet portions. However, the visible and IR portions are comparatively safer than microwaves and radio. The merits of visible light achieve energy efficiency by the transmission over illumination sources, although the optical wireless-based visible light communication (VLC) from the automation and sensor devices creates flickering, which will influence the users' visual comfort. It is also known as a green technology (Jenila and Jeyachitra, 2019).

PON is a "last mile" optical access network. It is also called a local loop. Here, the final stage is mostly in residential places, consisting of coaxial cable and copper telephone wires. Where there is a large level of business customer concentration, especially in metropolitan cities, the access networks are equable to the high-capacity and high data rate synchronous optical network (SONET) rings. Only an extended business undertaking can supply to pay higher prices to let out optical carrier connections. Medium- and large-scale residential and establishment customers are trouble with no choice but to use dial-up internet access and plain old telephone service. Cable modems and digital subscriber lines provide a more inexpensive data option, but they lead to implementation difficulty and time-consuming operation. Also, quality and distance of existing wiring restrict the bandwidth. However, these networks are still expensively performing voice applications (Obite et al., 2018).

Some IoT devices have costlier electrical-to-optical conversions and require more power, so they may have limitations. Therefore PON is a promising candidate that provides both long reach and high bandwidth for such devices. An unexplored hybrid IoT-NG-PON connectivity consists of optical fiber wired network directly connected to IoT devices. The major requirements for hybrid IoT-NG-PON connectivity are shown in Table 5.1 (Díaz et al., 2019).

Table 5.1 shows some common factors between PON connectivity and the desired hybrid IoT-NG-PON. The data output needed by each IoT device is usually a numerous order of amplitude lower than what the PON interface can provide to the IoT system. The long-distance and reliability from fibers are what hybrid IoT-NG-PON has to contribute to the IoT system. Installation, as well as maintenance in PON, is long-running, costly, and expensive at optical-to-electrical (O/E), electrical-to-optical (E/O), and O/E interfaces considering specialized splicing connectors and equipment, while the wireless process is virtually costless and effortless. Thus, a hybrid IoT-NG-PON should focus on very simple operations. Also, a PON's O/E and E/O are power consuming because of the requirement of cooling circuitry and biasing, whereas a hybrid IoT-NG-PON would focus, if possible, on passive fixes at IoT devices. In contrast, the exceedingly minimum cost demand from the IoT systems will encourage a hybrid IoT-NG-PON solution with bounded bandwidth at endpoints, where the spectral efficiency issue can be addressed (Díaz et al., 2019).

Fig. 5.1 shows the architecture of a hybrid IoT-NG-PON. It consists of central control at an optical line terminal (OLT), distribution of data through passive devices such as splitters, and broadcasting of data in different optical network units. After that the incoming data is forwarded to a large number of IoT devices through green VLC links. To put the hybrid IoT-NG-PON into IoT wireless connection context, there are two relevant parameters such as reach and throughput. The higher-frequency bands provide more bandwidth and channels, permitting high data output; nevertheless, minimum

TABLE 5.1 IoT and hybrid IoT-NG-PON minimum requirements (Díaz et al., 2019; Valcarenghi et al., 2012).

IoT requirements	Connectivity requirements in PON	Hybrid IoT-NG-PON minimum requirements
Data output	2.5 Gbps	100 bps
Distance	20 km	20 km
Power consumption	Approximately 1 W	0 W or passive

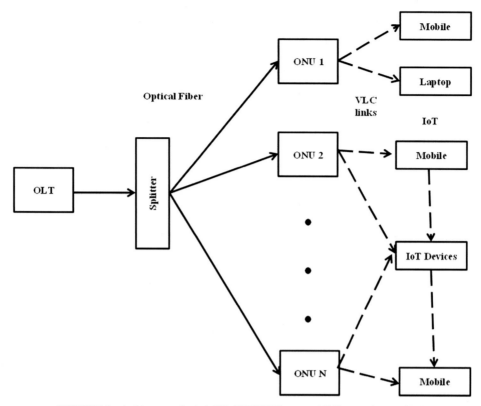

FIGURE 5.1   Architecture of a hybrid IoT-NG-PON system (Al-Shammari et al., 2019).

transmission length is attained. Lower frequency radio frequency waves are barley disturbed throughout the propagation compared to higher frequency radiations, achieving a larger operation range, having less data throughput. Hybrid IoT-NG-PON necessities should consternate at ranges beyond other traditional wireless systems, without negotiating minimal throughputs attained. An anticipated hybrid IoT-NG-PON is shown in Fig. 5.1. It has a long reach inflicted by a line of sight propagation of the earth's curvature, consisting of atmosphere refraction impacts. Coincidently, this is gigabit PON (G-PON)'s highest extended reach. A 20-km reach makes up the main wireless and optical landmark for a hybrid IoT-NG-PON to surpass and identify its slot (Díaz et al., 2019).

3.2 Hybrid IoT-NG-PON for transitional bioinformatics in healthcare

The fog, cloud, and IoT can be combined over a wireless fiber network, as shown in Fig. 5.2. Fig. 5.2 shows that a wireless fiber network is constituted of a PON as its backhaul and provides high reliability and capacity. While, ubiquitous connectivity, mobility, and coverage can be distributed by wireless frontend networks, e.g., long-term evolution and wireless fidelity (Wi-Fi). But PON supplies high capacity by utilizing various multiplexing techniques such as time division multiplexing PON (TDM-PON), wavelength division multiplexing PON (WDM-PON), etc., over the optical networks (Al-Shammari et al., 2019).

In the hybrid IoT-NG-PON, several IoT devices like cameras, motion sensors, temperature sensors, etc., are required to regularly monitor the patient's latest condition. To improve the hybrid IoT-NG-PON system, the command system should make a selection and execute several operations with improved efficiency and performance to serve the patients in hospitals. The service appeals are implemented by following the business processes (BP) and SOA in the data workflow. BP is regarded as the virtual topographic anatomy that contains virtual links and nodes. Here, the virtual nodes envelop the request processing, function requirements like actuating functions, or requested sensing and location. Also, virtual links envelop the communication requests requirements like neighbor connections and traffic demands (Al-Shammari et al., 2019).

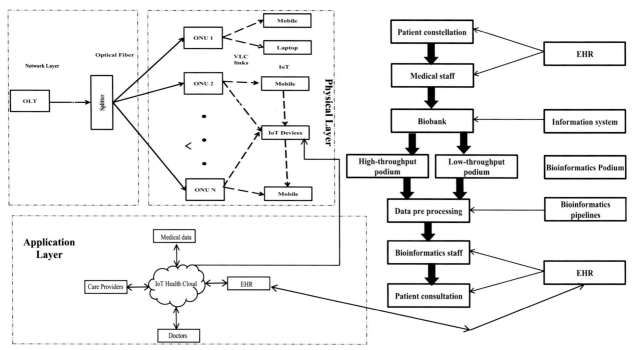

FIGURE 5.2 Architecture of a hybrid IoT-NG-PON system for translational bioinformatics in healthcare (Al-Shammari et al., 2019; Servant et al., 2014).

Fig. 5.2 describes the several practitioners implicated in a tough process, illustrates the data flow initializing from and returning to the specific patient to address the therapy, and presents the bioinformatics infrastructure handling the workflow. Here, to construct the therapeutic purpose, the most exhaustive information ranging from biologic to clinical, family, and environmental information requires to be composed along a very tough healthcare way. As the illness develops, novel experiments like high-output biomarkers detection or screens by immunohistochemistry have to be accomplished to measure appropriate biologic data need to select superior therapy. In this process, biologists, physicians, pharmacists, computational biologists, bioinformaticians, biostatisticians, biobank managers, informaticians, clinical research associates, biotechnologic platform managers, and technical employees will provide their skill for the patient's benefit. Different cultures and miscellaneous constraints, together with deadline meetings for results delivery, make the bioinformatics application on a daily basis extremely challenging. Thus, clinical decision support (CDS) and EHR are concerns for delivery because of the knowledge discovery acceleration and its influence on the potential clinical decisions. Also, the advancement in CDS is needed to maintain the large data heterogeneity along with complications. Here, the precision health monitoring of patients depends on the capacity to disseminate, collect, and study the information process. Truly, each stakeholder constructs information during the medical care pathway at specific time points at different locations.

In this design, the physical layer contains IoT nodes connected to end users through VLC. Each end user is linked to an ONU (optical network unit). The application layer contains the service requests presented in the framework by numbers of BPs. In brief, this design consists of the following (Al-Shammari et al., 2019):

- physical layer:
    - a processing module having RAM and a CPU
    - a network module having a transmitter power amplifier, transmitter/receiver circuit to provide access with a minimum one end user
    - the function module links to the actuators and supportable sensors
- network layer:
    - various network elements of OLT, ONUs, end users, and splitters

- application layer:
  - virtual nodes access
  - virtual nodes memory requirements and processing
  - zone request in virtual nodes
  - traffic demands for every virtual link

3.3 Aims of the hybrid IoT-NG-PON system

The aims of the hybrid IoT-NG-PON for transitional bioinformatics in healthcare are discussed as follows (Chowdhary et al., 2016):

1. to arrange the biologic information in a simple way to help researchers and biologists to access and store exiting information,
2. to design and develop a system that helps in data management with software tools,
3. to utilize and transfer the biologic information in the interpretation and analysis of results in an energy-efficient, economical, secure, and high-speed method,
4. to help magician for gene structures understanding diagnosing disease.

3.4 Tools

The main aim of bioinformatics tools is to deliver the data about quality portrayal, deciding auxiliary, protein physicochemical properties, and phylogenetic examinations. This is very important for the behavior of biomolecules in the cell. The distinct bioinformatics tools utilized for several applications are listed in Table 5.2.

3.5 Algorithms used

The important algorithmic used in the system are as follows (Chowdhary et al., 2016):

1. find the likeness among proteins of district organisms,
2. detect genes patterns in strings,
3. find the likeness among spatial structures parts,
4. construct phylogenetic trees,
5. categorize new information per previous clustered sets.

TABLE 5.2 Types of tools used in IoT and hybrid IoT-NG-PON (Aamer Mehmood, 2014).

S. No.	Type of tools	Description
1	Primary sequence analyses	Primary sequence analysis tools refer to the knowledge of several features of a biomolecule such as protein or nucleic acid, which provide its attractive functions
2	Phylogenetic analyses	Phylogenetic analysis tools are used to reconstruct the relationship among a large number of corresponding organisms or molecules, to identify features of a molecule with undefined functions
3	Structure-function analyses	These tools are used to identify structural elements in a protein sequence like sheets, helices, coils, strands, and domains
4	Molecular interactions	These tools are used to identify the protein–protein interactions for transportation, signaling, cellular metabolism, and various other biochemical processes
5	Molecular dynamics simulation (MDS)	MDS tools are used to provide information on the dynamic processes, fluctuations, and proteins' small- and large-scale conformational changes along with their occurring complexes

4. Applications

The major applications of bioinformatics are given as follows:

1. **Analysis of sequence**: The genetic organism basis depends on overall genome genes. Analysis of sequence is an approach utilized to understand the infrastructure, function, and features. There are various strong tools present in computer science and every tool has its merits and demerits. These are utilized to find the sequence concerned with organism DNA mutations. The analysis of the sequence of several fragments can be completed by utilizing the shotgun sequence method (Majhi et al., 2019).
2. **Protein structure prediction:** The 3D protein structure can be predicted from its amino acid. It is complex to find the secondary to quaternary protein structures. Thus, bioinformatics tools or crystallography methods can be utilized.
3. **Genome annotation:** Regulatory sequence, as well as protein coding, can be obtained utilizing genome annotation. It is the method to find the gene locations, genome structure, and coding regions (Majhi et al., 2019).
4. **Genomics comparative:** Various genomics features like messenger RNA, transfer RNA, and ribosomal RNA can be compared to find the biologic species functions and genomic structure. The researchers utilize the maps of the intergenomic to trace the path of a generation that be produced in various species. The data about the large chromosomal segments and point mutations can be identified through these maps.
5. **Drug discovery and health:** The bioinformatics tools on the basic molecular diseases are utilized in drug discovery. Based on diagnosis and disease management the researchers can develop the drugs and medicines suitable for 500 genes. The drug delivery depends on computational tools and targeted cells (Majhi et al., 2019). Some other applications are also shown in Fig. 5.3.

5. Open challenges

As the bioinformatics area is new, manpower demands cannot be fulfilled to manage the increasing data problems. Also, the sequence data size, characterized genes, and protein structures are increasing rapidly from several organisms. The primary need for all this is that data require being stored. Secondly, new techniques for analyzing huge databases are required. Thirdly, a powerful hardware structure is required for analyzing the database. Again, bioinformatics is increasing globally very fast, so academia is not able to generate the trained bioinformaticians (Rashid, 2006).

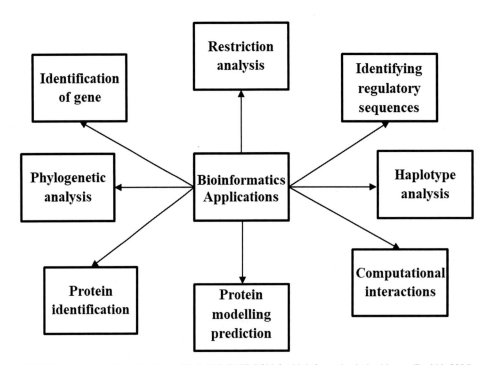

FIGURE 5.3 Potential applications of hybrid IoT-NG-PON for bioinformatics in healthcare (Rashid, 2006).

The sequencing genome projects are generating incredible sequential data amounts. There is a notable requirement in the scientific community at the moment for people who will fill the gap. As without bioinformatics, the latest research in most areas of biology and medicines would fester or remain handicapped. However, there is a lack of investigators who may be able to handle the challenges posed by current biologic developments in specific and in general science. Moreover, there is very little participation by scientists in some countries in developing genome resources process to fight diseases. This is mainly because of the minimum absorption rate of new advanced technology due to the shortage of financial resources and crucial network to meet future demands (Rashid, 2006). The other challenges are discussed as follows:

- **Sensors sensitivity:** The sensitivity of sensors is significant in turbulent environmental conditions. The sensory devices transducers are influenced by labor work (e.g., sweat), causing degradation in sensor sensitivity.
- **Deployment:** In a sensor network, sensor node implementation is a major problem to be fixed. A suitable node implementation method can minimize the complications of the problem. Handling and implementing a huge number of sensor nodes needs some particular skills and techniques.
- **Design impairments:** The primary aim of sensor network design is to generate economical, small-scale, and effectual devices. The sensor design as well as sensor nodes are influenced by various kinds at an additional cost.
- **Security:** It is one of the prime issues in the sensor network. Security problems consist of node authentication and data confidentiality. The implemented sensors must pass a data confidentiality and node verification examination by its related manager sensor nodes. However, a WSN requires a novel solution for better distribution, establishment, and security.
- **Bandwidth:** Limited bandwidth directly influences data exchange among sensor nodes. Recently, wireless communication has been restricted to an information rate of up to 100 kbps. Thus, lower power is used in processing the information than sending it. These wireless links work in the optical or radio infrared spectrum.
- **Cost:** A sensor network comprises a huge group of sensor nodes. The cost of a single node is too high. Thus the cost of all nodes should be kept minimum for approval of WSN globally. If the total cost of the nodes is suitable, then consumers will be further motivated to accept the WSNs.
- **Energy:** Energy management is one of the significant issues in WSNs. Power consumption is significant to functional areas such as communication, sensing, and data processing, and each needs optimization. The lifetime of a sensor node is linked to the battery life span. Sensors work with a restricted energy budget. In WSNs, batteries are efficient for recharged and power sensors. A sensor node should be capable to process until either the battery can be replaced or a target time has ended, which depends on application type.
- **Compatibility issues:** These issues arise while trying to merge various sensor appliances at different frequencies. The communicated sensor devices use different types of protocols and brands that can cause interference among devices.

6. Conclusion and future scope

In this book chapter, a novel hybrid IoT-NG-PON system for TBI in healthcare applications has been studied. This leads to a new evolution in data-driven medical care. TBI in the hybrid IoT-NG-PON system continues to make a good healthy life for patients. The design, aims, tools, and algorithms are the features of this system. It has various major challenges, but its applications for the future healthcare system are beneficial and countless. Thus, for the scientists, researchers, and bioinformaticians working at the hybrid IoT-NG-PON system for TBI, new opportunities abound, and the healthcare future looks shining. In the future, there will be the lots of potential applications of the hybrid IoT-NG-PON system for TBI such as discovering the reality of DNA-based life and determining the portable economical wireless devices that can be utilized by several industries and people in a hybrid IoT-NG-PON system for TBI applications.

References

Aamer Mehmood, M., 2014. Use of bioinformatics tools in different spheres of life sciences. J. Data Mining Genomics Proteomics. 05, 1–13. https://doi.org/10.4172/2153-0602.1000158.

Al Kawam, A., Sen, A., Datta, A., Dickey, N., 2018. Understanding the bioinformatics challenges of integrating genomics into healthcare. IEEE J. Biomed. Heal. Informatics. 22, 1672–1683. https://doi.org/10.1109/JBHI.2017.2778263.

Al-Azez, Z.T., Lawey, A.Q., El-Gorashi, T.E.H., Elmirghani, J.M.H., August 2016. Energy efficient IoT virtualization framework with passive optical access networks. Int. Conf. Transparent Opt. Networks. 1–4. https://doi.org/10.1109/ICTON.2016.7550472.

Aleksic, S., 2019. A survey on optical technologies for IoT, smart industry, and smart infrastructures. J. Sens. Actuator Netw. 8 https://doi.org/10.3390/jsan8030047.

Al-Shammari, H.Q., Lawey, A., El-Gorashi, T., Elmirghani, J.M.H., July 2019. Energy efficient service embedding in IoT over PON. Int. Conf. Transparent Opt. Networks. Angers, France. 1–5. https://doi.org/10.1109/ICTON.2019.8840429.

Browning, C., Farhang, A., Saljoghei, A., Marchetti, N., Vujicic, V., Doyle, L.E., Barry, L.P., 2017. 5G wireless and wired convergence in a passive optical network using UF-OFDM and GFDM. 2017 IEEE Int. Conf. Commun. Work. ICC Work. 2017, 386–392. https://doi.org/10.1109/ICCW.2017.7962688.

Chowdhary, M., Rani, A., Parkash, J., Shahnaz, M., Dev, D., 2016. Bioinformatics: an overview for cancer research. J. Drug Deliv. Therapeut. 6, 69–72. https://doi.org/10.22270/jddt.v6i4.1290.

Díaz, C.A.R., Leitão, C., Marques, C.A., Alberto, N., Fátima Domingues, M., Ribeiro, T., Pontes, M.J., Frizera, A., Antunes, P.F.C., André, P.S., Ribeiro, M.R.N., 2019. IoToF: a long-reach fully passive low-rate upstream phy for iot over fiber. Electron 8, 1–14. https://doi.org/10.3390/electronics8030359.

Farooqi, M.R., Iqbal, N., Singh, N.K., Affan, M., Raza, K., 2019. Wireless Sensor Networks Towards Convenient Infrastructure in the Healthcare Industry: A Systematic Study. Elsevier Inc. https://doi.org/10.1016/b978-0-12-819361-7.00002-6.

Fenstermacher, D., 2005. Introduction to bioinformatics. J. Am. Soc. Inf. Sci. Technol. 56, 440–446. https://doi.org/10.1002/asi.20133.

Jenila, C., Jeyachitra, R.K., 2019. Design of green indoor IoT networking through optical wireless communication using passive optical reflectors. 2018 IEEE Recent Adv. Intell. Comput. Syst. RAICS 2018, 159–163. https://doi.org/10.1109/RAICS.2018.8635049.

Majhi, V., Paul, S., Jain, R., 2019. Bioinformatics for healthcare applications. Proc. - 2019 Amity Int. Conf. Artif. Intell. AICAI 2019, 204–207. https://doi.org/10.1109/AICAI.2019.8701277.

Manrai, A.K., Kohane, I.S., 2017. Bioinformatics, and Precision Medicine. Elsevier Inc. https://doi.org/10.1016/B978-0-12-809523-2.00011-X.

Min, S., Lee, B., Yoon, S., 2017. Deep learning in bioinformatics. Briefings Bioinf. 18, 851–869. https://doi.org/10.1093/bib/bbw068.

Nagaraj, K., Sharvani, G.S., Sridhar, A., 2018. Emerging trend of big data analytics in bioinformatics: a literature review. Int. J. Bioinf. Res. Appl. 14, 144. https://doi.org/10.1504/ijbra.2018.10009206.

Obite, F., Jaja, E.T., Ijeomah, G., Jahun, K.I., 2018. The evolution of ethernet passive optical network (EPON) and future trends. Optik 167, 103–120. https://doi.org/10.1016/j.ijleo.2018.03.119.

Parihar, J., Kansal, P., Singh, K., Dhiman, H., 2019. Assessment of bioinformatics and healthcare informatics. Proc. - 2019 Amity Int. Conf. Artif. Intell. AICAI 2019, 465–467. https://doi.org/10.1109/AICAI.2019.8701262.

Qian, F., Guo, J., Jiang, Z., Shen, B., 2018. Translational bioinformatics for cholangiocarcinoma: opportunities and challenges. Int. J. Biol. Sci. 14, 920–929. https://doi.org/10.7150/ijbs.24622.

Qin, Z.S., 2017. Special collection of bioinformatics in the era of precision medicine. Quant. Biol. 5, 277–279. https://doi.org/10.1007/s40484-017-0128-z.

Rashid, S., 2006. Bioinformatics resource development in Pakistan: a review. Proc. Pakistan Acad. Sci. 43, 295–307.

Raza, K., Qazi, S., 2019. Nanopore Sequencing Technology and Internet of Living Things: A Big Hope for U-Healthcare. Elsevier Inc. https://doi.org/10.1016/b978-0-12-819361-7.00005-1.

Servant, N., Roméjon, J., Gestraud, P., La Rosa, P., Lucotte, G., Lair, S., Bernard, V., Zeitouni, B., Coffin, F., Jules-Clément, G., Yvon, F., Lermine, A., Poullet, P., Liva, S., Pook, S., Popova, T., Barette, C., Prud'homme, F., Dick, J.G., Kamal, M., Le Tourneau, C., Barillot, E., Hupé, P., 2014. Bioinformatics for precision medicine in oncology: principles and application to the SHIVA clinical trial. Front. Genet. 5, 1–16. https://doi.org/10.3389/fgene.2014.00152.

Sethi, P., Theodos, K., 2009. Translational bioinformatics and healthcare informatics: computational and ethical challenges. Perspect. Health Inf. Manag. 6, 1–13.

Shameer, K., Badgeley, M.A., Miotto, R., Glicksberg, B.S., Morgan, J.W., Dudley, J.T., 2017. Translational bioinformatics in the era of real-time biomedical, health care and wellness data streams. Briefings Bioinf. 18, 105–124. https://doi.org/10.1093/bib/bbv118.

Stefani, L., Galanti, G., 2017. Translational informatics in smart healthcare. In: Translational Informatics in Smart Healthcare - Advances in Experimental Medicine and Biology, pp. 47–61. https://doi.org/10.1007/978-981-10-5717-5.

Tenenbaum, J.D., 2016. Translational bioinformatics: past, present, and future. Dev. Reprod. Biol. 14, 31–41. https://doi.org/10.1016/j.gpb.2016.01.003.

Tsai, E.A., Shakbatyan, R., Evans, J., Rossetti, P., Graham, C., Sharma, H., Lin, C.F., Lebo, M.S., 2016. Bioinformatics workflow for clinical whole genome sequencing at partners healthcare personalized medicine. J. Personalized Med. 6 https://doi.org/10.3390/jpm6010012.

Valcarenghi, L., Van, D.P., Raponi, P.G., Castoldi, P., Campelo, D.R., Wong, S.W., Yen, S.H., Kazovsky, L.G., Yamashita, S., 2012. Energy efficiency in passive optical networks: where, when, and how? IEEE Netw. 26, 61–68. https://doi.org/10.1109/MNET.2012.6375895.

Chapter 6

IoT applications in translational bioinformatics

Rejaul Karim Barbhuiya[1],* and Naeem Ahmad[2]

[1]National Council of Educational Research and Training, New Delhi, Delhi, India; [2]Department of Computer Applications, Madanapalle Institute of Technology and Science, Madanapalle, Andhra Pradesh, India

*Corresponding author: E-mail: rejaul.ncert@nic.in

Chapter outline

1. Introduction

The internet of things (IoT) is a rapidly evolving interdisciplinary domain that integrates computer hardware, software, other electronic devices, and physical objects, whether living or nonliving, over a network. All such things or objects, once part of a network, can seamlessly interact, communicate, collect, and exchange data with each other. Starting with the radio frequency identification (RFID) system, the IoT today has evolved a lot through integration with fog and grid computing, data mining, and cyber-physical systems (Butte, 2008; Tenenbaum, 2016). The emerging IoT models include communication through technologies such as Bluetooth, Wi-Fi, ZigBee, RFID, as well as portable wireless personal area networks (LoWPAN) (Atzori et al., 2010). The IoT ecosystem includes sensors, actuators, advanced algorithms, communication interfaces, and cloud interface. Sophisticated algorithms are used for data processing and result in the analysis by integrating with application program interfaces.

Bioinformatics is an interdisciplinary field arising out of computer science, biology, mathematics, and statistics. Here, computational tools and methods are applied to huge biologic data to discover new insights. The large storage and processing power of computers are leveraged to store, analyze, and visualize biologic processes. Translational bioinformatics, an application domain of bioinformatics, helps us achieve further insight into diseases and their complex cause-effect relations. Using a well-integrated IoT system, multidimensional real-time data of every patient can be collected. These data can be analyzed using the bioinformatics tools and methods for more personalized and timely care of patients. This will help in monitoring the impact of every dose of a drug or other intervention and help us better understand diseases and their cure. Already, there are many healthcare applications of the IoT such as sensing and monitoring blood glucose, heart disease diagnostics, monitoring artificial heart valves and pacemakers, cancer diagnostics, etc.

The next section covers a brief introduction of translational bioinformatics and IoT. The remaining sections of the chapter explore the application of IoT in translational bioinformatics in terms of collection and exploration of biologic data as well as how IoT is useful in healthcare through sophisticated monitoring. The generic four-layer architecture of IoT is covered after that. The chapter ends with a discussion about the challenges involved in the application of IoT in healthcare.

2. Translational bioinformatics and IoT

This section briefly introduces the two broad domains: translational bioinformatics and the IoT. We have also introduced how the application of IoT can significantly enhance the outcomes in the area of translational bioinformatics, particularly in healthcare.

2.1 Translational bioinformatics

The American Medical Informatics Association defines translational bioinformatics as "the development of storage, analytic, and interpretive methods to optimize the transformation of increasingly voluminous biomedical data, and genomic data, into proactive, predictive, preventive, and participatory health" (Butte, 2008). Translational bioinformatics (hereafter TBI) involves the application of computational techniques that can analyze the enormous volumes of biologic data being collected and organized for different purposes like drug discovery, disease diagnosis, creation of tools for medicine, etc.

TBI, although a relatively new field, has proved to be an important discipline in the area of personalized and precision patient care and medicine. It aims to take advantage of the developments in the field of information processing to get insight from voluminous biologic data. Its application in healthcare links biologic parameters related to genes, proteins, etc., to clinical processes and looks for solutions to health challenges. The use of sequencing techniques for DNA and RNA, microarrays for DNA, proteomics, and metabolomics are becoming increasingly common. This necessitates the need for the design and application of novel computational techniques to extract information from these new data and ultimately get new knowledge (Tenenbaum, 2016). Thus, we can say that TBI approaches are used to determine the clinical significance of new biologic data when there is limited prior knowledge to be used for interpretation of results (Shameer et al., 2017).

TBI is broadly categorized into four major subfields (Denny, 2014):

i. use of electronic health records (EHRs) for genomic discovery through biobanks and as big data for clinical purpose,
ii. adoption of genomics and pharmacogenomics as part of "routine" clinical care through EHRs,
iii. use of omic technologies for drug discovery,
iv. personal genomic testing for the guidance of current and further clinical care, including the changing scenarios in direct-to-consumer genetic testing.

The invention of the electron microscope has enabled doctors and scientists to investigate and observe the detailed structure of tissues, cells, organelles, and macromolecular complexes. With the advent of magnetic resonance and other imaging techniques, it is possible to visualize tissues and organs at a much finer level. All these advancements have resulted in the generation of huge data that demands advanced tools and techniques to process the data and interpret results. It, therefore, requires advancement in the development of sophisticated molecular tools, high-end data processing machines, advanced computational techniques, and publicly accessible massive molecular measurement data. This has attracted investigators in the field of computer science, biomedical engineering, biotechnology, bioinformatics, and biomedical research to come together and work in TBI.

2.2 The internet of things

The internet's evolution has revolutionized the world and impacted almost every aspect of human society. The IoT is a popular area in the field of communication, primarily the wireless and sensor-based communication mechanism. IoT is expected to make a larger impact on the way information is recorded and processed and how automated decisions are taken.

The IoT recognizes the presence of various things around us that can connect to a network and communicate with others. Through sophisticated sensors, IoT enables each object to be able to connect to the internet, share data, and carry out specific instructions.

Such things can be RFID tags, sensors, wearables, actuators, smartphones, cameras, and all such objects that can handle data without human intervention (Atzori et al., 2010). A great deal of research is going on to develop various sensors and other devices that can securely communicate over a network without any direct human—computer interaction. The IoT has already brought a large number of home appliances, vehicles, wearable, etc., to the internet. It is promised to revolutionize the way we live, work, and communicate with objects. IoT has been in use for industrial and manufacturing domains for quite some time. The main application had been in machine-to-machine communication using RFID as well as different sensors. However, two recent developments have led to a significant emergence of IoT. The first one is the growth in mobile devices and their applications. The second is the widespread availability of wireless connectivity.

2.3 IoT, bioinformatics, and computational intelligence

Bioinformatics is advancing rapidly due to its widespread applications in healthcare and also facilitating other fields. The recent progress in the IoT promises to make a paradigm shift in the field of TBI. IoT-enabled computational intelligence techniques in bioinformatics have become the best possible tool to solve medical problems. Here, different types of devices, computer algorithms, programming solutions, and computing paradigms play an important role in analyzing and predicting the future treatment policies of healthcare.

Computational intelligence (CI) tools are mathematical tools inspired by nature and natural phenomena. CI techniques aim to create a closer alliance with human intelligence. Following are some of the most widely adopted and CI tools and techniques (Alansari et al., 2019):

- *Evolutionary computation* includes a set of evolutionary algorithms such as the genetic algorithm inspired by the theory of evolution and genetics.
- *Swarm intelligence* includes a large number of simple and low-intelligence agents that collaborate or compete among themselves to form what is called a swarm intelligence or collective intelligence. The ant colony optimization algorithm is one of the most popular swarm intelligence algorithms.
- *An artificial neural network* is inspired by neuroscience findings regarding the structure of neurons in the human brain.
- *Fuzzy systems* work based on concepts of high or low to describe the value of a variable instead of concrete yes/no. Fuzzy systems are being used to design smart appliances.

2.4 Limitations of IoT in translational bioinformatics

The globally acceptable protocol standards for the IoT are still evolving. This makes it difficult to create a coherent solution by application of IoT in TBI. Ideally, for IoT-enabled healthcare devices to talk to others and understand each other's requirements, standardization of protocols working at the application layer and other network interfaces is a must.

Storage and memory are other limitations for IoT in TBI. The consecutive records of health parameters are crucial to understanding the cause-effect relations of drugs. For example, the sensors deployed at the patient's end may require maintaining blood pressure, glucose, heartbeat, and pulse rate measured at short intervals for days. But, those devices usually do not have much storage to keep all that data.

Another key limitation of IoT in the context of bioinformatics is the regular upgradation of patch updates of software in those IoT devices.

3. Application of IoT for better healthcare

Like many other fields, the IoT is being applied in a big way in the fields of biomedical engineering, medicine, and healthcare. But healthcare is one such field where IoT has the potential to revolutionize every aspect of patient care, monitoring of vital parameters, emergency management, diagnosis of disease, treatment, drug discovery, as well as furthering our understanding about diseases and their behaviors. Researchers have been using various methods for collection, storage, and analysis of data related to health.

It is expected that in the near future, the application of IoT technologies will revolutionize healthcare environments (Ahmadi et al., 2018). For example, IoT is going to play a significant role in patient monitoring and care in hospitals as well as in homes. There exist various sensors and wearable gadgets, such as Global Positioning System (GPS), Electro-encephalogram (EEG), Electrocardiogram (ECG), and inertial sensors that are deployed to observe and record different types of health data such as weight, BMI, blood glucose, location, pulse rate, blood pressure, etc. (Qi et al., 2017).

Some of the potential benefits of the application of IoT in healthcare (Farahani et al., 2018) are listed next:

- Personalized service: IoT helps to monitor and communicate health data using multiple sensors, in real time. This can vastly expand the possibilities to provide personalized healthcare and treatments.

- Handling big data: IoT can easily integrate with cloud services to process and analyze massive real-time data produced by connected sensors that are multimodal, distributed, and heterogeneous in nature. This facilitates almost real-time knowledge discovery from health data.
- Lifetime monitoring and advanced prediction: The health data of a patient can be collected through the application of IoT for a continuous period also. Application of machine learning techniques and big data analytics on those data may help in predicting major illnesses like heart attacks, cancers, or infections before they occur.
- Ease of use: IoT devices can be easily used by health workers, patients, or their attendants as many of the wearable devices can be operated through only button clicks or through smartphone apps.
- Seamless integration: IoT in healthcare lets different devices and things to work together without much concern for the difficulty of technologic integration.
- Cost-effective: The deployment of IoT enables services in health to experience a reduction of costs in two ways. First, patients can self-monitor their health and consult doctors when required per recommendation. Second is the cost of precious human life that can be saved through timely intervention in terms of treatments.
- Round the clock accessibility: Since IoT can be integrated to the larger healthcare system through the internet, patients can also have access to healthcare services at a time and place of their convenience, without any barriers.
- Better diagnosis: Since doctors can get data about patients' current health status in real time, it can save their effort in examining patients. Besides, with all the vital data, doctors can diagnose health conditions with improved efficacy.
- Global collaboration and access: Health professionals around the globe get connected via the IoT-based healthcare ecosystem. This enables doctors to collaborate with their global peers in more complex cases of health conditions. Likewise, patients also can have access to healthcare consultants across the world at their fingertips.

3.1 IoT devices for healthcare

There are various IoT-enabled services that are being experimented with in healthcare. The sensors and RFID tags are key enabler technologies, which drive the concept of the smart healthcare system (Ramsden, 2015). This healthcare system connects the patients to the healthcare units remotely through the IoT network. The IoT-based smart wearable devices can be used in patients to collect data related to different key health parameters such as heartbeat, blood pressure, and glucose level. Such devices will have specialized sensors designed to work with wearable technologies (Raza and Qazi, 2019). The sensors are the most powerful means of measuring heart rate, blood pressure, and much more. The periodic data collected by those devices can be sent to smartphones for different stakeholders. This remote access of patients helps in performing healthcare activities including diagnosis, monitoring, and remote surgeries. Here is the list of important IoT devices used in medical care units and also available sensors.

Awair: A medical IoT device that is used by people with asthma and allergies. It continuously senses the air quality for patients and sends an alert message to improve air quality inside the room/house.
Fitbit: A fitness band that is used by people to monitor their calories, heart rate, etc.
Theatro: An IoT device that is used in the retail and hospitality industry. This device is used to track the staff and deploy accordingly to efficiently utilize the workforce and improve productivity.
Aware Point: This device with low-energy beacons is used to manage assets like wheelchair, bed, trolley, etc., in the hospitals in real time.
Withings Health Monitor: An IoT device that monitors blood pressure, sleep, and temperature and sends immediate feedback to the smartphone.

3.2 IoT sensors for healthcare

Sensors are key elements of IoT devices through which monitoring of people and assets, and data collection is possible. Sensors continuously sense the environmental temperature or pressure and send an electronic signal if any change is triggered. Different types of sensors are available in the IoT industry, which are used for different purposes. The rapid growth of IoT and the maturation of some of the wearable biosensors have created new opportunities for personalized healthcare and services. The IoT industry is focusing on building smarter, automated sensors that can solve the growing needs of society. These sensors are smaller, low cost, have low power consumption, and are capable of communicating with remote devices. They should give accurate and precise results. In healthcare, people are using advanced sensors and biosensors (Farooqi et al., 2019) to make the system more advanced and smarter in its automation. Various types of sensors are available in the market. We have listed some of the healthcare-centric sensors in Table 6.1.

TABLE 6.1 Sensors used in healthcare.

Sensor type	Sensors	Healthcare application
Environment	Smoke	To monitor air quality for allergy patients
	Temperature	To monitor body temperature
Biosensors	Glucose testing	To analyze blood features through invasive tests, e.g., daily monitoring of blood glucose
	Electrocardiogram Sensor and finger chip sensor	To monitor pulse rate using an electrode that detects electrocardiogram trace and pulse rate, which can be worn on the skin
	Muscle contraction/tightening (EMG)	To monitor situations related to muscles and related motor neurons. The ECG electrode is used for EMG also
	Breathing and temperature	Plethysmograph can be used to monitorbreathing or to monitor body temperature
	Blood flow (SpO2)	Photocell is taken to determine pigmentation changes. Accordingly, oxygen can be sent into the bloodstream
Location trackers	GPS sensor	To manage assets in hospitals
	Altimeter	Used for medical application and weather monitoring
	Magnetometer	Used for medical and biomedical purposes
Other sensors	Inertial measurement unit (IMU)	Human motion tracking, health monitoring, and analysis
	Image sensor	Used in endoscopy, dentistry, oncology, X-rays, and microscopy

4. Soft computing techniques for healthcare data

4.1 Data mining techniques

Data mining is a process to automatically extract knowledge and patterns from large data sets. The obtained knowledge or pattern assists in predicting future policies for the business or treatment. Data mining approaches include pattern recognition, classification, clustering, statistics, mathematics, artificial intelligence, and visualization. The primary tasks of data mining approaches involve clustering, classification, association, prediction, estimation, and data representation. Data mining techniques have an immense application in health-related data in an IoT-integrated environment. Ramsden (2015) describe that analysis of DNA sequencing is one of the most interesting domains for the bioinformatics research community. Generally, biologic data are classified into three main categories including sequential, structural, and functional databases (Tramontano, 2006). Nowadays the methodology of analysis in bioinformatics is shifting to data mining approaches. These approaches are being applied to extensive biologic datasets to describe properties like protein−protein interaction, protein folding trajectories, frequent motifs from DNA sequences, and much more.

Datasets collected by mobile apps through sensors in mobile phones such as accelerometer are very large in size. They include data related to physical activities like walking, jogging, running, jumping, climbing stairs, standing idle, etc. (Qi et al., 2017). Data mining techniques such as clustering, classification, regression, and multilayer perceptron networks are applied to discover useful knowledge from those data.

For clustering, k-means is one of the most commonly used algorithms. In the context of IoT, the unlabeled input for clustering can be behavioral data about patients recorded by different sensors (Tsai et al., 2013). Such data can be mined to decide the services required by the patient.

4.2 Cloud computing

For large-scale data, cloud computing has become the most feasible solution for analysis and predicting the future policies of any business. Cloud data centers consist of several servers or high computing machines, which is one of the means to store big data and compute complex calculations due to dynamic capacity augmentation. The idea of using high computing resources at low costs has attracted small- to large-scale business entities to use cloud environments. Gradually, cloud computing is being integrated with IoT to solve real-time problems such as smart homes, smart cities, and smart healthcare systems. Now mobile phones are common for people, and they have started to be utilized in monitoring patients without bothering about limited computing power. The cloud has solved this problem by providing access to high computing resources remotely. With this feature, complex IoT applications are possible, which are being accessed by low-power mobile phones through high network connection on high computing machines. Cloud providers are providing these services at low cost. These services are software-as-a-service, platform-as-a-service, and infrastructure-as-a-service. These services are making our healthcare system easy, low cost, automated, and speedy.

Fog computing is the decentralized version of cloud computing. Here, computing resources are placed at each edge of an IoT system. That means data can be processed quickly at the sensor level where it gets generated, so decision-making can be faster (Merelli et al., 2018).

4.3 IoT and AI

The integration of two or more technologies in bioinformatics is enabling continuous quality improvement in healthcare. This transformation in healthcare is playing a central role in patient treatment, asset management, and monitoring health. IoT devices are generating patient health data, which can be used for patient health recovery and also in predicting future treatment policies, which could help to make the healthcare system smarter and automated. It requires computer-based intelligence or artificial intelligence (AI), which is one of the most powerful tools. The integration of IoT and AI has widespread application from data collection to data analytics. The Consumer Electronics Show, 2018, demonstrated the use of AI, big data analytics, and IoT in bioinformatics. Such innovations are helping hands for the healthcare worker in health monitoring, diagnosing, and treating diseases, and many others. For example, chatbots-AI simulation software can have conversations with patients about their symptoms. Afterward, this conversation helps in assessing and diagnosing patient health. With this additional AI assistance, physicians and health workers are saving time by getting quick healthcare consultation.

5. IoT beneficiaries in healthcare

In the traditional healthcare system, patients interact with doctors by visiting their clinics or hospitals or sometimes the interaction happens over the phone. There was limited scope to monitor patients and make prescriptions for them. But now, integration of IoT is rapidly changing the healthcare system by transforming the patients' interactions with doctors by remote monitoring through an integrated system. IoT undoubtedly has reduced healthcare and treatment costs by providing personalized healthcare solutions. IoT solutions in the healthcare system benefit various stakeholders like patients, physicians, hospitals, and insurance companies. Here are some detailed discussions about how different beneficiaries are using IoT-based solutions.

Patients: IoT devices are being used in many forms like fitness bands, heart rate monitor, glucometer, blood pressure monitor, etc. These wearable IoT devices connect people to the healthcare system wirelessly through the internet. They continuously monitor blood pressure, heart rate, glucose, and much more and provide personalized access to patients. Moreover, these devices can be set as a reminder for calorie counting, exercise checking, variation in blood pressure, etc.

Undoubtedly, IoT has made people's lives easy by continuous monitoring of health conditions, especially elderly patients whose regular/daily checkup is very difficult. IoT solutions in healthcare directly impact people living alone and their families. On any disturbance in the health of a person, wearable IoT devices send an alert message to family members and concerned health providers.

Physicians: IoT devices have made healthcare professionals more watchful and proactively connected with the patients. By using wearable devices in combination with the previous history of the patient, physicians can easily monitor patient health conditions effectively and make prescriptions accordingly. These devices generate health data for the patients, which is used in treatment plans or for patients requiring any immediate medical care. With this data, physicians can also easily identify the best possible treatment process for the patients and achieve better health conditions of the patients.

Hospitals: In smart hospitals, IoT devices are a central part to monitor patients or manage their assets. To run day-to-day operations smoothly, hospitals rely on advanced technologies, and IoT can be of great help for them. A smart ambulance equipped with medical sensors for diagnosis and a secure communication link with the hospital can perform many of the simpler diagnoses on the go, so medical staff at the hospital can make required arrangements before the arrival of the patient in that ambulance.

In addition to tracking patient health conditions, IoT devices are also being used in the management of hospitals. The real-time locations of the medical equipment are being tracked using sensor-enabled IoT devices. The medical equipment may be wheelchairs, defibrillators, nebulizers, oxygen pumps, or others. Similarly, we can integrate IoT in other wings of the hospital such as intensive care units, primary care units, surgery wards, etc. In big hospitals, the deployment of the health workers can also be monitored in real time.

As we know, viral diseases like SARS-COV-2 (COVID-19) spread very rapidly among humans (Raza, 2020a,b). It is a major challenge in hospitals where infected people can transmit to others. Sensor-enabled IoT devices can help in monitoring and preventing patients and hospital staff from getting infected. Moreover, hospitals can also use IoT devices for the management of different activities such as pharmacy inventory control, checking refrigerator or air conditioner temperature, humidity, and temperature control.

Health insurance companies: IoT-enabled devices have created various opportunities for health insurers in insurance claims. Previously, insurance companies were getting too many fraud claims. Data on patient health generated from the IoT devices are being used by insurance companies for their underwriting and claims operations. Insurance companies can easily detect false claims and identify prospects for underwriting. Now, companies and customers have transparent processes of insurance claims, pricing, underwriting, and risk assessment. In the presence of collected data of the patients, customers would have acceptable visibility in all decision processes.

Additionally, it is one of the driving factors for the business of the third party for sharing patient data to the insurance company. Companies may also use other options like offering incentives to their customers for using and sharing their patients' data. Companies may also generate this data at their end by rewarding their customers for tracking their daily activities, treatment process, and precautionary health measures. It will help the company significantly in reducing claims as well as claiming time period because insurance companies can validate claims very quickly using data collected through IoT devices.

6. IoT architecture

In general, IoT consists of a multilayer architecture. In this section, we present an IoT architecture for healthcare, which consists of four layers, as shown in Fig. 6.1. From the bottom-up view, these layers are (i) sensor layer, (ii) internet layer, (iii) processing layer, and (iv) application layer. This architecture is inspired by general IoT architecture given by well-known studies (Qi et al., 2015; Acampora et al., 2013; Yang et al., 2012; Gyrard, 2013).

The sensor layer aims to connect heterogeneous sensor networks to gather data from different sources. This collected data contains personalized health and medical information. IoT-enabled wearables such as ECG, EFG, and GPS are capable of monitoring, reporting, and recording patient health conditions including blood pressure, location, weight, heart

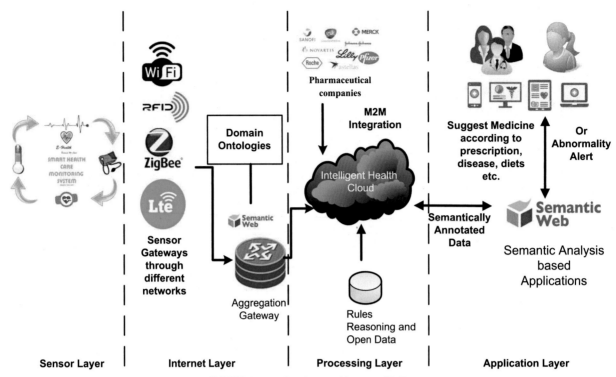

FIGURE 6.1 A four-layer architecture of IoT.

rate, etc. Moreover, healthcare units have begun to use mobile applications on smartphones to collect patient emotion and behavior data. A community of researchers is focusing on building low-cost and noninvasive sensing technology to automatically observe accurate, precise, and reliable health data in IoT-based uncontrolled environments.

M2M technology is advancing very fast in the market, which enables the use of any sensor to communicate. It makes a monitoring system automatically respond to environmental changes, which means less human interaction is needed. With the M2M integration platform, companies have started to develop new-generation services, wearables, and monitoring devices for healthcare. These devices can collect, transmit, and process patient health data to respond faster than medical professionals.

The internet layer is responsible for connecting sensor-enabled IoT devices and other hardware resources such as mobile phones, laptops, PCs, and machines in cloud environments for health data to be collected, shared, and processed under IoT infrastructure. This layer is also responsible for providing interoperability and security required for IoT healthcare. Interoperability is one of the key driving factors to integrate heterogeneous fixed devices and mobile devices, thus allowing machine-to-machine communication (also called hybrid computing grids). This interoperability is also needed to support heterogeneous protocols such as WiFi, RFID, Bluetooth, LTE-4G, and Zigbee. State-of-the-art IoT healthcare networks and related issues are studied in depth in Islam et al. (2015).

Regarding the IoT interoperability standard, Cummins (Shaikh et al., 2009) proposed service-oriented architecture (SOA) validated by a community of researchers as a promising solution for IoT healthcare architecture. Many standards have been designed and developed to preserve interoperability under SOA. Extensible Markup Language and Simple Object Access Protocol are a couple examples of such standards. It is observed that large-scale IoT healthcare is facing issues of cost, risk, and profit while implementing SOA standards. In addition to this, other network-related factors including management of heterogeneous networks, energy, security, and privacy also need to be addressed (Cummins, 2009; Sarvabhatla et al., 2014; Zhao et al., 2016).

The processing layer is responsible for defining computational approaches that aim to add semantics to health data. In the early stage of smart healthcare, researchers designed and developed disease-related algorithms based on available data instead of developing general approaches to handle health and medical data. Various such computational algorithms have been developed and employed (Islam et al., 2015). Nowadays, studies are focusing on developing generic algorithms or data analytics tools at the processing layer. These studies aim to improve the accuracy and validity of health data and to provide scalable, assessable, and sustainable data structure as well. This layer uses different data processing algorithms for IoT healthcare, which includes data-driven approaches, knowledge-based approaches, and hybrid approaches. The data-driven category covers mainly machine learning methods; the knowledge-based category includes modeling and semantic reasoning methods; the hybrid category contains a hybrid approach of data-driven and knowledge-based approaches by integrating machine learning into knowledge reasoning.

Generally, RFID tags of any product have very specific information about that product (e.g., name, expiry date). Medical professionals and patients require more than that information (e.g., soft drinks contain sugar, caffeine, etc.). To get this additional information, sensor technology is integrated with sensor measurements such as RDF, RDFS (RDF Schema), OWL (Ontology Web Language), and other domain ontologies. It converts raw health data into semantic measurement, thus providing an explicit description of any product or medical information. For example, RDF works on triplets, which describe a sentence as a subject, verb, and object. A sentence "Ahmad likes soft drinks" can be split into "Subject: Ahmad, Verb: Likes, Object: Soft drinks." This sentence further can be detailed as "Soft drinks are carbonated water, and they contain high carbohydrate content. Ahmad is allergic to carbohydrate content." OWL is a language that allows people to create properties and their relationships (e.g., soft drinks contain carbohydrate content, a person is allergic to carbohydrates).

The application aims to offer high-quality services and an easy interface for the end users. In recent years, mobile device technologies have been playing an important role in healthcare monitoring and services. Handheld devices such as PDA, smartwatches, and smartphones are embedded with inertial sensors and biosensors to monitor patients and collect personalized health data. Moreover, they are meant to run the application's interface to view updates, reports, and warnings. The layer combines the application interface into the algorithm layer. With the use of M2M integration, collected data at the cloud is analyzed, and necessary medical processes are adopted. An example of a common application is for regular checkups, where a wearable reminds or updates the patient about regular checkups if a patient has scheduled it on a particular day. A similar application is also used by the medical professional to report to them about the patients. The application layer covers different types of healthcare applications from medicine to academia.

7. Challenges in the adoption of IoT in healthcare

There lie many challenging issues that need to be addressed for IoT to have large-scale adoption in different fields. The application of IoT in healthcare looks promising where patients, doctors, pathologists, radiologists, and hospitals can join seamlessly and share data as well as decisions in almost real time. However, there still exist many challenging areas in IoT research to be overcome to create a more autonomous healthcare system (Farahani et al., 2018).

- *Data acquisition*: Data collection is one of the important activities in bioinformatics, which involves data from different sources including the data generated from IoT devices, experiments, and their analysis. The myriad of biologic data collection mechanisms has resulted in numerous publicly accessible databases (Jameson et al., 2008). The data-capturing tools whether collecting primary or secondary data should meet certain requirements, so the captured data can be used by multiple agencies. The standardization of data format is so the import and export of data can be easily accomplished.
- *Data management*: Various biosensors attached to the human body keep on generating large volumes of data. These are categorized as big data with inherent challenges related to volume, velocity, and variety. Thus, the management of such data is a major concern.
- *Scalability*: Billions of internet-enabled devices and data sources are expected to connect and create a huge network. These devices will produce massive amounts of data. This will create the challenge to store, organize, and process those data at scale, in a relatively quick period.
- *Interoperability*: Technologic standards in IoT are still evolving. There needs to be standardized models for designing IoT devices and their communication protocols. Otherwise, the interoperability of devices across healthcare applications will be a challenge, and this may hinder the utilization of the potential of IoT.
- *Ease of use*: Most of the IoT devices in healthcare will be required to be used and operated by the end users, particularly elderly patients. They may not have prior experience to deal with such devices and may have limited knowledge about wireless networks, the process of syncing data, etc. Hence, IoT devices for healthcare need to have an easy interface, so end users can self-train. Moreover, in remote areas, such devices will require to be set up with minimal access to experts. Thus, their setup needs to be straightforward and user friendly.
- *Security and privacy*: When applied to healthcare, IoT devices pose certain challenges that need to be taken care of. There lies the potential risk that can be exploited to either cause harm to users (patients) or compromise their privacy. If the security is breached, there can be unauthorized access to end user data. To minimize these challenges, efforts are going on at different layers of the IoT ecosystem: data, network, cloud, and human.

While it is certain that IoT-enabled technologies in personalized healthcare systems have huge potential, the IoT technologies are still largely considered to be in their infancy. This is because there are many open issues as highlighted earlier including the cost-effectiveness of sensing technologies, computational tools for processing high volume life-logging data sets recorded through sensors, the ability to deal with uncontrolled environments, security, and privacy. The efforts are going on to address these issues, and as IoT technology matures, it will unfold many other possibilities of enhancing healthcare facilities.

8. Conclusion

This chapter explains the possibilities of IoT contributing to faster development in the field of TBI. It is no more being called ambitious when people talk about the possibility of IoT revolutionizing bioinformatics, and particularly healthcare. With smart devices, wearables, robots doing surgeries, and other autonomous sensors monitoring health parameters, the future of healthcare is going to be patient centric. Researchers across the world are exploring various ways to enhance healthcare facilities by leveraging the potentials of IoT in a manner that complements existing services. In this, IoT is considered to be a great enabler by seamlessly integrating different devices, cloud services, as well as stakeholders such as patients, doctors, hospitals, clinical labs, etc., over a secure network. The collection of smart mobile apps in the areas of medication management, yoga, exercise, fitness, sleep pattern recording, pregnancy monitoring, etc., are already integrating with IoT devices and seamless experience to users.

After introducing both IoT and TBI, the chapter discussed the applications of IoT in healthcare with the use of advanced smart sensors. The role of various soft computing techniques in healthcare is covered. It then presents a generalized layered architecture of IoT in the context of application in the healthcare domain. The chapter then brings to focus some of the key challenges to be resolved for better integration of IoT. There are ongoing advances in sensors, devices, and internet technologies leading to the development of affordable healthcare gadgets and connected health services. This can significantly expand further developments in realizing the potential of IoT-based healthcare solutions. However, due to the vast amount of data being generated through different devices with different quality of service, the IoT poses the challenge of storage, latency, and bandwidth requirements, in addition to ethical and secure ways of handling personal data.

References

Acampora, G., et al., 2013. A survey on ambient intelligence in healthcare. Proc. IEEE 101 (12), 2470–2494.

Ahmadi, H., et al., 2018. The application of internet of things in healthcare: a systematic literature review and classification. In: Universal Access in the Information Society, pp. 1–33.

Alansari, Z., et al., 2019. Evaluation of IoT-based computational intelligence tools for DNA sequence analysis in bioinformatics. In: Progress in Advanced Computing and Intelligent Engineering. Springer, Singapore, pp. 339–350.

Atzori, L., Iera, A., Morabito, G., 2010. The internet of things: a survey. Comput. Network. 54 (15), 2787–2805.

Butte, A.J., 2008. Translational bioinformatics: coming of age. J. Am. Med. Inf. Assoc. 15 (6), 709–714.

Cummins, F.A., 2009. Service-oriented architecture. In: Enabling the Agile Enterprise. Morgan Kaufmann, Burlington, p. 27.

Denny, J.C., 2014. Surveying recent themes in translational bioinformatics: big data in EHRs, omics for drugs, and personal genomics. Yearb. Med. Inform. (01), 199–205, 23.

Farahani, B., et al., 2018. Towards fog-driven IoT eHealth: promises and challenges of IoT in medicine and healthcare. Future Generat. Comput. Syst. 78, 659–676.

Farooqi, M.R., et al., 2019. Wireless sensor networks towards convenient infrastructure in the healthcare industry: a systematic study. In: Sensors for Health Monitoring. Academic Press, pp. 31–46.

Gyrard, A., 2013. A machine-to-machine architecture to merge semantic sensor measurements. In: Proceedings of the 22nd International Conference on World Wide Web.

Islam, S.M.R., et al., 2015. The internet of things for health care: a comprehensive survey. IEEE Access 3, 678–708.

Jameson, D., et al., 2008. Data capture in bioinformatics: requirements and experiences with Pedro. BMC Bioinform. 9 (1), 183.

Merelli, I., et al., 2018. Low-power portable devices for metagenomics analysis: fog computing makes bioinformatics ready for the internet of things. Future Generat. Comput. Syst. 88, 467–478.

Qi, J., et al., 2015. Towards knowledge driven decision support for personalized home-based self-management of chronic diseases. In: 2015 IEEE 12th Intl Conf on Ubiquitous Intelligence and Computing and 2015 IEEE 12th Intl Conf on Autonomic and Trusted Computing and 2015 IEEE 15th Intl Conf on Scalable Computing and Communications and its Associated Workshops (UIC-ATC-ScalCom). IEEE.

Qi, J., et al., 2017. Advanced internet of things for personalised healthcare systems: a survey. Pervasive Mob. Comput. 41, 132–149.

Ramsden, J., 2015. Bioinformatics: an Introduction, vol. 21. Springer.

Raza, K., Qazi, S., 2019. Nanopore sequencing technology and internet of living things: a big hope for U-healthcare. In: Sensors for Health Monitoring. Academic Press, pp. 95–116.

Raza, K., 2020a. Artificial intelligence against COVID-19: a meta-analysis of current research. In: Big Data Analytics and Artificial Intelligence Against COVID-19: Innovation Vision and Approach. Studies in Big Data, vol. 78. Springer, Cham. https://doi.org/10.1007/978-3-030-55258-9_10.

Raza, K., 2020b. Computational intelligence methods in COVID-19: surveillance, prevention, prediction and diagnosis. In: Studies in Computational Intelligence (SCI), vol. 923. Springer, Singapore.

Sarvabhatla, M., Kodavali, L.N., Vorugunti, C.S., 2014. An energy efficient temporal credential based mutual authentication scheme for WSN. In: 2014 3rd International Conference on Eco-Friendly Computing and Communication Systems. IEEE.

Shaikh, A., et al., 2009. The role of service oriented architecture in telemedicine healthcare system. In: 2009 International Conference on Complex, Intelligent and Software Intensive Systems. IEEE.

Shameer, K., et al., 2017. Translational bioinformatics in the era of real-time biomedical, health care and wellness data streams. Briefings Bioinf. 18 (1), 105−124.

Tenenbaum, J.D., 2016. Translational bioinformatics: past, present, and future. Dev. Reprod. Biol. 14 (1), 31−41.

Tramontano, A., 2006. Introduction to Bioinformatics. Crc Press.

Tsai, C.-W., et al., 2013. Data mining for internet of things: a survey. IEEE Commun. Surv. & Tutor. 16 (1), 77−97.

Yang, P., et al., 2012. Efficient object localization using sparsely distributed passive RFID tags. IEEE Trans. Ind. Electron. 60 (12), 5914−5924.

Zhao, M., Ho, I.W.-H., Chong, P.H.J., 2016. An energy-efficient region-based RPL routing protocol for low-power and lossy networks. IEEE Internet Things J. 3 (6), 1319−1333.

Chapter 7

Blockchain technology in healthcare: making digital healthcare reliable, more accurate, and revolutionary

Md Tauseef Alam and Khalid Raza*

Department of Computer Science, Jamia Millia Islamia, New Delhi, Delhi, India
Corresponding author: E-mail: kraza@jmi.ac.in

Chapter outline

1. Introduction

Healthcare has played a critical and crucial role in human civilization by saving millions of billions of lives. But the years from 1970 to 90 saw the emergence of modular information technology systems in healthcare institutions that can be called Healthcare 1.0. Then there was an advancement in existing systems that started getting networked and electronic health records were produced and combined with clinical imaging, helping doctors to work more effectively and efficiently. This period lasted for one and a half decades after 1990 and was Healthcare 2.0. The decade from 2005 onward saw the event of genomics information, the emergence of wearables, and implantables. The mixing of all this data in conjunction with networked electronic health record systems saw the emergence of Healthcare 3.0. The increased use of artificial intelligence and automation coupled with real-time data collection along with high tech technology nowadays can be seen as Healthcare 4.0 (Khan, 2017).

However, today's digitization of medical science faces many issues when it comes to the interoperability of records among different parties. The cyberattacks on healthcare institutions, the problem of counterfeit drugs, transparency in organ donation, and trust issues prevailing in this field are some of the limitations that are yet to be solved. There are already many efforts going on to overcome these, but blockchain technology here fits perfectly to solve these existing issues along with providing many use cases for the healthcare sector.

Blockchain first came into existence with the Bitcoin white paper by Satoshi Nakamoto in the year 2008 as an outcome of the global recession of 2008–09 (Nakamoto, 2012). It was first to solve the double-spending problem that is spending an amount more than once to a different person at the same time. Bitcoin and blockchain should not be confused with each other: they are not same. Bitcoin is a cryptocurrency, which is an application of blockchain technology. To understand this, as email was an application of the internet web but not limited thereto. Now Amazon, Google, Facebook, and lots more are on the web. Similarly, cryptocurrency is an application of blockchain but is not limited to it. Being a technology more or less a decade old, it has many things to supply. Fig. 7.1 depicts the blockchain network, and the components of blockchain are these:

(a) Decentralized: The info is not stored in any single location but is stored with each node (computer) within the network having equal opportunity and significance.
(b) Distributed: The info is distributed among the nodes and is accessible to everyone on the platform.
(c) Shared public digital ledger: The record of transactions happening is stored in an exceedingly digital ledger form that is public and shared with each node within the blockchain network, i.e., each node features a copy of the shared digital ledger.
(d) Consensus: This is often an algorithm by which various active nodes within the network validate and verify a block that gets added later to the chain. The nodes performing this are called miners.

Blockchain has evolved very quickly from blockchain 1.0 to 4.0 (Unibright.io, 2017). Blockchain 1.0 started in the year 2008 with the cryptocurrency that acts as the "Internet of Money" and does not need any third party for transferring money with trust. In the year 2013 started the period of scripting programmable smart contracts on top of blockchain architecture to make blockchain tamperproof and transparent, which was blockchain 2.0. The year 2015 onward saw the development of Dapps (decentralized applications), which have a frontend similar to traditional apps and backend running on the blockchain. This period was blockchain 3.0, and now the technology is moving toward blockchain 4.0 to meet the business and industry needs.

This chapter makes an effort to give readers insight and awareness of making digital healthcare reliable, more accurate, and revolutionary by using blockchain technology. Section 2 explains why blockchain is needed and what are its potential features. In Section 3 and subpart, various use cases of blockchain in healthcare are discussed. In Section 4, some of the popular blockchain platforms are described that can be used for implementing proof-of-concept ideas in the medical science and healthcare sector. In Section 5, one gets to know about various ongoing blockchain projects and startups in the healthcare sector. In Section 6, SWOT analysis of the blockchain in the medical health sector is done, and finally, Section 7 concludes our chapter by discussing blockchain technology in healthcare.

2. Why blockchain?

There is no specific definition of blockchain accepted globally. Blockchain in simple words is a decentralized, distributed, publicly shared digital ledger to record transactions across various nodes in the network, so any transaction record can not be changed retroactively without changing all the subsequent blocks. Suppose there are 90 blocks mined at present and a malicious user wants to alter the 49th block, then it is nearly impossible for him because he will then have to make changes

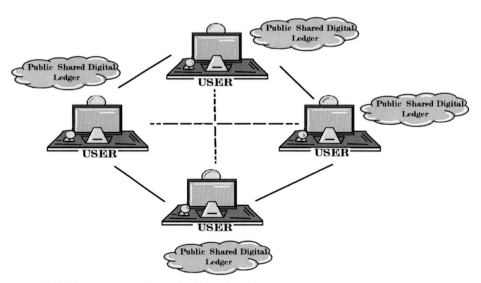

FIGURE 7.1   A decentralized, distributed, shared ledger network, i.e., backbone of blockchain.

in all the blocks from 50th to 90th block to add his fake block in the network. To understand this lets one become aware of the blockchain structure. A blockchain supports a hash pointer linked list structure in which every time a new block is appended at the end. Each block is connected one after the other with a hash created using a cryptographic one-way hash function like SHA256 (Nakamoto, 2012). A blockchain's first block is the genesis block, and the longest valid accepted chain is the canonical chain, and the chain rejected from the main chain is the orphaned and rejected chain.

A block along with the transaction data contains block number, previous block hash, timestamp, and nonce (Nakamoto, 2012). Fig. 7.2 shows the block in the blockchain. Generally, a one-way cryptographic hash function is applied to get a hash of a block that is a means to connect a new, unique block after it. The block nonce is the value calculated by the miners within the network to validate a block. A nonce is difficult to seek out and is found employing a brute force approach based on the difficulty of the block puzzle. So, here, this approach of validation uses proof-of-work consensus. The consensus among nodes in the network is achieved using different consensus algorithms depending on the use case of blockchain (Zheng et al., 2018). Some of the popular consensus algorithms other than proof-of-work are (A) proof-of-stake, (B) practical Byzantine fault tolerance (PBFT) based (C) proof of elapsed time (D) Raft BFT or Istanbul BFT, and so on (Zheng et al., 2018).

Fig. 7.3 shows how a generalized transaction happens in the blockchain network. A transaction request is made in step 1, and in step 2, it gets in the block. Then in step 3, all the nodes in the network get notified. Then miners mine the block in step 4 per the consensus algorithm used and validate the transactions in the block by solving the puzzle. The miners get a percentage of the incentives for validating the block (Nakamoto, 2012). Then the quantity of transactions is bundled up together to make a singular block. The new block mined is then added to the chain in step 5 to become a neighborhood of the blockchain. Thus, a transaction is completed in step 6. Some features of blockchain that make it different are as follows:

(a) persistent in that it helps in securing storage and provides integrity protection of data
(b) audit ability of the records
(c) the data on-chain are immutable
(d) privacy and ownership of data is guaranteed
(e) transparency and trust are strongly created because of smart contracts.

Programmable smart contracts on top of blockchain architecture and consensus methods provide blockchain its beauty. The smart contracts help in building the decentralized applications on a blockchain platform. DApps are different from apps and provide more security as they run on blockchain architecture rather than traditional client-server architecture. As blockchain technology is becoming mature, many of the significant features and uses cases are getting disclosed. As time passes, blockchain will prove its potential more practically in various industries or domains. While each of the concerns of the healthcare sector are addressed separately with the proper use of cryptography algorithms and privacy-preserving technologies, the key concerns in such solutions have always been the governing trust model. In such solutions, blockchain as a trustworthy, decentralized, shared ledger technology can act as a trust-binding glue. The next section describes and explores how blockchain can transform digital healthcare to make it more counterrevolutionary.

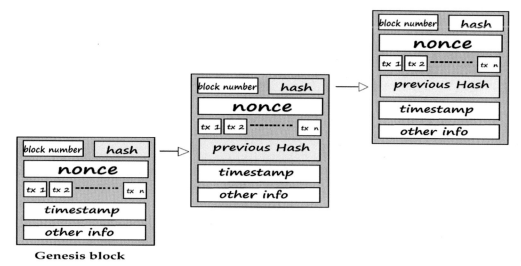

Genesis block

FIGURE 7.2   A generalized blockchain with blocks.

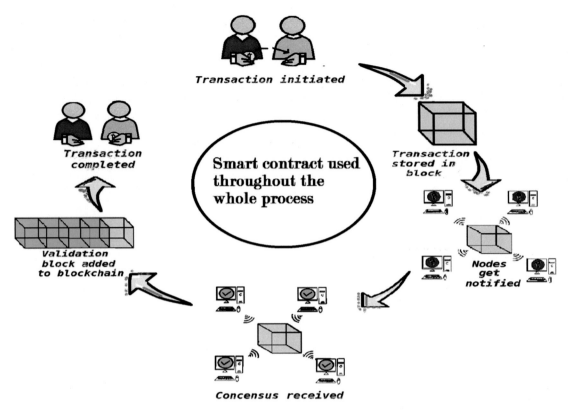

FIGURE 7.3 Workflow of a transaction in a blockchain network.

3. Use cases of blockchain in healthcare

Blockchain technologies have a noteworthy role to play in the healthcare systems of tomorrow. The possible use cases of the nascent blockchain technology are numerous. However, this is an infant technology and a conservative industry; we are just in the beginning. Having known the potential of blockchain, this section and Fig. 7.4 give a short and few use cases of blockchain and its implementation in medical science. There can be more than these use cases discussed in this section, but it is just to give readers a fragrance and importance of adopting new emerging technology within the changing healthcare institutions at a greater pace.

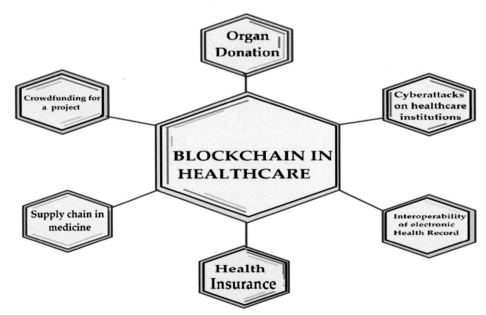

FIGURE 7.4 Use cases of blockchain in healthcare.

3.1 Cyberattacks on healthcare institutions

The international criminal police organization, also known as Interpol, issued a purple notice (a notice giving information about the methods used by criminals) to 194 nations warning the hospitals about cyberattacks during the COVID-19 pandemic (Vijay Kumar, 2020). Cybercriminals are using ransomware to digitally make hostage and lock systems to prevent access to anything from the system. They lock the system and data by using malware and in return demand ransom to unlock the system. WannaCry ransomware attack of May 2017 resulted in over 200,000 victims and more than 300,000 computers infected (Liptak, 2017). The US Department of Health gives us a report of cyberattacks in various years that affected millions of people (U.S. Department of Health, 2017). It is rightly said that nothing is safe when it is online, and the viruses and malware along with technical challenges affect productivity. It is high time to prefer security as a most pressing matter. Most of the digital systems and healthcare organizations in this world use the traditional server/client paradigm. The data storage and security systems are highly centralized in hospitals, which means there is a single point of failure. The distributed denial of service attacks on healthcare institutions are also a great distress. The triumph of these attacks lies in the fact that the point of failure is single (Akpan, 2016). Even if the decentralized distributed network is used in the client-server architecture, there remains the problem of consensus and synchronization among networks. To overcome these issues, blockchain comes to the rescue with its decentralized, distributed, shared ledger technology.

The blockchain has the strength to possess unique ways out in dealing with security threats. For example, a blockchain network assign unique hashes to downloads and updates, so this lets the users compare the hash value on the to-be downloaded data with the developer's hash value and remarkably reduces the chances of infecting their systems with any fraudulent activity or malware. The security feature delivered by the blockchain is because of the components in its functioning like secure hashing, append-only linked list data structure, and consensus mechanism.

Suppose a malicious attacker tries to attack the centralized server of hospitals. It will be easy for him to attack it, but if there is a decentralized structure, an attacker cannot harm it. If in case the system is intruded and locked, there are multiple copies of data present with each authorized node in the network. The hospitals can use private and permissioned blockchain architecture to overcome the fear of cyberattacks in the form of ransomware or distributed denial of service. If a malicious user enters the network and tries to modify the content, it is impossible in blockchain, as he will have to change all the blocks coming after it, which will be a nightmare for any attacker. Another way remaining for a malicious user to attack the network is by owning 51% of the blockchain network resource, which is also an impossible task to achieve (Joshi et al., 2018).

The sequential hashing and cryptography along with the decentralized structure of blockchain prevent any authorized user to alter or modify data on the ledger. This immutability feature of blockchain replaces the use of public key infrastructure and shift toward keyless signature infrastructure, where the challenges of basing the security on the secret keys and letting a group of people manage the same have dropped down in probability. Thus the hospitals and healthcare institutions along with many startups are shifting toward decentralized storage of data and use blockchain as its backbone.

3.2 Supply chain in medicine

Drug counterfeiting is an urgent global problem with significant risk to common people. According to a world health organization report, in 2009, a 5-month operation by Interpol across china and its south Asian neighbors seized 20 million pills that were adultrated and fake (Bulletin of the World Health Organisation, 2010). According to WHO, 10% of drugs worldwide are counterfeit, and it is 30% in developing countries. More than 50% of cases of online purchased medicine are counterfeit (Bulletin of the World Health Organisation, 2010). These are the statistics from a decade ago issued as articles in the news. These counterfeit medicines have their effect not only on so-called lifestyle products like muscle building supplements but also on the treatment of cancer and heart disease, painkillers, antibiotics, and other drugs. Sometimes, these drugs contain correct ingredients but are produced in an impure manner, making the dose too high or too low, which is an extremely dangerous case for human beings.

Supply chain management (SCM) is how goods are managed and processed from raw material to the finished good, which is from point of origin to point of consumption. It is delineated in such a way that it incorporates industry best practices for management of the entire delivery process. SCM is a thought-provoking prospect in the healthcare industry, with disconnected arrangement settings of medical supplies, drugs, and critical medical resources. There are many uninvited risks associated with the supply chain process that directly or indirectly have an impact on patient safety (Kim and Kim, 2019). The challenges in medical supply are several.

- tracking them down
- verifying drug authenticity and condition as well as the reputation of the supplier
- moving quickly where the medicines are needed
- keeping production rate up with or ahead of the demand

The supply chain thus needed must be transparent and driven by cooperation and collaboration, not simply competition. Because of these shortcomings, it is an ideal blockchain use case. Blockchain preserves an individual's privacy, the integrity of data, protects intellectual property rights, and provides flexibility in the medical supply chain. It diminishes the time and cost of numerous stakeholders involved in the traditional supply chain. The key features of blockchain that are used for keeping alive trust among various parties in the supply chain are as follows:

(a) immutability
(b) transparency
(c) smart contracts

A paper (Sylim et al., 2018) describes the developed pharmacy surveillance blockchain system and its functionality in the simulated test network. A distributed application running smart contracts on the Ethereum platform and Hyperledger Fabric platform is developed using delegated proof-of-stake or PBFT consensus algorithm for scalability. Transparency and accountability are seen throughout the supply chain process.

Fig. 7.5 depicts the operational working of the blockchain network in the supply chain. First, the pharmaceutical companies' research and development teams or clinical labs report the new medicine details on the shared ledger, which becomes the first block of the chain network. In the second step, the manufacturer updates the block after manufacturing. Third, the warehouse inventory and transportation team validate the update and further update the block after they execute work. Fourth the hospitals and retailers selling the drug verify the chain and update it on sale. Finally, the end client can verify the whole chain and make sure that medicine is genuine. Thus, everything is transparent, and because the blocks are immutable, there is trust among various entities in the supply chain.

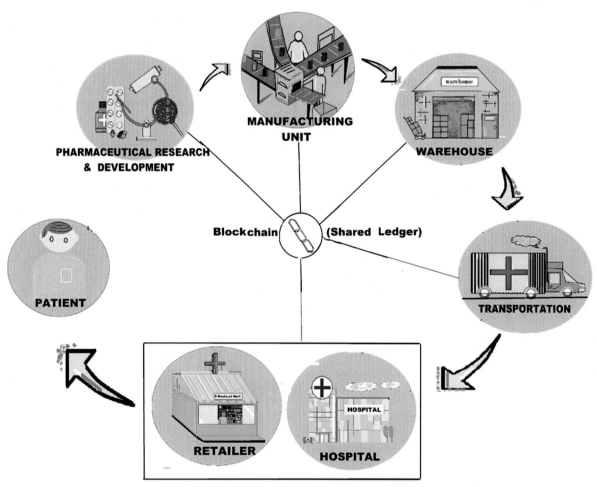

FIGURE 7.5 Supply chain in healthcare using blockchain technology.

3.3 Interoperability of the electronic health record

The interoperability of electronic health records in healthcare is described as the ability to exchange data and communicate among modern heterogeneous information technology systems and software applications, such as the EHR system, and across organizational boundaries to improve diagnostic accuracy. The process of obtaining and sharing hardcopy medical records is ineffective because of the following (Zhang et al., 2018):

- It is slow in delivery and access by patients as multiple copies are maintained.
- It is insecure because there are chances of copies to be stolen during physical transmission.
- It is incomplete since there is no single source that stores all medical data of any particular individual.
- It lacks context as most healthcare systems are not patient-centric, so they have no control over their data.

The security, privacy, and lack of trust between stakeholders technology-related issues, such as scalability, incentives, and governance are existing concerns. Other reasons for ineffective interoperability are (A) information blocking and (B) trouble in patient identification. Information blocking is the unreasonable constraint imposed on an individual's medical data to be accessed anywhere with anyone on patient consent. Shaun Grannis, Director of Center for Biomedical Informatics, pointed out the importance of a correct match of an individual's health data with that individual and the extent to which today's system is faulty in achieving this (Siwicki, 2017).

These obstacles can be resolved by increasing transparency, accountability, collaboration, and security (Mettler, 2016). Hence, blockchain comes up with a very effective use case in the interoperability of electronic health records. The distributed shared ledger used for recording data provides transparency and collaboration. Security and accountability are achieved by the immutability feature of blockchain. Programmable smart contracts can then guarantee patients (A) control of their medical data, (B) a known origin of the aggregated data source, and (C) getting informed when anyone accesses their data. Kaur et al. (2018) proposes the development of a blockchain-based platform for storing and managing electronic medical records in a cloud environment. The transaction request sent to blockchain nodes gets verified over the cloud, and a new block is then appended for the transaction to complete. Gordan describes how blockchain helps in the management of digital access rules, data availability, rapid access to clinical information, and patient identity (Gordon and Catalini, 2018). Various promising projects working in this sector of healthcare are introduced in Section 4. The public or private blockchain can be preferred on the usage basis. The amount of data produced can be kept on-chain or off-chain depending on the situation in which it is used. For example, during genome sequencing where the data of individuals are huge, to store on-chain then off-chain is a better choice. Blockchain limitations around these are covered in Section 6.

Ancile is a blockchain framework for safe, interoperable, and secure access to electronic health records by providers, patients, and other participants while taking care of preserving the privacy of sensitive information of patients. It uses programmable smart contracts in the Ethereum blockchain platform to increase access control and security of data. Cryptographic techniques are used along with the smart contract to address the longstanding security and privacy drawback in healthcare institutions while interacting with different needs of patients, providers, and others.

3.4 Organ donation

Organ donation is the procedure of extracting an organ from an organ donor (living or deceased) and then surgically replacing that organ in a recipient. According to the United Network for Organ Sharing, a nongovernment organization, every 10 min registration is done on the national transplant waiting list. Approx 20 individuals lose their lives each day waiting a long time for a transplant of organs. A single organ donor can save eight people's lives approximately. Due to the high importance in the supply and demand of transplantable organs, the transparency and efficiency of the organ donation system is a priority. The effective and fair working of the system used is directly correlated and linked with the patient's medical information as well as the organ allocation process (US Government Information on Organ Donation and Transplantation).

The life of a few organs outside the body is given in this list (US Government Information on Organ Donation and Transplantation):

(a) heart: 4−6 h
(b) lungs: 4−6 h
(c) liver: 8−12 h
(d) pancreas: 12−18 h
(e) kidney: 24−36 h
(f) intestine: 8−16 h

By looking at these statistics, an individual can get the importance of time wasted in modern healthcare systems that are not up to date, in tune, compatible, and the time it takes, makes the auditing process difficult. Problems faced by organ donation systems around the globe are more or less the same that there are more people on the waiting list than actual donors, and this gap is increasing every year. Modern systems handling the organ donation process face various issues:

(a) There is a lack of transparency.
(b) They are usually slow in a life-threatening matter.
(c) They are rarely up to date in terms of security, processing power, and algorithms.
(d) They use traditional databases and do not have a uniform system for communicating data with hospitals, the health ministry, or other parties involved.

The blockchain technology can thus help to address and overcome these issues easily. It can improve the process (A) by providing a reliable and easy way to check the compatibility among organ donor and its recipient, (B) an expedited way to match availability with demand, and (C) secure tools for storing personal choices like willingness to donate, together with medical health information useful in the most serious situations, where time is a critical factor. It also improves transparency and traceability of the whole donation process, thus helping in the fight against organ trafficking.

GBA partner DHONOR blockchain, a nonprofit organization, is working on projects for organ and blood donation and supporting millions of patients in need of organs (De Malde, 2018). The transplantChain, a decentralized application built on the Ethereum platform, is a medical SCM tool that fixes donor matching issues to make the process fast and more efficient (transplantChain). A decentralized application using blockchain technology is proposed and developed for organ donation (Dajim et al., 2019).

3.5 Crowdfunding in healthcare

Crowdfunding is an open invitation on the internet for the provision of monetary and financial resources in the form of (A) donation, (B) a future reward, product, or some service, or (C) exchange for organization shares or debt securities (Vismara, 2018; Wallmeroth et al., 2018). Thus, crowdfunding is classified into three categories: (A) donation based, (B) reward based, and (C) investment based (Ahlers et al., 2015). Donation-based crowdfunding is generally used for personal treatment or charity projects. In reward-based crowdfunding, donors receive a product or service in return for their contributions. Investment-based crowdfunding in healthcare is used by companies for the development of new technology like the diagnostic test for uncommon pathologies. The donors contribute relatively small sums of money to raise a much larger goal amount. Bassani et al. (2019) have examined the worldwide healthcare crowdfunding platforms to offer global and cross-platform evidence where healthcare crowdfunding platforms emerge. The coverage and reach of healthcare crowdfunding in public sector health systems is poor and fund amount collected is also minimal. Up to October 2017, 76 medical crowdfunding platforms operated worldwide to raise over $132 million in 13,633 health projects. The United States of America is a country with the highest number of successfully funded healthcare projects. Crowdfunding becomes essential for countries where public healthcare is dominated by a private player.

According to a recent report, the funding done by pharmaceutical companies on COVID-19 is far much more than the total fund given in tuberculosis. This difference clearly shows how companies fund only those ideas that give them profit. Thus medical crowdfunding is a recent and fast-developing phenomenon that has attracted global public interest. The issues with crowdfunding in today's scenario are (i) high transaction fee, (ii) restrictions faced by intergovernmental bodies at the global level of crowdfunding, (iii) involvement of middlemen, and (iv) enforcement of the funding terms.

The transparency and cyberattacks on these fundraising platforms are also a great concern. Blockchain technology with all its potential advantages can best overcome these issues in healthcare. The programmable smart contract used by blockchain platforms helps to enforce the funding terms. The need for people living in remote areas can be met to overcome government restriction with the help of cryptocurrency and crypto tokens. Many people globally do not have a bank account, especially in some of the African countries, so they can benefit from crypto tokens and cryptocurrency on decentralized applications. The decentralized distributed shared ledger and smart contract remove middlemen and reduce the transaction fees. The commission or percentage share is taken by middlemen to reduce the holy cause of saving a patient's life. The immutability feature provides transparency and security for the receiver, donor, and other parties involved.

3.6 Health insurance

Health insurance offers individual financial coverage for medical expenses during a medical emergency. A health insurance policy is defined as a bond signed between the policyholder and insurance underwriter in which the insurance company bears the cost spent by the insured during a medical emergency. A health policy provides the cash reimbursement facility or cashless treatment as mentioned in the contract. Healthcare insurers have very complex billing requirements and often contradict or delay claimed medical financial expenses. Moreover, many healthcare providers experience significant cash flow issues with insurance claim denials that seem arbitrary. Each insurance company has different reimbursement amounts and procedures, so the complexity of accepting patients from all major insurers is irresistible.

There is an issue of trust missing in the way the insurance industry operates. But, what if an individual could securely process claims in seconds instead of weeks or months?

Deloitte's Center for Health Solutions and Center for Financial Services aims to decrease costs, improve operational effectiveness, and strengthen relationships with the insured. DokChain is a blockchain solution offered by PokitDok that works in the health insurance field. The characteristics of blockchain that makes it useful to meet the needs of health insurance in healthcare are consistent accessibility, strong data integrity, no central point of control, and network-wide public accountability. Here are some examples of how blockchain is helpful:

(a) facilitating a dynamic insurer and client relationship: because of the EHR stored on a blockchain and the smart contract
(b) moving toward interoperable, comprehensive electronic health records
(c) effectively detecting fraud involved in insurance: because of the immutability feature of blockchain and smart contracts
(d) improving provider directory accuracy: because of the decentralized consensus protocol used
(e) simplifying the application operation by making it more client-centric
(f) supporting administrative and strategic imperatives with smart contracts
(g) reducing regulatory and compliance costs

4. Some popular blockchain platforms that can be used in healthcare

Many blockchain platforms are being developed by different companies either starting from scratch or using the existing platform and making advancement in it. Some of the popular and trending blockchain platforms and how they are impacting the healthcare organizations are discussed in this section.

4.1 Ethereum

In November 2013, Vitalik Buterin proposed a white paper intending to have a scripting blockchain technology for generalized use cases. This later became an open source project to make a public blockchain distributed platform and operating system having smart contract functionality. It overcame the existing limitation in the first blockchain-based application, Bitcoin. It is a platform to develop decentralized applications on top of blockchain technology by just writing a smart contract. Ethereum does this by building what is essentially the ultimate abstract foundational layer, a blockchain with a built-in Turing-complete programming language (White Paper).

The smart contract written in Ethereum is done presently using solidity and Vyper programming language. The code written in these high-level languages is converted to the low-level, stack-based bytecode language, also known as Ethereum Virtual Machine code. or EVM code. Ethereum Virtual Machine is a 256-bit register stack machine that provides a runtime environment for smart contracts in Ethereum. It is designed to run the bytecode exactly as intended. Galvin Wood, cofounder of Ethereum, describes Ethereum and EVM working in more detail (Wood, 2014). EVM has been implemented in OOP (object-oriented programming) languages such as C++, C#, Go known as Geth, Haskell, Java, Python, JavaScript, and Erlang. The transaction happening in Ethereum among users charges some transaction fee amount in the form of 'gas' units. The Ethereum platform is the foundation for a new era of the internet (Ethereum):

(a) an internet where money and payments are built in
(b) an internet where users can own their data and your apps do not spy nor steal from you
(c) an internet where everyone has access to an open financial system
(d) an internet built on neutral, open-access infrastructure, controlled by no company or person

The present consensus mechanism followed for mining is proof-of-work, which becomes a problem when we talk of scalability. Ethereum is currently fixing the issue to make it easily scalable, and this is known as Serenity or Ethereum 2.0 and is expected to launch by July 2020 (Baker, 2020). Ethereum 2.0 will be using a proof-of-stake consensus algorithm instead of proof-of-work, but this will take time to be implemented. Many healthcare projects are using and going for Ethereum because of its large number of nodes using the network. In the following years, there can be growth in its utilization because of new updates coming. Time will only reveal the reality of usage in the coming years.

4.2 Quorum

Quorum is an open source Ethereum-based distributed ledger protocol that was developed by J.P. Morgan company to provide various industries and organizations with a private or with permission implementation of Ethereum that supports transaction and contract privacy. It includes the most essential elements forked off the Go Ethereum client, also called Geth. Hence, it supports both public contracts as well as private contracts. In other words, the Quorum platform is not a decentralized network but is a distributed shared digital ledger, as the node operators in the network are all known parties and do not use proof-of-work or proof-of-stake consensus algorithms (Morgan, 2016).

In Quorum, the Transaction Manager and Enclave are included along with the Go Ethereum node to provide the functionality of privacy. The Transaction Manager is responsible for private transactions, and Enclave supports it by providing encryption and decryption facilities. The working can be further explored in the Quorum docs (Go Quorum Docs). The consensus algorithms used are generally Raft BFT and Istanbul BFT instead of proof-of-work or proof-of-stake.

The main features of Quorum that make it more useable over public Ethereum are listed:

(a) transaction and contract privacy that helps in peer-to-peer encrypted message transfer
(b) multiple voting-based consensus mechanisms for on-demand creation of blocks
(c) network/peer permissions management, so only known parties can join the network
(d) higher performance than Ethereum, as the transaction fees are eliminated

The decentralization feature of blockchain is traded for the scalability in Quorum. The limitation of Quorum is that private contracts in Quorum result in lower throughput at higher load on the system due to extra overhead involved in secure communication and encryption/decryption operations employed between peers for confidentiality (Baliga et al., 2018). Many health insurance companies and supply chain managers in the medical industry are working on Quorum to build decentralized applications using this platform. This platform attracts many users and developers of the most widely accepted Ethereum network, as a transition from one to another is relatively easy.

4.3 Corda

R3, an enterprise blockchain company, was founded by David E Rutter to build the Corda blockchain platform, on top of which distributed apps can be built known as CorDapps. Currently, more than 200 firms are working on top of Corda across various domains like insurance, finance, healthcare, digital assets, and so on (Clark, 2018). Corda is an open source blockchain project providing a platform to build blockchain applications that transact directly among nodes in strict privacy. At present, Corda supports two Java Virtual Machine (JVM) languages: Java and Kotlin. Smart contracts are often written in one of the programming languages mentioned.

The communication in Corda network among the nodes is one to one, and the network needs permission, i.e., taking permission, from the network operator to join the network. The shared ledger concept is different for Corda: it is of different size and contains information that a party is a part of, or else the transaction or block for which a party is not involved is ignored in the shared ledger. This feature makes it attractive and straightforward to take care. The consensus achieved is done by validating with each user signature or by the notary node. This is a unique node having the authority to prevent double spending in the network. The State and Flow are two crucial setups that are coded in Java or Kotlin along with smart contracts to develop a CorDapp. The State represents on-ledger facts and Flow automates the process of agreeing to ledger updates (Corda docs).

The main advantages of Corda are that it is highly scalable, highly interoperable, provides confidentiality, and handles disintermediation (every participant can verify every transaction themselves) quite well. The limitation, however, is that it is not a full blockchain technology; rather, it can be said to be a distributed ledger technology (Greenspan, 2018). The concept of notary node/s which is/are an important feature of CorDapps, if owned by a particular organization, can defeat the very purpose of trust if they behave maliciously in the network. Corda recently has been working on many proof-of-concept ideas in the healthcare sector, one of which is sharing efficient and secure healthcare data (Maurya, 2019). The features provided by CorDapps make it a popular choice to be used for the healthcare domain. The impact of the platform can be seen in the upcoming years.

4.4 Hyperledger Fabric

Hyperledger is an open source blockchain and related tools project started by Linux Foundation in December 2015, later joined by big companies like IBM and Intel. Hyperledger Fabric is one of the most active, popular, and widely used Hyperledger projects. The various Hyperledger projects are (A) Hyperledger Besu, (B) Hyperledger Burrow, (C) Hyperledger Caliper, (D) Hyperledger Cello, (E) Hyperledger Explorer, (F) Hyperledger Indy, (G) Hyperledger Iroha, (H) Hyperledger Sawtooth, and (I) Hyperledger Composer. Each has its specific feature that they deal with. For further query and exploration of each, refer to www.hyperledger.org/use/tutorials.

The Fabric platform is permissioned, highly modular, and has configurable architecture, making it a very popular choice for healthcare, supply chain, and insurance domains. The smart contract, also called chaincode, is written here in a general purpose programming language like Go, Node.js, or Java. The workflow followed for a transaction is execute−order−validate (Androulaki et al., 2018). The features provided are resiliency, flexibility, scalability, performance, and confidentiality. But, it has the limitation that it has a very complex architecture setup for a node. It has a smaller number of APIs and SDKs, and it is not network fault tolerant. However, due to the features provided, it is used in the healthcare industry to develop applications on top of blockchain technology. KitChain works on the pharmaceutical clinical supply chain, MyClinic.com works to schedule appointments, review medical reports, and request further investigations or assistance, and Verified.Me is a digital identity network; these are some of the use cases implemented in Hyperledger Fabric (Five Healthcare, 2020).

Some of the other blockchain platforms worth mentioning are Ripple, EOS, Multichain, and TRON (Table 7.2).

5. Popular projects or startups in healthcare using blockchain

The improvements and research ongoing in emerging blockchain technology have created and opened doors to new investors in this technology. Many companies and startup projects are being funded and are working on exploring various possibilities of this new technology. According to a study, there has been an increase in the use of blockchain technology in the healthcare domain from 2015 to 2019 (Holbl et al., 2018). Let us discuss some of the popular projects or startup companies working in healthcare using blockchain to address different problems.

  i. *MedRec* is an MIT Digital Currency Initiative that utilizes blockchain technology for handling medical records, providing auditability, interoperability, and accessibility. The whole project is developed on top of the Ethereum platform, which acts as a framework and can be used as a platform for further development (Azaria et al., 2016).
  ii. *BlocHIE* is a blockchain-based platform for healthcare information exchange, supported by Huawei Technologies Co., Ltd. The two categories of data, electronic medical records and personal healthcare data, are handled on two loosely coupled blockchains (Jiang et al., 2018).
  iii. *Guardtime* is a data security startup based out of Estonia working on blockchain healthcare. It works on data visibility and liquidity management, supply chain accountability and visibility, and clinical trial data management. It provides multiple APIs that can be used to develop a decentralized application using it (Guardtime Health, 2019).
  iv. *Kidner* is a blockchain-based kidney donation system that proposes a Kidney Paired Donation module instead of using the usual kidney waiting list. It is working in France and is developed on top of the Ethereum platform, and the next version will be developed on the Hyperledger Fabric platform (Zouarhi, 2017).
  v. *Doc.AI* is a company based in Palo Alto, California, started in 2016, that works for the combination of precision medicine, AI, and blockchain. It uses blockchain technology to help medical facilities gain insight from medical data and research. It allows for the creation of predictive medical models (Disruptordaily, 2018).
  vi. *Patientory:* The company founded in 2015 is based in the United States. It aids in securing and obtaining patient medical data for healthcare providers and patients. Users can trace and track their health profile through a mobile application. Medical billings, doctor visits, insurance, and vaccinations are some of the things that are also trackable (Forging The Path).
  vii. *Cyph MD* is an Australia-based startup working on blockchain technology to make advancements in healthcare. It uses the Ethereum platform to execute the smart contract to handle the creation of secured digital identities. It works on building a digital identity for secure communication among healthcare providers (Brennan, 2017).
  viii. *Dentacoin:* The startup working through the ERC20 token of the Ethereum platform was founded in 2017. It aims at creating a dental industry community by rewarding users, who provide valuable contributions, with cryptocurrency. It works on improving the quality of dental care worldwide, reducing treatment costs, and creating a dental community (Dentacoin, 2018) (Table 7.1).

TABLE 7.1 Summary of blockchain in the healthcare domain.

Blockchain use case in healthcare	Type of blockchain suitable	Summary
Cyberattacks on healthcare institutions	Private blockchain	Decentralization and distributed shared ledger property of blockchain prevent cyberattacks on healthcare institutions
Supply chain in medicine	Hybrid blockchain	Transparency, immutability, and easy traceability provided by blockchain prevents drug counterfeiting
Interoperability of electronic health record	Private blockchain	Immutability, security, transparency, decentralized, and tamperproof shared ledger in blockchain helps in the interoperability of data
Organ donation	Hybrid blockchain	Traceability and transparency build trust in blockchain for organ donation
Crowdfunding in healthcare	Public blockchain	Immutability, transparency, anonymity, and decentralization of the blockchain network excluding middlemen make crowdfunding in healthcare more effective
Health insurance	Hybrid blockchain	Decentralized, distributed, immutable ledger provides transparency and trust among health insurance institutions to use blockchain, benefiting both customers and institutions

TABLE 7.2 Comparison among various popular blockchain platforms.

Blockchain platforms	Owned by	Domain	Ledger type (permissioned/permissionless)	Open source	Smart contract
Ethereum	Community	Cross-industry	Both	Yes	Yes
Quorum	J P Morgan	Cross-industry	Permissioned	Yes	Yes
Corda	R3 Consortium	Finance	Permissioned	Yes	Yes
Hyperledger Fabric	Linux Foundation	Cross-industry	Permissioned	Yes	Yes
Ripple	Ripple Labs	Finance	Permissioned	-	No
EOS	Block.one	Cross-industry	Permissioned	Yes	Yes

    ix. *Blockpharma:* The company is based in France and, founded in 2016, works mainly with blockchain and machine learning technology. It uses a mobile app to detect counterfeit drugs. It uses blockchain technology for anticounterfeiting and traceability of drugs, thus alerting parties involved in the supply chain (Blockpharma).

    x. *Medicalchain:* It is a UK-based company using blockchain technology in the healthcare domain. It securely records the health data of the user on the blockchain that can be shared when required with hospitals, medical labs, pharmaceutical companies, and doctors. It works on improving user experience along with tackling current issues in healthcare. Hyperledger Fabric is used for developing the application, and Ethereum is used for developing MedToken (Medicalchain).

    xi. *Cronicled:* It works on blockchain technology and IoT (internet of things) to improve the supply chain in the healthcare domain. It enhances the accountability and speed of healthcare logistics and decreases data discrepancies (Chronicled).

    xii. *Nebula Genomics:* This is a human genome sequencing and health big data company founded in 2016 that is using blockchain technology to ensure that users have control of their data and are compensated for its usage. The user can either choose to keep it private or they can get rewarded for securely and anonymously sharing their data with medical researchers (Nebula).

6. SWOT analysis of blockchain technology in healthcare

After getting an idea of blockchain technology use cases and projects in healthcare, let us analyze to identify the strength, weaknesses, opportunities, and threats of it in healthcare. This will help one to know and obtain a broad overview of the technology's impact on medical science and healthcare. Strength and weakness are judged on internal parameters and environment, whereas opportunities and threats are judged on the external environment and parameters.

    Strengths:

- smart contract automation, where the smart contract provides trust among parties
- tamper-proof information sharing among nodes
- speedy access to data
- immutability, where once a transaction is recorded in a block, it cannot be changed
- eliminates middlemen and reduces the chance of fraud
- nonrepudiation
- decentralized and stable

    Weaknesses:

- energy consumption is high for the platforms following proof-of-work consensus algorithms like Bitcoin and Ethereum
- immaturity of blockchain technology
- potential healthcare client lacks clear and coherent vision for blockchain
- potentially in conflict with existing digital healthcare infrastructure
- 51% attack logic for proof-of-work where an attacker owns 51% of computing resources
- users access data through a private key, which is unique, and if it is lost, then the data it accesses becomes irretrievable

    Opportunities:

- transparency since the exchange happening in the network is transparent and avoids the double spending problem
- reduced time to process and audit any activity
- secure in terms of malicious attacks
- cost-efficient
- users get more control of data

    Threats:

- Standardization challenges: there is no universally defined guideline or organization keeping an eye on blockchain usage and misuse; government involvement is also minimal as one can see cryptocurrency is illegal in many countries.
- Social acceptance: the society and audience are not fully aware of the technology and are thus not interested in it.
- Managing storage capacity: the data stored on-chain is increasing at a very fast rate to store, but alternatives are being worked on.
- Scalability: there is always a trade-off between the decentralization of the network and the scalability of the network. If the network is fully decentralized, then it is difficult to scale it up.
- The privacy of an individual loophole exists.

In the current digital transformation in healthcare, a lot is moving toward the better. If handled and approached correctly, blockchain could lead on to real, actionable improvements in digital healthcare. Having known the benefits and opportunities of the technology in healthcare, one cannot blindly place confidence in it. The appliance of this hyped technology to healthcare is in its infancy, and there are several challenges for adaption within the health sector, such as regulatory challenges, conservative attitudes, and to some extent a broken health information system, lack of common definitions, and high stakes.

7. Conclusion, discussion, and future works

In this chapter, we explored the potential and features of blockchain technology and how it can be used in solving the issues that exist in modern digital healthcare. The problem of interoperability, cyberattacks, SCM in pharmaceutical industries, crowdfunding limitations, organ donation transparency, and health insurance trust are explained and a possible use case of blockchain is suggested. Various projects and startups along with popular blockchain platforms are discussed and a SWOT analysis of the blockchain in digital healthcare is done. Most of the issues of modern healthcare are tackled in the chapter in light of blockchain technology, further opening the doors for future research opportunities. It was observed that the healthcare ecosystem can be made more secure and effective by blockchain, but there remain the complexities and limitations of blockchain. This technology is immature and is still evolving as the limitations are tackled and improved further. The study conducted shows the increase in the use of blockchain in healthcare starting from the year 2015 to 2019 (Holbl et al., 2018). The current trend of application of blockchain use in healthcare is generally in the field of data sharing, health records, access control, medical billing, or anti-counterfeiting drugs (Holbl et al., 2018). Most research presents a novel framework, architecture, or model using blockchain technology in healthcare. Particularly, smart contracts could be more used as they enable the automation of processes within a blockchain platform (Holbl et al., 2018). The more implementation using a popular platform like Ethereum and Hyperledger Fabric will further boost the interest of people to work on this technology. It is easy to implement blockchain technology in a healthcare system where the institution is not very developed and digital. But for the institutions already having a digital infrastructure, it is very difficult to change everything with blockchain technology at once. When it comes to users, they do not care for the background system or implementation; they care more about the outcome or result they get to make their work easy. So social awareness and acceptance are important for the blockchain to bring a revolution. Moreover, governments and regulatory bodies must look after this emerging technology and support it to nurture and grow.

The healthcare industry is changing and moving toward healthcare 4.0, which will be a healthcare system that gently transforms into a virtual reality environment, and health services will be using AI services. Blockchain has a significant role to play here to increase trust and transparency in this updated healthcare system. Trust comes in various forms like trust in the treatment that one receives, even if it is from an AI healthcare worker, trust in health data management, and trust in health research. The reader can take up a proof-of-concept idea to make a Dapp or propose a solution on blockchain to check whether the license of a doctor is real or fake in this virtual interacting world. This can be taken as an exercise and along with this, one can try to approach some of the open questions and solve them. The scalability, speed in transaction processing, or mining block along with the storage capacity issue arising in blockchain can be worked on.

References

Ahlers, G.K.C., Cumming, D., Günther, C., Schweizer, D., 2015. Signaling in equity crowdfunding. Enterpren. Theor. Pract. 39, 955–980.

Akpan, N., March 23, 2016. Has health care hacking become an epidemic? PBS News Hour. http://www.pbs.org/newshour/updates/has-health-care-hacking-become-an-epidemic.

Androulaki, E., Manevich, Y., Muralidharan, S., Murthy, C., Nguyen, B., Sethi, M., Laventman, G., 2018. Hyperledger fabric: a distributed operating system for permissioned blockchains. In: Proceedings of the Thirteenth EuroSys Conference on - EuroSys'18.

Azaria, A., Ekblaw, A., Vieira, T., Lippman, A., August 2016. Medrec: using blockchain for medical data access and permission management. In: 2016 2nd International Conference On Open and Big Data (OBD). IEEE, pp. 25–30.

Baker, P., May 11, 2020. Vitalik Buterin Says Much Delayed Ethereum 2-0 Still on Track for July Launch. Coindesk. https://www.coindesk.com/vitalik-buterin-says-much-delayed-ethereum-2-0-still-on-track-for-july-launch.

Baliga, A., Subhod, I., Kamat, P., Chatterjee, S., 2018. Performance Evaluation of the Quorum Blockchain Platform. arXiv preprint arXiv:1809.03421. https://arxiv.org/abs/1809.03421. (Accessed 25 May 2020).

Blockpharma, n.d. https://www.blockpharma.com/. Accessed 25 May 2020.

Bassani, G., Marinelli, N., Vismara, S., 2019. Crowdfunding in healthcare. J. Technol. Tran. 44, 1290–1310. Springer. https://doi.org/10.1007/s10961-018-9663-7.

Brennan, B., January 23, 2017. Cyph MD puts healthcare information on the blockchain. Blockchain Healthc. Rev. https://blockchainhealthcarereview.com/cyph-md-puts-healthcare-information-on-the-blockchain/.

Bulletin of the World Health Organisation, April 2010. Growing Threat From Counterfeit Medicines, 88, pp. 241–320, 4. https://www.who.int/bulletin/volumes/88/4/10-020410/en/.

Chronicled, n.d. https://www.chronicled.com/. Accessed 25 May 2020.

Corda docs, n.d. https://docs.corda.net/docs/corda-os/4.4.html. Accessed 25 May 2020.

Clark, J., March 29, 2018. Blockchain initiative of the year 2018: the nominees. Dow Jones Financ. News. https://www.fnlondon.com/articles/blockchain-initiative-of-the-year-2018-the-nominees-20180325.

Dajim, L.A., Al-Farras, S.A., Al-Shahrani, B.S., Al-Zuraib, A.A., Merlin Mathew, R., 2019. Organ donation decentralized application using blockchain technology. In: 2019 2nd International Conference on Computer Applications & Information Security (ICCAIS), Riyadh, Saudi Arabia, pp. 1—4.

De Malde, M., October 28, 2018. GBA Healthcare Working Group Launches Blockchain Project (Organ & Blood Donation Blockchain). GBA. https://www.gbaglobal.org/gba-healthcare-working-group-launches-blockchain-project-organ-blood-donation-blockchain/.

Dentacoin: The Blockchain Solution for the Global Dental Industry Whitepaper v.2.2, November 28, 2018. https://dentacoin.com/assets/uploads/whitepaper.pdf. (Accessed 25 May 2020).

Doc.ai: Leveraging AI and Blockchain to Break Down Data Silos in Healthcare, February 27, 2018. Expert Insight Disruptordaily. https://www.disruptordaily.com/disruption-blockchain-part-47-walter-de-brouwer-doc-ai/.

Ethereum, n.d. http://ethereum.org.

Five Healthcare Projects Powered by Hyperledger You May Not Know About, January 29, 2020. Hyperledger Blog. https://www.hyperledger.org/blog/2020/01/29/five-healthcare-projects-powered-by-hyperledger-you-may-not-know-about. (Accessed 25 May 2020).

Forging The Path To Consumer Directed Health Through Blockchain Technology A Case Study. n.d. https://patientory.com/. Accessed 25 May 2020.

Go Quorum Docs, n.d. http://docs.goquorum.com/en/latest/Privacy/Lifecycle-of-a-private-transaction/. Accessed 25 May 2020.

Gordon, W.J., Catalini, C., 2018. Blockchain technology for healthcare: facilitating the transition to patient-driven interoperability. Comput. Struct. Biotechnol. J. 16, 224—230.

Guardtime Health Whitepaper, April 2019. https://m.guardtime.com/files/Guardtime_whitepaper_A4_april_web.pdf. (Accessed 25 May 2020).

Greenspan, G., May 8, 2018. R3 Corda: Deep Dive and Technical Review. Private blockchains. https://www.multichain.com/blog/2018/05/r3-corda-deep-dive-and-technical-review.

Holbl, M., Kompara, M., Kamisalic, A., Zlatolas, L.N., 2018. A systematic review of the use of blockchain in healthcare. Symmetry 10 (10), 470. https://doi.org/10.3390/sym10100470.

Jiang, S., Cao, J., Wu, H., Yang, Y., Ma, M., He, J., June 2018. Blochie: a blockchain-based platform for healthcare information exchange. In: 2018 IEEE International Conference on Smart Computing (Smartcomp). IEEE, pp. 49—56.

Joshi, A.P., Han, M., Wang, Y., May 2018. A survey on security and privacy issues of blockchain technology. Math. Found. Comput. 1 (2), 121—147.

Kaur, H., Alam, M.A., Jameel, R., Mourya, A.K., Chang, V., 2018. A proposed solution and future direction for blockchain-based heterogeneous medicare data in cloud environment. J. Med. Syst. 42 (8). Article 156. Springer.

Khan, S., June 18, 2017. The Health 4.0 Revolution. ETHealthWorld, 59187378. https://health.economictimes.indiatimes.com/news/health-it/the-health-4-0-revolution/59187378. (Accessed 25 May 2020).

Kim, C., Kim, H.J., 2019. A study on healthcare supply chain management efficiency: using bootstrap data envelopment analysis. Health Care Manag. Sci. 22, 1—15.

Liptak, A., May 14, 2017. The WannaCry Ransomware Attack Has Spread to 150 Countries. Verge. https://www.theverge.com/2017/5/14/15637888/authorities-wannacry-ransomware-attack-spread-150-countries.

Maurya, D., December 20, 2019. Secure and Efficient Healthcare Data Sharing (POC) Using Corda Blockchain. OodlesBlockchain. https://blockchain.oodles.io/blog/healthcare-data-sharing-poc-corda-blockchain/.

Medicalchain, n.d. Whitepaper. https://medicalchain.com/Medicalchain-Whitepaper-EN.pdf. Accessed 25 May 2020.

Mettler, M., September 2016. Blockchain technology in healthcare: the revolution starts here. In: 2016 IEEE 18th International Conference on e-Health Networking, Applications and Services (Healthcom). IEEE, pp. 1—3.

Morgan, J.P., 2016. Quorum Whitepaper. https://github.com/jpmorganchase/quorum-docs. (Accessed 25 May 2020).

Nakamoto, S., 2012. Bitcoin: a Peer-to-Peer Electronic Cash System, 1. Consulted. http://nakamotoinstitute.org/bitcoin/.

Nebula, n.d. https://nebula.org/whole-genome-sequencing/. Accessed 25 May 2020.

Siwicki, B., November 16, 2017. CHIME Drops National Patient ID Challenge. Healthcare. https://www.healthcareitnews.com/news/chime-drops-national-patient-id-challenge.

Sylim, P., Liu, F., Marcelo, A., Fontelo, P., 2018. Blockchain technology for detecting falsified and substandard drugs in distribution: pharmaceutical supply chain intervention. JMIR Res. Protoc. 7, e10163.

TransplantChain, n.d. https://github.com/talha-atta/transplantChain.

U.S. Department of Health, 2017. Breaches Affecting 500 or More Individuals. https://ocrportal.hhs.gov/ocr/breach/breach_report.jsf.

U.S. Government Information on Organ Donation and Transplantation, n.d. Matching Donors and Recipients. https://www.organdonor.gov/about/process/matching.html.

Unibright.io, December 7, 2017. Blockchain Evolution: From 1.0 to 4.0. Medium. https://medium.com/@UnibrightIO/blockchain-evolution-from-1-0-to-4-0-3fbdbccfc666. (Accessed 25 May 2020).

Vijay Kumar, S., April 08, 2020. Interpol Warns of Cyberattacks on Hospitals. Hindu.

Vismara, S., 2018. Signaling to overcome inefficiencies in crowdfunding markets. In: Cumming, D., Hornuf, L. (Eds.), The Economics of Crowdfunding. Palgrave Macmillan, Cham.

Wallmeroth, J., Wirtz, P., Groh, A.P., 2018. Venture Capital, Angel Financing, and Crowdfunding of Entrepreneurial Ventures: a Literature Review, 14. Foundations and Trends in Entrepreneurship, pp. 1—129.

White Paper Ethereum/wiki Wiki GitHub, n.d. https://github.com/ethereum/wiki/wiki/White-Paper.

Wood, G., 2014. Ethereum: a Secure Decentralised Generalised Transaction Ledger. Byzantium Version. Ethereum project yellow paper. https://ethereum.github.io/yellowpaper/paper.pdf.

Zhang, P., Schmidt, D.C., White, J., Lenz, G., 2018. Blockchain technology use cases in healthcare. In: Advances in Computers, vol. 111. Elsevier, pp. 1—41.

Zheng, Z., Xie, S., Dai, H.-N., Wang, H., 2018. Blockchain challenges and opportunities: a survey. Int. J. Web Grid Serv. 14 (4), 352—375. https://doi.org/10.1504/IJWGS.2018.095647.

Zouarhi, S., 2017. Kidner-A worldwide decentralised matching system for kidney transplants. J. Int. Soc. Telemed. & eHealth 5, 1—4.

Chapter 8

Integrity promised: leveraging blockchain technology for medical image sharing

S. Sridevi, S. Vishnuvardhan*, B. Vinoth Kumar, G.R. Karpagam and P. Sivakumar

PSG College of Technology, Coimbatore, Tamil Nadu, India

Corresponding author: E-mail: greenmatrix22@gmail.com

Chapter outline

1. Introduction

The emergence along with the success of blockchain technology over various fields for its realm of distributed, decentralized data sharing by preserving security, transparency, and privacy plays a vital role in storing and sharing medical images. Blockchain technology has the potential for storing medical images and making them available when needed for medical professionals. Medical imaging is a technique and procedure of generating visual exemplification of internal parts of the body for medical assessment, and clinical healthcare organizations have started to incorporate blockchain technology for medical image management, information management, and patient identity (Computerworld). By 2025, 55% of medical and healthcare applications will be incorporating blockchain technology for commercial purposes. BIS Research says the estimation of incorporating blockchain in healthcare will jump to $5.61 billion from the present $170 million (Research and Markets). The objective of this paper is to explore the contemporary research trends in the usage of blockchain technology for medical image sharing.

Medical imaging involves different imaging techniques and processes for observing the human body for diagnosis, therapeutic purposes, and pharmacologic intervention, so it plays a significant role in efforts to improve public health for all ethnic community groups (World Health Organization; Wani and Raza, 2018; Vinoth Kumar et al., 2019; Kumar et al., 2020). Many researchers have concentrated in applying artificial intelligence techniques for medical image analysis (Vinoth Kumar et al., 2017, 2018; Raza and Singh, 2021). While interpreting the body's clinical images, a physician may evaluate diseases such as pneumonia, diabetes, internal bleeding, brain injury, etc. (Hosny et al.). Henceforth, a clinical medical image affords essential information about the human's health and body condition. Over the past three decades, a revolution has happened in the healthcare industry precipitated by medical images. They have modernized the diagnosis, treatment, and interpretation of the medical condition of body parts. Hence, they provide a great prospect for physicians and medical professionals to guard the patient from life-threatening diseases. Medical imaging is consistently ranked as one of the leading research advances in modern medical history (meaning throughout the past 100 decades), so both patients and healthcare professionals have already

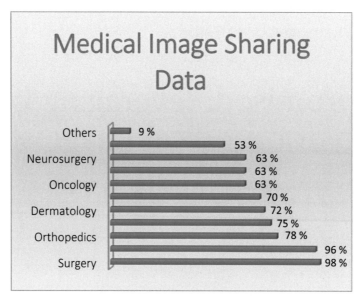

FIGURE 8.1 Medical image sharing statistics.

witnessed and recognized the phenomenal advantages of life-saving medical image analysis. The most common types of medical visual representations (medical imaging) are as follows (Ausmed):

- X-rays
- ultrasound
- computed tomography scan (CT)
- magnetic resonance angiography
- magnetic resonance imaging (MRI)
- positron emission tomography
    - **Care facilities:** Medical image exchange is used by hospitals to enable transfers between other facilities that may or may not be on the same network. The reports can be submitted immediately to referring physicians in the area as well as to patients directly.
    - **Physicians:** Instead of waiting for physical media to arrive, physicians use the software to have immediate access to photos. A doctor may need a patient's medical history stored in different hospitals to choose the best body-based treatment. Physicians may need the patient's history of records for detailed analysis.
    - **Patients:** Patients may undergo their imaging tests remotely without having to carry and store physical media. There is also decreased radiation exposure for patients. Patients have remote access to information and professional advice (Sandberg et al.).

Statistics of various types of medical images, which are used in the medical industry, are shown in Fig. 8.1. During surgery, the patient's entire medical history is shared for examining the condition. Generally, 98% of medical images are shared for the period of surgery. In radiology, patients may go through high radiation if medical images are taken frequently. To reduce this effect, radioactive medical images are shared among physicians or medical scientists for analysis. At present, 96% of medical radiology images are from dermatology, and 70% of gynecology, 78% of orthopedics, 75% of trauma, and 72% of images are shared. Usually, 63% of medical images are shared in oncology, cardiology, and neurosurgery, 53% of medical images are shared in neurology, and 9% of other medical images are shared via cloud (Reactiondata.com; Advaiya).

1.1 Blockchain: a decentralized technology

Don and Alex Tapscott, authors of the "Blockchain Revolution" (2016), said that blockchain is an incorruptible digital ledger that can be applied to anything that has a value (Alyson).

A blockchain is a digital database that records all transactions that are being processed. In other words, it is a distributed ledger and will have a copy of the ledger for each block in the network. Using cryptographic principles, all

TABLE 8.1 Real-time implementation of blockchain in healthcare.

MedRec 2.0 Ethereum blockchain is developed for enhanced access to a medical record by the joined contribution of Robert Wood Johnson Foundation and MIT Media Lab. Currently, MedRec 2.0 is being tested and hosted at Israel Deaconess Medical Hub. The code is open source.

MTBC, which includes medical images, intends to enhance the traditional electronic health record system (EHR) by changing the application program interface (API). Blockchain is entrenched on API, which puts medical records in control of the patients. Using MTBC a patient can transfer his/her reports from one doctor to another. Currently, the hyperledger blockchain platform is available. MTBC project can be accessed via MTBC's website.

FarmaTrust was developed by ICO, which intends to end counterfeit drugs. It monitors manufacturer and regulatory compliance aids that have been following government guidelines. Inventory is traced easily via blockchain. Using supply chain visibility management, anyone can easily track if any alteration has been made on the product.

Coral's health discovery and research blockchain technology accelerates patient care, self-governing administrative processes, and integrates smart contracts among patients and doctors to ensure accurate lab data and treatments.

Digital Treasury Corporation and Taipei Medical University. The aim of PhrOS is to increase transparency among patient records by placing various medical centers' patient records on a blockchain. The project is already completed and can be accessed via the phrOS website.

blocks in the blockchain are bound to each other. In the medical industry, privacy and trust are the key factors for success. Many industries are currently using the cloud for sharing medical images due to economic reasons and simplicity. Even though the users are making use of current encryption formats to secure their data, they are always hesitant to store their data in the cloud (Xue and Xin, 2016). Since it is sensitive data, many risks are involved in tampering with the images. This is why the concept of using blockchain is used for transferring the images in a more secure manner (SemanticMD). A consortium blockchain includes shared cryptographic features, which allows for greater control of a centralized source from a few different nodes. The consortium blockchain will be useful for implementing medical image sharing.

The advantages of blockchain that are useful for medical image sharing are as follows:

- Transparency: The success of implementing blockchain for storing medical images is due to the transparency of the system. It also maintains traceability of stored data, documents, records, and works.
- Proof of tampering: As it is difficult to achieve tampering of data in a blockchain, it promotes the user's trust about integrity preservation of storing medical images.
- Cooperation: The introduction of blockchain for medical imaging will increase collaboration with many organizations since blockchain can be trusted.
- Decentralized administration: The implementation of medical image sharing using blockchain will give us a decentralized administration, which is far efficient than centralized administration.

The real-time applications of the blockchain in the healthcare sector are listed in Table 8.1.

The rest of the paper is organized as follows. Section 2 briefly discuss about literature survey, while Section 3 explains the proposed system architecture. Section 4 exemplifies the overall working of proposed system with the help of a use case. Implementation is elucidated in Section 5, and the recent trends are expounded in Section 6, which is followed by conclusion in Section 7 and references in Section 8.

2. Literature survey

For the last 20 years, the process of recording and exchanging patient health records has been changed considerably due to the requirement of effective care and diagnosis, stringent professional requirements, and boom of new technology to enhance the sharing of medical images. Medical images are usually exchanged as mail or hardcopies between hospitals, so patients and physicians know about the diagnosis, but the enactment of this technology may result in harm or interception of medical images (Erickson, 2011).

To address these limitations, a cloud-based system was developed to store, record, and exchange medical images through various healthcare organizations, typically as a layout called Digital Imaging and Medicine Communications (DICOM) (DICOM; Asan et al., 2018).

The Radiological Society of North America entrenched the e-transmission of medical images based on the image-sharing network (ISN) (Langer et al., 2014). The ISN network practices a cloud-based centralized medical image storage that allows a patient to access their own medical images using their own passwords. Here, doctors use edge servers to view unencrypted images of the patient and conclude with each local radiology site about the diagnosis. The edge server uses a significant technology called the Picture Archiving and Communication System (PACS) (Choplin et al., 1992) to provide easy access and cost-effective storage of medical images such as CT scanning, ultrasound, MRI, X-ray, etc. But, the current practice of medical image sharing depends on network centralization and third-party intermediaries, which paves the way to theft of images for profit and reduces patient privacy.

Research performed by leading cyber security firm McAfee found that poor security in sharing medical images can impel cybercrime revelation of medical data (Prince and Links). The researchers estimated that more than 1100 PACSs (cloud sharing network) access the medical images without any security or VPNs. After this investigation, it was found that cloud server vulnerabilities and default architecture raise questions about third-party involvement and a centralized network. Regarding this, a number of researchers have recently concentrated on creating a platform incorporating a cloud service and a blockchain to exchange medical records. A breadcrumb method, MedBlock, for searching medical records was proposed (Beek, 2018). Breadcrumbs were intended to record block addresses containing data relating to the patient. Unfortunately, due to a rise in fragmented data, these approaches are not relevant to the method of searching the data over the blockchain. Then, a hybrid cloud-based image sharing solution, MedShare, was proposed that follows a centralized cloud server provider (Fan et al., 2018).

A two decentralized architecture named MedChain is proposed to replace the drawback of cloud-based MedShare medical image sharing (Xia et al., 2017). Here, a digest-chain structure and session-based data sharing scheme are implemented using mutable P2P storage combined with an immutable blockchain, which enhances the secure transfer of medical data (Shen et al., 2019). However, owing to the mutable P2P storage architecture, there are possibilities of manipulating the stored patient health records, prompting high risk to medical data. However, no attempt had been proposed to address the privacy concerns to facilitate the sharing of medical images through a blockchain.

Since the medical images are of high quality, they consume a lot of storage. If we store the images directly in the blockchain, the size of each block will increase, and it will be tedious to maintain the blockchain. Economically, centralized solutions are better, but if we combine both the advantages of centralized and decentralized solutions, it will do wonders. Hence, the images are stored in a secure cloud environment along with the calculated hash value of the image, which improves the latency of the images. The third-party cloud can be trusted since they provide us with their agreement on our data. For example, Amazon AWS provides agreements as mentioned in the reference (Amazon).

3. Proposed architecture

To increase the security in sharing the medical images, a detailed architecture is proposed in Fig. 8.2. The medical images cannot be stored in the blockchain directly since the storage in the blockchain is limited. Since cloud storage provides large storage, we can combine the benefits of both cloud and blockchain. On the other hand, storing medical images directly in the cloud is also not secure. For solving this problem, a technique of hashing the images using hashing functions is given subsequently.

A hashing function is one that represents the given image as a string of binary values. The hash value generated is unique for each image. The value generated will be different even if there is a small change in the image. There are different hash functions used for image hashing. The first is average hash. The average hash algorithm converts and scales the image into a gray scale. Then, the average of grayscale values is taken from grayscale image, and the image pixels are tested from left to right one by one. If the grayscale value is larger than the average value, a "1" will be added to the hash, or else a "0" will be added. The second type is block hash. Here an image will be divided into many blocks, and the value will be generated for each block that is either 0 or 1. In the end, these values are combined. The division of an image into N blocks depends upon the N bit hash that we require. Third is difference hash. This hash function is similar to the average hash function. The difference hash algorithm also generates a grayscale image of the given image and then is scaled to a different size. Here, the first N pixels are examined from left to right for each row and compared to their neighbor on the right. Fourth is median hash. This is more similar to the average hash algorithm; the only difference is that the gray values are taken instead of the average gray values.

The fifth type, wavelet hash, is similar to the average hash function. It generates gray values of the image, and then the two-dimensional wavelet transform is applied over the image. Next, the perceptual hash algorithm is followed to generate the hash, and the sixth type, perceptual hash function. The perceptual hash transforms the image given into a grayscale image and then scales it down. Then, the discrete cosine transformation is applied to the scaled-down image.

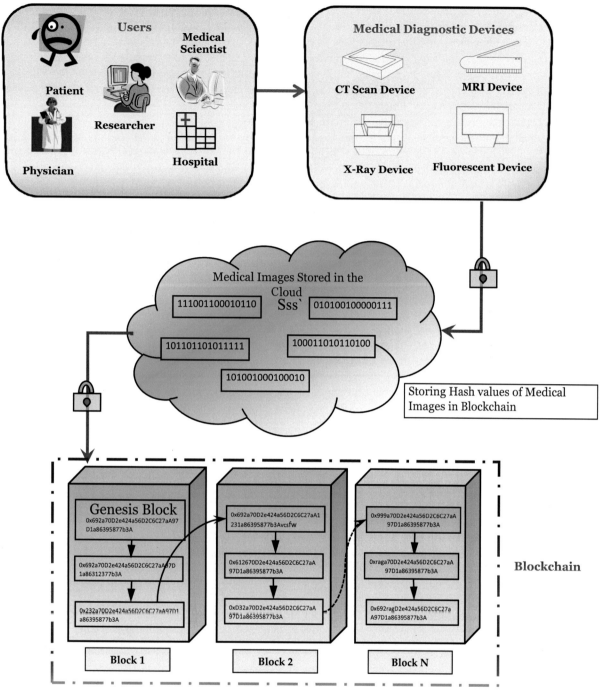

FIGURE 8.2 Overall architecture diagram.

The formula is applied first per row, then per column. The discrete transformation of cosine is given by

$$\text{Xk} = \sum_{n=0}^{N-1} 2n^* \cos\left(\pi^* k^* \frac{2n+1}{2N}\right) \quad \forall k \in [0, N]$$

This will move the pixels with high frequencies to the top left corner and that part is cropped. Then the median hash algorithm is applied to the resultant image (Content Blockchain).

Comparing with other hash functions, the perceptual hash function should preserve the invariant of the image even for lossy transformation and perpetuate content preservation. It also tolerates the differences in the quality and format of the encoded image and retains the actual image if decoded (Monga and Evans). The medical images are obtained from the medical devices that are then uploaded in the cloud environment. A perceptual hash is generated for the image uploaded, and it can be stored in the blockchain. If the image has been tampered with, the hash that is generated after the change will not match with the hash that is present in the block. Hence, the medical image cannot be tampered with, thereby increasing the security of the cloud platform.

Fig. 8.2 explains the flow of the system at different stages. The users take the medical image of the patients using any of the medical diagnostic devices. Once the images are taken, they are uploaded to the cloud along with the image hash values. Consequently, the hash value of the image is computed locally and uploaded to the cloud. This hash value is also stored in the blockchain. Since the blockchain data are not able to tamper with this methodology, the hash value is securely stored. If any hacker tries to modify the image in the cloud, the hash that will be computed after the hacking will not be the same as that of the value stored in the blockchain. From this, we can find that the image has been tampered with.

4. Use case

A complete use case is depicted in Fig. 8.3. Let us consider a scenario in which the medical image needs to be shared between different healthcare organizations to examine it.

The medical image of the patient is generated using the medical instruments available. Once the images are created, a hash value for the image is calculated using the perceptual hash technique.

The image is stored in the cloud along with the hash value, and the hash value is alone stored in the Ethereum blockchain network. To store the data in the Ethereum blockchain network, we use smart contracts. Smart contracts are deployed in the blockchain network to store the hash values generated for the medical images. Since the blockchain is a tamper-proof system, the generated hash value stored in it cannot be tampered with. In a worst-case scenario, if the cloud servers are hacked and the medical images in the cloud have been tampered with, the hash value of the image will also be changed. This can be verified by calculating the hash value again for the image that is stored in the cloud and comparing it with the value stored in the blockchain. In this way, both the merits of cloud and blockchain are utilized for storing and sharing the medical images.

5. Implementation

The aforementioned technique is implemented as a blockchain application using Ethereum blockchain, React JS, and Truffle framework.

The doctors can register themselves in the application to securely store the medical records of the patients, as shown in Fig. 8.4.

The doctors can upload the details about the patients along with the EHR (electronic health record). The medical images are stored securely using blockchain and cloud servers, as shown in Fig. 8.5.

Once the details are stored in the application, they can be sent to other doctors who are available when needed, as shown in Fig. 8.6. Since the transaction is done using blockchain, the data cannot be tampered with. This application enables doctors to share medical images with minimal effort.

6. Recent trends

Many healthcare organizations are struggling to share medical images using the conventional method of sharing the hard copies of the images. Even though many cloud solutions exist, they are not completely secure. Recently, a solution was proposed using the only blockchain with Hyperledger (Seo and Cho, 2020). Applications of medical images in a blockchain are also explored (McBee and Wilcox, 2020).

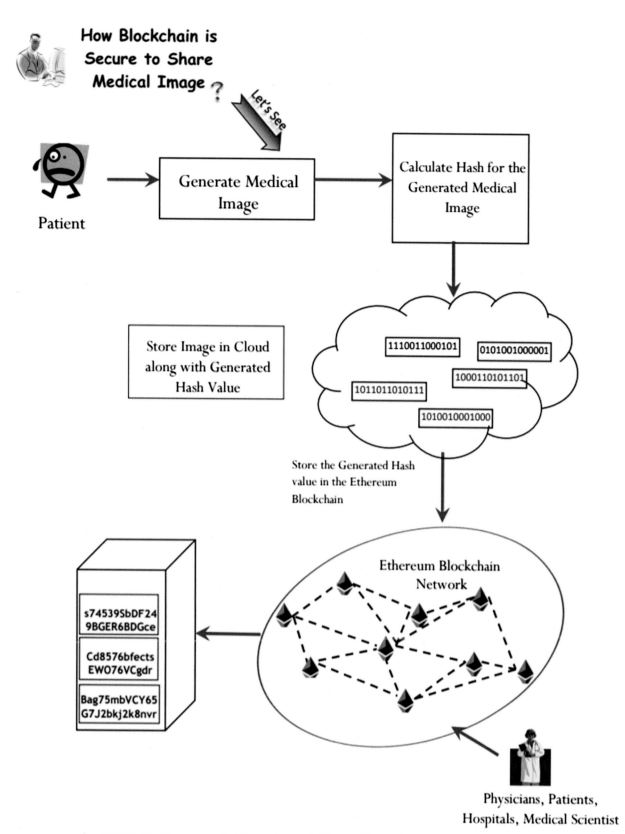

FIGURE 8.3 Use case: medical image sharing via Ethereum blockchain network that ensures integrity.

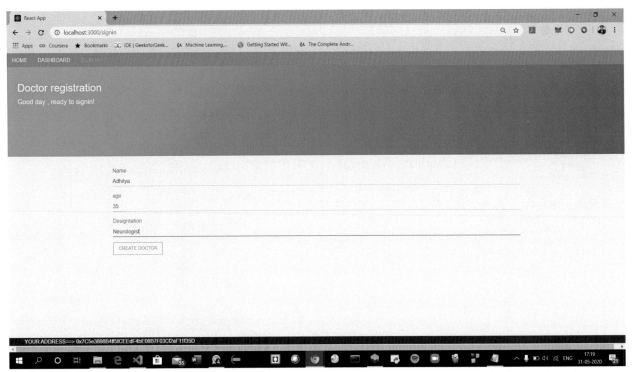

FIGURE 8.4 Doctor registration.

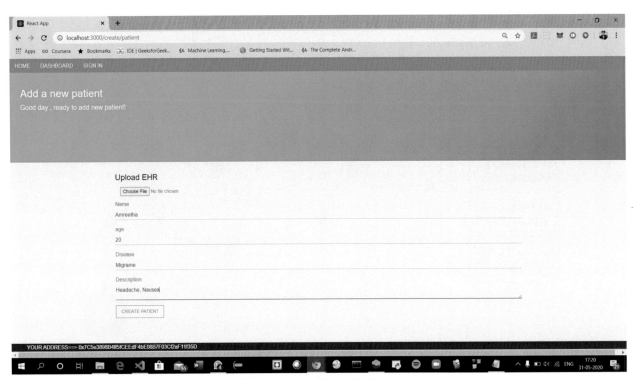

FIGURE 8.5 Uploading medical images.

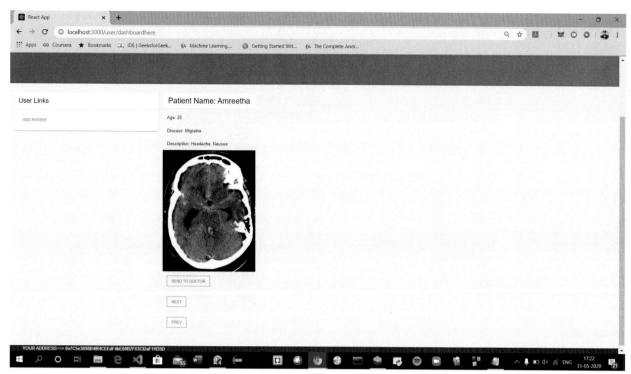

FIGURE 8.6 Sharing medical images.

7. Conclusion

Cutting-edge, secure sharing of medical images over the cloud is multifarious due to a lack of integrity. Medical images may undergo vulnerability or data modification due to malicious attackers inside a cloud, lack discernibility, and lack strong protection on access control, leading to security breaches. Taking these breaches into consideration, one potential solution is blockchain technology. The impending of blockchain for secure medical sharing hinges on the acceptance of the new technology within the medical image sharing industry to create technical infrastructure. Though incorporating medical image sharing in a cloud with blockchain has certain concerns and speculations for cultural adoption, the blockchain has the capability to prove its uniqueness, vital role, and is necessary to achieve integrity. In the future, the research can be done to prevent malicious attacks happening in the cloud, the lack of storage protection, and the security breaches.

References

Advaiya. Healthcare Analytics. https://www.advaiya.com/services/business-analytics/healthcare-analytics/.

Alyson. What is Blockchain Technology? https://support.blockchain.com/hc/en-us/articles/211160223-What-is-blockchain-technology-#:~:targetText=The%20term%20%22blockchain%20technology%22%20typically,and%20proof%20of%20work%20methods.

"Amazon", AWS Customer Agreement. https://aws.amazon.com/agreement/.

Asan, O., Crotty, B., Nagavally, S., Egede, L.E., 2018. Patient centered communication and E-health information exchange patterns: findings from a national cross-sectional survey. IEEE J. Transl. Eng. Heal. Med. 7, 2168–2372.

Ausmed. Medical Imaging Types and Modalities. https://www.ausmed.co.uk/cpd/articles/medical-imaging-types-and-modalities.

Beek, C., 2018. McAfee Researchers Find Poor Security Exposes Medical Data to Cybercriminals [Online]. Available from:https://securingtomorrow.mcafee.com/other-blogs/mcafee-labs/mcafee-researchers-find-poor-security-exposes-medical-data-to-cybercriminals/. (Accessed 9 May 2019).

By Lucas Mearian, By 2020, 1-in-5 Healthcare Orgs Will Adopt Blockchain; Here's Why. https://www.computerworld .com/article/3294996/by-2020-1-in-5-healthcare-orgs-will-adopt-blockchain-heres-why.html.

Choplin, R.H., Boehme, J.M., Maynard, C.D., 1992. Picture archiving and communication systems: an overview. Radiographics 12 (1), 127–129.

Content Blockchain. Testing Different Image Hash Functions. %https://content-blockchain.org/research/testing -different-image-hash-functions/.

DICOM. [Online]. Available from: http://en.wikipedia.org/wiki/DICOM. (Accessed 5 June 2019).

Erickson, B., 2011. Experience with importation of electronic images into the medical record from physical media. J. Digit. Imaging 24 (4), 694–699.

Fan, K., Wang, S., Ren, Y., Li, H., Yang, Y., 2018. Systems-Level Quality Improvement MedBlock: Efficient and Secure Medical Data Sharing Via Blockchain, pp. 1−11.

Hosny, A., Parmar, C., Quackenbush, J., Schwartz, L.H., Aerts, H.J. W. L. Artificial Intelligence in Radiology. https://www.ncbi.nlm.nih.gov/pmc/articles/PMC6268174/.

Kumar, B.V., Jeneesha, P., Nivethitha, M., January 8−10, 2020. A differential evolution approach for segmentation of white blood cells in acute lymphoblastic leukemia images. In: 4th International Conference on Inventive Systems and Control. Coimbatore, India.

Langer, S.G., et al., 2014. The RSNA image sharing network. J. Digit. Imaging 28 (1), 53−61.

McBee, M.P., Wilcox, C., 2020. Blockchain technology: principles and applications in medical imaging. J. Digit. Imaging. https://doi.org/10.1007/s10278-019-00310-3.

Monga, V., Evans, B.L. Perceptual Image Hashing Via Feature Points: Performance Evaluation and Trade-Offs. IEEE Explore Digital Library. https://ieeexplore.ieee.org/document/1709989.

Prince, J., Links, J. Medical imaging signals and system. Pearson Education, 2006.7. Alyson. What is Blockchain Technology?, https://support.blockchain.com/hc/en-us/articles/211160223 -What-is-blockchain-technology-#:∼: targetText=The%20 term%20%22blockchain%20technology%22%20typically,and%20proof%20of%20work%20methods.

Reactiondata.com. Medical Image-Sharing Quick Report. https://www.nuance.com/content/dam/nuance/en_us/collateral/healtsihcare/report/rpt-medical-image-sharing-quick-report-en-us.pdf.

Research and Markets. Global Blockchain in Healthcare Market: Focus on Industry Analysis and Opportunity Matrix - Analysis and Forecast, 2018−2025. https://www.research and markets.com/reports/4519297/global-blockchain-in-healthcare-market-focus-on.

Raza, K., Singh, N.K., 2021. A tour of unsupervised deep learning for medical image analysis. Curr. Med. Imaging. https://doi.org/10.2174/1573405617666210127154257.

Sandberg, J.C., Ge, Y., Nguyen, H.T., Arcury, T.A., Johnson, A.J., Hwang, W., Gage, H.D., Reynolds, T., Carr, J.J. Insight into the Sharing of Medical Images, Physician, Other Health Care Providers, and Staff Experience in a Variety of Medical Settings. https://www.ncbi.nlm.nih.gov/pmc/articles/PMC3613038/.

SemanticMD. A Blockchain for Medical Imaging. https://medium.com/@ semanticmd/a-blockchain-for-medical-imaging-b0bacb356374.

Seo, J., Cho, Y., 2020. Medical image sharing system using hyperledger fabric blockchain. In: 2020 22nd International Conference on Advanced Communication Technology (ICACT), Phoenix Park, PyeongChang, Korea (South), pp. 62−64. https://doi.org/10.23919/ICACT48636.2020.9061384.

Shen, B., Guo, J., Yang, Y., 2019. MedChain: efficient healthcare data sharing via blockchain. Appl. Sci. 9 (6), 1207.

Vinoth Kumar, B., Karpagam, G.R., Zhao, Y., 2019. "Evolutionary algorithm with memetic search capability for optic disc localization in retinal fundus images" intelligent data analysis for biomedical applications: challenges and solutions. In: Intelligent Data-Centric Systems. Elsevier, pp. 191−207.

Vinoth Kumar, B., Sabareeswaran, S., Madumitha, G., August 3−5, 2018. A decennary survey on artificial intelligence methods for image segmentation. In: International Conference on Advanced Engineering Optimization through Intelligent Techniques, SardarVallabhbhai National Institute of Technology, Surat, Gujarat, India. Springer. Available from:

Vinoth Kumar, B., Janani, K., Priya, N.M., January 19−20, 2017. A survey on automatic detection of hard exudates in diabetic retinopathy. In: IEEE International Conference on Inventive Systems and Control, JCT College of Engineering and Technology, Coimbatore, Tamil Nadu,.

Wani, N., Raza, K., 2018. Multiple kernel learning approach for medical image analysis. In: Dey, N., Ashour, A., Shi, F., Balas, E. (Eds.), Soft Computing Based Medical Image Analysis. Elsevier, pp. 31−47.

World Health Organization. Diagnostic Imaging. https://www.who.int/diagnostic_ imaging/en/RadiologyInfo. org for Patients. Professions in Diagnostic Radiology. https://www.radiologyinfo.org/en/info.cfm?pg=professions-diagnostic-radiology.

Xia, Q., Sifah, E.B., Asamoah, K.O., Gao, J., Du, X., Guizani, M., 2017. MeDShare: trust-less medical data sharing among cloud service providers via blockchain. IEEE Access 5, 14757−14767.

Xue, C.T.S., Xin, F.T.W., December 2016. Benefits and challenges of the adoptheion of cloud computing in business. Int. J. Cloud Comput. Services Architect. 6 (6).

Chapter 9

From molecules to patients: the clinical applications of biological databases and electronic health records

Ayyagari Ramlal[1,a,*], Shaban Ahmad[2], Laxman Kumar[3], Fatima Nazish Khan[2,b] and Rubina Chongtham[4,*]

[1]Department of Botany, University of Delhi, New Delhi, Delhi, India; [2]Department of Computer Science, Jamia Millia Islamia, New Delhi, Delhi, India; [3]Department of Botany, Jamia Hamdard, New Delhi, Delhi, India; [4]Department of Botany, Deshbandhu College, University of Delhi, New Delhi, Delhi, India

*Corresponding authors: E-mail: ramlal.ayyagari@gmail.com, chrubina1@yahoo.co.in

Chapter outline

a Division of Genetics, ICAR — Indian Agricultural Research Institute (IARI), Pusa, New Delhi, Delhi, India.

b Division of Genomic Resources, ICAR — National Bureau of Plant Genetic Resources (NBPGR), Pusa, New Delhi, Delhi, India.

Translational Bioinformatics in Healthcare and Medicine. https://doi.org/10.1016/B978-0-323-89824-9.00009-4

1. Introduction

The chapter deals with important biological databases and electronic health records. First, it describes nature, types, and roles of both databases and electronic health records (EHRs). Then, it focuses on the role of biological databases in transitional bioinformatics. At last, it deals with the challenges in the usage of databases and EHRs.

"Biological informatics" or "bioinformatics" is the use of computer-assisted algorithms and analytical tools to extract and elucidate the biological data (Pevsner, 2009). According to the National Institutes of Health (NIH), this branch is defined as "research, development or application of computational tools and approaches for expanding the use of biological, medical, behavioral or health data, including those acquire, store, organize, analyze, visualize such data" (Pevsner, 2009). In the past few years, many organisms have been used in studying various processes, which include structural analyses like morphology and anatomy, biochemical and molecular, evolutionary, and inheritance-based studies, all of which have resulted in the accumulation of huge biological data (Committee to Update Science, Medicine, Animals & National Research Council, 2004). There are three main public databases that store huge amounts of information about protein and nucleotide sequences and provide easy access to them, namely, National Center of Biotechnology Information (NCBI) of the NIH in Bethesda, USA, European Molecular Biology Laboratory (EMBL) at the European Institute of Bioinformatics (EBI) in Hinxton, and the DNA Database of Japan (DDBJ) at the National Institute of Genetics in Mishima. These three databases share their sequences regularly and are part of the International Nucleotide Sequence Database Collaboration (INSDC) (Pevsner, 2009). Apart from these databases, there are many other databases like genetic disorders and diseases, bibliographic, metabolic pathways, and biomolecular structure databases along with the Search Tool for the Retrieval of Interacting Genes/Proteins database and plant peptide database (Pevsner, 2009; Das et al., 2020; Kaul et al., 2019). Model organisms are being used for experimental purposes to study various diseases (Committee to Update Science, Medicine, Animals & National Research Council, 2004). To understand the molecular and linkage maps, for genome sequencing as well as functional genomics and transcriptomic analyses, researchers have worked on many model organisms, which include *Drosophila*, *Caenorhabditis elegans*, mice, yeast, and plants like *Arabidopsis*, *Medicago*, *Oryza sativa*, etc. Thus, the obtained data is deposited in the form of either molecular coordinates or sequences in various formats, which enables the researchers easy extraction and retrieval (like sequencing file formats for DNA and protein, molecular file formats for coordinates for molecules, and three-dimensional (3D) structural formats representing macromolecular structures) in databases referred to as "biological databases" (Pevsner, 2009). The collection of data stored in the databases is structured, searchable, and they are cross-referenced and updated regularly. The amount of biological information (data) has increased due to the development of powerful technologies and is rapidly increasing as the outcome of new and automated sequencing techniques, which has resulted in important findings, including next-generation sequencing (NGS) techniques like PacBio, Illumina, and Nanopore (Pevsner, 2009; Raza and Ahmad, 2019). As a result, biological sciences have become extremely data rich.

The main functions of biological databases include (a) providing platforms for cross-referencing between experiments and inferences made from the results and data generated from different laboratories, thereby providing us with the scope of standardization and validation of the obtained results with those existing data/results. This will help avoid duplication of experiments, thus saving time and resources, (b) making data storage and access possible from anywhere with cross-checking, and (c) making data available in a readable manner, providing a medium for user-friendly analysis.

The major timeline in the development of biological databases is as follows:

1. The first protein to be sequenced and made available in the year 1956 was insulin. As soon as insulin was sequenced, it caused a necessity to be put in the database. Following this, in the year 1965, *Atlas of Protein Sequences and Structures* by Margaret et al. became the first published book with all the structures of the proteins available then. Later on, its revised editions came in the 1970s.
2. In 1972, the Protein Data Bank consisted of only 10 entries of 3D protein structures and increased to 43,755 entries until May 2007, and as of now, it has more than 150,000 structures (https://www.rcsb.org/pages/about-us/history).
3. In 1986, Swiss-Prot was developed, which contains 2,69,293 protein sequences (till May 2007) to 550,000 (to date) from 10,917 model organisms (https://www.sib.swiss/pages/10290-history-of-swiss-prot).

The major characteristic features of biological databases are as follows:

(a) Data heterogeneity: There are many types of data that are stored in databases. For instance, they contain sequence-based information, DNA and RNA of many organisms (humans, mouse, etc.), also store high-dimensional data, including data generated using microarray experiments, etc. They also have graphic information (regulatory networks, genetic maps) and shapes (docking sites of molecules, etc.).

(b) High volume: Biological databases contain a huge amount of data.

(c) Data sharing: Data stored in these can be used by any scientific community from any place (laboratory or workstation).

(d) Dynamic: Data stored is subject to change with the arrival of new information.

(e) Large-scale data integration: Data shared and collected from across the world contain different multitudes like structural or sequence-based information, etc.

The EHRs are contemporaneous, patient-centered digital documentation that contains information about the health and medical condition of a patient starting from their history to present condition. It will provide the caregivers and doctors with an insight to proceed with the treatment. The EHRs contain data of patients that include their medical history, diagnoses, treatments, information about allergies, and medical record (X-rays, dates of immunization, test results). It also contains retrospective as well as prospective particulars about the patients, helping in providing continuous medical treatment (HEALTHIT, n.d.; Häyrinen et al., 2008). Per the International Organization of Standardization, an EHR is defined as "a repository of patient data in digital form, stored and exchanged securely, and accessible by multiple authorized users" (Häyrinen et al., 2008).

2. Biological databases

The field of biology is advancing toward a new era in which all the technologies and techniques are either automated or computer-based from a simple BLAST to NGS, which include single-molecule real-time, PacBio, nanopore, and also microarray (Robbins, 1994; Raza and Ahmad, 2019; Raza, 2016). The volume of data is increasing daily with the advancement in technology, so the number of DNA sequences is rising (Rehm, 2001). Depending upon their role and type of data, biological databases can be classified into different types, including sequence (NCBI, DDBJ, EMBL) (Pevsner, 2009; NCBI Resource Coordinators, 2013), structural (Protein Data Bank (PDB), nucleic acid database (NDB)) (Pevsner, 2009; Bank, 1971), metabolic pathways databases (KEGG, MetaCyc) (Pevsner, 2009; Kanehisa and Goto, 2000), literature databases (PubMed, Scopus) (NCBI Resource Coordinators, 2013; Burnham, 2006), disease databases (Online Mendelian Inheritance in Man (OMIM), Online Mendelian Inheritance in Animals (OMIA), Genecard, Pathcard) (Lenffer et al., 2006), and many more.

2.1 Electronic health records

The concept of EHRs came into existence in the 1990s. It defines a comprehensive, repeated observation of the same variables ranging from short to long period (commonly called longitudinal collection) and inter- and intrainstitutional record of patients (Hoerbst and Ammenwerth, 2010). The patient is solely responsible for the addition, access, and managing of the health-related data in the EHRs. The roles of EHRs and the data that it stores are also diverse. The aim of using EHRs is to frame objectives and plan strategies for taking care of the patient, determining the tests, and analyzing results (Häyrinen et al., 2008). The database also contains information about the different requirements of the patient as assessed by different caregivers during their treatments. Another important upcoming electronic tool is telemedicine, used for varied purposes including diagnosis, nursing, and treatment, and it serves many more purposes (Qazi et al., 2019).

2.2 Importance of biological databases and electronic health records

In bioinformatics, biological databases play a central role. They provide a broad scope of opportunity to all and enable us to access the data stored in it. They provide different kinds of data from human genome data with human sequence variation information to genomic sequence related from the model organisms (Baxevanis, 2009). EHRs play a primary role in enhancing the condition of a patient's health. After the implementation of the American Recovery and Reinvestment Act (2009); Burke, 2010, care providers and hospitals have started incorporating EHRs in their treatments (Sittig and Singh, 2012). They play an important function in the decision-making process for the patient and aid in supporting them in their needs, which in turn helps in the policymaking and management (Häyrinen et al., 2008). It is anticipated that the electronic data of patients will be used more precisely and effectively for clinical research, planning services for health, managing health care, policymaking, and for governmental purposes (Häyrinen et al., 2008). The EHRs are used both in general practice and in hospitals. There are other advantages associated with the EHRs, which include improvement in the clinical records, as they enhance quality and reduce medical errors (Menachemi and Collum, 2011).

3. Classification of biological databases and electronic health records

Based on the different criteria like data type (shown in Table 9.1), source of data, maintainer status, etc., biological databases can be classified. The classification of databases into different categories will reduce the redundancy and provide a better overview of all the information available and aid in easy analysis and understanding.

TABLE 9.1 Showing different types of important databases with some examples.

S No.	Data type	Examples	References/web links
1	Sequence information	NCBI, DDBJ EMBL, Swiss-Prot	1. https://www.ncbi.nlm.nih.gov/ 2. https://www.ddbj.nig.ac.jp/index-e.html 3. https://www.embl.org/ 4. https://www.uniprot.org/
2	Biomolecular structures	PDB	https://www.rcsb.org/
3	Bibliographic databases	PubMed, SCOPUS	https://pubmed.ncbi.nlm.nih.gov/ https://www.scopus.com/home.uri
4	Metabolic pathways	KEGG	https://www.genome.jp/kegg/
5	Genetic disorders	OMIM, OMIA	https://omim.org/ https://omia.org/home/
6	The Human Protein Atlas	–	https://www.proteinatlas.org/

A. Source of information (data)

   I primary databases

   II secondary databases

   III composite databases

   IV integrated databases

B. Type of data

There are various types of EHRs, namely problem oriented, source oriented, and time oriented. In time-oriented type, data is arranged sequentially, while in problem-oriented type the medical records and problems of the patients are described in subjective information, objective information, assessment, and plan (SOAP) format. Finally, in the source-oriented medical records, the medical information is arranged based on methodology obtained for the patient like blood testing, X-ray reports, etc.

There are different types of EHRs, per the International Organization of Standardization (ISO), and the different categories are given in Table 9.2.

TABLE 9.2 Major types of electronic health records (Hayrinen et al., 2008).

S No.	Record type	Nature	References
1	Departmental electronic medical record (EMR)	It contains information from single departments	Häyrinen et al. (2008), Raghavendra and Marilyn (2016), ISO/TR 20514: 2005 (en)
2	Interdepartmental electronic medical record (EMR)	Includes information from different hospitals (two or more)	Häyrinen et al. (2008), Raghavendra and Marilyn (2016), ISO/TR 20514: 2005 (en)
3	Electronic patient record (EPR)	Contains patient's medical records from a single infirmary	Häyrinen et al. (2008), Raghavendra and Marilyn (2016), ISO/TR 20514: 2005 (en)
4	Computerized patient record (CPR)	Contains patient's medical records from a single clinic	Häyrinen et al. (2008), Raghavendra and Marilyn (2016), ISO/TR 20514: 2005 (en)
5	Hospital EMR	Includes patient's medical records from a single health center	Häyrinen et al. (2008), Raghavendra and Marilyn (2016), ISO/TR 20514: 2005 (en)
6	Interhospital EMR	Includes patient's information from many hospitals	Häyrinen et al. (2008), Raghavendra and Marilyn (2016), ISO/TR 20514: 2005 (en)
7	Virtual EMR	–	Häyrinen et al. (2008), Raghavendra and Marilyn (2016), ISO/TR 20514: 2005 (en)
8	Population health record	Contains aggregated data	Häyrinen et al. (2008), Raghavendra and Marilyn (2016), ISO/TR 20514: 2005 (en)

3.1 National Center for Biotechnology Information

NCBI was founded in 1988 at the NIH of the National Library of Medicine, Bethesda (USA), for the development of molecular systems (Pevsner, 2009; NCBI Resource Coordinators, 2013). The ideology behind this creation was to assist in the research in computational biology by creating publicly available databases and programming tools developed for the inspection of sequences and genomic data and to disseminate information on biomedical data (Pevsner, 2009). NCBI also shares its collaboration with other major international databases like the EMBL and DDBJ. NCBI provides a variety of facilities, and one among them is GenBank, a unit of INSDC, a primary nucleotide sequence archive. This can be used by researchers across the world (Pevsner, 2009; NCBI Resource Coordinators, 2016).

The NCBI has created a biomedical database, Medical Literature, Analysis and Retrieval System Online, abbreviated MEDLINE, as one of the bibliographic databases. It includes data from fields like preclinical sciences, veterinary medicine, nursing, and many more. Apart from these, it also involves clinical care, behavioral sciences, bioengineering, and health policy development, and caters to the needs of biomedical practitioners, educators, and researchers (MEDLINE: Description of the Database, n.d.). The database has more than 25 million articles from life science journals including biomedicine (Pevsner, 2009; MEDLINE: Description of the Database, n.d.). These are indexed in Medical Subject Headings of National Library of Medicine (NLM). It is part of PubMed and can be accessed through the Entrez system (MEDLINE: Description of the Database, n.d.), and it includes all publications from 1966 to the present.

3.1.1 Pathogen detection

The NCBI developed a project known as Pathogen Detection (www.ncbi.nlm.nih.gov/pathogens/) wherein it facilitates the easy retrieval of bacterial pathogens and foodborne diseases. This database helps in the genomic analysis of pathogens to unravel genetic relatedness of strains and trace the pathogenesis, which can be used in the prevention of foodborne diseases. It was created in collaboration with several agencies concerning public health like the Food and Drug Administration and the Centers for Disease Control, etc. NCBI collects all the data (sequences) from these agencies and provides the scope for further analysis and studies, which will lead to the identification of plausible sources of contamination causing problems to the environment and humans. The database primarily focuses on data collected from *Salmonella*, *Campylobacter*, *E. coli*, *Listeria*, and *Shigella*, including other bacterial species (https://www.ncbi.nlm.nih.gov/pathogens/organisms/) (https://www.ncbi.nlm.nih.gov/pathogens/about/) (NCBI Resource Coordinators, 2016).

3.1.2 ClinVar

This database maintains and allows the investigation or determination of the relationship between phenotype and human sequence variation. The two main reports are "record" and "variation." In the record report, it consolidates the interpretations submitted about a variation and its condition, whereas the variation report contains information about each variant in an organized manner. This database also throws light on the connection between phenotype and human sequence variation (Database Resources of the National Center for Biotechnology Information, 2013). This database is also connected with different other databases like dbSNP, dbVar, Gene, MEdGen, and PubMed. MedGen contains information about human genetic disorders that are inherited in nature (genetic disorders) (www.ncbi.nlm.nih.gov/clinvar/) (NCBI Resource Coordinators, 2016; Database Resources of the National Center for Biotechnology Information, 2013). The MEdGen also facilitates access to the tests recorded that are inherited in nature through the NCBI's Genetic Testing Registry (Database Resources of the National Center for Biotechnology Information, 2013).

PubMed Health provides information on the treatment and prevention of diseases or conditions to consumers and clinicians. It also includes summaries and complete technical reports on clinical research and its effectiveness (NCBI Resource Coordinators, 2016).

3.2 European molecular biology laboratory

The EMBL Data Library was founded in 1980 to assemble, arrange systematically, and dispense the sequences and their associated facts and figures. The work of maintaining and establishing the database has been carried out in partnership with the GenBank of NCBI, Bethesda, USA, and the DDBJ, Mishima, since 1982. EMBL is one of the most recognized organizations in the world that is dedicated to life science research and provides the facility of data retrieval from varied sources for various study purposes, as well as tools for analysis and submission, and lastly, it shares them with the research community (Pevsner, 2009). EMBL is playing a very crucial role in providing information to researchers throughout the nation, including industry and healthcare sectors. The "Nucleotide Sequence Database" of the EMBL is a comprehensive collection of both RNA and DNA sequences that have been directly submitted by research groups and also contains information gathered from the scientific literature and patents. EMBL services are an extension of EMBL Data Library, Heidelberg, Germany, and share its data with DDBJ and GenBank of NCBI (Stoesser et al., 1997). EBI's services allow the user to access up-to-date data through searches and also provide data analysis facilities along with additional databases (Pevsner, 2009; Schumacher, n.d.).

In addition to generating nucleotide sequence databases, the EBI also aids in maintaining and distributing protein sequence databases through SWISS-PROT in combination with Amos Bairoch, University of Geneva. TrEMBL is a protein database that is associated with SWISS-PROT consisting of translated forms of the available sequences from databases like the Radiation Hybrid Database (Rhdb) (Stoesser et al., 1997).

EST data (expressed sequence tags) is produced in enormous amounts and is integrated with this database. Rather than sequencing the complete genome, small and short pieces of the genome are sequenced that are expressed in particular tissues from varied organisms, thereby yielding dynamic expression patterns. Per the EMBL Release 48, the EST entries are 6,06,286 and still increasing. This number will increase further exponentially due to the advancement in technologies (Stoesser et al., 1997).

EMBL is working in partnership with many groups working on sequencing of the genome, making huge numbers of new sequences daily. It also continues to update bibliographic references and all the major European molecular biology journals.

3.2.1 Data submissions methods of EMBL

World Wide Web: Submissions can be made through EBI's common form, the World Wide Web (WWW), a submission tool. The WWW browser earlier supported MacWeb, Netscape and now JAVA, while it is used for larger submission of data. This tool has become one of the preferred media for submission (Stoesser et al., 1997; Stoesser et al., 1999).

Authorin: It is another wanted submission tool. The data is prepared in an interactive manner using available methods by the authors. Submission of manuscripts and sequences is mechanical and computerized and controlled by the staff (curators) of the Authorin. Authorin can be accessed from the EBI FTP server.

Webin and Sequin: The process is used for submitting a huge amount of data together. EMBL has various submission tools, which include Webin and Sequin. Webin is used for submitting annotation-related information along with nucleotide sequence data and mostly preferred for bulk submissions. It allows submission of very large and multiple sequences very rapidly and efficiently. Whereas, Sequin was developed by NCBI, but it is used by EMBL for submission of sequences (Stoesser et al., 2002).

EBI forms: Nucleotide sequences are directly submitted using the forms available in the EBI network server.

3.2.2 EMBL in healthcare

The EMBL also provides the facility to the healthcare industry and professionals to use the database and for analyzing purposes (Annual Scientific Reports, 2018).

EMBL has launched new data resources, namely, PhenoMeNal and Single Cell Expression Atlas. PhenoMeNal stands for phenome and metabolome analysis, and it is an electronic standardized and comprehensive resource used mainly for analysis of phenotypes and metabolomic studies (https://phenomenal-h2020.eu/home/). The Single Cell Expression Atlas was started in the year 2018, and it is used to retrieve single-cell ENA sequences from different species. It has now more than 50 datasets belonging to nine species from 40,000 cells (Annual Scientific Reports, 2018).

3.3 DNA Database of Japan

It is one of the biological databases that deal with DNA sequences. It was founded in 1986 and is situated at the National Institute of Genetics, Shizuoka. Japan (Pevsner, 2009). It has a major role in the exchange of data with EMBL-EBI and with GenBank at the NCBI daily.

This database stores both phenotypic and genotypic data collected from individuals for research usage. The data access is strictly regulated like NCBI Genotypes and Phenotypes database and the European Genome-Phenome Archive of the EBI. The National Bioscience Database Center provides the rules and regulations for mutually distributing data obtained from humans and reviews requests of users and data submitted.

3.3.1 Data submissions methods of DDBJ

SAKURA: This submission tool runs through the World Wide Web server of DDBJ and is used for the submission of nucleotide sequences. It allows the users to submit either nucleotide sequences or amino acid sequences (or translated version) (Pevsner, 2009).

MSS (Mass Submission System): It is generally used for long sequences (not reads) and genomic data submissions (Pevsner, 2009). The sequences are submitted in text files. It is used when the Nucleotide Sequence Submission System is not valid to use for this kind submission, the sequence is more than 500 kb in length, sequence length exceeds 1024, and it contains many features (>30 features).

3.4 SWISS-PROT

SWISS-PROT was established in 1986 and primarily deals with protein sequence and its annotation (Bairoch and Boeckmann, 1991). It is handled by the Universal Protein Resource Consortium (UniProt) (earlier maintained by Swiss Institute of Bioinformatics, Switzerland, and EBI), and since 1988, it has also been overseen by the Department of Medical Biochemistry, University of Geneva, and EMBL Data Library (Bairoch and Boeckmann, 1991). The database has been derived from three sources, namely, translated protein sequences of nucleotide sequences of EMBL, Protein Identification Resource (Protein Sequence Database), and from the literature. A curated protein sequence database with nonredundancy and having standardized rules as it describes a protein predicts its structure of the domain, PTMs, variants, etc. This database is integrated and shares its resources with other databases as well (Bairoch and Apweiler, 1996). Swiss-Prot has three main principles: minimal redundancy, annotations, and integration with other databases (Pevsner, 2009). It contains different types of sequences (Bairoch et al., 2000).

Translational of EMBL Nucleotide Sequence Database, abbreviated TrEMBL, was automatically annotated using computer-based software and acts as a supplementary database to Swiss-Prot (Pevsner, 2009).

3.5 Biomolecular structural databases

Structure databases contain information and data on 3D structures of proteins and nucleic acids, of crystallographic or nuclear magnetic resonance (NMR) coordinate data, constraint files for the NMR structures, as well as structure factors for X-ray structures, and the information about the experimental methods used to identify and determine the structure. There are many sources for information related to structures of chemical compounds, for example, NDB, PDB, SCOR, DALI, and MMDB. These provide data about molecular structures. The details of some of the most important bimolecular structural databases are described in the following sections.

3.5.1 Protein data bank

The PDB is the main global repository containing biological macromolecules and their 3D structures, which are experimentally determined using techniques like X-ray crystallography, electron (cryo-) microscopy, etc., and it was set up in 1971 with less than 10 X-beam protein structures using the technique of crystallography available at http://www.pdb.org/ (Bank, 1971). The structural biology community started their discussions soon after the submission of structures of myoglobin (Kendrew et al., 1958, 1960) as well as hemoglobin (Bolton and Perutz, 1970; Perutz et al., 1960), which is how to best find about protein crystallography and how can it be made globally available. Therefore in 1971, during a broad conversation in a Cold Spring Harbor Laboratory Conference on protein crystallography, data sharing was announced (Cold Spring Laboratory, 1972). Walter C. Hamilton, one of the participants, offered to give the main home to what is currently the PDB (Berman, 2008). Presently, the PDB is propelled from inside the Department of Chemistry at Brookhaven National Laboratory, expanding on the Protein Structure Library system (Meyer, 1997).

During the initial years of PDB, the submissions were not so good, but after the 1980s, the structural biology community made data deposition mandatory and issued publication guidelines in 1989 (International Union of Crystallography, 1989). In 2003, the wwPDB was shaped to keep up a solitary PDB archive of macromolecular structural information that is openly accessible to the worldwide network, available from wwpdb.org. In May 2016, PDB contained about 80% of experimental data. A bibliometric examination performed by Clarivate Analytics (PDF) in 2017 shows PDB persuaded top-notch research all through the world. The Research Collaboratory for Structural Bioinformatics (RCSB) PDB is an individual from the wwPDB, a collective exertion with PDBe (UK), PDBj (Japan), and BMRB (USA) to guarantee the PDB document is worldwide and uniform (Standley et al., 2008; Ulrich et al., 1989, 2007; Markley et al., 2008).

3.5.1.1 Salient features

(A) The PDB database is updated weekly, and it is supported by the RCSB PDB. (B) The RCSB PDB has a global network of clients, including scholars in all fields like biochemistry, structural biology, etc., different researchers and academicians and other public entities. (C) The RCSB PDB Advisory Committee is a global group of specialists in X-beam crystallography, cryoEM, NMR, bioinformatics, and training. (D) The main webpage of RCSB (http://www.rcsb.org) offers a few fundamental administrations such as archive search, submission of new structures, investigation of structures, and others. The PDB has created numerous tools for submission and structure validations, all effectively accessible from the web. (E) The structures that can be queried can be downloaded in mmCIF format or in the historical PDB format, which can be browsed, and the properties selected by users are arranged in tabular form. (F) X-ray diffraction and NMR (about 10%) techniques are used to investigate the structures in the PDB. (G) For any of the structures involving X-ray diffraction, determination in PDB can be viewed through a structure factor file and its electron density map, which are stored on the electron density server. (H) The structure files can be viewed by using software such as Jmol, MDL Chime, Pymol, and many more.

3.5.2 Nucleic acid database

NDB was founded in the year 1991 for experimentally determining nucleic acid structures and their complex assemblies, and it contains the structures of both X-ray and NMR having di-nucleotide and longer sequences. It contains the data of annotations particularly about the structure and function of nucleic acids and provides many tools that help to download, search, analyze, and know more about them. The NDB's core is a relational database having both primary and derived data, which offers rich query and reporting features (Berman et al., 1992, 2003).

3.5.2.1 Salient features

(i) It provides the facility of searching DNA, RNA, and its complexes and enables advanced searching as well (chemical and structural features, binding modes, and information of experimental data and citations).
(ii) RNA 3D Motif Atlas: It is a repository of RNA 3D internal and hairpin loop motifs.
(iii) Nonredundant List: It is a list of RNA, which contains 3D structures.
(iv) RNA Base Triple Atlas: It contains motifs made up of two RNA base pairs.
(v) WebFR3D: It is a web server for the geometric and symbolic finding of 3D structures of RNA.
(vi) R3D Align: It is a software for alignments of RNA 3D structures (Coimbatore Narayanan et al., 2014).

3.6 Bibliographic databases

These are scientific literature databases that contain many articles and research papers from different journals. The most widely used bibliographic database is PubMed, available at NCBI. There are many sources for information related to literature databases, for instance, PubMed, MEDLINE, Scopus, and Web of Science, which provide data and information related to scientific literature. The details of some of the most important bibliographic databases are described as follows.

3.6.1 PubMed

The NLM first gave a database that is both interactive and searchable (Medline) in 1971, which in 1996, further added the database of "Old Medline" that covered publications from 1950 to 1965 (Falagas et al., 2008). In 1997, PubMed (the combined version of both Medline and Old Medline) was started by NLM, and it is considered a bibliographic database of freely accessible online literature searches and contains about 30 million or so abstracts of biomedical resources from MEDLINE, online books, and life science journals. In addition to abstracts, it also contains molecular biology data and clinical trial databases and so on. It is a literature database, and it contains more than 30 million citations from biomedical journals (https://pubmed.ncbi.nlm.nih.gov/about/) (NCBI Resource Coordinators, 2013).

PubMed is a standalone service, but it has most of the links to other resources. PubMed contains the information about search facilities and restrictions of the database, covering many journals, and updates occasionally. The search for any keyword with PubMed includes online early articles and usually offers optimal update frequency. Currently, it includes MEDLINEplus (www.medlineplus.gov/), a database containing current and new clinical information provided by the NLM. PubMed provides links to full-text articles in abstracts and journal publisher information. PubMed Central (PMC) works on this trend initiative of the NIH to provide full-length access to many journals of life science online without any barrier (Falagas et al., 2008).

3.6.2 Scopus

The Scopus is an indexing and abstract database containing full-text links and provides access to 14,000 STM and social science journal articles from 4000 publishers and the references present in those articles. It is produced by Elsevier, which allows a researcher to search the database containing past as well as present articles. There are more than 4500 health science titles that contain 100% of EMBASE coverage and 100% MEDLINE coverage, as well as 100% of Compendex coverage. This database is utilized for research as well as for collection. Instead of American journals, it also includes the Asian Pacific and European literature (Burnham, 2006).

(1) It provides links to both cited documents as well as citing, allowing a researcher to search the database.
(2) The titles in the index are openly accessible to users, and over 167 million web pages are present as indexed web pages and patents.
(3) It offers both online and offline training and offers guides, tips, quick reference, and online technical support to the users.

Uses of Scopus: (a) It can be utilized to know which is the most-cited journal for any subjective area, and (b) it allows the user to search a journal year wise to find the total number of citations using a citation overview tool.

3.6.3 Web of Science

Web of Science, previously known as Web of Knowledge, is a database of bibliographic citations of multidisciplinary areas that covers the various journals of medical, scientific, and social sciences including humanities. It was inaugurated in 2004 by Thomson Reuters (Thomson Scientific), which is a part of Thomson Cooperation, to incorporate the citation indices and provides a scope for analysis of indexing and citations. It usually requires a commercial subscription and also helps in viewing the references. It is also utilized for searching of a subject and cited references; for instance, it retrieves the articles that are cited by a reference article and also helps in the viewing of the references that are already cited in a relevant article. It shows 10−15 results per page, which contains details like name of authors and source. The articles can be searched by using entries like author name, country, title, and source. The benefit of utilizing this database is that it will retrieve a number of articles from various disciplines and therefore saves time (Falagas et al., 2008; Krieger et al., 2016).

3.7 Metabolic pathways database

These types of databases contain information and data related to biochemical pathways and enzymes present in different organisms. For instance, KEGG and MetaCyc are the most important metabolic pathway databases, which provide data and information related to an organism's biochemical pathways. Metabolic pathway databases also contain organism-specific databases that include organism-related information and data individually such as Flybase, EcoCyc, and CCDB.

3.7.1 KEGG

Kyoto Encyclopedia of Genes and Genomes, commonly referred to as KEGG, started in the year 1995 and is an updated and freely accessible pathway database (http://www.genome.ad.jp/kegg/). It is primarily used for comprehension of the functioning of genes and linking to genomic information and the applicability in biological systems (molecular-level information of the cell to ecosystem levels). These datasets of genomic information and higher order functional information are generated by the methods of high-throughput experimental technologies and sequencing. It has been found that KEGG contains many databases such as GENES, PATHWAY, LIGAND, etc. GENES database contains the genomic information, which is the information of genes for some partial genomes and all the completely sequenced genomes, along with updated gene functions (annotation). The PATHWAY database contains higher order functional information, which provides the graphic information of cellular processes including membrane transport to cell cycle to metabolism. LIGAND is a database that provides information about enzyme molecules, chemical compounds, and enzymatic reactions (Kanehisa and Goto, 2000).

3.7.1.1 Salient features

(1) KEGG is globally used as a reference knowledge base for the analysis of large datasets. (2) It is being utilized for practical applications for human disease and genetic disorders, medicines, and other substances related to health. (3) KEGG has also the feature of Java graphics tools, which help in the browsing of genome maps and their comparison, manipulation of expression maps, and provides the tools for comparing graphs, sequences, and path computation.

3.7.2 BioSilico

BioSilico is a heterogeneous and web-based metabolic database system that is used for searching and analyzing metabolic pathways. It includes KEGG/LIGAND, ENZYME, BRENDA, EcoCyc, and MetaCyc (Hou et al., 2004). All these databases are combined systematically to allow users to easily take out the relevant data and information about metabolic pathways, enzymes, biochemical compounds, and reactions, which are important for identification and characterization of physiologic and metabolic characteristics of organisms.

3.7.2.1 Salient features

(1) Empower clients to scan for the data and to rebuild the network of reactions. (2) A coordinated information structure and an assortment of questioning rationales are created to permit simple and efficient recovery of different information in the metabolic network. (3) The framework is bolstered by a chemical structure database (Chem DB). (4) It has a relational structure for data integration, and the databases are persistently restored by a DB updating system, stored in a local server. (5) The relations in BioSilico are founded on the data of Enzyme Commission (EC) number, protein, compound, and metabolic reaction. For example, ENZYME, LIGAND (enzyme), EcoCyc (reaction), and MetaCyc (reaction) are connected by utilizing the EC number. (6) BioSilico provides data on 9994 enzymes, 13554 compounds, and 12248 fundamental processes (reactions).

3.8 Genetic disorders database

There are many sources of information related to disease and genetic disorders. For example, OMIM and OMIA provide data and information related to an organism's genes and genetic disorders. These databases provide significant therapeutic value in the clinical, medical, and research fields. The details of some of the most important genetic disorder databases are described as follows.

3.8.1 OMIM

OMIM was started around the 1960s by Dr. Victor A. McKusick and is an openly accessible and daily updated database of an extensive and concise collection of human genes and their genetic phenotypes that contains information of over 15,000 genes of all known Mendelian disorders (http://www.ncbi.nlm.nih.gov/omim/). It mainly focuses on the connection between genotype and phenotype, where each entry contains links to other resources (Hamosh et al., 2000).

It has a list of Mendelian characteristics and disorders, as Mendelian Inheritance in Man. The online version of the database, OMIM, was made in 1985 by a joint effort between the NLM and the William H. Welch Medical Library at Johns Hopkins and was made commonly accessible on the web beginning in 1987. It was developed for the World Wide Web by NCBI in 1995. Instead of other databases that only maintain primary sequence, mapping, or reference material, it gives free access to text overviews about gene loci as well as genetic disorders that can be utilized by anyone.

3.8.1.1 Importance

OMIM can be utilized by clinicians as a guide in differential conclusions via looking through the database utilizing key clinical features of a patient. It gives students a brisk and simple approach to discover and audit basic data about a given gene or hereditary issue.

In the research field, it provides information about genes connected with a specific disorder. It also helps in recognizing genetic disorders caused by various mutation events and about hereditary information. It maintains primary sequence, mapping, or reference material, and gives free access to text overviews about gene loci as well as genetic disorders.

3.8.1.2 Salient features

The entries present in the OMIM contain a standardized format, having many features, as follows:

Entries present in OMIM are assigned a unique number for each unique gene as well as a genetic disorder. The information that is present in gene entries has a recognized gene name, gene symbol, vernacular name, data of map location in mouse and human, information about the protein and DNA sequence, cloning method, related genes in man or other species, functional and clinical information such as key allelic variants, and variations from the usual case. It also includes the text entries that are usually diachronic, i.e., they are added in chronological order, having most recent information at the end.

1. Clinical synopsis
   It contains entries that give information about phenotype, particularly important for making lists for differential diagnosis.
2. Allelic variants
   Allelic variants are the mutations that cause disease and also include common polymorphisms that are unable to produce any type of disease. OMIM only includes the variants that are relatively common, have some historical aspect, or have a new mechanism of mutation.

3. The OMIM Gene Map

It includes information about the "morbid map," like mapping of disorders, and gives information of the chromosomal location, mapping techniques, and disorders about the specific gene. It also includes links to the human/mouse homology maps and NCBI and GDB.

4. Neighboring

OMIM contains a key feature called neighboring shown as a light bulb icon help in MEDLINE searches for the users by using keywords from the preceding paragraph. It searches the MEDLINE articles that are closely related to the paragraph of OMIM. From time to time the NEIGHBOR algorithm is updated against MEDLINE.

5. Links

OMIM provides links to other resources such as Entrez databases, which include UniGene, LocusLink, PubMed, RefSeq, protein and nucleic acid databases, mapping databases, etc., and permits direct access from the entry (Hamosh et al., 2000).

3.8.2 OMIA

OMIA is an annotated and extensive compendium of genetic disorders, single locus, and familial traits found in animals except for humans, mice, and rats. This database is authored by Professor Frank Nicholas of the University of Sydney, Australia, and information of OMIA is stored in a database that has references as well as textual information. It also provides links to OMIM and Ensembl and PubMed and Gene records present at the NCBI. Australian National Genomic Information Service moved OMIA to a MySQL database in 1995 (Lenffer et al., 2006).

3.8.2.1 Importance

Future headings incorporate clarifying quality changes seen as related with specific phenes by connecting dbSNP record, with phenes, and the joining of a pseudonym file to cover any equivalent words at any point utilized for a specific gene. Revamped on a flexible, secluded establishment of MySQL and Python, OMIA is currently effectively extensible and better situated to adapt to the ever-increasing influx of new genomic and phenotypic data. Genomic research has been uplifted with the integration of the NCBI's Entrez framework with OMIA.

3.8.2.2 Salient features

(1) Curators can edit and update entries using a dynamic interface created using a programming language (Python). (2) Both OMIA into NCBI's Entrez interface offers further developed search facilities empowering complex questions, it and gives complete direct connections to other NCBI databases and outside bioinformatics assets. (3) NCBI OMIA contains joins registered between specific phene-species records and related records in Entrez Gene, Protein, OMIM, PubMed, Taxonomy, UniGene, HomoloGene, and UniSTS. The links menu, found at the right-hand edge of each NCBI OMIA record, gives advantageous access to these related records.

3.8.3 GeneCards

GeneCards (www.genecards.org) is an authoritative and comprehensive platform containing the annotated data of genes present in humans. Users can automatically pull out the information of genes that are already consolidated from about 100 digitally available resources, providing information of a deep-linked card of more than 80,000 genes present in a human, containing data such as genetic locus, protein-coding genes, RNA gene, pseudogene, and clusters of genes. It mainly focuses on the analysis of a set of genes containing combinatorial annotated information of biomedical wealth, which include GeneALaCart, which helps in the formation of tables for multiple annotated genes selected by users, and GeneDecks, which helps in the identification of the same genes sharing their annotative information by the analysis of their descriptors. It also helps in the visualization of patterns of expression of both normal and cancerous genes and patterns found in alternative splicing and single-nucleotide polymorphisms (SNPs) and integrated pathway analysis. It also provides many direct links to chemicals and reagents related to research for genes such as recombinant proteins, antibodies, inhibitory RNAs, and cloned DNA (Safran et al., 2010).

3.8.4 MalaCard

MalaCards (www.malacards.org) is an annotated and integrated database of maladies present in humans, designed on the strategy and idea taking from the GeneCards database. It helps in the mining and merging of information of more than 44 resources available and helps in the making of a digitalized card for 16,919 human ailments. It is relationally linked with

GeneCards and also contains the information of analysis of GeneDecks. It also shares data and information about clinical features and etiology and even is considered an effective software for biomedical research (Rappaport et al., 2013).

3.8.5 PathCards

PathCards (http://pathcards.genecards.org/) is another cumulative database containing information about annotated biological pathways of human genes, and it contains entries of more than 1300 SuperPaths, integrated from 12 available resources. Based on gene similarity, the pathways of humans were merged as SuperPaths, and a single PathCard contains the information of single SuperPath containing one or more integrated pathways present in humans (Belinky et al., 2015).

Table 9.3 provides a summary of important biomolecular structure, bibliographic, metabolic pathways, and genetic disorders and diseases databases.

3.9 Human Protein Atlas

In 2003, HPA was announced in Sweden intending to annotate all the proteins of each cell, tissue, and organ primarily of humans. It can be accessed freely from https://www.proteinatlas.org/, and all the data submitted are open access for the user to allow the investigation of the proteome of humans including scientists both from academia and industry, as well as the general population. This project was succeeded after the amalgamation of omics technologies such as antibody-based imaging, transcriptomics, mass spectrometry-based proteomics, and systems biology (Uhlen et al., 2010). It stores data for the inspection of candidate proteins that may have implications for human biology in both disease and health and the data derived from the tissue and cell type-specific expression patterns. This atlas project includes the cumulative efforts of many Swedish universities including the Uppsala University, Royal Institute of Technology, Karolinska Institute, and Chalmers University, as well as the national infrastructure SciLifeLab as major contributors. The queries during the search include the name of the protein of interest; along with this, it provides conditional advanced queries like inclusion/exclusion of tissue types, types and line of cells, protein classes, etc. (Uhlén et al., 2005; Pontén et al., 2008). The gene-centered summary is obtained from the search that provides a general and large-scale overview on expression patterns both at the mRNA and protein level and also provides specific expression patterns of all tissues, cancers (Pathology Atlas), and cells (Cell Atlas) (Berglund et al., 2008). It also incorporates expression-related data ranging from blood and brain to metabolic atlases covering blood cells and plasma, mammalian brain regions (*Homo sapiens* L., *Sus* sp. (pig) and *Mus musculus*), and metabolic data.

The HPA data shows comprehensive summaries for cell types or organ-specific proteomes in interactive charts and illustrations. Fig. 9.1 represents the homepages (HPA) of six different components of the Atlas, while Fig. 9.2 gives the overview of the process of data generation and analysis. It also provides more than 20 datasets that can be downloadable for large-scale analyses.

It majorly has six parts, which emphasize different aspects of human proteins, providing the scope of genome-wide analysis. They are as follows.

A. **Tissue Atlas**: It contains most of the human proteins expressed in all tissues and organs.
B. **Cell Atlas**: It has the subcellular localization of proteins in each cell.
C. **Pathology Atlas**: It contains the mRNA and expression of proteins involved in different cancers.
D. **Brain Atlas**: It contains mammalian brain-related protein information by the cumulating data from pig, *Homo sapiens*, and mouse.
E. **Blood Atlas**: It carries information on various blood cell types of humans and about the distribution of secreted proteins from different cell types around the body.
F. **Metabolic Atlas**: It is a concoction of the metabolic pathway data and organ-specific mRNA expression.

3.9.1 Research projects at HPA

Expansion to the high-throughput protein profiling center task, a few undertakings with progressively explicit research goals are run dependent on the assets created inside the HPA, as a team with Swedish or worldwide analysts. Some major projects are as follows.

3.9.2 Antibody-related project

The venture aims to create assays and methodologies for additional approval of antibodies in tissues and cells. Strategies incorporate refinement of rules for counteracting agent approval utilizing standardized immunohistochemistry, yet

TABLE 9.3 Various important biological databases along with their web links.

Categories of databases	Database name	Description (primary roles)	Links
Biomolecular structure databases	PDB	3D structures of proteins, nucleic acids, and complex assemblies	www.rcsb.org
	NDB	Experimentally determined data on DNA, RNA, and complex assemblies	http://ndbserver.rutgers.edu/
	MMDB	Proteins, RNA, and DNA, (experimentally resolved structures) derived from the PDB	https://www.ncbi.nlm.nih.gov/Structure/MMDB/mmdb.shtml
	Gene3D	Globular domains in proteins	http://gene3d.biochem.ucl.ac.uk/Gene3D/
	E-MSD	Search macromolecular structure data in the Protein Data Bank (PDB) and other integrated bioinformatics data resources	http://www.ebi.ac.uk/msd/
	TOPS	Topologic descriptions of protein structures	http://www.tops.leeds.ac.uk/
	FSSP	3D protein folds and comparison with structures available in PDB	EMBL file server and by anonymous ftp (file transfer protocol)
	DALI	Comparing protein structures in 3D	http://ekhidna2.biocenter.helsinki.fi/dali/
	SCOR	RNA motif structure, function, tertiary interactions, and their relationships	http://scor.berkeley.edu/
Bibliographic databases	PubMed	Bibliographic database of freely accessible online literature searches	www.ncbi.nlm.nih.gov/entrez/query.fcgi
	MedlinePlus	Medical information (NLM)	www.medlineplus.gov/
	Scopus	Abstract and citation database of peer-reviewed literature	https://www.scopus.com/home.uri
	Web of Science	Publisher-neutral citation index and research intelligence platform	www.webofknowledge.com
Metabolic pathways databases	KEGG	A knowledgebase resource for understanding and analysis of gene functions	http://www.genome.ad.jp/kegg/
	BioSilico	A heterogeneous and web-based metabolic database system that is used for searching and analyzing metabolic pathways	http://biosilico.kaist.ac.kr
	BRENDA	Enzyme information	https://www.brenda-enzymes.org/
	MetaCyc	Metabolic pathways from all domains	https://metacyc.org/
	EcoCyc	*Escherichia coli* K-12 MG1655database.	https://ecocyc.org/
	Flybase	*Drosophila* genes and genomes database	https://flybase.org/
	CCDB	A comprehensive community resource for plant chromosome numbers	http://ccdb.tau.ac.il/
Genetic disorders and diseases databases	OMIM	Genes and phenotypes of humans	http://www.ncbi.nlm.nih.gov/omim/
	OMIA	Inherited disorders, single locus, and familial traits found in animals (except for humans, mice, and rats)	http://omia.angis.org.au/

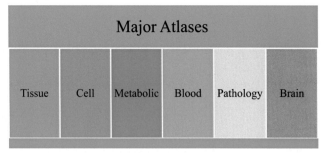

FIGURE 9.1 Basic classification of Human Protein Atlas showing six parts of the database.

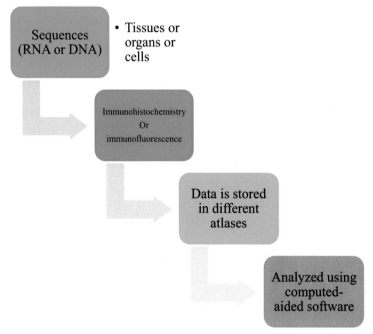

FIGURE 9.2 Schematic overview of the process of Human Protein Atlas. The HPA breaks down the human genome on various levels, for example, in organs, tissues, cells, and organelles. The proteomic examination is joined with RNA-seq on the organ, tissue, and cell level, and all information is uninhibitedly open on the HPA online interface.

additionally strategy advancement of new methods, for example, multiplexed recognition of proteins in paraffin-implanted tissue areas utilizing immunofluorescence. Different methods utilized for counteracting agent approval incorporate nearness ligation measure. The strategies utilized have various preferences and impediments regarding affectability, particularity, goals, and execution in a high-throughput work process (Uhlén et al., 2005).

3.9.3 Machine learning for cancer diagnosis

It develops algorithms for the identification of malignant growth tissues in specific organs like prostate and lung. Immunofluorescence is utilized to stamp explicit proteins related to malignancy and typical tissues. After checking the tissues are recolored with hematoxylin and eosin (H&E) and examined in brightfield. The immunofluorescence recoloring is overlaid with H&E and utilized to identify and lay out disease regions (Gibbs et al., 2015).

3.9.4 Organ-explicit proteomics

Worldwide RNA expression levels across 37 distinctive typical tissues and organs have taken into consideration the grouping of every human gene into classes dependent on abundance and dispersion. Genes raised or explicitly communicated in specific organs give intriguing beginning stages to tissue-explicit research in wellbeing and illness. A few ongoing projects centered on such genes joined with procedures targeting decisions on the cell type-explicit restriction in the tissue utilizing immune response-based strategies.

3.9.5 Single-cell omics

An enormous extent of genes elevated in specific organs have a place with male and female regenerative organs, and studies have indicated that a significant number of the corresponding proteins have an obscure capacity. Utilizing organ-explicit antibody panels and multiplexed imaging apparatuses, high-goal spatial protein maps of human tissues are worked to decide the specific area of cell type-explicit articulation examples, and how these genes and proteins are identified with contraceptive science.

3.9.6 Biomarkers for cancer

With the advent of high throughput technologies, identification of markers associated with various types of cancers provides a new paradigm in the discovery and development of cancer markers. The Human Atlas Protein has provided numerous high resolution and annotated images of both normal and cancerous cells which would help in the studies with the developed or candidate markers against specific cancer-type using the protein expression profiling and immunohistochemical staining techniques (Chiang et al., 2013).

3.10 Classical types of electronic health records

In 1970, two general categories were made for the classification of medical health records; Weed instigated the problem-oriented type of medical record, and Fries gave the concept of the medical record of the time-oriented type.

Under the leadership of Weed in the year 1969, the Problem-Oriented Medical Information System was formed at the Medical Center Hospital, Vermont. In the problem-oriented medical record, each problem is carefully observed and noted from the predefined list of problems and organized per the medical reasoning and SOAP. This can be helpful for the caregivers in keeping a record, organizing, and aids in using the computerized database (Tange et al., 1997).

In the time-oriented type, physical and history examinations are arranged in a matric form. The American Rheumatism-Association Medical Information System was headed by Fries and developed the computerized medical history database. In this, all the examinations and medical history of patients are stored in an orderly manner and can be referred thereon (Tange et al., 1997).

Regenstrief Medical Record System was developed at the Wishard Memorial Hospital in 1972. This medical record database generates automatic reminders to the patients regarding the prevention and diet followed per their medical conditions based on the recommendations from the physicians (Tange et al., 1997).

4. Role of biological databases in translation bioinformatics

Biological databases play a crucial role in computation biology and translational bioinformatics as they provide an opportunity to researchers and scientists to avail and get a vast diversity of biological information of their interest, like sequenced genomes and transcriptomic and proteomic data for their analyses and visualization (Altman, 2012; Sethi and Theodos, 2009). Translational bioinformatics is an advanced combination of both translational medicine and bioinformatics wherein it involves information from DNA, proteins, etc., and pathologic data (reports and tests) also (Altman, 2012). Translational bioinformatics aims to develop novel methodologies that would plausibly deal with analyzing cellular and molecular topics, which thereby can be used in diagnostics, prevention, and formulations of therapeutic strategies. With the use of principles of translational medicines, scientists are working to discover new molecules that could act as potential drugs. It primarily focuses on the development of new diagnostics, prognostics, immunization systems, and treatments strategies (Altman, 2012).

Three significant specialized capacities empower translational bioinformatics. Firstly, the highly increased computing power has propelled capacities for information storage, analyses, and representation. Secondly, high-throughput sequencing provides the scope of whole genomes sequencing, along with the identification and investigations about the transcriptome and metabolome. Lastly, with the technologic advancement leading to an increase in the electronic medical records (EMRs), they also provide an opportunity to get information about clinical data (Altman, 2012). The data being generated should be easily available with minimum costs to all. With an ultimate aim of synthesizing and providing new drugs, translational bioinformatics has extended its horizons and made it possible to elicit various downstream processes, viz, (1) pharmacogenomics that is used to study the relationship between sequence variation and its phenotype upon the delivery of drugs, (2) a scope to relate the biomarkers with drug responses including its efficacy and other effects, and (3) numerous upcoming sources that provide information about various drugs and their ill effects, which eventually lead to enhancing the current understanding of the usage and application of drugs (Altman, 2012).

4.1 Biomedical informatics

Biomedical informatics deals with two major fields, namely, biomedical and health informatics. It is defined as an "interdisciplinary field that studies and pursues the effective use of biomedical data, information and knowledge for scientific inquiry, problem-solving and decision making driven by efforts to improve human health" (taken from Chapter 1, Shortliffe and Blois†, 2006) Biomedical informatics includes bioinformatics, imaging, public health, and clinical informatics as major domains (Sarkar, 2010). The ability to quantify DNA sequences (in terms of sequencing) has experienced noteworthy changes in the past few years. For instance, with the help of techniques like expression arrays, one can easily identify genetic variations both precisely and in an economical manner (Altman, 2012). The transformation in our capacity to gauge genetic data of humans opens doors of translational medicine. The primary focus is to apply the results of biological research on human beings and at the same time improve the longevity of humans using the clinical data (Butte, 2008). The important application of this field involves in assessing and identifying genetic variations both through sequencing and clinical results, which include ailment risk, infection forecast, and remedial reaction. Statistical analyses of these genetic variations are thus quite considerably important in population studies. The identification of mutations in individuals with healthy phenotypes is often difficult as sometimes the changes occur in noncoding regions of the genome (Altman, 2012). Thus, understanding the genetic variations and how these variations are related to the noncoding genomic regions is extremely important to improve health and develop new treatment strategies (Altman, 2012; Sarkar, 2010).

The field of translational bioinformatics can be used in clinical medicine with a vision of applying this for genome-informed medication. Taking advantage of this field, genomes of all patients can be sequenced to utilize the grouping data to organize disease observation and avoidance and also to choose efficient treatment strategies with negligible side effects. For instance, the sequenced genome of an elderly person with a family ancestry of coronary illness may be used to evaluate the risk for other regular infections and the data about alleles associated with genetic risk, the nearness of uncommon alleles related with a disease that show Mendelian inheritance, which may then be used to explore novel medications. The analysis may help in suggesting an early commencement of treatment. Additionally, such analyses could help in profiling individual risks and advantages of drugs commonly used for the treatment of various diseases. For example, statins are prescribed to patients suffering from heart-related diseases, and the personal risk/advantage profile obtained from the analysis could be considered in evaluating the treatment and drug delivery (Altman, 2012). Phenotyping using the EMR and its utilization in hereditary disclosure are attainable and cost significantly lower than traditional sequencing technologies. Self-reports of patients can act as a significant instrument for the phenotyping. Genome-Wide Association Studies (GWAS) can also be fruitful in recognizing SNPs related to phenotypes. Morphology-related, photic sneeze reflex (autosomal dominant disorder), and pigment-patched skin, etc., can be detected using GWAS (Altman, 2012). Molecular systems show incredible applications in assisting with interpreting genetic information. It is easier to analyze and reduce the workload of researchers in estimating DNA along with estimating RNA expression, protein expression, small biomolecules, and metabolites. The possibility of utilizing this information as markers in identifying diseases is immense. The fundamental analysis incorporates portraying cell populaces dependent on these estimations and grouping them dependent on comparative profiles. Earlier studies were based on expression information: malignancies related with blood that showed up phenotypically the same had distinctive molecular signatures. These markers are related to clinical results, proposing that molecular profiles can be used to generate data that can predict the risk of disease, its prognosis, and possible therapeutics. Disease states that look similar in phenotype can have different molecular signatures that are related to clinical outcomes. Thus, genetic markers are important in prognosis and treatment, for example, those utilized in analytical stages for studying breast cancer based on gene expression (Altman, 2012). In ongoing investigations, researchers are concentrating on the discovery of biomarkers, sequencing for rare Mendelian diseases, and searching for novel phenotypic outcomes of genetic variation, among different applications. In a study carried out by the Wellcome Trust Case-Control Consortium, there are 14,000 instances of seven basic ailments that were reported, wherein GWAS analysis utilized 500,000 SNPs. Rare genetic diseases are focused targets for new sequencing advancement (Altman, 2012).

5. Barriers and drawbacks

Both biological databases and EHRs possess great usability and are being widely used for both academic and industrial purposes; despite this fact, both of them have some lacunae, which are as follows.

1. Proprietary issues of the databases: Though some databases are widely available, not all papers and resources are easily available to all. For instance, databases owned by private companies are not freely accessible (Pool and Esnayra, 2000).
2. The disparity in terminology: As the field of bioinformatics is dynamic, new terms and words are also evolving, which is a hindrance in free exchange and access of resources due to a lack of proper and standard terminology (Pool and Esnayra, 2000).
3. Lack of interoperability: Another common drawback of using databases is regarding interoperability. Every database has its means of deciphering its resources, and this results in a lack of access due to failure of understanding of their respective website properly (Pool and Esnayra, 2000).
4. Capital challenge: EHRs are very useful; however, they face financial issues in terms of maintenance and purchasing costs, implementation and adoption costs, and revenue loss and also may be due to cost-prohibitive infrastructure like regular upgrading of software and hardware (Menachemi and Collum, 2011; Kaul et al., 2019).
5. Disturbance in the workflow: Sometimes, disturbance in the process gets hampered due to the medical staff or service providers (Menachemi and Collum, 2011).
6. Privacy and security issues: An associated problem with EHRs is violations in the privacy of records of patients. Due to electronic transferring of data, the incidence of loss of personal information increases (Menachemi and Collum, 2011).
7. Unprecedented problems: EHRs have other issues also, which include errors caused during updating the records and technology-dependent and medical errors (Menachemi and Collum, 2011).
8. Lack of adequate support: The dearth of technical support or staff and lack of technology (high-speed internet connectivity or storing devices) adds to the limitation of EHRs (Kruse et al., 2016).
9. Interpersonal relations: Sometimes lack of organizational cooperation and coordination (irregularities in updating and communication gaps) also lead to mismanagement while handling EHRs (Kruse et al., 2016).

6. Conclusion

Bioinformatics includes algorithms to prescribe, store, and examine fundamental organic information, including DNA arrangement, RNA expression, and protein and small particle bounty inside cells. This new field is emerging, as well as the availability of numerous databases being used at large scale by researchers globally for their research in biomedical and allied fields because of the potential ability for developing novel algorithms for analyzing genomic sequences, protein structures, vaccines, therapeutics, and diagnostics along with understanding the underlying mechanisms of various diseases. The databases help in the identification of genes that are susceptible to diseases and their associated studies. So, the unraveling of the differences in the genetic constitution not only provides the opportunity in understanding the genes that cause disease but will help in prescribing the correct medication in the right amount to all.

The trend from the past few years in the field of science has increased with a huge amount of research data. But there remains a challenge of how to store and annotate such huge information. Therefore, the biological databases paved a new way to store and organize information in a specific manner, so the process of analyzing the information is facilitated. Further, new paths should be discovered from scientific research to clinical application as simply as possible. The chapter primarily focused on information about clinical applications of biological databases and EHRs. The biological databases are classified into major categories such as sequence databases, structural databases, metabolic pathways databases, literature databases, disease databases, etc. NCBI, EMBL, and DDBJ are nucleotide sequence databases that were established in 1988, 1980, and 1986, respectively, with the key goals to build, maintain, and prepare biological databases and other computational services to support data deposition and data analysis (Pevsner, 2009). These biological databases offer researchers the ability to submit their findings and sequences isolated from organisms either in the form of DNA or RNA. Each database works collaboratively by sharing its resources (Stoesser et al., 1997). For instance, the structural databases include the information and data on the 3D structure of proteins and nucleic acids of X-ray crystallographic or NMR coordinate data and also the information about the experimental methods used to determine the structure. Bibliographic databases contain information about scientific literature from different journals. The information and data related to biochemical pathways and enzymes present in different organisms are represented in metabolic pathways databases. Similarly, the genetic disorders database provides data and information related to an organism's genes and genetic disorders and also provides significant therapeutic value in the clinical, medical, and research fields.

Applications of these fields not only apply to a researcher for structural and functional analysis but are extended to development and implementation of computational algorithms and various computer software tools that facilitate our understanding of the biological process intending to serve primarily agriculture and pharmaceutical sectors. Translational bioinformatics ranges in these two fields; it includes the advancement of calculations to break down essential atomic and cell information with an unequivocal objective of influencing clinical consideration.

References

Altman, R.B., 2012. Translational bioinformatics: linking the molecular world to the clinical world. Clin. Pharmacol. Ther. 91 (6), 994–1000.

American Recovery and Reinvestment Act, 2009. Pub. L. No. 111-5 (2009 Feb 17).

Annual Scientific Reports, EMBL. https://www.embl.de/aboutus/communication_outreach/publications/ebi_ar/ebi_ar_2018.pdf.

Bairoch, A., Apweiler, R., 1996. The SWISS-PROT protein sequence data bank and its new supplement TREMBL. Nucleic Acids Res. 24 (1), 21–25.

Bairoch, A., Boeckmann, B., 1991. The SWISS-PROT protein sequence data bank. Nucleic Acids Res. 19 (Suppl. l), 2247.

Bairoch, A., Apweiler, R., Campus, W.T.G., 2000. The SWISS-PROT Protein Sequence Database User Manual. Swiss Institute of Bioinformatics and Central Medical University.

Bank, P.D., 1971. Protein data bank. Nat. New Biol. 233, 223.

Baxevanis, A.D., 2009. The importance of biological databases in biological discovery. Curr. Protoc. Bioinform. 27 (1), 1.1.1–1.1.6. https://doi.org/10.1002/0471250953.bi0101s27.

Belinky, F., Nativ, N., Stelzer, G., Zimmerman, S., Iny Stein, T., Safran, M., Lancet, D., 2015. PathCards: multi-source consolidation of human biological pathways. Database 2015.

Berglund, L., Björling, E., Oksvold, P., Fagerberg, L., Asplund, A., Szigyarto, C.A.K., et al., 2008. A genecentric Human Protein Atlas for expression profiles based on antibodies. Mol. Cell. Proteomics 7 (10), 2019–2027.

Berman, H.M., Olson, W.K., Beveridge, D.L., Westbrook, J., Gelbin, A., Demeny, T., et al., 1992. The nucleic acid database. A comprehensive relational database of three-dimensional structures of nucleic acids. Biophys. J. 63 (3), 751.

Berman, H., Henrick, K., Nakamura, H., 2003. Announcing the worldwide protein data bank. Nat. Struct. Mol. Biol. 10 (12), 980-980.

Berman, H.M., 2008. The protein data bank: a historical perspective. Acta Crystallogr. A: Found. Crystallogr. 64 (1), 88–95.

Bolton, W., Perutz, M.F., 1970. Three dimensional Fourier synthesis of horse deoxyhaemoglobin at 2.8 Å resolution. Nature 228 (5271), 551–552.

Burke, T., 2010. The health information technology provisions in the American Recovery and Reinvestment Act of 2009: implications for public health policy and practice. Public Health Reports 125 (1), 141–145.

Burnham, J.F., 2006. Scopus database: a review. Biomed. Digit. Libr. 3 (1), 1.

Butte, A.J., 2008. Translational bioinformatics: coming of age. J. Am. Med. Inf. Assoc. 15 (6), 709–714.

Chiang, S.C., Han, C.L., Yu, K.H., Chen, Y.J., Wu, K.P., 2013. Prioritization of cancer marker candidates based on the immunohistochemistry staining images deposited in the human protein atlas. PloS One 8 (11), e81079.

Coimbatore Narayanan, B., Westbrook, J., Ghosh, S., Petrov, A.I., Sweeney, B., Zirbel, C.L., et al., 2014. The Nucleic Acid Database: new features and capabilities. Nucleic Acids Res. 42 (D1), D114–D122.

Cold Spring Laboratory, 1972. Cold Spring Harbor Symposia on Quantitative Biology, vol. 36. Cold Spring Laboratory Press; Cold Spring Harbor, NY.

Committee to Update Science, Medicine and Animals, National Research Council, 2004. Science, Medicine, and Animals. National Academies Press (US).

Das, D., Jaiswal, M., Khan, F.N., Ahamad, S., Kumar, S., 2020. PlantPepDB: a manually curated plant peptide database. Sci. Rep. 10 (1), 1–8.

Database resources of the national center for biotechnology information. Nucleic Acids Res. 42 (D1), 2013, D7–D17. https://doi.org/10.1093/nar/gkt1146.

Falagas, M.E., Pitsouni, E.I., Malietzis, G.A., Pappas, G., 2008. Comparison of PubMed, Scopus, Web of Science, and Google Scholar: strengths and weaknesses. FASEB J. 22 (2), 338–342.

Gibbs, S.L., Genega, E., Salemi, J., Kianzad, V., Goodwill, H.L., Xie, Y., et al., 2015. Near-infrared fluorescent digital pathology for the automation of disease diagnosis and biomarker assessment. Molecular imaging 14 (5), 1–9.

Hamosh, A., Scott, A.F., Amberger, J., Valle, D., McKusick, V.A., 2000. Online mendelian inheritance in man (OMIM). Hum. Mutat. 15 (1), 57–61.

Häyrinen, K., Saranto, K., Nykänen, P., 2008. Definition, structure, content, use and impacts of electronic health records: a review of the research literature. Int. J. Med. Inf. 77 (5), 291–304.

n.d. What is an electronic health record (EHR)?. Retrieved from: https://www.healthit.gov/faq/what-electronic-health-record-ehr.

Hoerbst, A., Ammenwerth, E., 2010. Electronic health records. Methods Inf. Med. 49 (04), 320–336.

Hou, B.K., Kim, J.S., Jun, J.H., Lee, D.Y., Kim, Y.W., Chae, S., et al., 2004. BioSilico: an integrated metabolic database system. Bioinformatics 20 (17), 3270–3272.

International Union of Crystallography, 1989. Policy on publication and the deposition of data from crystallographic studies of biological macromolecules. Acta Crystallogr. 45, 658.

n.d. ISO/TR 20514: 2005 (en) - Health Informatics — Electronic Health Record — Definition, Scope and Context. Retrieved from: https://www.iso.org/obp/ui/#iso:std:iso:tr:20514:ed-1:v1:en.

Kanehisa, M., Goto, S., 2000. KEGG: Kyoto encyclopedia of genes and genomes. Nucleic Acids Res. 28 (1), 27–30.

Kaul, T., Eswaran, M., Ahmad, S., Thangaraj, A., Jain, R., Kaul, R., et al., 2019. Probing the effect of a plus 1bp frameshift mutation in protein-DNA interface of domestication gene, NAMB1, in wheat. J. Biomol. Struct. Dyn. 1–15.

Kendrew, J.C., Bodo, G., Dintzis, H.M., Parrish, R.G., Wyckoff, H., Phillips, D.C., 1958. A three-dimensional model of the myoglobin molecule obtained by x-ray analysis. Nature 181 (4610), 662−666.

Kendrew, J.C., Dickerson, R.E., Strandberg, B.E., Hart, R.G., Davies, D.R., Phillips, D.C., Shore, V.C., 1960. Structure of myoglobin: a three-dimensional Fourier synthesis at 2 Å. resolution. Nature 185 (4711), 422−427.

Krieger, M., Tao, D., Royeen, C.B., 2016. Foundations of evidence-based gerontological occupational therapy practice. In: Occupational Therapy with Aging Adults, pp. 52−73.

Kruse, C.S., Kristof, C., Jones, B., Mitchell, E., Martinez, A., 2016. Barriers to electronic health record adoption: a systematic literature review. J. Med. Syst. 40 (12), 252.

Lenffer, J., Nicholas, F.W., Castle, K., Rao, A., Gregory, S., Poidinger, M., et al., 2006. OMIA (Online Mendelian Inheritance in Animals): an enhanced platform and integration into the Entrez search interface at NCBI. Nucleic Acids Res. 34 (Suppl. 1_1), D599−D601.

Markley, J.L., Ulrich, E.L., Berman, H.M., Henrick, K., Nakamura, H., Akutsu, H., 2008. BioMagResBank (BMRB) as a partner in the Worldwide Protein Data Bank (wwPDB): new policies affecting biomolecular NMR depositions. J. Biomol. NMR 40 (3), 153−155.

MEDLINE®: Description of the Database, n.d. Retrieved from: https://www.nlm.nih.gov/bsd/medline.html.

Menachemi, N., Collum, T.H., 2011. Benefits and drawbacks of electronic health record systems. Risk Manag. & Healthcare Pol. 4, 47.

Meyer, E.F., 1997. The first years of the protein data bank. Protein Sci. Publ. Protein Soc. 6 (7), 1591.

NCBI Resource Coordinators, 2013. Database resources of the national center for biotechnology information. Nucleic Acids Res. 41, D8 (Database issue).

NCBI Resource Coordinators, 2016. Database resources of the national center for biotechnology information. Nucleic Acids Res. 44, D7 (Database issue).

Perutz, M.F., Rossmann, M.G., Cullis, A.F., Muirhead, H., Will, G., North, A.C.T., 1960. Structure of hæmoglobin: a three-dimensional Fourier synthesis at 5.5-Å. resolution, obtained by X-ray analysis. Nature 185 (4711), 416−422.

Pevsner, J., 2009. Bioinformatics and Functional Genomics, second ed. John Wiley and Sons, Hoboken, New Jersey.

Pontén, F., Jirström, K., Uhlen, M., 2008. The human protein atlas—a tool for pathology. J. Pathol. J. Pathol. Soc. G. B. & Irel. 216 (4), 387−393.

Pool, R., Esnayra, J., 2000. Bioinformatics: Converting Data to Knowledge: A Workshop Summary. National Academies Press.

Qazi, S., Tanveer, K., El-bahnasy, K., Raza, K., 2019. From telediagnosis to teletreatment: the role of computational biology and bioinformatics in tele-based healthcare. Telemed. Technol. 153−169. https://doi.org/10.1016/B978-0-12-816948-3.00010-6. Elsevier.

Raghavendra, K., Marilyn, W., 2016. Prospect of big data technologies in healthcare. In: Tomar, G.S., Chaudhari, N.S., Bhadoria, R.S., Deka, G.S. (Eds.), The Human Element of Big Data: Issues, Analytics, and Performance. CRC Press.

Rappaport, N., Nativ, N., Stelzer, G., Twik, M., Guan-Golan, Y., Iny Stein, T., et al., 2013. MalaCards: an integrated compendium for diseases and their annotation. Database 2013.

Raza, K., Ahmad, S., 2019. Recent advancement in next-generation sequencing techniques and its computational analysis. Int. J. Bioinform. Res. & Appl. Indersci. 15 (3), 191−220. https://doi.org/10.1504/IJBRA.2019.10022508.

Raza, K., 2016. Analysis of microarray data using artificial intelligence based techniques. In: Handbook of Research on Computational Intelligence Applications in Bioinformatics. IGI Global, USA, pp. 216−239. https://doi.org/10.4018/978-1-5225-0427-6.ch011.

Rehm, B., 2001. Bioinformatic tools for DNA/protein sequence analysis, functional assignment of genes and protein classification. Appl. Microbiol. Biotechnol. 57 (5−6), 579−592.

Robbins, R.J., 1994. Biological databases: a new scientific literature. Publish. Res. Q. 10 (1), 3−27.

Safran, M., Dalah, I., Alexander, J., Rosen, N., Iny Stein, T., Shmoish, M., et al., 2010. GeneCards version 3: the human gene integrator. Database.

Sarkar, I.N., 2010. Biomedical informatics and translational medicine. J. Transl. Med. 8 (1), 22.

Schumacher S., n.d. European Molecular Biology Laboratory's Position Paper on the Interim Evaluation of Horizon 2020. Retrieved from: https://www.embl.es/aboutus/international-relations/european-science-policy/downloads/EMBL-position-paper-on-the-interim-evaluation-of-Horizon-2020.pdf.

Sethi, P., Theodos, K., 2009. Translational bioinformatics and healthcare informatics: computational and ethical challenges. In: Perspectives in Health Information Management/AHIMA, vol. 6. American Health Information Management Association (Fall).

Shortliffe, E.H., Blois†, M.S., 2006. The computer meets medicine and biology: emergence of a discipline. In: Shortliffe, E.H., Cimino, J.J. (Eds.), Biomedical Informatics. Springer, New York, NY, pp. 3−45.

Sittig, D.F., Singh, H., 2012. Electronic health records and national patient-safety goals. N. Engl. J. Med. 367 (19), 1854.

Standley, D.M., Kinjo, A.R., Kinoshita, K., Nakamura, H., 2008. Protein structure databases with new web services for structural biology and biomedical research. Briefings Bioinf. 9 (4), 276−285.

Stoesser, G., Baker, W., van den Broek, A., Camon, E., Garcia-Pastor, M., Kanz, C., et al., 2002. The EMBL nucleotide sequence database. Nucleic Acids Research 30 (1), 21−26.

Stoesser, G., Sterk, P., Tuli, M.A., Stoehr, P.J., Cameron, G.N., 1997. The EMBL nucleotide sequence database. Nucleic Acids Res. 25 (1), 7−13.

Stoesser, G., Tuli, M.A., Lopez, R., Sterk, P., 1999. The EMBL nucleotide sequence database. Nucleic Acids Research 27 (1), 18−24.

Tange, H.J., Hasman, A., de Vries Robbé, P.F., Schouten, H.C., 1997. Medical narratives in electronic medical records. Int. J. Med. Inf. 46 (1), 7−29.

Uhlén, M., Björling, E., Agaton, C., Szigyarto, C.A.K., Amini, B., Andersen, E., et al., 2005. A human protein atlas for normal and cancer tissues based on antibody proteomics. Mol. Cell. Proteomics 4 (12), 1920−1932.

Uhlen, M., Oksvold, P., Fagerberg, L., Lundberg, E., Jonasson, K., Forsberg, M., et al., 2010. Towards a knowledge-based human protein atlas. Nat. Biotechnol. 28 (12), 1248−1250.

Ulrich, E.L., Markley, J.L., Kyogoku, Y., 1989. Creation of a nuclear magnetic resonance data repository and literature database. Protein Seq. Data Anal. 2 (1), 23−37.

Ulrich, E.L., Akutsu, H., Doreleijers, J.F., Harano, Y., Ioannidis, Y.E., Lin, J., et al., 2007. BioMagResBank. Nucleic Acids Res. 36 (Suppl. 1_1), D402−D408.

Chapter 10

Translational bioinformatics methods for drug discovery and drug repurposing

Salim Ahmad, Sahar Qazi and Khalid Raza*

Department of Computer Science, Jamia Millia Islamia, New Delhi, Delhi, India

Corresponding author: E-mail: kraza@jmi.ac.in

Chapter outline

1. Introduction

Translational bioinformatics (TBI) is an extension of its ancestor bioinformatics, which rose to popularity back in the early 2000s after the success achievement of the Human Genome Project, and it mainly aims to provide a *person-centric platform* that holds the power to integrate all the biomedical data with the existing research in the scientific domain for a better healthcare system. TBI accelerates drug discovery and drug repurposing not only in an efficacious manner but also has minimal long-term negative effect on the patient (Buchan et al., 2011; Wilke et al., 2007).

Drug discovery (DD) is a time-consuming, convoluted, and expensive process wherein pharmaceutical companies invest a lot of money just to identify and develop a specific drug and also manufacture it. The concept of DD has altered significantly after the research of *Paul Ehrlich* that provided a perception shift from *experiential* to *knowledge-based* DD. Translational approaches are a demand of modern DD to understand the progression and proliferation of disease stages and also play a pivotal role in identifying a specific drug for the same. TBI highlights the potential of knowledge-based DD pipelines to reduce the time taken, cut on the expenditures, and thus, lead to a more specific drug lead identification (Denny, 2014). This chapter provides an insight of the current trends of TBI in DD along with some existing issues that need to be resolved for personalized medicine (PM) in the healthcare scenario.

2. Translational bioinformatics

TBI has grown from its ancestor bioinformatics, which amalgamates all the scientific domains such as physics, biology, chemistry, computer sciences, statistics, and mathematics to provide insights into complex biologic problems. TBI rose to prominence after the culmination of the Human Genome Project in the early 2000s and since then has motivationally worked toward the betterment of the human healthcare system. Fig. 10.1 highlights the potential of TBI, which acts as a bridge between its predecessor (bioinformatics) and successor (health informatics).

Butte and Chen (2006) first used the term "*translational bioinformatics.*" TBI reflects a new era of progressive transdisciplinary science that assembles, processes, and integrates a broad collection of biologic informatics domain to transform biomedical findings into clinical care (Londin and Barash, 2015; Tanenbaum, 2016; Butte and Chen, 2006).

The American Medical Informatics Association (AMIA) has described TBI as the amalgamation of three important methods, namely, storage, analytics, and interpretive, to modify and optimize humongous medical data and utilize it for developing a more generic medical healthcare platform (https://www.amia.org/applications-informatics/translational-bioinformatics). Simply, TBI is computer-related activities designed to get clinically feasible information from very large datasets for the advancement of human health and wellness.

TBI employs novel tools and techniques to trigger clinical applicable knowledge by analyzing massive biomedical data and focuses on the proliferative biomedical domain for integrative analyses and summarization of crucial interdisciplinary challenges (Butte, 2008; Ma, 2014). Finally, TBI is integrating heterogeneous biomedical information sources to illuminate the latest biomedical knowledge by interlacing the chasm between the molecular and the clinical world (Fig. 10.2).

2.1 Main methodologies of TBI

An important application of TBI approach lies in the pharmaceutical industry, i.e., the identification of drug candidates for various diseases. As far as the modern drug development process is concerned, TBI is well equipped to provide major contributions when compared to traditional DD processes (Readhead and Dudley, 2013). Massive biologic data is now available and continues to grow exponentially and can be retrieved from repositories, namely, NCBI (https://www.ncbi.nlm.nih.gov/), DDBJ (htbj.nig.ac.jp/index-e.htmltps://www.dd), and EMBL (https://www.embl.org/). TBI has mainly using storage, analytics, and integrative methodologies to access more than a half million samples.

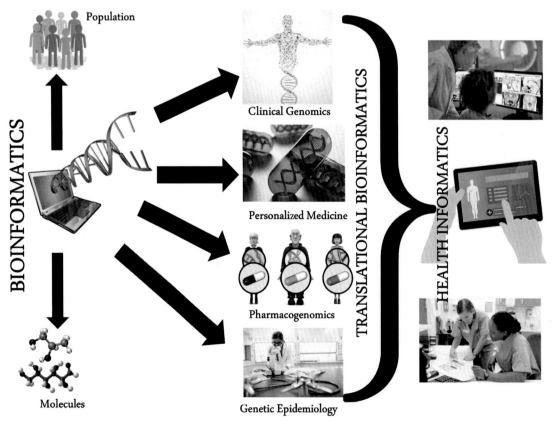

FIGURE 10.1 Translational bioinformatics (TBI) bridges between bioinformatics and health informatics.

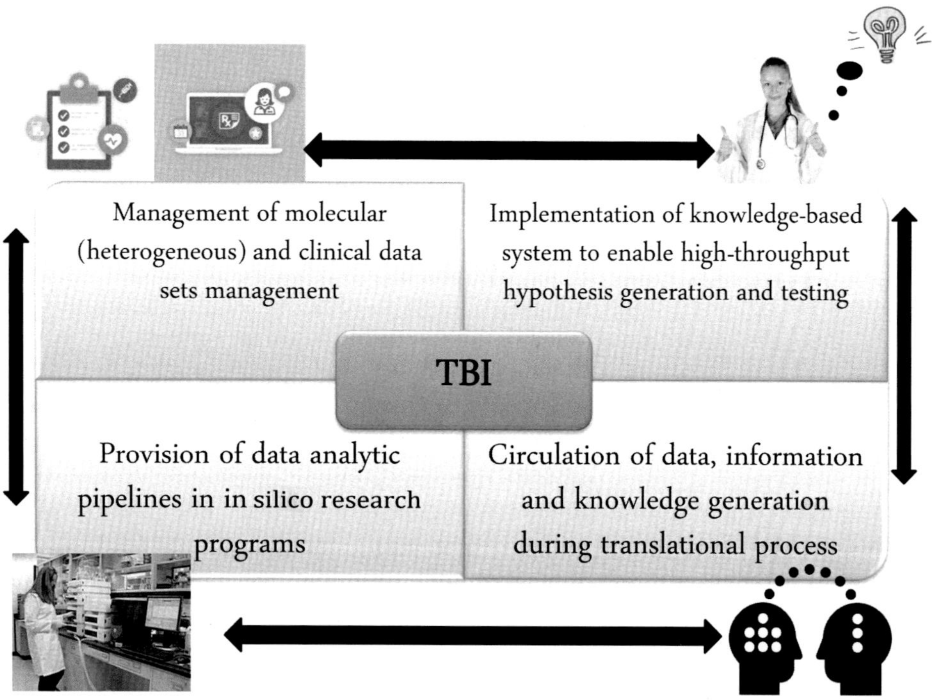

FIGURE 10.2 Vital areas of translational bioinformatics.

2.1.1 Storage

Methods, namely, *data consolidation*, *data federation*, and *data warehousing*, have been deployed extensively to derive useful data from humongous datasets to aid in information retrieval, diagnosis, and to lead compound identification.

a. **Data consolidation** approach is nothing but data derivation from myriad sources in a single database like a warehouse or data lake. This approach enables standardization of heterogeneous data by removing any redundancies and cleaning up any errors before centralization.
b. **Data federation approach** enables common data services by simplifying data reusage. Also, it connects many databases together and retrieves data periodically and then integrates as a single unit for queries, aiding the user to access data in real time.
c. **Data warehousing approach** provides a central repository of information originating from one or more data sources, thus enabling a large platform for data maintenance. Data warehousing integrates structured, semistructured, and unstructured data from myriad sources into a single format that is employed in devising decision support systems (Yan, 2010).

2.1.2 Analytics

To decipher biologic data into clinically relevant information, TBI deploys analytic techniques using high-throughput techniques. *Weka*, a machine learning software for data mining, has also been developed, which is one of the analytical tools available today (Butte, 2009; Sahu et al., 2020a,b).

2.1.3 Integration

It encapsulates interlacing data localized in different sources to enable a consolidated framework (Lenzerini, 2002). It helps a consultant to access data easily and aids in making a decision regarding a disease diagnosis and its treatment. For example, *decision support systems* based on TBI are used to identify correlations in patient electronic medical records and other clinical information systems for diagnoses (Yan, 2010). Integration of TBI resources helps in easy and quick drug reprofiling.

3. Drug discovery

DD is a complex process wherein novel potential leads are identified and designed that can be used against a disease (Xia, 2017). In 1905, *John Newport Langley* stated how targets bind some specific small molecules (drugs) that trigger a biochemical phenomenon in the body, which is now known as "pharmacologic" research (Maehle, 2004). However, it was by consistent efforts of the father of modern DD, Paul Ehrlich, that current DD and design have taken a solid shape (Blass, 2015). The process of DD involves (A) lead "*druggable*" candidate identification, (B) classification of the product, (C) assays for therapeutic efficacy, (D) rigorous screening, and (E) toxicology testing before entering into the clinical trials (Giersiefen et al., 2003). The DD process can be divided into different subsets such as chemical drug candidate's acquisition, screening (pharmacodynamic testing of a huge amount of compounds), and optimization of pharmacokinetic and pharmaceutical properties (Karwasra et al., 2020, Fig. 10.3).

3.1 Five major phases

DD process mainly include the following steps: (i) *target identification*, (ii) *target validation*, (iii) *lead discovery*, (iv) *lead optimization*, and (v) *preclinical and clinical development*.

(a) *Target identification*: Identifying a "*target*" in hope of formulating a novel drug leads to the first step in understanding a disease. A gene or a protein is the "target" that is associated in the progression of a disease. Drug targets can be established drug targets or potential drug targets (depending on their scientific knowledge). **Target deconvolution** process is also known as reverse target validation, which might be used to identify therapeutic targets (Ferreira et al., 2015; Terstappen et al., 2007).

(b) *Target validation*: Target validation is disease—causative effect establishing process. Target validation is helpful in providing a better comprehension into the proliferation and progression of diseases. The validated target is a centerpiece of innovative DD. Validation starts by the identification of a target evidence and evaluation of its potential to design assay for measuring its biologic activity. Target validation also looks over pharmacokinetic and pharmacodynamic factors of the therapeutic target to reduce its failure rate in clinical trials (Wang et al., 2004).

(c) *Lead discovery*: A molecule that holds the potential to trigger a biologic response on binding to a target could be referred to as a "*lead*" compound. Different approaches like serendipity (luck), chemically modified active molecules, rational drug discovery (RDD), and critical examining are deployed to rectify lead compounds (Hughes et al., 2011).

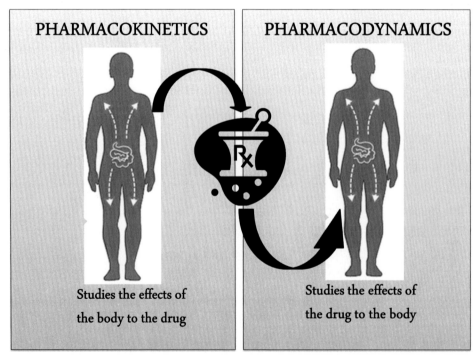

FIGURE 10.3 The main difference between pharmacokinetics (PK) and pharmacodynamics (PD).

(d) *Lead optimization*: This is a process that gives out a drug lead compound whose structure is used as a motivation for alterations. Small structural modifications are guided by evaluation of the pharmacokinetic and pharmacodynamic properties introduced to improvise the physiocochemical properties of a lead compound during the lead optimization process. In the optimization process, the main objective of reiterations is the selection of a drug candidate for preclinical development (Knowles and Gromo, 2003; Rai et al., 2020).

(e) *Preclinical and clinical development*: Preclinical study is inclusive of the development of gigantic-scale synthesis of selected compounds, their animal model studies, toxicity assessments, drug formulations, and efficacy examinations. The clinical development is more inclined toward clinical trials, prevention, and diagnosis of diseases for which the drug has been prepared (Herrling, 2005).

4. Drug reprofiling

Drug reprofiling or repurposing aims to find existing FDA-approved drugs for diseases (Hodos et al., 2016). Drug repurposing or, simply, drug repositioning/rediscovery or reprofiling is a strategy to identify advanced uses for pre-approved drugs or existing medications. The basic idea of repurposing is to discover new useful activity for a distinct malady in an older clinically used drug or one that failed in later stages of development (Chong and Sullivan, 2007). Fig. 10.4 highlights the strategies for drug repurposing for DD studies.

The drug development process is tedious, time-consuming, and heavily expensive one that comes with a high risk of failure because of the selective nature of the drug for a mechanism. Drug repurposing reduces the risk of disintegration as it is based on FDA-approved drugs, so there is no need for human trials. Moreover, low risk of failure, shorter time frame cycle, high success rate, and less investment are expediencies of drug repurposing (Flower, 2020). Table 10.1 summarizes all the repurposed drugs that are widely being used to treat severe diseases and disorders such as cancers, psychiatric diseases, gastrointestinal issues, respiratory infections, etc.

After 2010, the number of researches related to drug repurposing enhanced enormously. The most common examples of drug repurposing are *sildenafil* and *thalidomide*. They were designed for angina and sickness, while their implementation has further been curated for diseases, namely, erectile dysfunction and leprosy, respectively (Masoudi-Sobhanzadeh et al., 2019).

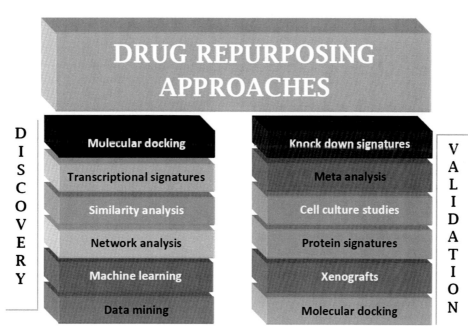

FIGURE 10.4 Drug repurposing approaches for drug discovery and validation.

TABLE 10.1 Some of the widely used prominent repurposed drugs.

Drug name	Original indication	Disease name	Formula
Aspirin	Analgesia	Colorectal cancer	$C_9H_8O_4$
Azathioprine	Rheumatoid arthritis	Renal transplant	$C_9H_7N_7O_2S$
Cycloserine	Urinary tract infection	Tuberculosis	$C_3H_6N_2O_2$
Duloxetine	Depression	Stress urinary incontinence	$C_{18}H_{19}NOS$
Galantamine	Polio and paralysis	Alzheimer	$C_{17}H_{21}NO_3$
Gemcitabine	Antiviral	Cancer	$C_9H_{11}F_2N_3O_4$
Finasteride	Benign prostatic hyperplasia	Hair loss	$C_{23}H_{36}N_2O_2$
Imatinib	Chronic myelogenous leukemia	Gastrointestinal tumors	$C_{29}H_{31}N_7O$
Topiramate	Epilepsy	Obesity	$C_{12}H_{21}NO_8S$
Minoxidil	Hypertension	Hair loss	$C_9H_{15}N_5O$
Phentolamine	Dermal necrosis (hypertension)	Autism	$C_{17}H_{19}N_3O$
Raloxifene	Osteoporosis	Breast cancer	$C_{28}H_{27}NO_4S$
Sildenafil	Angina	Erectile dysfunction	$C_{22}H_{30}N_6O_4S$
Sunitinib	GIST, renal cell carcinoma	Pancreatic tumors	$C_{22}H_{27}FN_4O_2$
Thalidomide	Nausea	Leprosy and multiple myeloma	$C_{13}H_{10}N_2O_4$
Zidovudine	Cancer	AIDS	$C_{10}H_{13}N_5O_4$

5. Role of TBI in drug discovery and drug repurposing

5.1 Resources for drug discovery and drug repurposing

The foundation of TBI is accessing relevant information from enormous databases and other resources. Retrieval of useable platform data for DD development is the key demand of TBI. Several examples of TBI resources for DD and drug repurposing are depicted in Table 10.2.

5.2 Biomarker discovery using TBI strategies

Prognostic markers (biomarkers) are essential for DD and development (Colburn, 2003; Jabeen et al., 2019). Nowadays, biomarker discovery and validation are challenges due to emerging complexities and changing dynamics in diseases. TBI along with the "*omics*" fields aid to get rid of obstacles in biomarker identification (Yan, 2012; Matthews et al., 2016). Fig. 10.5 represents the major "*omics*" strategies that are widely employed for making TBI essential for prognostic marker identification and studies.

Data integration promises to aid in biomarker detection as it is important in amalgamating various types of biomarkers with clinical data with specific biologic context (Perera-Bel et al., 2018). For instance, *bortezomib* resistance is considered to be a potential biomaker in multiple myeloma (Fall et al., 2014). Potential useful biomarkers in gastroenterology were identified using TBI method by microarrays executed on formalin-fixed paraffin-embedded tissue samples (Sharaf et al., 2011). Translational strategies are beneficial for promoting biomarker discoveries. However, the application of TBI in biomarker identification has been more limited.

5.3 TBI methods for drug discovery and drug repurposing

TBI approaches are inclusive of an amalgamation of computational, biologic, chemical, physical, and statistical domains useful for providing immense support in organizing and integrating analyses, data mining, disease prediction, prognostic marker identification, lead compound identification targeting, and repurposing. Multiscale disease network models can be created by combining information about various related and relevant parameters. Such network inferencing approaches surely will help in determining specific and sensitive prognostic indicators (Readhead and Dudley, 2013). TBI methods have laid a way for improvising the safety and use amongst currently available drugs.

TABLE 10.2 Translational bioinformatics-based resources.

Database	URL	Description	References
DrumPID	http://drumpid.bioapps.biozentrum.uniwuerzburg.de/compounds/index.php	The database inclusive of protein interactions with small drug ligands that allows accessing useful information	Kunz et al. (2016)
CREDO	http://marid.bioc.cam.ac.uk/credo	It is a relational database to store pairwise atomic interactions of inter/intramolecular contacts between micromolecule and macromolecules	Schreyer and Blundell (2013)
Protein–Drug Interaction Database (PDID)	http://biomine.ece.ualberta.ca/PDID	Allows users to access protein–drug interactions in the complete human interactome	Wang et al. (2016)
European Union Drug Regulating Authorities Clinical Trials Database (EudraCT)	https://eudract.ema.europa.eu/	A database for all clinical trials on medicinal products that have been authorized by the European Union	Krafft (2005)
SIDER	http://sideeffects.embl.de/	Encapsulates adverse drug reaction (ADR) information on marketed medicines	Kuhn et al. (2016)
DrugBank	https://www.drugbank.ca/	A database integrating detailed drug information with elaborated information of drug targets	Wishart et al. (2008)
The General Practice Research Database (GPRD)	http://www.gprd.com/home/	A repository of medical data taken from primary healthcare based in the United Kingdom	Hansell et al. (1999)
The Drug-Gene Interaction Database (DGIdb)	http://www.dgidb.org/	A database that arranges, stores, and highlights drug–gene interactions and provides druggability information from existing literature sources	Wagner et al. (2016)
Virtually Aligned Matched Molecular Pairs Including Receptor Environment (VAMMPIRE)	http://vammpire.pharmchem.uni-frankfurt.de	A database and a web interface describing useful information on structure-based lead optimization	Weber et al. (2013)
PhID	http://phid.ditad.org/	Provides detailed information on drug–target associations, diseases, disease network biology, associated genes, etc.	Deng et al. (2017)
PROMISCUOUS	http://bioinformatics.charite.de/promiscuous	Network-based drug reprofiling platform	von Eichborn et al. (2011)
Therapeutic Target Database (TTD)	http://db.idrblab.net/ttd/	It provides vital information about drug targets, network biology, associated diseases, and useful drugs	Chen et al. (2002)
IDAAMP	http://idaapm.helsinki.fi/	A database for ADMET and adverse drug reactions (ADRs) based on FDA drug data	Legehar et al. (2016)
CancerDR	http://crdd.osdd.net/raghava/cancerdr/	A database of anticancer drugs against thousands of cancer cell lines	Kumar et al. (2013)
ChEMBL	https://www.ebi.ac.uk/chembl/	Database entails comprehensive information about one million bioactive compounds with more than 8000 drug targets	Gaulton et al. (2003)
Orphan Nuclear Receptor Ligand Binding Database (ONRLDB)	http://www.onrldb.org/	A database that collects and connects information about small orphan ligands available from scientific literature	Nanduri et al. (2015)
The Adverse Event Reporting System (AERS)	https://healthdata.gov/dataset/adverse-event-reporting-system-aers	A surveillance system for all FDA-approved drugs	Wang et al. (2014)

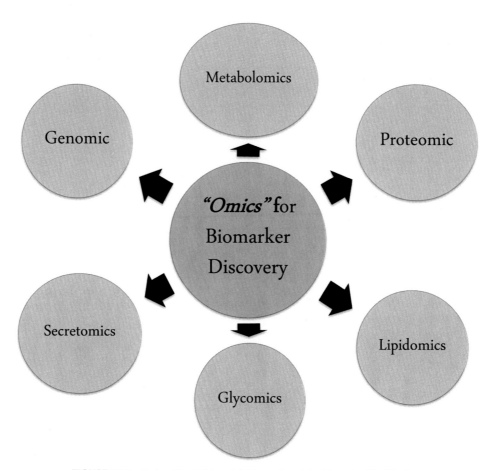

FIGURE 10.5 Various "*omics*"-based fields employed for biomarker identification.

6. Impact of TBI on drug discovery and drug repurposing

The accomplishment of TBI in the drug development field has led to an improvement in the quality of drug identification and design modus operands for molding a better and effective treatment system. The main impact of TBI in DD is the perception shift from traditional reliance on animal models to more unified in silico and in vitro frameworks including different areas, namely, molecular bioinformatics, clinical informatics, and health informatics (Kulikowski and Kulikowski, 2009). The considerable impact of TBI on DD and the development pipeline might be illustrated in preclinical, clinical, and postclinical phases (Buchan et al., 2011).

6.1 The *preclinical* phase

6.1.1 Understanding the dynamics

Various TBI approaches open the door to understanding novel relationships between diseases and treatments via fraternization with clinical and healthcare domains. Use of platform approaches like pharmacogenomics, genome characterization, transcriptomics studies, gene expression data, etc., lead to better opportunities in decision-making for medical consultants, disease biology dynamics understanding, and better treatment protocols design. Jones et al. (2010) suggested the classification of an oncogene (*adenocarcinoma of the tongue*) and discerned the tumor arises because of the RET oncogene.

6.1.2 Drug repurposing

As it has been already mentioned in the previous sections, TBI approaches have been dexterously deployed for reprofiling of drugs for new directions, such as connectivity *approaches*, disease—drug association, literature mining methods, etc. Chiang and Butte (2009) suggested that *rituximab*, a drug deployed against non-Hodgkin lymphoma and rheumatoid arthritis, now also be used for treating cataracts, gastric problems, and cancers (Sahu et al., 2020a).

6.1.3 Drug safety

An unexpected impairment that is usually caused by either overdose or a prolonged administration of drugs is referred to as an *adverse drug reaction* (ADR), and it is highly mandatory to predict and prevent such adverse drug reactions (ADRs). TBI techniques help in amalgamating already known information of genes and networks that are affiliated with ADRs. Such a study is mainly deployed during the preclinical assessment of the DD process (Yeung, 2015).

6.2 The *clinical* phase

6.2.1 Participation for clinical trials

Patient selection for clinical trials in another important step in DD, and TBI has been highly beneficial in its execution as it uses artificial intelligence (AI) techniques for the same. For instance, PARADIGM is one such platform that sorts and selects the best participants for clinical trials by taking their genomic composition as an input and combining it with an already existing database, namely, the NCBI Pathway Interaction Database (http://pid.nci.nih.gov), to check for network interactions (Vaske et al., 2010).

6.2.2 Prognostic markers

TBI has encouraged framing a simpler analysis of metadata, which has led to improved and better possibilities of rectifying prognostic markers (biomarkers) to check a patient's disease stage and support medical consultants for better decision-making for diagnosis and prognosis (Strimbu and Tavel, 2010).

6.3 The *post* launch

6.3.1 Diagnostics

Parallel molecular screenings are getting widely accepted as a "*part and parcel*" for patient diagnosis. TBI uses next-generation sequencing data for screening and identifying relevant motif signatures or patterns that can be aligned to receptor targets. For example, lamination of various breast cancer tumor samples was used to determine relevant specific signature patterns in the breast cancer network (Gatza et al., 2010). This could surely aid in generating specific disease biomarkers (Buchan et al., 2011).

6.3.2 Theranostics

Theranostics, a word formed from two terms "therapeutics" and "diagnostics," is an aspect in DD that uses radioactive drugs for the diagnosis and treatment in two consecutive phases. Currently, innovative approaches of TBI take genomic content of the patient, the complete human interactome, and ADRs into account to frame a biologic reasoning for a drug candidate that may lead to some altered effect in the human body (Berger et al., 2010). Goldenberg et al. (2008) have deployed this technique and have discerned its potential in long-QT syndrome, which is a congenital disease. Fig. 10.6 depicts the basic mechanism of theranostics.

7. Advent of *AIM* in drug discovery

Artificial intelligence in medicine (AIM) is one such promising domain that has grown from TBI that utilizes the potential of existing medical data and uses this knowledge with a little help from computational algorithms to develop medical

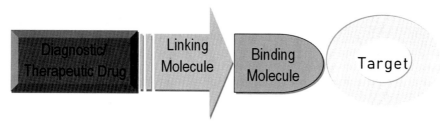

FIGURE 10.6 Principle mechanism of theranostics.

decision support systems (MDS) employed by medical consultants to detect, diagnose, and prescribe a better person-centric treatment. With the advent of AI in healthcare, major developments have been accomplished for betterment of RDD (Mak and Pichika, 2019). AIM has proved its success with various accomplishments such as virtual reality (VIREAL) for diseases like psychiatric disorders (ASD) (Qazi and Raza, 2020a), biosensors for achieving a *point of care* in healthcare management (Qazi and Raza, 2020b), remote-based healthcare assistance and checkup with the development of tele-based healthcare (Qazi et al., 2019), and internet of living things for a ubiquitous healthcare management (Raza and Qazi, 2019).

Currently, the pharmaceutical fraternity lacks DD approaches that are pocket friendly with better efficiency. AIM can significantly improve the efficacy of the drug development process. The basic difficulty in DD is to find a suitable drug candidate that can be deployed for treatment of diseases. This drug must be stable, druggable, with few or no side effects and toxicity, and due to the gargantuan size of the chemical space, it becomes very tedious to identify such drug compounds. Therefore, AI becomes very helpful in identifying and sorting such drug compounds that can be used for further analysis (Segler et al., 2018; Raza, 2020). AIM-based DD approaches have become rapid, robust, and more efficient with the identification, evaluation of drug targets, developing novel drugs, drug repurposing, and in refining the MDS that selects patients for clinical trials (Huang et al., 2017; Zhang, 2017; Mamoshina et al., 2016). The main purpose of AIM in DD is to minimize bias and human interference (Seddon et al., 2012). Many researchers working in this domain have suggested myriad applications of AIM in DD, namely, identification of potential lead compounds (Merk et al., 2018), pharmacologic properties (Klopman et al., 2004), drug repurposing (Mak and Pichika, 2019), drug–receptor interactions (Nascimento et al., 2016), and determination of novel biomarkers (Matthews et al., 2016). For instance, Amgen, a pharmaceutical company that deployed AIM for DD, has developed a platform namely MELLODDY that allows machine learning models to be trained on datasets from myriad sources for optimal drug compounds for diseases (https://www.melloddy.eu/). Deep learning has also showcased magnanimous power in predicting drug ADME properties and toxicity risks (Hughes et al., 2011). With all such impactful resources, pharmaceutical industries and R&D have been able to rapidly work toward person-centric systems for healthcare management.

8. The road ahead: challenges and future directions

TBI has been greatly appreciated in DD as it has eased human intervention and reduced expenditure and time drastically. Furthermore, it has also aided in various aspects of drug target identification, drug bioactivity prediction, drug repurposing, drug lead prediction, etc. Howbeit, there are many clinical challenges that still exist in the road of TBI in drug identification processes. DD is a tedious process and takes time. Although TBI has made it quite rapid, it still lags behind in many aspects. Firstly, the unknown functioning of various diseases makes drug target identification very difficult. Another challenge is that relying completely on animal model trials cannot suffice in TBI approaches for DD studies. Furthermore, a patient's genomic composition varies greatly, so incremental phenotyping and endotyping may lead to variant results. Currently, there are hardly any specific biomarkers that can be used to detect diseases, thus leading to no specific drug development for the same. Although most of these challenges are now being resolved with the aid of computational approaches and AI, the apex challenge that still lies is the lack of trained professionals who can handle and use the TBI-based platforms for better DD and repurposing strategies (https://www.ncbi.nlm.nih.gov/books/NBK195047/).

The future prospect of TBI in DD research is to train individuals who are well aware about the benefits of this platform and who can regulate the TBI approaches for drug candidate identification and discovery and designing processes. Furthermore, there is also a need to devise more computationally intensive machines that can aid in critically selecting patients who can participate in clinical trials. Also, a common integrated platform is also underway that can help in determining the potential drug targets, target receptors, biomarkers, drug–target associations, potential gene expression, and genomic content of patients for efficient healthcare management (Redhead and Dudley, 2013).

9. Conclusions

Drug discovery and development is a convoluted, time-consuming, and extravagant process. TBI has grown from its ancestor bioinformatics that amalgamates all the scientific domains such as physics, biology, chemistry, computer sciences, statistics, and mathematics to provide insights to complex biologic problems. TBI rose to prominence after the annotation of the complete human genome in the early 2000s and since then has motivationally worked toward the betterment of the human healthcare system. TBI has no precise nor widely held definition.TBI employs novel tools and techniques to trigger clinical applicable knowledge by analyzing massive biomedical data, and it focuses on a proliferative biomedical domain for integrative analyses and summarization of crucial interdisciplinary challenges. Drug repurposing refers to the deployment of an existing FDA-approved drug to a new disease and to minimize costs, time, and human resources, so there is no requirement for human clinical trials. Moreover, low risk of failure, shorter time frame cycle, high success rate, and less investment are expediencies of drug repurposing.

The accomplishment of TBI is gaining momentum in the drug development field. TBI emphasizes its potential to improve the methods of DD for a more effective treatment for patients, leading to a person-centric platform system in healthcare. TBI's main objective is nothing but the "perception shift from traditional approaches to modern strategies for personalized healthcare." *AIM* is one such promising domain that has grown from TBI that utilizes the potential of existing medical data and uses this knowledge with a little help from computational algorithms to develop MDS employed by medical consultants to detect, diagnose, and prescribe a better person-centric treatment. With the advent of AI in healthcare, major developments have been accomplished for betterment of RDD.

With all these accomplishments of TBI in DD, there still are many loopholes that need to be taken care of. Some of the crucial challenges are (A) diseases that are not well annotated nor understood, making it difficult to identify targets; (B) dependence on animal models cannot be sufficient; (C) a patient's genomic composition varies greatly, so incremental phenotyping and endotyping may lead to variant results; and (D) there are hardly any specific biomarkers that can be used to detect diseases, leading to no specific drug development for the same. The future for TBI is quite bright as many novel researches are being conducted to improve the approaches of current DD. There is a need to train more individuals who are well aware about the benefits of this platform and can regulate the TBI approaches for drug candidate identification and discovery and designing processes. Moreover, computationally intensive machines that can aid in critically selecting patients who can participate in clinical trials must also be developed for aiding medical consultants. A platform that encapsulates determining the potential drug targets, target receptors, biomarkers, drug—target associations, potential gene expression, and genomic content of patients for an efficient healthcare management is under development and would surely be helpful to improve the current healthcare scenario, making it more personalized in nature.

Acknowledgments

SQ is supported by DST-INSPIRE Fellowship, Department of Science and Technology (DST), Govt. of India.

Conflict of Interests
None.

References

Berger, S.I., et al., 2010. Systems pharmacology of arrhythmias. Sci. Signal. 3, 1—15.

Blass, B.E., 2015. The Drug Discovery Process. https://doi.org/10.1016/B978-0-12-411508-8.00002-5.

Buchan, N.S., Rajpal, D.K., Webster, Y.W., Alatorre, C.I., Gudivada, R.C., Zheng, C., Sanseau, P., Koehler, J., 2011. The role of translational bioinformatics in drug discovery. Drug Discov. Today 16 (9—10), 426—434.

Butte, A.J., 2008. Translational bioinformatics: coming of age. J. Am. Med. Inf. Assoc. JAMIA 15 (6), 709—714.

Butte, A.J., 2009. Translational bioinformatics applications in genome medicine. Genome Med. 1 (6), 64.

Butte, A.J., Chen, R., 2006. Finding disease-related genomic experiments within an international repository: first steps in translational bioinformatics. In: AMIA Annual Symposium Proceedings. AMIA Symposium, 2006, pp. 106—110.

Chen, X., Ji, Z.L., Chen, Y.Z., 2002. TTD: therapeutic target database. Nucleic Acids Res. 30 (1), 412—415.

Chiang, A.P., Butte, A.J., 2009. Systematic evaluation of drug—disease relationships to identify leads for novel drug uses. Clin. Pharmacol. Ther. 86, 507—510.

Chong, C.R., Sullivan Jr., D.J., 2007. New uses for old drugs. Nature 448 (7154), 645—646.

Colburn, W.A., 2003. Biomarkers in drug discovery and development: from target identification through drug marketing. J. Clin. Pharmacol. 43 (4), 329—341.

Deng, Z., Tu, W., Deng, Z., Hu, Q.N., 2017. PhID: an open-access integrated pharmacology interactions database for drugs, targets, diseases, genes, side-effects, and pathways. J. Chem. Inf. Model. 57 (10), 2395—2400.

Denny, J.C., 2014. Surveying recent themes in translational bioinformatics: big data in EHRs, omics for drugs, and personal genomics. Yearb. Med. Informatics 9 (1), 199—205.

Fall, D.J., Stessman, H., Patel, S.S., Sachs, Z., Van Ness, B.G., Baughn, L.B., Linden, M.A., 2014. Utilization of translational bioinformatics to identify novel biomarkers of bortezomib resistance in multiple myeloma. J. Canc. 5, 720—727.

Ferreira, B.I., Hill, R., Link, W., 2015. Special review: caught in the crosshairs: targeted drugs and personalized medicine. Canc. J. 21 (6), 441—447.

Flower, D.R., 2020. Drug discovery: today and tomorrow. Bioinformation 16 (1), 1—3.

Gatza, M.L., Lucas, J.E., Barry, W.T., Kim, J.W., Wang, Q., Crawford, M.D., Datto, M.B., Kelley, M., Mathey-Prevot, B., Potti, A., Nevins, J.R., 2010. A pathway-based classification of human breast cancer. Proc. Natl. Acad. Sci. U. S. A 107 (15), 6994—6999.

Gaulton, A., Hersey, A., Nowotka, M., Bento, A.P., Chambers, J., Mendez, D., Mutowo, P., Giersiefen, H., Hilgenfeld, R., Hillisch, A., 2003. Modern methods of drug discovery: an introduction. EXS (93), 1—18.

Giersiefen, H., Hilgenfeld, R., Hillisch, A., 2003. Modern methods of drug discovery: an introduction. Mod. Meth. Drug Disc. 1—18. https://doi.org/10.1007/978-3-0348-7997-2_1.

Goldenberg, I., et al., 2008. Long QT syndrome. Curr. Probl. Cardiol. 33, 629−694.

Hansell, A., Hollowell, J., Nichols, T., McNiece, R., Strachan, D., 1999. Use of the general practice research database (GPRD) for respiratory epidemiology: a comparison with the 4th morbidity survey in general practice (MSGP4). Thorax 54 (5), 413−419.

Herrling, P.L., 2005. The drug discovery process. Progress in drug research. In: Fortschritte der Arzneimittelforschung. Progres des recherchespharmaceutiques, vol. 62, pp. 1−14.

Hodos, R.A., Kidd, B.A., Shameer, K., Readhead, B.P., Dudley, J.T., 2016. In silico methods for drug repurposing and pharmacology. Wiley Interdiscip. Rev. Syst. Biol. & Med. 8 (3), 186−210.

Huang, Z., et al., 2017. Data mining for biomedicine and healthcare. J. Healthc. Eng. 2, 7107629.

Hughes, J.P., Rees, S., Kalindjian, S.B., Philpott, K.L., 2011. Principles of early drug discovery. Br. J. Pharmacol. 162 (6), 1239−1249.

Jabeen, A., Ahmad, N., Raza, K., 2019. Differential expression analysis of ZIKV infected human RNA sequence reveals potential genetic biomarkers. In: Lecture Notes in Bioinformatics, vol. 11465. Springer, pp. 1−12. https://doi.org/10.1007/978-3-030-17938-0_26.

Jones, S.J., et al., 2010. Evolution of an adenocarcinoma in response to selection by targeted kinase inhibitors. Genome Biol. 11, R82.

Karwasra, R., Fatihi, S., Raza, K., Singh, S., Khanna, K., Sharma, N., Sharma, S., Sharma, D., Varma, S., 2020. Filgrastim loading in PLGA and SLN nanoparticulate system: a bioinformatics approach. Drug Dev. Ind. Pharm. 46 (8), 1354−1361. https://doi.org/10.1080/03639045.2020.1788071. Taylor & Francis.

Klopman, G., et al., 2004. ESP: a method to predict toxicity and pharmacological properties of chemicals using multiple MCASE databases. J. Chem. Inf. Comput. Sci. 44, 704−715.

Knowles, J., Gromo, G., 2003. A guide to drug discovery: target selection in drug discovery. Nat. Rev. Drug Discov. 2, 63−69.

Krafft, H., 2005. Die EudraCT-Datenbankbei der EMEA zurErfassungklinischer Prüfungen in Europa [The community clinical trial system EudraCT at the EMEA for the monitoring of clinical trials in Europe]. Bundesgesundheitsblatt - Gesundheitsforsch. - Gesundheitsschutz 48 (4), 453−458.

Kuhn, M., Letunic, I., Jensen, L.J., Bork, P., 2016. The SIDER database of drugs and side effects. Nucleic Acids Res. 44 (D1), D1075−D1079.

Kulikowski, C.A., Kulikowski, C.W., 2009. Biomedical and health informatics in translational medicine. Methods Inf. Med. 48, 4−10.

Kumar, R., Chaudhary, K., Gupta, S., et al., 2013. CancerDR: cancer drug resistance database. Sci. Rep. 3, 1445.

Kunz, M., Liang, C., Nilla, S., Cecil, A., Dandekar, T., 2016. The drug-minded protein interaction database (DrumPID) for efficient target analysis and drug development. Database J. Biol. Databases & Curation 2016, baw041.

Legehar, A., Xhaard, H., Ghemtio, L., 2016. IDAAPM: integrated database of ADMET and adverse effects of predictive modeling based on FDA approved drug data. J. Cheminf. 8, 33.

Lenzerini, M., 2002. Data Integration: A Theoretical Perspective. PODS, pp. 233−246.

Londin, E.R., Barash, C.I., 2015. What is translational bioinformatics? Appl. & Transl. Genomics 6, 1−2.

Ma, T., 2014. Integrative and interdisciplinary challenges in translational bioinformatics. ACM SIGBioinform. 4 (2), 1−6.

Maehle, A.H., 2004. "Receptive substances": John Newport Langley (1852-1925) and his path to a receptor theory of drug action. Med. Hist. 48 (2), 153−174.

Mak, K.K., Pichika, M.R., 2019. Artificial intelligence in drug development: present status and future prospects. Drug Discov. Today 24 (3), 773−780.

Mamoshina, P., et al., 2016. Applications of deep learning in biomedicine. Mol. Pharm. 13, 1445−1454.

Masoudi-Sobhanzadeh, Y., Omidi, Y., Amanlou, M., Masoudi-Nejad, A., 2019. Drug databases and their contributions to drug repurposing. Genomics 112. https://doi.org/10.1016/j.ygeno.2019.06.021.

Matthews, H., Hanison, J., Nirmalan, N., 2016. "Omics"-Informed drug and biomarker discovery: opportunities, challenges and future perspectives. Proteomes 4 (3), 28.

Merk, D., et al., 2018. De novo design of bioactive small molecules by artificial intelligence. Mol. Inform. 37, 1700153.

Nanduri, R., Bhutani, I., Somavarapu, A.K., Mahajan, S., Parkesh, R., Gupta, P., 2015. ONRLDB–manually curated database of experimentally validated ligands for orphan nuclear receptors: insights into new drug discovery. Database J. Biol. Databases & Curation 2015, bav112.

Nascimento, A.C.A., et al., 2016. A multiple kernel learning algorithm for drug-target interaction prediction. BMC Bioinf. 17, 46.

Perera-Bel, J., Leha, A., Beißbarth, T., 2018. Bioinformatic methods and resources for biomarker discovery, validation, development, and integration. In: Predictive Biomarkers in Oncology, pp. 149−164.

Qazi, S., Raza, K., 2020a. Towards a VIREAL platform: virtual reality in cognitive and behavioural training for autistic individuals. In: Advanced Computational Intelligence Techniques for Virtual Reality in Healthcare, Studies in Computational Intelligence SCI, vol. 875. Springer, pp. 25−47.

Qazi, S., Raza, K., 2020b. Smart biosensors for an efficient point of care (PoC) health management. In: Smart Biosensors in Medical Care. Elsevier, pp. 65−85.

Qazi, S., Tanveer, K., El-bahnasy, K., Raza, K., 2019. From telediagnosis to teletreatment: the role of computational biology and bioinformatics in tele-based healthcare. In: Telemedicine Technologies. Elsevier, pp. 153−169.

Rai, A., Qazi, S., Raza, K., 2020. In silico analysis and comparative molecular docking study of FDA approved drugs with transforming growth factor beta receptors in oral submucous fibrosis. Indian J. Otolaryngol. Head Neck Surg. Springer. In press. https://doi.org/10.1007/s12070-020-02014-5.

Raza, K., 2020. Computational Intelligence Methods in COVID-19: Surveillance, Prevention, Prediction and Diagnosis, Studies in Computational Intelligence (SCI). Springer, p. 923.

Raza, K., Qazi, S., 2019. Nanopore sequencing technology and internet of living things: a big hope for U-healthcare. In: Sensors for Health Monitoring, vol. 5. Elsevier, pp. 95−116.

Readhead, B., Dudley, J., 2013. Translational bioinformatics approaches to drug development. Adv. Wound Care 2 (9), 470−489.

Sahu, A., Qazi, S., Raza, K., Varma, S., 2020a. COVID-19: hard road to find integrated computational drug repurposing pipeline. In: Computational Intelligence for COVID-19: Surveillance, Prevention, Prediction and Diagnosis, Studies in Computational Intelligence (SCI). Springer, p. 923.

Sahu, A., Pradhan, D., Raza, K., Qazi, S., Jain, A.K., Verma, S., 2020b. In silico library design, screening and MD simulation of COX-2 inhibitors for anticancer activity. In: Proc. Of 12th International Conference on Bioinformatics and Computational Biology (BICOB-2020), San Francisco, USA, March 23-25, 2020. EPiC Series in Computing, vol. 70, pp. 21–32. https://doi.org/10.29007/z2wx.

Schreyer, A.M., Blundell, T.L., 2013. CREDO: a structural interactomics database for drug discovery. Database J. Biol. Databases & Curation 2013, bat049.

Seddon, G., et al., 2012. Drug design for ever, from hype to hope. J. Comput. Aided Mol. Des. 26, 137–150.

Segler, M.H.S., et al., 2018. Generating focused molecule libraries for drug discovery with recurrent neural networks. ACS Cent. Sci. 4, 120–131.

Sharaf, R.N., Butte, A.J., Montgomery, K.D., Pai, R., Dudley, J.T., Pasricha, P.J., 2011. Computational prediction and experimental validation associating FABP-1 and pancreatic adenocarcinoma with diabetes. BMC Gastroenterol. 11, 5.

Strimbu, K., Tavel, J.A., 2010. What are biomarkers? Curr. Opin. HIV AIDS 5 (6), 463–466.

Tenenbaum, J.D., 2016. Translational bioinformatics: past, present, and future. Dev. Reprod. Biol. 14 (1), 31–41.

Terstappen, G., Schlüpen, C., Raggiaschi, R., et al., 2007. Target deconvolution strategies in drug discovery. Nat. Rev. Drug Discov. 6, 891–903.

Vaske, C.J., et al., 2010. Inference of patient-specific pathway activities from multidimensional cancer genomics data using PARADIGM. Bioinformatics 26, i237–i245.

von Eichborn, J., Murgueitio, M.S., Dunkel, M., Koerner, S., Bourne, P.E., Preissner, R., 2011. PROMISCUOUS: a database for network-based drug-repositioning. Nucleic Acids Res. 39, D1060–D1066.

Wagner, A.H., Coffman, A.C., Ainscough, B.J., Spies, N.C., Skidmore, Z.L., Campbell, K.M., Krysiak, K., Pan, D., McMichael, J.F., Eldred, J.M., Walker, J.R., Wilson, R.K., Mardis, E.R., Griffith, M., Griffith, O.L., 2016. DGIdb 2.0: mining clinically relevant drug-gene interactions. Nucleic Acids Res. 44 (D1), D1036–D1044.

Wang, C., Hu, G., Wang, K., Brylinski, M., Xie, L., Kurgan, L., 2016. PDID: database of molecular-level putative protein-drug interactions in the structural human proteome. Bioinformatics 32 (4), 579–586.

Wang, L., Jiang, G., Li, D., Liu, H., 2014. Standardizing adverse drug event reporting data. J. Biomed. Semant. 5, 36.

Wang, S., Sim, T.B., Kim, Y.S., Chang, Y.T., 2004. Tools for target identification and validation. Curr. Opin. Chem. Biol. 8, 371–377.

Weber, J., Achenbach, J., Moser, D., Proschak, E., 2013. VAMMPIRE: a matched molecular pairs database for structure-based drug design and optimization. J. Med. Chem. 56 (12), 5203–5207.

Wilke, R.A., Lin, D.W., et al., 2007. Identifying genetic risk factors for serious adverse drug reactions: current progress and challenges. Nat. Rev. Drug Discov. 6 (11), 904–916.

Wishart, D.S., Knox, C., Guo, A.C., Cheng, D., Shrivastava, S., Tzur, D., Gautam, B., Hassanali, M., 2008. DrugBank: a knowledgebase for drugs, drug actions and drug targets. Nucleic Acids Res. 36, D901–D906 (Database issue).

Xia, X., 2017. Bioinformatics and drug discovery. Curr. Top. Med. Chem. 17 (15), 1709–1726.

Yan, Q., 2012. Translational bioinformatics in psychoneuroimmunology: methods and applications. Methods Mol. Biol. 934, 383–400.

Yan, Q., 2010. Translational bioinformatics and systems biology approaches for personalized medicine. Systems Biology in Drug Discovery and Development Methods Mol. Biol. 662, 167–178.

Yeung, E.Y., 2015. Adverse drug reactions: a potential role for pharmacists. Br. J. Gen. Pract. J. R. Coll. Gen. Pract. 65 (639), 511.

Zhang, Y., et al., 2017. Computer-aided clinical trial recruitment based on domain-specific language translation: a case study of retinopathy of prematurity. J. Healthc. Eng. 2017, 7862672. https://doi.org/10.1155/2017/7862672.

Further reading

Atkinson, F., Bellis, L.J., et al., 2017. The ChEMBL database in 2017. Nucleic Acids Res. 45 (D1), D945–D954.

Hamet, P., Tremblay, J., 2017. Artificial intelligence in medicine. Metabolism 69, S36–S40.

Hidalgo, C.A., et al., 2009. A dynamic network approach for the study of human phenotypes. PLoS Comput. Biol. 5, e1000353.

Isa, M.A., Mustapha, A., Qazi, S., Raza, K., Allamin, I.A., Ibrahim, M.M., Mohammed, M.M., 2020. In silico molecular docking and molecular dynamic simulation of potential inhibitors of 3c-like main proteinase (3clpro) from severe acute respiratory syndrome-2 (sars-cov-2) using selected african medicinal plants. Adv. Trad. Med., Springer, (In Press). https://doi.org/10.1007/s13596-020-00523-w.

Jabeen, A., Ahmad, N., Raza, K., 2018. Machine learning-based state-of-the-art methods for the classification of RNA-seq data. In: Dey, N., Ashour, A., Borra, S. (Eds.), Classification in BioApps. lecture notes in computational vision and biomechanics, 26. Springer, pp. 133–172.

Karwasra, R., Singh, S., Raza, K., Sharma, N., Varma, S., 2020. A brief overview on current status of nanomedicines for treatment of pancytopenia: focusing on chemotherapeutic regime. J. Drug Deliv. Sci. Technol., Elsevier, (In Press). https://doi.org/10.1016/j.jddst.2020.102159.

Mazumder, J., Khan, E., Perwez, M., Gupta, M., Kumar, S., Raza, K., Sardar, M., 2020. Exposure of biosynthesized nanoscale ZnO to Brassica juncea crop plant: morphological, biochemical and molecular aspects. Sci. Rep. Nat. 10, 8531. https://doi.org/10.1038/s41598-020-65271-y.

Menden, M.P., et al., 2013. Machine learning prediction of cancer cell sensitivity to drugs based on genomic and chemical properties. PLoS One 8, e61318.

Schneider, G., 2017. Automating drug discovery. Nat. Rev. Drug Discov. 17, 97–113.

Chapter 11

Role of Bioinformatics in cancer research and drug development

Anam Beg* and Rafat Parveen

Department of Computer Science, Jamia Millia Islamia, New Delhi, Delhi, India

*Corresponding author: E-mail: anamrazabeg@gmail.com

Chapter outline

1. Introduction

Cancer has been around forever, but in recent times our ability to diagnose the disease and treat it has improved greatly. People with cancer are living longer. Cancer is a deadly disease with many subtypes and it is also a leading cause of deaths globally with numbers reaching 13.1 million in 2030. Genetic and epigenetic alteration in a human body defines cancer. Easy management of cancer is possible with early diagnosis and prognosis. This is also a leading trend in cancer research today. There are several challenges that cancer patients and oncologists face while treating a cancer patient. Cancer treatment is costly due to the high price patients have to pay for drugs. Secondly there is no surety that the drug will have the same effectiveness for all patients and the response to the drug may vary on a case to case basis. In addition to both these factors there is a psychologic battle the patients and caregivers have to fight on an everyday basis. Failure of drugs and limited financial resources often push patients into depression and financial crises. Often patients have to deal with severe side effects ranging from headache and nausea to thrombocytopenia and leukopenia, leading to admission to hospitals for supportive care. Cancers are usually classified based on the origin/primary site/location in the body where it first develops. The importance of cancer classification is extreme because it addresses problems related to drug discovery and cancer diagnosis (Lu and Han, 2003). DNA microarray enables us to monitor several hundred gene expressions and with this we are left with a myriad of gene expression data, so researchers are now exploring opportunities of cancer classification using gene expression data. To get a deeper understanding many issues still need to be addressed (the problem of gene contamination or statistical significance vs. biologic significance of a cancer classifier and the asymmetrical classification errors for cancer classifier). For this, classification can be based on feature detection because of the biomedical and bioinformatics fields (Lu and Han, 2003). Bioinformatics is playing a major role in healthcare and here are certain views. The computational techniques like Bayesian network, fuzzy logic, artificial neural network, genetic algorithm, data mining, machine learning etc. have a high impact on the early diagnosis of cancer and its prognosis.

Cancer bioinformatics deals with organizing and analyzing data to identify important movements and motifs: the penultimate goal being the innovation of new therapies and diagnostic entente for cancers. In today's time a large sum of data for example clinical data, SNP data (single nucleotide polymorphism), structure data, microarray data, proteomic, and expressed sequence tag (EST) provides a chance to understand cancer. In recent years, virtual repositories—or "data clouds"— have been in great use to improve and integrate access to research data. Many of these developments are still in their early stages. Cancer research is being greatly assisted by the creation and utilization of public data banks and the emphasis is being laid on cancer tissue resourcing and EST data. Cancer-related genes and their functions can be best understood with the help of EST data because EST are single DNA sequencing reads made from complementary DNA (cDNA) clone libraries constructed from a known tissue source. Computational analysis of EST clustering and EST tissue is being done to understand the concept behind inherent carcinogenesis (Xie et al., 2002). Since researchers do not have access to primary data created by computational tools it is challenging to analyze and integrate data from these platforms.

Cancer bioinformatics plays a major role in the recognition and verification of biomarkers and it also measures disease progression and how the patients are responding to different therapies. So bioinformatics plays a major role in selecting drug targets. Cancer drug research has come a long way with new therapies like targeted therapy, immunotherapy (Charoentong et al., 2012) and nanomedicines (Blanco et al., 2011) showing promise. Cancer unlike other diseases acts differently in different patients/cases. No two cancer patients are the same or respond in the same way to therapy or drugs, hence making therapies ineffective for some and very effective for a select few. It is found that chemotherapy is a major stressor in cancer patients other than those who have not received chemotherapy. The life quality among cancer patients is reduced and this can be inferred from the statistics that 16.8%−45% of people suffer from depression, and 12%−18% of people suffer from depressive order among cancer patients undergoing chemotherapy (Wen et al., 2019). It is also ascertained that the psychologic health of patients took a beating as 418 (54.4%) of the total number of patients surveyed usually felt depressed, and 755 (98.3%) are uncomfortable attending social functions. Most of them, i.e., 585 (76.2%), were insecure about recurrence 755 (98.3%) of respondents felt that their income status was reduced as a result of illness and physical well-being and 658 (85.7%) were worried and dissatisfied about body image (Nayak et al., 2017). This problem has challenged researchers for a long time and now some claim to have found an answer in targeted therapies. With recent advancements in drug design and developments researchers have come up with a new class of drugs e.g., PARP inhibitors and angiogenesis inhibitors. Research is also underway to develop a vaccine for several types of cancers and immunotherapy is also being widely researched as an alternative to chemotherapy and radiotherapy. With a wide variety of natural and artificial proteins and peptides available it is a daunting challenge and a rigorous exercise to figure out the target and proteins that are most likely to work in a given condition, hence giving rise to the use of molecular dynamic (MD) simulation. Biomedical researches create a bulk of biologic data and over the years it has increased exponentially but the computational tools and techniques of bioinformatics help a lot to store and analyze those data. The information we gain from these data leads toward the progress of precision medicine i.e. the patient disease is now based on molecular characteristics that are tailored in diagnosis treatment and prevention.

2. Bioinformatics advancement in cancer research till date

Sequencing of the genome has provided a major breakthrough in understanding cancer, its effects and possible treatment options. One of the major advantage was to predict the disease by analyzing mutation and also manage the disease by treating the patient with drugs that inhibit proteins. Genes events of the disease can now be processed for mutation and disease progression can be predicted. This helps in the development of therapies that revolve around drug-resistant cancers and recurrences in patients that have received first-line therapy. Oncology programs today are focused on understanding drug resistance. The processing and analysis of biologic data via computational statistical mathematical methods is what bioinformatics is all about. Microarray expression profiling DNA sequencing and genomic sequence analysis is all based on the statistical algorithm. Gene expression profiling of tumors with the help of DNA microarray is a potent tool for pharmacogenomic targeting of treatment (Simon, 2005). For example Oncotype DX assay is required for positive breast cancer patients for whom chemotherapy is not required; it identifies node-negative estrogen receptors (Paik et al., 2004). These genomic tests are validated by a team of biostatisticians a biological scientist and clinical investigators. Some of the advancement in cancer research related to bioinformatics is mentioned subsequently.

Microarray experiments: Over many years scientists have been focusing on the entire genome rather than a single gene for the substantial component and with this a huge quantum of data is being generated and is being used for patient record-keeping, so there is a necessity to store the genetics of cancer. Bioinformatics plays an essential role by using its computational tool and methods to collect and store these data. All human genes are simultaneously interrogated by DNA microarray and it has been used for the past many years in the study of cancer. In past we applied biologic classes to identify differential gene expression but later on attempts were being made in clinical cancer investigation to predict outcomes and guide the use of therapeutics. With the passing years, microarrays contributed a lot towards the development of biomarkers that predict cancer etiology and patient response to therapies. After the microarray experiment the analysis parts start which include data normalization (linear regression, global ratio, curvilinear analysis, or internal control) and background subtraction (global or local) (Zhang, 2011). These data analyses involve class prediction, class discovery, and class comparison, and all these analyses are followed by data interpretation. Hence to complete the process of microarray analysis, numerous databases and software are available and each one is different in characteristics and functions (Zhang, 2011; Raza, 2016). For example Bio-conductor and BRB tools are the freely accessible array analysis software. Besides these the annotation databases that are used for biologic interpretation are KEGG, GO, GenMAPP, etc. The microarray tools that are specific to cancer are also available, e.g., caArray, Oncomine databases, caWorkbench, etc. Various repositories are available to store microarray data, and these are SMD (Stanford Microarray Databases) and GEO (National Cancer Institute (NCI) Gene Expression Omnibus) (Zhang, 2011). Since these archives offer limited data analysis choices for example hierarchic clustering, bioinformatics approaches were developed to find a high level of gene expression (Raza, 2014; Raza and Hasan, 2015; Zhang, 2011).

Bioinformatics techniques: Clustering the traditional methods is informative but these methods have limitations for a single experimental run and are limited to specific cancer types. Researches therefore move beyond single-chip like **Module Maps, SLAMS and COPA** have been developed to follow a novel algorithm to find gene expression across a heterogeneous microarray experiment and the only limitations with all these bioinformatics approaches are that these are not ideal for large-scale microarray data analysis and interpretation (Hanauer et al., 2007). For a large scale, we have come up with the Cancer Genome ATLAS project and Cancer Biomedical Informatics.

CaBig: The bottleneck of the aforementioned approaches is that they could not connect cancer on a broader aspect, and investigators were unable to investigate and examine data in unusual ways. Cancer biomedical informatics grid, CaBig, connects many research institutions and cancer centers in the network to share and analyze biomedical data. Tools developed by TCGA are freely available across all communities.

Bio-conductor and dChip: Bioinformatics also provides data-intensive research on the cellular expression of cancer. Bio-conductor and dChip are the two software that are being used in the cellular expression of cancer. Bio-conductor is based on R language, and dChip is menu-oriented software. The former is used for analyzing gene expression, while the later helps to manage data generated by microarray. Simultaneously, both will help in the interrogation of thousands of genes (Chaudhuri and Chaudhuri, 2010).

EBImage and RNA splicing: Bioinformatics is a boon in analyzing imaging cells with specific markers to localize cellular structure and proteins. EBImage provides multidimensional processing and analysis of images (Pau et al., 2010). It segments cells and extracts quantitative cellular descriptors. RNA splicing also plays a role in cancer research. It is a process in which to produce many protein isoforms a part of a gene is excluded or included. Hence the resulting isoforms may have altogether different functions, and it plays an important part in early carcinogenesis (Chaudhuri and Chaudhuri, 2010). Bioinformatics and high-throughput sequencing help to identify cancer-specific protein isoforms that serve as potential biomarkers in the early detection of cancer.

Bioinformatics for cancer immunology and immunotherapy: After years of research from preclinical studies, we came to realize the interaction between the immune system and tumor. In fact, immunity plays a major role in tumor pathogenesis (Charoentong et al., 2012). Also, it is found that the recurrence of cancer is influenced by the immune system. Our immune system reacts toward cancer cells by acting against either tumor-associated antigens or tumor-specific antigens. Hence, these findings pave a new way toward antitumor activity in immunotherapy. In previous times the conventional techniques to treat/cure different cancers were chemotherapy, radiation therapy, surgery, or a combination of these, and they would fail to prevent or treat malignancy. Therefore, to overcome the cancer progression, immunotherapy is now being accepted as an alternative to conventional methods of treatment like chemotherapy radiation therapy etc., and is being used in clinical practice. Bioinformatics showed a new ray of hope in cancer immunology; it paved the way for network modeling, epitope prediction tools and integrative data analysis and also provided techniques to analyze next-generation sequencing data. It is very difficult to complete entire genome sequence data analysis because it involves various steps, and it relies upon a number of algorithms, programs, and databases. Hence, it was challenging to deal with vast sums of heterogeneous data. Hence, bioinformaticians developed 11 workflow systems and 168 individual tools to address the analysis steps (Charoentong et al., 2012). But to get meaningful biologic results remains a challenge because combining all these different tools is a tedious process. To overcome this, different pipelines have been introduced that comprise software tools that are capable of analyzing all steps starting from raw sequences to a set of final annotations, e.g., HugeSeq (Lam et al., 2012), Treat (Asmann et al., 2012), SIMPLEX (Fischer et al., 2012), etc.

With the help of these, we are able to discover some checkpoint inhibitors. Checkpoint inhibitors are specific classes of drugs that fight the body's immune response against various tumor types. As a class of anticancer agents, immunotherapies are designed to harness the patient's own immune system to fight cancer (Pennock and Chow, 2015). T cells, with the aid of checkpoint inhibitors, find cancer cells and destroy it. For example, CTLA-4 (**Ipilimumab**), PD-1 (**Nivolumab and Pembrolizumab**), and PD-L1 (**Atezolizumab, Avelumab, and Durvalumab**) are the various checkpoint inhibitors to treat lymph nodes, renal cell, and urothelial carcinoma, respectively (Davies and Duffield, 2017).

Systems clinical medicines and cancer bioinformatics: To improve therapies, diagnosis, and prognosis of cancer research, it was necessary to integrate clinical science, systems biology, bioinformatics, omics-based technology and computational science. The introduction of this new concept is what we call systems clinical medicines. Cancer bioinformatics focuses on bioinformatics methods in cancer related to disease specificity, proliferation, communication and signaling, while clinical bioinformatics is an emerging science that combines mathematics, medical informatics, and clinical informatics. Cancer bioinformatics is a critically important aspect of the systems clinical medicine for cancer and the focal tool and approach for testing of cancers in systems clinical medicine (Wu et al., 2012). The idea of clinical bioinformatics was initially conceived to facilitate researchers to search biologic databases on the web, to use bioinformatics in medical practice. It also helped researchers in selecting required software for the analysis of microarray data that is further used in medical decision-making, as well as to optimize the identification of protein-based, disease-specific biomarkers, administer identification of drug targets, and clinical validation (Wang and Liotta, 2011; Wu et al., 2012). The traditional methods of bioinformatics and statistics for analysis of the genome, large-scale "omic" data sets, and three-dimensional protein structure could become the backbone for computational cancer research (Wang and Liotta, 2011). Clinical informatics is entirely different from other informatics; it focuses more on the patient's history, clinical symptoms, and signs, therapies given to date, biochemical analysis, pathologies reports, their data, etc. It was recommended that the evaluation of clinical and basic research together has the potential to improve medical care and methods for data utilization in disease treatment and algorithms that are used for analyzing heterogeneous data sets (Wang and Liotta, 2011; Wu et al., 2012). To improve current healthcare information and technology, translational bioinformatics is required, and it can consolidate multiple biomedical data streams, healthcare, and wellness data streams. These applications could prove useful in three areas, i.e., predictive modeling, data-driven clinical trials, and diagnostic alerts (Shameer et al., 2017).

3. The current mode of therapy and drug development

Small molecule inhibitors: To overcome traditional cancer therapies the approach for targeted drugs has now been shifted toward small-molecule inhibitors, which include metalloproteinases (MMPs), tyrosine, serine, threonine kinases, proteasome, and matrix heat shock proteins. These molecular targets are for the selective elimination of cancer cells. They constitute high structural diversity, a chemical moiety that leads to the development of new lead compounds for the development of potential targets for chemotherapeutic intervention in certain cancers and validates them in clinical trials. The only cost-effective method available is virtual high-throughput screening (vHTS). This computational technique is used in the process of drug design to identify small compounds similar to drugs. Virtual screening has helped a lot in identifying potential drug targets for kinases like CaMK4 (Beg et al., 2019), MARK4 (Mohammad et al., 2019), etc. These days, small molecule drugs and monoclonal antibodies are used in combination with radiotherapy with these potential drug targets, which act very effectively in treating the diseases. To improve the current drug design scenario, it is necessary to identify specific genes and proteins involved in the progression of cancer cells (Lavanya et al., 2014).

Cancer vaccines: The science of designing and developing the latest vaccines with the aim of developing bioinformatics-based acquisition, calculations, and analysis of biologic data of human immunology and disease agents is called vaccine informatics (Raman et al., 2014). Emphasis is being laid on target prescreening, analysis of big data, and experimental validation by a small number of key experiments. Immunoinformatics is based on the mining of immunologic data, data warehousing, and prediction of immunogenicity. For a better understanding of human immunome and the design of new vaccines, researchers are now involving bioinformatics approaches, along with experimental validation to identify and select key experimental designs. Vaccines are made from cancer cells. Hence, many computational approaches are applied to study cancer vaccines. For example, **VaccImm** (von Eichborn et al., 2013) is a vaccination made up of peptides and is helpful in cancer therapy. One cancer vaccine, **sipuleucel-T** (**Provenge**), is used to cure prostate cancer (Cheever and Higano, 2011). Vaccines are under clinical trials against brain, lung, and breast cancers.

4. The latest in cancer prevention and screening

Genetic and genomic tests: Genetic and genomic tests are the frontier in the screening of cancer tests. Genetic tests focus on alteration in genes and look for the mutated segment and further predict how the tumor might behave when treated with a particular drug during treatment. One such genetic test looks for the BRCA1 and BRCA2 genes (Berry et al., 2002). Women carrying BRCA1/BRCA2 mutations are at higher risk of developing breast and ovarian cancers. Men with BRCA1 mutations are at a greater lifetime risk of getting prostate cancer and male breast cancer (Bonn, 2002). Genetic testing is also used as a preventive tool to find patients who are at a greater risk of developing cancers throughout their lives. Individuals having a family history of cancers like ovarian, breast, and lung cancer are often advised to get genetic testing to estimate the risk posed by a genetic mutation. One such case is that of famous hollywood actress Angelina Jolie who had preventive surgeries done as her genetic tests were positive, and she was at a high risk of developing breast and ovarian cancer. Her mother also had cancer. Today, genetic testing is being used to customize cancer treatment. BRCA mutation in the case of ovarian cancer in women will respond better to platinum but not so well to hormonal therapy in general (Dann et al., 2012). Drugs like olaparib have been found to be more effective for BRCA-positive patients than those who do not test positive. Such analysis helps in predetermining the course of treatment (Ledermann et al., 2012). This helps the patients with saving time and money and doctors with disease progression and prognosis. DNA testing-based kits are available today for self-testing at home for colon cancers. It is noninvasive, unlike colonoscopy. In case the test is positive for colon cancer, a colonoscopy is performed for confirmation. Hence, considering the healthcare system in case of cancers, it has improved a bit with the help of bioinformatics tools and technologies.

Angiogenesis inhibitor in cancer: The creation of new blood vessels is called angiogenesis, but in the case of cancer, this growth is uncontrollable. To inhibit this uncontrolled growth, angiogenesis inhibitors (also called antiangiogenics) are designed. The different types of drugs are **axitinib (Inlyta)** [kidney cancer] (Tzogani et al., 2015); **bevacizumab (Avastin)** [colorectal, kidney, lung cancers (Mukherji, 2010)]; **cabozantinib (Cometriq)** [medullary thyroid cancer and kidney cancer (Hoy, 2014)]; **everolimus (Afinitor, Zortress)** [kidney cancer, advanced breast cancer (Curran, 2012)]; **sunitinib (Sutent)** [kidney cancer (Chouhan et al., 2007)]; **ziv-aflibercept (Zaltrap)** [colorectal cancer (Perkins and Cole, 2014)], and so on.

Role of new drugs in cancer research: Today, we have several classes of drugs for treating cancer with this approach. This has been made possible only due to genome sequencing and analyzing the protein structure. Naturally occurring products are rich in therapeutic agents and are being used in practice for the development of new drugs. This constitutes high structural diversity, a chemical moiety that leads to the development of new lead compounds for the development of potential targets for chemotherapeutic intervention in certain cancers and validates them in clinical trials. The only cost-effective method available is virtual high-throughput screening (vHTS). For a particular protein–drug interaction, it is important that the drug efficiently hold together in the active site of the protein. Hence, for its structure–function relationship, the protein structure is essentially important. The principal basis of drug activity is molecular recognition in which drug molecules show pharmacologic action by binding to a target protein and making a stable protein-ligand complex. Molecular recognition uses the criteria of docking and scoring (Wang et al., 2003) to characterize the compounds in the virtual library. Prediction of the ligands conformation and orientation of the receptor's active site are two main analyses of the docking algorithms (Halperin et al., 2002), while the interaction between the target protein and the ligands binding is predicted by scoring methods. Natural compounds are virtually stored in different repositories for drug discovery and development and are available from various stores and merchant sites in the form of the virtual library. These libraries are accessible at various public domains such as DrugBank, NCI database, PubChem and ZINC library that consist of natural products and include many synthesizable and purchasable small compounds, which can be screened against different biologic targets for lead discovery.

High-throughput screening is performed using protein-ligand docking methods for a particular target protein for which the ligand is being searched in the various databases mentioned earlier. The screening is being carried out by Autodock Vina. Different orientations of ligands are searched in the active site of the receptor using a docking algorithm. The most suitable docked confirmation was then taken for further analysis. PyMol (DeLano, 2002), Discovery Studio Visualiser (BIOVIA, 2015) and LigPlot (Wallace et al., 1995) were used for the visualization and structure analysis of the docked complex. After the selection of top hits, we used Lipinski criteria to sort out the best possible hits. The Lipinski criterion is based on certain parameters along with their threshold values on which the drug-likeness of chemical compounds is to be predicted. The pharmacokinetic profile for the selected hits is evaluated to address the putative bioavailability for the inhibitors. The physicochemical properties, of selected compounds, are evaluated using the Pre-ADMET web server (https://preadmet.bmdrc.kr/). Carcinogenicity and toxicity of compounds are predicted by the CarcinoPred-EL server (http://ccsipb.lnu.edu.cn/toxicity/CarcinoPred-EL). After filtering compounds from toxicity and carcinogenicity the selected compounds then undergo MD simulation. MD simulations are done to analyze the conformational changes, stability, and the underlying molecular interaction at the atomic level of protein alone, first, and then further in comparison with the selected ligands. Hence, these computational approaches are used to search and find drug-like compounds for lead discovery (Sahu et al., 2020).

5. Translational Bioinformatics and Precision Medicine in Cancer: The future scenario

Translational bioinformatics is a multidisciplinary field of informatics and biomedical data sciences that translates cellular, clinical, genetic and molecular data into clinical products, while precision medicine is an approach that is based on clinical entities to select a particular treatment that is based on patient genetics (Shameer et al., 2017; Ritchie et al., 2020).

Integrating translational bioinformatics with the basic science community (bioinformatics, statistics, genomics and computer science) along with the translational community (pharmacogenomics, medical and clinical informatics and genomic medicine) will mutually benefit biomedical research into precision medicine (Ritchie et al., 2020). Most complex human diseases, i.e., cancer, drug repositioning, biomarkers, and pharmacogenomics, are among the active areas for translation of genomic discoveries into clinical care. Translational bioinformatics applies novel methods for the storage, analysis and interpretation of a massive volume of genetics, genomics, multiomics and clinical data; this includes diagnosis, medications, laboratory measurements, imaging, and clinical notes (Tenenbaum, 2016). Translational bioinformatics in precision medicine attempts to determine individual solutions based on the genomic, environmental, and clinical profiles of each individual, providing an opportunity to incorporate individual genomic data into patient care (Ritchie et al., 2020). A brief representation is described in Fig. 11.1.

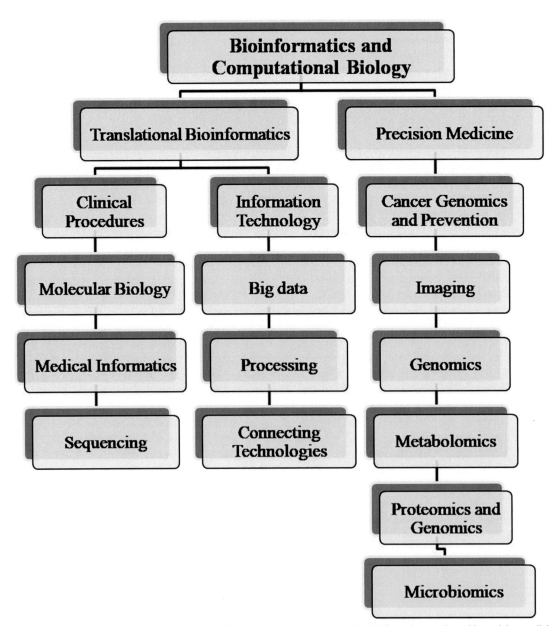

FIGURE 11.1 Bioinformatics technologies are booming in the healthcare system. Translational bioinformatics together with precision medicine bridges the gap in healthcare technologies.

6. Conclusion

The use of big data in cancer research has provided a boost but also poses challenges for the researchers as the data, though available in large quantities, had to be analyzed to draw inferences. The generation of bulk data needs to be stored, so we have made completely different databases for the use of cancer only (Cancer3D database, Cancer Genomic Hub, MTB Mouse Tumor Biology database, The Osteosarcoma Database, etc.). Bioinformatics provides researchers with the inferences they need by eliminating noise from big data and providing relevant information. The current drug discovery processes within pharmaceutical companies remain conservative, typically focused on the discovery of a novel therapeutic target and new potential compound that modulates the activity of the identified target. Subsequently, clinical and preclinical investigations are often slow, risky, and expensive processes taking up to 15 years and up to 800 million USD to one billion USD to introduce a compound to the market (Gill et al., 2016). Hence, an innovative approach is required to predict the drug efficacy, to strengthen the success of the drug development process. Toxicity at the cellular level and poor pharmacokinetic profile are two reasons why drugs fail in clinical trials. Hence, different software and web servers can predict the possible toxicities (Lipinski Filter, CarcinoPred, and Pre-ADMET) and interactions (PyMol, Discovery Studio), thereby accurately defining the success of a compound or the repositioning for a new one. The cost and time of pharmaceutical compounds and drugs can be reduced greatly with the help of the drug design process. Drug likenesses are predicted by computational methods, genetic algorithms, and neural networks. With the help of these, the best candidate molecule can survive in later stages of drug development and eliminate compounds with limited scope for further use (Gill et al., 2016). The progression of the pharmaceutical drug discovery process goes from drug target to lead compound and ultimately to drug.

References

Asmann, Y.W., Middha, S., et al., 2012. TREAT: a bioinformatics tool for variant annotations and visualizations in targeted and exome sequencing data. Bioinformatics 28 (2), 277–278.

Beg, A., Khan, F.I., et al., 2019. High throughput screening, docking, and molecular dynamics studies to identify potential inhibitors of human calcium/calmodulin-dependent protein kinase IV. J. Biomol. Struct. Dyn. 37 (8), 2179–2192.

Berry, D.A., Iversen Jr., E.S., et al., 2002. BRCAPRO validation, sensitivity of genetic testing of BRCA1/BRCA2, and prevalence of other breast cancer susceptibility genes. J. Clin. Oncol. 20 (11), 2701–2712.

BIOVIA, D.S., 2015. Discovery Studio Modeling Environment, Release 4.5. Dassault Systèmes, San Diego.

Blanco, E., Hsiao, A., et al., 2011. Nanomedicine in cancer therapy: innovative trends and prospects. Canc. Sci. 102 (7), 1247–1252.

Bonn, D., 2002. Prostate-cancer screening targets men with BRCA mutations. Lancet Oncol. 3 (12), 714.

Charoentong, P., Angelova, M., et al., 2012. Bioinformatics for cancer immunology and immunotherapy. Canc. Immunol. Immunother. 61 (11), 1885–1903.

Chaudhuri, A., Chaudhuri, S., 2010. Role of Bioinformatics in Cancer.

Cheever, M.A., Higano, C.S., 2011. PROVENGE (Sipuleucel-T) in prostate cancer: the first FDA-approved therapeutic cancer vaccine. Clin. Canc. Res. 17 (11), 3520–3526.

Chouhan, J.D., Zamarripa, D.E., et al., 2007. Sunitinib (Sutent®): a novel agent for the treatment of metastatic renal cell carcinoma. J. Oncol. Pharm. Pract. 13 (1), 5–15.

Curran, M.P., 2012. Everolimus. Pediatr. Drugs 14 (1), 51–60.

Dann, R.B., DeLoia, J.A., et al., 2012. BRCA1/2 mutations and expression: response to platinum chemotherapy in patients with advanced stage epithelial ovarian cancer. Gynecol. Oncol. 125 (3), 677–682.

Davies, M., Duffield, E.A., 2017. Safety of checkpoint inhibitors for cancer treatment: strategies for patient monitoring and management of immune-mediated adverse events. ImmunoTargets Ther. 6, 51.

DeLano, W.L., 2002. The PyMOL Molecular Graphics System. http://www.pymol.org.

Fischer, M., Snajder, R., et al., 2012. SIMPLEX: cloud-enabled pipeline for the comprehensive analysis of exome sequencing data. PloS One 7 (8).

Gill, S.K., Christopher, A.F., et al., 2016. Emerging role of bioinformatics tools and software in evolution of clinical research. Perspect. Clin. Res. 7 (3), 115.

Halperin, I., Ma, B., et al., 2002. Principles of docking: an overview of search algorithms and a guide to scoring functions. Proteins Struct. Funct. & Bioinform. 47 (4), 409–443.

Hanauer, D.A., Rhodes, D.R., et al., 2007. Bioinformatics approaches in the study of cancer. Curr. Mol. Med. 7 (1), 133–141.

Hoy, S.M., 2014. Cabozantinib: a review of its use in patients with medullary thyroid cancer. Drugs 74 (12), 1435–1444.

Lam, H.Y., Clark, M.J., et al., 2012. Performance comparison of whole-genome sequencing platforms. Nat. Biotechnol. 30 (1), 78.

Lavanya, V., Mohamed Adil, A., et al., 2014. Small molecule inhibitors as emerging cancer therapeutics. Integr. Cancer Sci. Ther.

Ledermann, J., Harter, P., et al., 2012. Olaparib maintenance therapy in platinum-sensitive relapsed ovarian cancer. N. Engl. J. Med. 366 (15), 1382–1392.

Lu, Y., Han, J., 2003. Cancer classification using gene expression data. Inf. Syst. 28 (4), 243–268.

Mohammad, T., Khan, F.I., et al., 2019. Identification and evaluation of bioactive natural products as potential inhibitors of human microtubule affinity-regulating kinase 4 (MARK4). J. Biomol. Struct. Dyn. 37 (7), 1813–1829.

Mukherji, S., 2010. Bevacizumab (avastin). Am. J. Neuroradiol. 31 (2), 235–236.

Nayak, M.G., George, A., et al., 2017. Quality of life among cancer patients. Indian J. Palliat. Care 23 (4), 445.

Paik, S., Shak, S., et al., 2004. A multigene assay to predict recurrence of tamoxifen-treated, node-negative breast cancer. N. Engl. J. Med. 351 (27), 2817–2826.

Pau, G., Fuchs, F., et al., 2010. EBImage—an R package for image processing with applications to cellular phenotypes. Bioinformatics 26 (7), 979–981.

Pennock, G.K., Chow, L.Q., 2015. The evolving role of immune checkpoint inhibitors in cancer treatment. Oncol. 20 (7), 812.

Perkins, S.L., Cole, S.W., 2014. Ziv-aflibercept (Zaltrap) for the treatment of metastatic colorectal cancer. Ann. Pharmacother. 48 (1), 93–98.

Raman, H., et al., 2014. Bioinformatics for vaccine target discovery. Asia Pacific Biotech News 18 (9), 25–53.

Raza, K., 2014. Clustering analysis of cancerous microarray data. J. Chem. Pharmaceut. Res. 6 (9), 488–493.

Raza, K., 2016. Analysis of microarray data using artificial intelligence based techniques. In: Handbook of Research on Computational Intelligence Applications in Bioinformatics. IGI Global, pp. 216–239.

Raza, K., Hasan, A.N., 2015. A comprehensive evaluation of machine learning techniques for cancer class prediction based on microarray data. Int. J. Bioinf. Res. Appl. 11 (5), 397–416.

Ritchie, M.D., Moore, J.H., et al., 2020. Translational bioinformatics: biobanks in the precision medicine era. Pac. Symp. Biocomput. World Scientific.

Sahu, A., Pradhan, D., et al., 2020. In silico library design, screening and MD simulation of COX-2 inhibitors for anticancer activity. In: Proceedings of the 12th International Conference.

Shameer, K., Badgeley, M.A., et al., 2017. Translational bioinformatics in the era of real-time biomedical, health care and wellness data streams. Briefings Bioinf. 18 (1), 105–124.

Simon, R., 2005. Bioinformatics in cancer therapeutics—hype or hope? Nat. Clin. Pract. Oncol. 2 (5), 223-223.

Tenenbaum, J.D., 2016. Translational bioinformatics: past, present, and future. Dev. Reprod. Biol. 14 (1), 31–41.

Tzogani, K., Skibeli, V., et al., 2015. The European Medicines Agency approval of axitinib (Inlyta) for the treatment of advanced renal cell carcinoma after failure of prior treatment with sunitinib or a cytokine: summary of the scientific assessment of the committee for medicinal products for human use. Oncologist 20 (2), 196.

von Eichborn, J., Woelke, A.L., et al., 2013. VaccImm: simulating peptide vaccination in cancer therapy. BMC Bioinform. 14 (1), 127.

Wallace, A.C., Laskowski, R.A., et al., 1995. LIGPLOT: a program to generate schematic diagrams of protein-ligand interactions. Protein Eng. Des. & Sel. 8 (2), 127–134.

Wang, R., Lu, Y., et al., 2003. Comparative evaluation of 11 scoring functions for molecular docking. J. Med. Chem. 46 (12), 2287–2303.

Wang, X., Liotta, L., 2011. Clinical bioinformatics: a new emerging science. J. Clin. Bioinform. BioMed Central.

Wen, S., Xiao, H., et al., 2019. The risk factors for depression in cancer patients undergoing chemotherapy: a systematic review. Support. Care Canc. 27 (1), 57–67.

Wu, D., Rice, C.M., et al., 2012. Cancer Bioinformatics: A New Approach to Systems Clinical Medicine. Springer.

Xie, H., Zhu, W.-y., et al., 2002. Computational analysis of alternative splicing using EST tissue information. Genomics 80 (3), 326–330.

Zhang, X., 2011. Omics Technologies in Cancer Biomarker Discovery. CRC Press.

Chapter 12

Application, functionality, and security issues of data mining techniques in healthcare informatics

Afroj Alam[1], Ismail Rashid[2] and Khalid Raza[3,*]

[1]Department of Computer Application, Integral University, Lucknow, Uttar Pradesh, India; [2]Computer Science Faculty, Bakhtar University, Kabul, Afghanistan; [3]Department of Computer Science, Jamia Millia Islamia, New Delhi, Delhi, India
*Corresponding author: E-mail: kraza@jmi.ac.in

Chapter outline

1. Introduction

Computing and understanding the structure of biologic data using data mining functionalities, including frequent pattern mining, associations, correlation, clustering, and outlier analysis, are some of the essential tasks that have been carried out in bioinformatics as a profession. The data mining profession is interdisciplinary and assimilates many techniques from other fields like machine learning, neural networks, deep learning, statistics, database management systems, data warehouses, visualization, multidimensional data modeling, advanced computer science algorithms, high-performance computing, and so on. Data mining may also extract knowledge from a vast amount of collected data using internet of things (IoT)-based smart sensor devices from the cloud computing data center, edge computing data center, and fog computing data center. As a result, knowledge discovery in data (KDD) is another name for data mining. This extracted knowledge is very useful in the field of bioinformatics and health informatics systems for the diagnosis, prediction, and analysis of disease (Zucco, 2018).

For prognosis and diagnosis of heart disease and various cancers, machine learning and data mining techniques play a role that is reliable and efficient with respect to cost and time for patient as well as doctors (Raza, 2019; Raza and Hasan, 2015). In other words, data mining is a cost-effective analytical tool for discovering the frequent hidden patterns within the biologic and medical data (Mia et al., 2018).

1.1 What kinds of patterns can be mined?

Fraud detection is one of the most popular applications of pattern mining in medical claims. Some of the common frauds in medical claims are repeated bills, misusing the code, up-coding, and unbundling (Verma et al., 2017). Scrutiny of the medical claims manually is an outdated and cost-expensive method. So, an innovative and cost-effective fraud detection technique is required in healthcare services. In healthcare, fraud detection is being automated by data mining and machine learning methods. For detailed assessment, these methods will be helpful for identifying the medical claims and also helpful for providing the fraud concerned security.

When an insurer involves himself in medical claims, the vendor has a mutual understanding by the state for claiming payment. The state verifies the claims by different prepayment processing checks for inspecting the legality of the claim. The current system cannot detect whether the services that are claimed by the provider are correct or not. Hence, we can find the fraud of expensive tests and illegal charges for services that are not provided to the provider. These are very complex tasks to detect because they need to find frequent patterns from huge medical data for the maximization of fraud detection. For example, the claims that have been done by doctors can be compared by us with the help of existing aggregated and precalculated computed data using predefined rules in systems that can detect which test has been done unnecessarily and which services have been charged with high rates. Frequent pattern mining methods help in finding these erroneous claims (Verma et al., 2017).

1.2 Data mining function in bioinformatics

Data mining function in the field of bioinformatics is not new. Clustering techniques, associated rule mining, outlier detection, frequent item set pattern mining, regression analysis, and classification techniques are some functionality of data mining, and they have several essential and critical applications that include *recognizing the frequent pattern of DNA, protein substructure and subsequences, healthy protein features reasoning inference, functional domain and operational concept diagnosis, health condition prognosis and diagnosis, and therapy improvement, protein and genetics interaction network reconstruction, data drawing out, purification and loading in the healthcare data warehouse,* and *protein sub-cellular location prognosis* (Raza, 2012).

1.3 Technologies used in data mining for bioinformatics

The interdisciplinary science of data mining is closely connected with several other computational approaches such as artificial intelligence, statistics, pattern acknowledgment, visualization, database and data warehouses, information retrieval, formulas, and high-performance processing (Han et al., 2011), as depicted in Fig. 12.1.

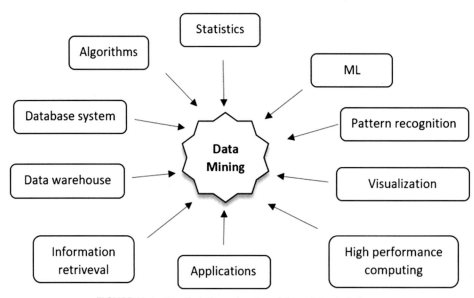

FIGURE 12.1 Interdisciplinary domains of data mining techniques.

1.4 Data warehouse and healthcare informatics

There is an enormous amount of data that is unprocessed in the clinical industry. This unprocessed data can be extracted from different branches and then transferred and loaded into the data warehouses, from where we can get meaningful patterns that are very useful for healthcare business intelligence. Data mining techniques can be applied in the clinical data houses to analyze and provide new insights for disease prediction and its prevention. As far as the classification of disease based on clinical data is concerned, several machine learning approaches have been applied to predict heart disease using UCI (University of California, Irvine) machine learning repository, including support vector machine and naïve Bayes (Amin et al., 2019) and ensemble learning (Raza, 2019). It is also used to predict viral epidemics and outbreaks including dengue (Iqbal and Islam, 2019), coronavirus disease (COVID-19) (Raza, 2020; Raza et al., 2021), and so on.

2. KDD in healthcare informatics

Knowledge discovery from the database is a looping process of data cleansing, integration, selection, mining frequent patterns in the form of structure and substructure, and knowledge presentation (Fig. 12.2). Data mining has some techniques to recognize the frequent pattern automatically and addresses to uncover the hidden patterns in the data, which is very difficult in traditional statistical methods (Kaur and Wasan, 2006).

IoT-based intelligent sensor devices generate a huge amount of data, especially in the healthcare sector. These data are coming from different sources like patient data, scientific data, doctor data, organizational data, hospital recorded data, and fiscal year data. Our healthcare informatics system should be highly optimized with quick responsiveness, so our system can continuously update the patient and doctor's queries in a small transaction.

Data that is coming from different sources in healthcare are of different formats. For example, one organization follows one date format, but another follows a different date format. One follows M for male and F for female. Another follows 0 for males and 1 for females. Hence, using data warehousing, we can integrate these healthcare data in a standard format to provide intelligent views of the health information concerning location, age, qualification, job, etc. We have different cube operations in multidimensional online analytical processing like slice and dice, rollup, drill down, etc., in the data warehouse to provide intelligent views of health information (Lu et al., 2015).

KDD is the other name of data mining, which infers hidden information and aquires knowledge by transforming the unprocessed data from given data sets. These pieces of knowledge are useful in healthcare. For example, a new treatment method is being forecasted by data mining for the treatment of patient based on past data, patient profile, health examination, location and diagnosis, and historical patient pattern treatment (Campbell et al., 2010). The hot research area of clinical data mining is being introduced in medicine and healthcare by applying the concepts of artificial intelligence. The impact of KDD in healthcare information applications has been addressed by the suggestion of many reviewers and surveyors (Jacob and Ramani, 2012). A review on formal concepts analysis for knowledge discovery from biologic data can be found in Raza (2017).

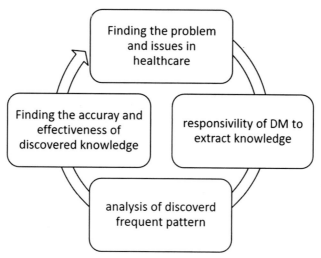

FIGURE 12.2 Data mining cycle (Kaur and Wasan, 2006).

2.1 Mining approach for breast cancer data

In breast cancer research, KDD functionality has already been applied with different datasets. Previously, an artificial neural network (ANN) was very popular for analyzing a complex dataset in which the input data and predicted patterns have many complicated nonlinear relationships. Determining breast cancer in a patient having chemotherapy that could survive a long time is recognized as a data mining problem. Lee and Clift (2018) proved it by clustering techniques where 253 samples of a breast cancer patient were taken into three groups: good, intermediate, and poor.

3. Data mining techniques in healthcare analytics

Currently, we have lot of healthcare information sectors, which makes our task easier. An example is fraud detection in healthcare where insurance companies by outlier analysis provide better facilities for patients at a cheaper cost, efficient healthcare policies, e-healthcare services, u-healthcare services, IoT-based intelligent sensor devices services in healthcare, and so on. Some important and hot topic areas of research in data mining are identification and prediction of the disease using some frequent pattern item sets that are occurring frequently in the transactional database.

In the healthcare sector, data mining functionalities play an essential role for making decisions based upon the analysis of the enormous scientific data. Data mining functionalities are class/concept description, classification and regression, clustering analysis, and outlier analysis. These functionalities have been implemented in healthcare industries for prediction and detection of disease and making intelligent decisions for the prevention of disease at an early stage. Classification, also called supervised machine learning, is an approach that is working on a given training data set of different objects into target class collection. In these techniques, objects are classified into different groups with some common characteristics. A new entered object belonging to which groups will be identified with the help of common characteristics of that object. Some classification algorithms as applied to healthcare informatics are listed in Fig. 12.3.

3.1 Apriori algorithm

Association rule mining is actually the base of the Apriori algorithm that uses the enormous medical datasets for discovering frequent patterns and interesting associations. Given subsequently is a two-step approach of an Apriori algorithm. (i) Finding all the frequent item sets is the first step. An item set will be considered frequent in which the occurrence exceeds the minimum support for which the threshold value is already given. (ii) Assuming that all the k-item set frequent

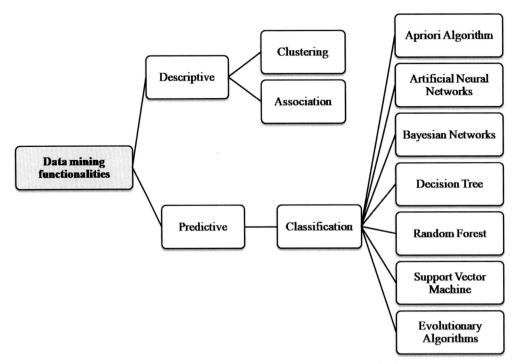

FIGURE 12.3 Various data mining techniques in healthcare informatics.

patterns already have been exceeded based on k-item set, then create another (k+1) item set, and frequent (k+1) item set is updated by frequent k-item set (Yuan, 2017). A large number of Apriori algorithm rules have been compared for cardiovascular disease prediction in data mining. In the Apriori algorithm, strong rules are compared among them for finding accurate support, improving accuracy, and also addressing strong rules (Mirmozaffari et al., 2017).

3.2 Artificial neural networks

Artificial neural networks (ANN) mimic the neuron network structure of the human brain. This ANN is also called a mathematical model or computational structure, which consists of several nodes that are connected with direct links in which each node is considered a processing unit or artificial neuron and the link specifying the path or cost or relationship among nodes. It is a powerful classification technique used for analyzing the complex clinical data for descriptive and predictive data mining purposes. Descriptive data mining describes information about what is happening in the data without any predefined information. Predictive data mining describes submitting a file with unknown field values and the system will automatically guess the missing values with the help of the previous pattern discovered in the transactional database.

3.3 Bayesian network

Bayesian network (BN) is a graphical model, which is represented in the form of a directed acyclic graph (DAG). BN contains a conditional based probability table. In DAG, nodes are connected through links that represent the relationship in a simple way. The node represents the computational unit, and the link represents the relationship among the nodes. *Tree augmented naive Bayesian network, general Bayesian network,* and *naive Bayesian networks* are known as popular Bayesian networks. Generally, we have three approaches for designing the Bayesian network: *data-driven, knowledge-driven,* and *hybrid.*

Although several machine learning and artificial intelligence approaches are very popular in healthcare for disease prognosis, prediction, and diagnosis, BN is more powerful and widely applied in healthcare informatics. The advantage of BN over other machine learning techniques is that it does not require massively huge clinical datasets. In some situations, BN may use the previous experience and current datasets then accumulate the knowledge of experts with limited data and generate more accuracy for decision-support systems.

3.4 Fuzzy sets

L.A. Zadeh in 1965 introduced the concept of a fuzzy set. It is defined as a continuous curve in which a value lies between 0 and 1 rather than the exact number. Fuzzy sets have been applied in so many fields like control systems and pattern recognition in the large clinical database. The fuzzy set technique is a very efficient and effective tool that handles different forms of uncertainties. Fuzzy set techniques perform more accurately and efficiently if they are associated with other decision-making techniques like probability and ANN. Hence, fuzzy sets can improve the accuracy of pattern recognition mining in a large healthcare database (Wang et al., 2017).

3.5 Regression analysis

For analyzing the relationship between the independent and dependent variables, regression analysis acts as a one of most important fundamental tools. The dependent variables are those whose values will be identified by the independent variable. R statistical language and RStudio are the popular integrated environment for conducting regression analysis (Abdallah et al., 2017). In healthcare informatics, we can use the regression analysis technique for fitting an equation on the clinical dataset, where $y = mx+c$ is a simple straight-line linear regression in which we can find the value of y based on x. The linear regression can depict the positive as well as negative and no relationship (Fig. 12.4). Linear regression executes the computational operation on a clinical large dataset for predicting numeric value where we have already defined the target value (Gupta, 2015).

4. Security and privacy issues related to biologic and clinical data

Security is a primary concern in a data warehouse where biologic and clinical data are stored. The goal of security and privacy is to pay attention to control data for making it secure. The architecture of security comprises different components

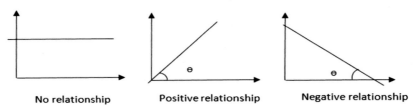

FIGURE 12.4   Three different types of the linear regression relationship.

from endpoint security practices to data flow in networks and storing it in a data warehouse. Whereas, privacy is a bit different issue having to do with the practice of creation and management of genetic data from an individual's biologic data, such as genetic sequences, cell populations, or protein samples. Both security and privacy are important operational goals that safeguard data for users.

Besides hoping to keep up the security of individual data itself, organizations and analysts need to ensure their business or research interests in an inexorably serious field. Considering all the aspects, it has become imperative to develop extremely up-to-date secure techniques to store and transfer information. Contingent upon the security needs of both the data and the user of data, just as the technique for information sharing, different protection issues are reported (Lee and Clift, 2018).

One appropriate case of potential concern confronting privacy, particularly in the health informatics subdiscipline of the bioinformatics field, is the increasing usage of enormous scope genomic databases. These data sets are utilized to learn the relationship between genomic composition and molecular, organ, and tissue-level frameworks, an investigation that has been demonstrated as basic to understanding the genetic inclination to entangled clinical issues. This data, which permits analysts to make progress in the information and treatment of sickness, brings dread of identification and segregation for those people conveying medicinally stereotyped genetic data.

Complication of patient privacy depends on the nature of data: by definition, genomic information is an ultimate tool of identification, which contains further vital information linking to family members. To secure individual privacy, steps are taken to anonymize the information, if the character is not required. This is frequently done consequently on collection by relegating every genome a randomized ID; however, further insurances must be taken with the genetic data itself to forestall potential reidentification of samples. Potential solutions incorporate erasing or changing incriminating sequences, including extra "noise" sequences, or giving just short, nonincriminating arrangements pertinent to the analyst's inquiry.

Sharing genomic information must be done in a secure manner using a trusted third party's potential software application which can provide an encryption framework as further layer of deidentification. There are still restrictions to securing information in this manner, as the idea of the genetic material that permits identification is persistently changing as science advances. This material should be ceaselessly checked for incriminating sequences.

4.1 Privacy issues

In this section, different threats to biometric data in terms of privacy are discussed.

Reidentification threats: Reidentification is one of the most widely considered privacy risk threats in dispersal and investigation of important human genomic information, as human genomes contain the identity information of humans, more specifically patient donors. Thus, it is necessary to be well protected and safe from unauthorized parties. To get these protected published human genomes, an unauthorized party tries to attack to retrieve information and the identity of individual patients involved. On successful attempts of such an attack by intruders, serious loss or damage could cause donors financial misfortune, etc. (Naveed et al., 2015; Gymrek et al., 2013).

Phenotype inference: Phenotype inference is also one of the threats to privacy in the case of biometrics data. This kind of threat can cause harm to an individual when an attacking party collects genomic data from a person. Due to this collected small portion set of single nucleotide polymorphisms, an attacker may find a similar sample in anonymous DNA sequence published in different available online datasets repositories, e.g., astudy on HIV phenotype. It will be straightforward due to the uniqueness of an individual's genome (Lin et al., 2004). Due to this reason, without agreements and consents of donors or owners of data, genomic researchers would agree that DNA sequences are too sensitive to be released in online repositories.

Anonymous paternity breach: As we know, the Y chromosome is inherited from father to son. Hence, genealogical databases associate this chromosome to the surname to model ancestry. In several cases, sperm donors were identified using this information. For instance, a boy who was currently 15 years old conceived through donor sperm easily traced his biologic father by performing an internet search and using a genealogy service by submitting his cheek swab (Motluk, 2005; Stein, 2005). In the same way, an adopted child could find his biologic father using a genealogy database (Naik, 2009). In conclusion, anonymous donors of sperm are easier to be traced by testing DNA, and theoretically, none of the sperm donors will be anonymous anymore (Lehmann-Haupt, 2010).

Legal and forensic: In legal and forensic sciences, DNA is collected from criminals and victims for legal and forensic purposes. Due to advancements in forensic techniques, it is becoming more promising and has wider applications (Pakstis et al., 2010; Kayser and Knijff, 2011). On the other side of the coin, misuses of DNA have already confused individuals and law enforcement agencies (Bobellan, 2010). There are few people like a famous singer Madonna and many more who were much suspicious regarding their DNA misuse. Therefore, they hired sterilization teams to clean up and sterilized leftover DNA in the form of saliva, hair, etc. (Villalva, 2012).

5. Conclusion

This chapter briefly presented the applications, functionalities, security, and privacy issues of data mining in health informatics. Today, we have a vast amount of collected biologic (DNA sequences) and clinical data (patient's profile) stored in various databases and data warehouses. Further, recent advancements in IoT-based sensor devices connected with cloud data storage have made it easier to collect health-related data very easily. Despite the availability of huge biologic and clinical data, we have a crisis of information. Hence, this chapter focused on the data mining technique, which is popular for knowledge discovery from data. Some of the important data mining techniques, including clustering, outlier detection, frequent pattern mining, association rule mining techniques, classification, and regression, are widely applied to understand the biologic structure of healthcare data (e.g., DNA, proteins) to uncover the hidden information. We also highlighted some of its applications including disease prediction and diagnosis, fraud detection in healthcare insurance companies, and planning better healthcare policies at chapter cost. Biologic data, such as the human genome, is very vital in terms of security and privacy. Compromising the integrity, confidentiality, and availability of these sensitive data may lead to abuse and misuse. To understand it, we discussed some of the main issues of privacy in genomic databases like reidentification threats, phenotype inference, and anonymous paternity breach. Along with these, we also discussed the legal and forensic purposes of data investigated. In the future, a new creative method would be for detecting, measuring, and analyzing biomedical information by integrating a mining approach of heterogeneous data (Wang and Preininger, 2019). Future challenges of data mining in terms of process mining in healthcare information is to improve the visualization techniques and visualization analytics that are necessary for the interpretation of obtained results in healthcare (Rojas et al., 2016).

References

Abdallah, S., Malik, M., Ertek, G., 2017. A data mining framework for the analysis of patient arrivals into healthcare centers. In: Proceedings of the 2017 International Conference on Information Technology, pp. 52−61.

Amin, M.S., Chiam, Y.K., Varathan, K.D., 2019. Identification of significant features and data mining techniques in predicting heart disease. Telematics Inf. 36, 82−93.

Bobellan, M., March/April 2010. DNA's dirty little secret. Washington Monthly. https://washingtonmonthly.com/2010/03/01/dnas-dirty-little-secret-2/. (Accessed 1 January 2021).

Campbell, K., Thygeson, N.N., Srivastava, J., Speedie, S., 2010. Exploration of classification techniques as a treatment decision support tool for patients with uterine fibroids. In: International Workshop on Data Mining for HealthCare Management. PAKDD.

Gupta, S., 2015. A regression modeling technique on data mining. Int. J. Comput. Appl. 116 (9).

Gymrek, M., McGuire, A.L., Golan, D., Halperin, E., Erlich, Y., 2013. Identifying personal genomes by surname inference. Science 339 (6117), 321−324.

Han, J., Kamber, M., Pei, J., 2011. Data Mining Concepts and Techniques, third ed. Morgan Kaufmann.

Iqbal, N., Islam, M., 2019. Machine learning for dengue outbreak prediction: a performance evaluation of different prominent classifiers. Informatica 43 (3).

Jacob, S.G., Ramani, R.G., 2012. Data mining in clinical data sets: a review. ISSN: 2249-0868 IJAIS vol. 4 (6). Foundation of Computer Science FCS, New York, USA.

Kaur, H., Wasan, S.K., 2006. Empirical study on applications of data mining techniques in healthcare. J. Comput. Sci. 2 (2), 194−200.

Kayser, M., de Knijff, P., 2011. Improving human forensics through advances in genetics, genomics and molecular biology. Nat. Rev. Genet. 12 (3), 179−192.

Lee, A.C., Clift, I.C., 2018. Bioinformatics. In: The SAGE Encyclopedia of Surveillance, Security, and Privacy. https://doi.org/10.4135/9781483359922.n49.

Lehmann-Haupt, R., March 1, 2010. Are sperm donors really anonymous anymore? DNA testing makes them easy to trace. Slate 5. http://www.slate.com/id/2243743/?gt1=38001Slate. (Accessed 1 January 2021).

Lin, Z., Owen, A.B., Altman, R.B., 2004. Genomic research and human subject privacy. Science 305 (5681), 183.

Lu, J., Hales, A., Rew, D., Keech, M., Fröhlingsdorf, C., Mills-Mullett, A., Wette, C., September 2015. Data mining techniques in health informatics: a case study from breast cancer research. In: International Conference on Information Technology in Bio-And Medical Informatics. Springer, Cham, pp. 56—70.

Mia, M.R., Hossain, S.A., Chhoton, A.C., Chakraborty, N.R., February 2018. A comprehensive study of data mining techniques in health-care, medical, and bioinformatics. In: 2018 International Conference on Computer, Communication, Chemical, Material and Electronic Engineering (IC4ME2). IEEE, pp. 1—4.

Mirmozaffari, M., Alinezhad, A., Gilanpour, A., 2017. Data mining apriori algorithm for heart disease prediction. Int. J. Comput. Commun. & Instrum. Engg 4 (1), 20—23.

Motluk, A., 2005. Anonymous sperm donor traced on internet. New Sci. 2524 (6).

Naik, G., 2009. Family secrets: an adopted man's 26-year quest for his father. Wall St. J. https://www.wsj.com/articles/SB124121920060978695. (Accessed 1 January 2021).

Naveed, M., Ayday, E., Clayton, E.W., Fellay, J., Gunter, C.A., Hubaux, J.P., et al., 2015. Privacy in the genomic era. ACM Comput. Surv. 48 (1), 1—44.

Pakstis, A.J., Speed, W.C., Fang, R., Hyland, F.C., Furtado, M.R., Kidd, J.R., Kidd, K.K., 2010. SNPs for a universal individual identification panel. Hum. Genet. 127 (3), 315—324.

Raza, K., Hasan, A.N., 2015. A comprehensive evaluation of machine learning techniques for cancer class prediction based on microarray data. Int. J. Bioinf. Res. Appl. 11 (5), 397—416. https://doi.org/10.1504/IJBRA.2015.071940. Inderscience.

Raza, K., 2012. Application of Data Mining in Bioinformatics arXiv preprint arXiv:1205.1125.

Raza, K., 2017. Formal concept analysis for knowledge discovery from biological data. Int. J. Data Mining & Bioinform. 18 (4), 281—300. https://doi.org/10.1504/IJDMB.2017.10009312. Inderscience.

Raza, K., 2020. Artificial intelligence against COVID-19: a meta-analysis of current research. In: Big Data Analytics Intelligence against COVID-19: Innovation Vision and Approach, 78. Springer, pp. 165—176.

Raza, K., 2019. Improving the prediction accuracy of heart disease with ensemble learning and majority voting rule. In: Advances in Ubiquitous Sensing Applications for Healthcare, U-Healthcare Monitoring Systems: Design and Applications. Academic Press, Elsevier, pp. 179—196. https://doi.org/10.1016/B978-0-12-815370-3.00008-6.

Raza, K., Maryam, Qazi, S., 2021. An introduction to computational intelligence for COVID-19: surveillance, prevention, prediction, and diagnosis. In: Computational Intelligence for COVID-19: Surveillance, Prevention, Prediction and Diagnosis, Studies in Computational Intelligence (SCI), 923. Springer, pp. 3—18.

Rojas, E., Munoz-Gama, J., Sepúlveda, M., Capurro, D., 2016. Process mining in healthcare: a literature review. J. Biomed. Inf. 61, 224—236.

Stein, R., 2005. Found on the web, with DNA: a boy's father. Wash. Post A9. https://www.washingtonpost.com/archive/politics/2005/11/13/found-on-the-web-with-dna-a-boys-father/11d74d45-6c0a-4ce2-8ec9-2a7fc20a12b8/. (Accessed 1 January 2021).

Verma, A., Taneja, A., Arora, A., August 2017. Fraud detection and frequent pattern matching in insurance claims using data mining techniques. In: 2017 Tenth International Conference on Contemporary Computing (IC3). IEEE, pp. 1—7.

Villalva, B.R., 2012. Madonna sterilization, star hires DNA team on tour. In: The Christian Post.

Wang, F., Preininger, A., 2019. Ai in health: state of the art, challenges, and future directions. Yearb. Med. Inf. 28 (01), 016—026.

Wang, H., Xu, Z., Pedrycz, W., 2017. An overview on the roles of fuzzy set techniques in big data processing: trends, challenges and opportunities. Knowl. Base Syst. 118, 15—30.

Yuan, X., March 2017. An improved Apriori algorithm for mining association rules. In: AIP Conference Proceedings, vol. 1820. AIP Publishing LLC, p. 080005. No. 1.

Zucco, C., 2018. Data mining in bioinformatics. In: Encyclopedia of Bioinformatics and Computational Biology. ABC of Bioinformatics, 328.

Chapter 13

Viroinformatics: a modern approach to counter viral diseases through computational informatics

Abhishek Sahu[1], Rutumbara Dash[1], Manasa Kumar Panda[1,2] and Yengkhom Disco Singh[3,*]

[1]School of Life Sciences, Sambalpur University, Burla, Odisha, India; [2]Environment & Sustainability Department, CSIR- IMMT, Bhubaneswar, Odisha, India; [3]Department of Post Harvest Technology, College of Horticulture and Forestry, Central Agricultural University, Pasighat, Arunachal Pradesh, India

*Corresponding author: E-mail: disco.iitg@gmail.com

Chapter outline

1. Introduction

For centuries, viruses have been known to confer irreparable loss to mankind. Each year, millions of people are dying due to viruses. These not only infect humans but also plants and other life forms. Zoonotic diseases caused by viruses are prevailing nowadays. Despite successful discoveries of vaccines and drugs to counter the viruses, new viruses are still emerging and posing serious threats to mankind. Along with that, some old viruses still persist without vaccines or medication like human immunodeficiency virus (HIV) (Singh, 2006). Some viruses are a successor to their previous strains due to mutation. Viruses like coronavirus are not new, but whenever they become virulent, they show a different strain. Some prominent viruses such as dengue virus, influenza virus, and HIV are still a problem for medical science. Researchers around the world are still in pursuit to find novel and effective ways to control these diseases. However, mutation and unidentified genomic construction are adding to the complexity and thus causing unsuccessful attempts.

In most cases, developing a drug/vaccine through proper protocol actually undergoes several experiments in a year, and the findings may not be easily accessible to other researchers in real time. Even if the results were extracted somehow, manual procedures were followed to test any hypothesis. It does not only consume time, but also with every failed attempt, it used to lose a lot of resources and thus delay in producing concrete results.

The solution was to bind together all the verified information and enable it to be accessed by researchers around the world. This was when computational technology came into the picture. A bioinformatic approach is taken to integrate all the viral data into a digital system. Not only any interaction with the host was given priority, but several tools could be constructed to perform various tasks like annotation and real-time simulation to ease the process of genomic study, interactome study, vaccine development, and therapeutic regime preparation. Viroinformatics is a new amalgamation of viral data and bioinformatics. To date, 1421 genera containing 6590 species have been classified by the International Committee on Taxonomy of Viruses (https://talk.ictvonline.org/). The National Center for Biotechnology Information (NCBI) has emerged as the biggest contributor to database analysis along with several other resources. Now, hundreds of databases are available to search for the required information (genome sequence, protein sequence, protein—protein interaction between virus and virus, or virus and host).

In this chapter, an attempt is made to bring all the resources under one umbrella, so the complexity of finding them can be minimized.

2. Virus database

A virus database is a collection of data related to viruses that are organized and stored in an electronic medium. Today, the size of virus databases has increased many fold, and it is all due to the exponential and rapid growth of biologic data related to viruses (Zou et al., 2015). Here, bioinformatics tools are mainly taken as the sole weapon to study the viruses and their genomic data. Bioinformatics is a multidisciplinary subject that combines entities like chemistry, mathematics, computing technology, and most importantly biology (Chowdhary et al., 2016; Gupta et al., 2020). So, the virus database contains data ranging from morphology to genomes and even more. Not only that, it comprises many application tools that can help in establishing many theories and developing drugs and other related things.

The virus database can be classified into many categories. They can be related to a particular virus (e.g., influenza virus, HIV, papillomavirus) or to a specific group of viruses like animal viruses, hemorrhagic fever viruses, etc. Also, many databases are widely available for analyzing diversity in viruses. These tools and their applications are an important part of the database that is used for speculating virus—host interaction, small RNA analysis, etc. (Sharma et al., 2015). So, the whole virus database contains information and simulating applications that help in making advanced products in researches. The database can be availed through different resources (Table 13.1), and as the resources are in huge quantity and each resource contains discrete data about particular information, that makes them a bit more complicated (Sharma et al., 2015). A comprehensive list of some available databases is given in Table 13.1.

Viral genomes can either consist of DNA or RNA. Irrespective of whatever it is, it can be single-stranded or double-stranded. As far as their structure is concerned, they can be circular or linear. The single-stranded RNA viruses show either positive $(+)$ sense or negative $(-)$ sense. Some rare single-stranded viruses show both kinds of sense, and they are being referred to as ambisense (Chaitanya, 2019). The coding transcripts code for required proteins, while the noncoding strands present help in the regulation of essential biochemical processes (Zhang et al., 2018).

3. Transcriptome of viruses

The complete set of coding and noncoding RNA transcripts of a virus is called the transcriptome of the virus. The transcriptome or the transcriptomic analysis is done to know the transcripts of RNA produced by the genome and the functions of the genes. The cellular response of the host to viruses can be tested when a virus infects a host. The factors that are involved directly or indirectly in the interaction can be identified by transcriptomic analysis (Huang et al., 2013). Use of high-throughput RNA sequencing with the help of bioinformatics has proved to be an important tool to get inside knowledge about cellular signaling mechanisms (Jones et al., 2014; Zou et al., 2013). RNA-seq can point out systematic changes in the host gene expression and the dynamic changes in the genome of the pathogen. This gives clarity about the negative effects of infection and interaction between them (Ertl and Klein, 2014; Jones et al., 2014; Wang et al., 2014; Xiao et al., 2013; Zou et al., 2013). The RNA-seq can give reads on the expression of genes and events related to DNA binding to generate transcription factors targets (Wani and Raza, 2019). This also helps in creating a precise and specific library as well as suitable bioinformatics databases for data processing and to quantify their abundance for functional analysis.

The RNA sequencing can be performed with the use of short-read method (by *illumine*). The short read produces transcripts that are then stitched digitally to construct the original transcript. So, in this method a large number of reads are produced. In contradiction to this, long-read method (by *PacBio* and *Nanopore*) produces fewer reads, but it is more effective than the former and eliminates the need of stitching them. But to create a very detailed viral transcriptome with high clarity, these two methods can be combined and later synchronized accordingly (Depledge et al., 2018; Moldován et al., 2018; O'Grady et al., 2016). This RNA sequencing can be implemented with different machine learning approaches

TABLE 13.1 Virus databases and their key feature.

Databases/tools	Key features	URL (checked on May 21, 2020)
RVDB	Viral transcriptome database	https://rvdb.dbi.udel.edu/ (Goodacre et al., 2018)
Viruses. STRING	Protein–protein database	http://viruses.string-db.org/ (Cook et al., 2018)
Virus HostNet 2.0	Virus–host protein interaction	http://virhostnet.prabi.fr/ (Guirimand et al., 2015)
Virus MINT	Virus–human protein–protein interaction	https://amp.pharm.mssm.edu/Harmonizome/resource/Virus+MINT (Chatr-Aryamontri et al., 2009)
NCBI-HHPID	HIV-1–human protein interactions	https://www.ncbi.nlm.nih.gov/genome/viruses/retroviruses/hiv-1/interactions/ (Fu et al., 2009)
Virus-host DB	Database showing virus and host relationship	https://www.genome.jp/virushostdb/ (Mihara et al., 2016)
GISAID	Database for sharing data related to influenza virus and hCoV-19	https://www.gisaid.org/ (Shu and Mc Cauley, 2017)
VIGOR	Prediction of gene program	https://www.jcvi.org/vigor (Wang et al., 2010)
NCBI genotyping tool	Viral sequence genotyping	https://ncbi.nlm.nih.gov/projects/genotyping/help.html (Rozanov et al., 2004)
GATU	Viral genome annotation	https://4virology.net/virology-ca-tools/gatu/(Tcherepanov et al., 2006)
VGO	Complete viral genome annotation	https://4virology.net/virology-ca-tools/vgo/ (Upton et al., 2000)
HPV-QUEST	HPV genotyping tool	http://www.ijbcb.org/HPV/ (Yin et al., 2012)
Virus-PLoc	Subcellular location of viral proteins prediction	http://www.csbio.sjtu.edu.cn/bioinf/virus/ (Shen and Chou, 2007)
AVPdb	Major medical viruses targeted antiviral peptides database	http://crdd.osdd.net/servers/avpdb/ (Qureshi et al., 2014)
VirOligo	Oligonucleotides of virus-specific database	http://viroligo.okstate.edu/ (Onodera and Melcher, 2002)
Geno2pheno	Prediction of resistance to drug in HIV-1, hepatitis B, and hepatitis C virus	https://www.geno2pheno.org/ (Beerenwinkel et al., 2003)
PrimeHunter	Subtyping of viruses using primer construction tool	https://dna.engr.uconn.edu/?page_id=85 (Duitama et al., 2009)
VaZyMolO	Viral protein-making tool	http://www.vazymolo.org/ (Ferron et al., 2005)
HIVSIM	Comparing HIV therapy regimens effectiveness	https://sites.google.com/site/hivsimulator/ (Lim et al., 2011)
LANL HIV	HIV sequences, immunologic epitopes Epitopes database	https://www.hiv.lanl.gov/ (Foley et al., 2018)
ViPR	Integrated data repository and analysis tool	https://www.viprbrc.org (Pickett et al., 2012)
IRD	Resource and tools for influenza virus host–pathogen interactions	https://www.fludb.org (Zhang et al., 2017)

Continued

TABLE 13.1 Virus databases and their key feature.—cont'd

Databases/tools	Key features	URL (checked on May 21, 2020)
NCBI-VVR	Resource for specific virus providing online recovery interfaces and analysis along with visualization tools	https://www.ncbi.nlm.nih.gov/genome/viruses/variation/ (Resch et al., 2009)
DengueNet	Dengue and dengue hemorrhagic fever monitoring at global level	http://www.denguevirusnet.com/ (Lawrence, 2002)
HepSEQ	Molecular, clinical, and epidemiologic information containing database with tools	http://labworm.com/tool/hepseq (Gnaneshan et al., 2007)
HBVdb	Digitally annotated sequences with common and specialized tools	https://hbvdb.lyon.inserm.fr/HBVdb/ (Heyer et al., 2013)
SeqHepB	HBV genome sequence analysis	http://www.seqhepb.com/ (Yuen et al., 2007)
HBVRegDB	Detection of regulatory elements	http://lancelot.otago.ac.nz (Panjaworayan et al., 2007)
LANL HCV	HCV sequence data and immunologic epitopes database	http://hcv.lanl.gov (Kuiken et al., 2005)
euHCVdb	Computer annotated sequence resource with analysis tools	http://euhcvdb.ibcp.fr (Combet et al., 2007)
PaVE	Papilloma virus genomes and protein sequence resource	https://pave.niaid.nih.gov/ (Van Doorslaer et al., 2012)
LANL HFV	Annotated HFV sequence database and several analysis tools hub	https://hcv.lanl.gov/ (Kuiken et al., 2012)
HVDB	Database of hepatitis A, B, C, D, and E virus sequences with phylogenetic analysis tool	https://hbvdb.lyon.inserm.fr/HBVdb/ (Belshaw et al., 2009)
phiSITE	Bacteriophage gene annotation tool	http://www.phisite.org/ (Klucar et al., 2010)
DPVweb	Data on viruses, viroids, and satellites of plants, fungi, and protozoa	http://www.dpvweb.net/ (Adams and Antoniw, 2006)
ViTA	Comprises known host/viral miRNAs and host miRNA targets	http://vita.mbc.nctu.edu.tw/ (Hsu et al., 2007)
Vir-Mir database	Hosts potential viral miRNA hairpins and viral miRNA target genes prediction	http://alk.ibms.sinica.edu.tw/ (Li et al., 2007)
HIVsirDB	HIV-inhibiting siRNAs database	http://crdd.osdd.net/raghava/hivsir/(Tyagi et al., 2011)
VIRsiRNAdb	Curated database of siRNA/shRNA with special focus on important human viruses	http://crdd.osdd.net/servers/virsirnadb/ (Thakur et al., 2012)
siVirus	Software for siRNA design	http://sivirus.rnai.jp/ (Naito et al., 2006)
viRome	Software for analysis of viral small RNA sequence datasets	http://virome.dbi.udel.edu/ (Watson et al., 2013)

All the links were working on May 21, 2020. Some links for many databases or tools were not working on May 21, 2020 so were not included.

like deep learning and shallow learning, which would learn from training data, and by using a specific algorithm, it will put forward an inference upon getting any experimental data (Jabeen et al., 2018).

The bioinformatics tools allow one to change primary sequencing data into stacks of regulated genes that can be optimized by statistically significant reads rectified with repeated testing. This makes sure that subsequent analysis will be made specifically for the viral genome of choice while eliminating any shortcomings. The two largest reservoirs of nucleic acid sequences are Gen Bank and NCBI, which are available in the public domain. But they have certain limitations like scarcity of closely associated sequence and their misannotation, or the availability of a huge amount of cellular sequences. This can camouflage a positive hit. Nowadays reference viral database (RVDB) 10.2 has overcome these issues (Goodacre et al., 2018). Its run proved to be faster for virus detection, and it is publicly available for high-throughput sequencing.

4. Virus–host interactomes

The virus–host interaction knowledge can prove to be more effective while producing broad-spectrum drugs and can be possibly more stable in terms of resistance development. Yeast 2 hybrid (Y2H) and RNA interference (RNAi) are being used to get inside knowledge about the interactions between host genome and viral proteins (Friedel and Haas, 2011). A large number of interactions are required to be examined for virus–host screening. Calderwood et al. were the first to do genome-wide Y2H screening for virus–host interaction in Epstein–Barr virus in 2007 (Calderwood et al., 2007). Y2H screening only detects direct interaction, but for indirect interaction, proteomic or RNAi screenings are required. RNAi assays identify host factors (HFs) embedded in protein complexes along with their involvement in signaling pathways and cellular processes. They also identify HFs binding to nonprotein components of the virus (Cherry, 2009). Genetic screening and genome-wide association studies provide insights into the involvement of HFs in infection (Awany et al., 2019; Carette et al., 2009). Along with all these, the results of expression profiling, structural analysis, kinetic studies, and localization studies are required to create an integrative bioinformatic database that can be used to analyze virus–host interactions (Friedel and Haas, 2011) (Fig. 13.1).

5. Virus–host interaction networks and modeling viral control of the host system

There are many databases conferring virus–host interactomes. **Viruses.STRING** is a protein–protein interaction database that contains data on virus–virus and virus–host interactions. To provide virus–host protein interactions, results of experiments as well as text-mining entities are combined. More than 170,000 interactions between 200 viruses and 300 hosts can be retrieved from this database (Cook at al., 2018).

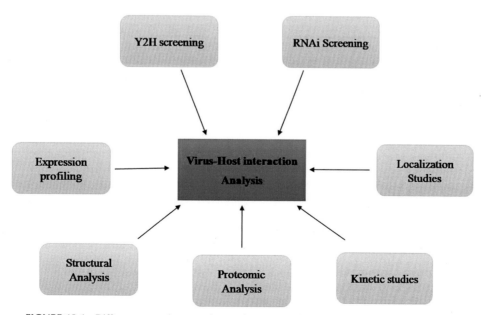

FIGURE 13.1 Different approaches to analyze and create an effective virus–host interaction database.

VirusHostNet 2.0 is another such database. The first version, VirusHostNet, was released in 2009. But this new version is based on Cytoscape to provide the most satisfactory access to the virus—virus and virus—host protein interaction along with their complementary host cell protein interaction networks (Guirimand et al., 2015).

VirusMINT is also a database that is dedicated to virus—human protein—protein interaction and contains data on more than 5000 interactions containing more than 490 viral proteins from 110 strains. Its data are collected and annotated in a structured way, and the data were collected from reported interactions from the literature between the virus and human proteins. It also contains data on some of the most medically important viruses like papillomaviruses, HIV 1, Epstein—Barr virus, hepatitis B virus, hepatitis C virus, herpes viruses, and Simian virus 40 (Chatr-Aryamontri et al., 2009).

Interactions between HIV-1 and host protein that are published in works of literature are curated and positioned in NCBI HIV-1/Human Protein Interaction Database (**NCBI-HHPID**). This lets the user explore the possibility of new HIV vaccines and targets for medical works (Fu et al., 2009). **CAPIH** helps in identifying genetic changes occurring in HIV-1 interacting host proteins. Humans and three model organisms are compared, and the information is put in this database for HIV-1 protein interaction of host. It is the first of its kind (Lin et al., 2009). **PhEVER** is a reservoir of data that holds virus-cell sequences as well as sequences of different viruses that are homologous (Palmeira et al., 2011).

The **Virus-Host DB** is another database that showcases the relationship between viruses and their hosts with their paired NCBI taxonomy IDs. The whole viral genome of the enlisted viruses can be retrieved here, which are harnessed from RefSeq, GenBank, UniProt, and ViralZone. Currently, it has 14,746 viral entries including 1316 viruses related to human hosts (Mihara et al., 2016).

GISAID is a database that helps in sharing data (genetic sequence, epidemiologic, clinical, geographic, and species-specific) related to influenza virus and the human coronavirus (Shu and Mc Cauley, 2017). The database includes Flu-Server Tool for identification, analysis, and interpretation of mutation in influenza virus sequences; Nextflu App for tracking the evolution of influenza A/H3N2 in real-time; and Next hCoV-19 App featuring data about genomic epidemiology of hCoV-19.

Genetic annotation is the next important thing after successful access to the genetic sequences. It would enable one to understand the structural and functional genome to mediate vaccine development and effective treatment. Several tools are made for annotation and classification of sequences: VIGOR (Viral Genome ORF Reader) (Wang et al., 2010); NCBI Genotyping Tool (Rozanov et al., 2004); Genome Annotation Transfer Utility (GATU) (Tcherepanov et al., 2006); Viral Genome Organizer (VGO) (Upton et al., 2000); Virus-Genotyping Tools (Alcantara et al., 2009); ZCURVE_V (Guo and Zhang, 2006); STAR (Subtype Analyser) (Myers et al., 2005); and HPV-QUEST (Yin et al., 2012).

There are other several resources that can be used to solve specific issues. **Virus-PLoc** is a fusion classifier that helps one to know viral protein sites inside host and virus-infected cells. It retrieves data primarily from Swiss Prot Database to give predictions of all viral proteins having no annotations for subcellular location or having uncertain annotations (Shen and Chou, 2007). **AVPdb** is a database that targets medically important viruses that are experimentally validated. It provides four different searches i.e., field search, advanced search, conditional search, and multidisplay search. It has many tools like AVPdb MAP, AVPdb BLAST, and physicochemical properties calculator (Qureshi et al., 2014). **VirOligo** is a database that contains oligonucleotides that are virus specific that contain data for PCR primers and hybridization probes as well as experimental conditions that helps to detect them (Onodera and Melcher, 2002). **Geno2pheno** can predict the drug resistance with regard to phenotypes of HIV-1, hepatitis B virus (HBV) and hepatitis C virus (HCV). It uses decision trees and support vector machines (Beerenwinkel et al., 2003). **PrimerHunter** is a primer designing tool for identification for PCR-based virus subtypes, and it guarantees the ideal enhancement by utilizing exact assessments of melting temperature with bungles, processed dependent on the closest model employing an effective fragmentary programming calculation (Duitama et al., 2009). **VIPS (Viral IRES Prediction System)** is a web server predicting internal ribosomal entry site secondary structure. To predict local RNA secondary structures by MFE, it uses RNAL fold program, whereas for comparing these predicted structures, RNA Align program is used. Pseudoknots structure is calculated using pknotsRG program (Hong et al., 2013). **VaZyMolO** targets characterizing viral protein modules that may be expressed in a solvent and practically dynamic structure, in this way distinguishing possibility for crystallization examines. It enables viral sequence handling at the protein level, which will define their modularity (Ferron et al., 2005).

6. HIV therapy simulator

HIV Therapy Simulator (HIVSIM) is a graphical user interface-based program that allows researchers and clinicians to find the efficacy of different models of therapeutic approaches such as induction maintenance therapies, structured treatment interruptions, and booster therapies. HIVSIM uses mathematical models that simulate the dynamics to find the outcome of therapies and overcomes limits of previous modeling programs by giving accessibility beyond theoretical research use (Lim et al., 2011). HIV simulator is a free application that is available at https://sites.google.com/site/hivsimulator/.

Dynamics of the simulator is that it harbors typical primary and chronic HIV infection, and it is a stochastic type based on random fluctuation of viral populations at low densities, while the model targets cells that limit viral load whenever the effects of antiretroviral agents are not restricted, and for this, it uses some earlier described models to simulate viral dynamics (Bonhoeffer et al., 1997; Curlin et al., 2007; Ribeiro and Bonhoeffer, 2000). It regulates the concentration of drugs, free virus particles, and uninfected $CD4^+$ cells according to time. It also updates short- to long-lived infected cells in the body. The phase-to-phase fall in viral load observed at the time of antiretroviral therapy is accurately presented here. To change the parameters of the model for other therapies, there is a provision to change host/virus, drug, mutation, and simulation.

HIVSIM is a potential tool for elucidating critical viral systems and clinical consequences. It can be easily modeled to check the drug efficacy period and its potential side effects while focusing on different washout period delivering potential percentage of success of that drug after simulation (Lim et al., 2011; Lockman et al., 2007).

HIVSIM is very useful for those who have no technical background, and it enables them to test and compare the effectiveness of primary and new HIV therapy regimens in controlling viral replication and inception of any strains having drug resistance. It is a tool to showcase the advantages and disadvantages of many HIV therapy strategies while focusing light on many concepts like genetics and epistasis. But along with that, it is also suggested that this simulation should not be used as a sole reason for use of any therapy into human patients directly without further confirmation from other platforms of testing and approval from an authority.

7. LANL HIV database

This is a database that is completely dedicated to HIV and simian immunodeficiency virus (SIV) to some extent, and it contains comprehensive HIV sequence data and immunologic epitopes besides tools for analysis of various data. It can be accessed through a website (https://www.hiv.lanl.gov/content/index) (Foley et al., 2018). In the HIV sequence database, there are different programs and tools such as the following:

Search interface: HIV sequence data can be extracted here, and these are used for alignment and model building.
Geography search interface: This is for recovery of the sequence according to its geographic distribution.
Genome browser: Diverse proteome and HIV-1 genome data can be seen using JBrowse.

This HIV sequence database contains different online tools that work with sequences, and they are organized by function. These tools help in analysis and quality control, alignment and sequence manipulation, creating phylogenetic trees, and analyzing homology. It also includes HIV premade alignments, which includes consensus and ancestral sequences, subtype reference alignments, and complete alignments.

The HIV immunology database can be used to search for annotated HIV-1 cytotoxic and T_H cell epitopes and antibody binding sites. There are various search interfaces such as CTL/CD8+ search; T helper/CD4+ search; antibody search; CTL variant search; T helper variant search; search help, and variant search help.

There are also database products like epitope maps, epitope tables, epitope alignments, and epitope density plots. Along with this, it also has tools that are categorized into tools produced by the Los Alamos HIV databases, external tools for epitope prediction, external tools for germline antibody reconstruction, external immunology databases and tools. So, this online website is a collection of a huge database and tools, and it hosts both of its modules as well as those from external sources.

8. Virus pathogen database and analysis resource and influenza resource database

Virus Pathogen Database and Analysis Resource (ViPR, https://www.viprbrc.org/) is an inclusive storehouse of information and analysis tool (Pickett et al., 2012). It contains a search tool for sequences and strains (genome, protein, and strain data), immune epitopes, 3D protein structures, host factor data, antiviral drugs, plasmid data, protein domains, and motifs. It also has data analysis tools like sequence alignment, phylogenetic tree, sequence variation, metadata-driven comparative analysis, BLAST, VIGOR4 genome annotator, and GATU genome annotator. It contains data from internal as well as external sources. Currently, ViPR has information regarding many human-pathogen viruses belonging to Arenaviridae, Caliciviridae, Coronaviridae, Filoviridae, Flaviviridae, Hantaviridae, Hepeviridae, Herpesviridae, Nairoviridae, Paramyxoviridae, Peribuniyaviridae, Phasmaviridae, Phenuiviridae, Picornaviridae, Pneumoviridae Poxviridae, Reoviridae, Rhabdoviridae, and Togaviridae families. Some important viruses like dengue virus, Ebola virus, enterovirus, HCV, Lassa virus, SARS-CoV-2, and Zika virus are contexed separately.

To import data, the external sources are NCBI-Genbank, NCBI-RefSeq, Immune Epitope Database, UniProt, RCSB Protein Data Bank, Catalytic Site Atlas, PATRIC, and VBRC Bioinformatics Resource Centers. There are several sources that submit data directly to ViPR, and they are NIAD Genome Sequencing Center, NIAD Systems Biology Program, and ViPR-funded Driving Biologic Projects.

Influenza Resource Database (IRD, https://www.fludb.org/) is a database that provides bioinformatic support for research of influenza virus. IRD provides an inclusive collection of influenza-related data and also gives facilities like visualization tools for hypothesis generation and mining of data. By this, it helps to discover new information about influenza virus transmission, virulence, host range and pathogenesis, and development of vaccines, diagnostics, and therapeutics against influenza virus (Zhang et al., 2017).

IRD has three main constituents: a comprehensive collection of data related to influenza, a module for analysis and visualization tools, and a personal interface for data storage and sharing facility. Its search module contains almost the same kind of features as ViPR. But it has some new features like search for PCR primer probe data, sequence feature variant type, human clinical studies and experiments (in beta stage), animal surveillance, and serology experiments (in beta stage). In the analysis section, it offers BLAST, sequence align, aligned sequence visualization, sequence annotation, point mutation identification, HPAI H5N1 clade classification, swine H1 classification, and metadata-driven comparative analysis tool for sequences (meta-CATS).

IRD is supported by the US National Institute of Allergy and Infectious Diseases, National Institutes of Health, and Department of Health and Human Services. Its sources of information for importing are NCBI-Genbank, NCBI-RefSeq, Immune Epitope Database, UniProt, RCSB Protein Data Bank, Catalytic Site Atlas, and AVI Base, whereas NIAID Genome Sequencing Center, NIAID Systems Biology Program, and NIAID Centers of Excellence for Influenza Research and Surveillance provide data directly to IRD.

9. Dengue and West Nile viruses databases

Dengue is an acute viral disease caused by dengue virus from Flaviviridae. It is an RNA virus and Aedes mosquito spreads this. Information about the virus is present in many databases. As mentioned earlier, it is present in ViPR. All the modules present in ViPR can be used to elucidate and extract information about this virus and can be used for any application. Currently, **NCBI-VVR** database contains data on dengue virus and West Nile viruses (Resch et al., 2009). West Nile viruses are the leading cause of mosquito-borne disease that is occurring in the continental United States.

The NCBI-VVR allows the user to retrieve information about metadata (time and place of sample collection, seriousness of disease, and serotype) and for aligning multiple sequences and creation of phylogenetic tree.

DengueNet is actually a WHO-created data management program serving as a global epidemiologic and virologic surveillance of dengue-related disease. It is designed to collect and combine the data in a timely manner and to show real-time prime indicators such as prevalence data, case-fatality rates, frequency and distribution of dengue and dengue hemorrhagic fever cases, death cases, and dengue virus serotypes spreading, as well as to give historical data (Lawrence, 2002).

10. Hepatitis viruses, papillomavirus, and ViPR

Hepatitis is caused by hepatitis A virus, HBV, HCV, hepatitis D virus, and hepatitis E virus (HEV). For HBV, there are many databases, and **HepSEQ** is one of them that is a repository for a vast library of molecular data related to the virus. This is controlled by the Center for Infections, Health Protection Agency, England. It is a database that has tools for tracking and managing HBV case and research. The organization of the database framework takes into account far-reaching molecular, clinical, and epidemiologic information to be kept into a utilitarian database, to look at and control the stored information, and to recover and envision epidemiologic, virologic, clinical, and nucleotide grouping data, and data on mutational parts of HBV contamination online. Programs such as Sequence Matcher, Genotyper, and Polymerase Annotator are also provided here (Gnaneshan et al., 2007).

Another database, **HBVdb**, also dedicated to HBV, provides suitable tools for testing genetic variability and viral resistance during treatment. Manually annotated reference genomes are collected and computationally annotated before being put into the database. It offers a static and dynamic query provision and also generic and specialized analysis tools (Heyer et al., 2013). HBVdb focuses on known genotype sequences, while HepSEQ takes on HBV variants from patients.

SeqHepB allows user to strike out main mutations from the collection linked to antiviral resistance, as well as pointing out clinically major mutants, and all this while determining HBV genotypes (Yuen et al., 2007). HBV sequences containing regulatory elements can be spotted, compared, and visualized by **HBVRegDB**. It can perform analyses based on selected HBV alignments. Integration of conserved regions is made, which includes primary conservation and RNA secondary predictions. Generic Genome Browser is considered for viral genome analysis. Annotated genomic modules are used for flexible queries, and annotated sequences can be analyzed to find novel regulatory motifs (Panjaworayan et al., 2007).

For HCV, **lanl HCV** database comprises two main segments, i.e., HCV sequence database and HCV immunology database, similar to that of lanl HIV database mentioned earlier. The HCV sequence data contains a user-friendly web interface and collates sequence data with annotation (Kuiken et al., 2005). The HCV immunology has a selective and organized pile of immunologic epitopes and their immune system interaction along with their recovery and analysis tools (Yusim et al., 2005).

European HCV database (**euHCVdb**) is another one that collects sequences that are digitally annotated built on genomes of reference. Subtyping and 3D molecular models of proteins along with genome mapping and utilization of nomenclature come under this computer annotation (Combet et al., 2007).

But nowadays, these two (lanl HCV and euHCVdb) are succeeded by more advanced ViPR, but these still can be utilized. The ViPR HCV contains HCV taxonomy browser containing seven known genotypes and one unknown genotype. Each of these has up to many thousands of strains and complete genomes.

For papillomavirus, the Papillomavirus Episteme (PaVE) provides an integrated resource for genome sequence analysis with relatable information. It enables storage, analysis, and sharing of sequence information based on relatable aspects in a freely accessible web-based (http://www.pave.niaid.nih.gov) tool. Annotated genomes used for open frame readings and cis-regulatory elements are provided by PaVE. It also gives access to data on genes, proteins, and structures (Van Doorslaer et al., 2012).

11. Virus group-specific databases

There are many databases that hold information about a group of related viruses rather than a specific virus. Hemorrhagic fever viruses is a group of several viruses that cause Ebola fever. The glycoprotein present on the envelope of these Ebola viruses helps in the pathogenesis of diseases (Khan et al., 2017). These viruses are mainly characterized by their pathogenicity and not by their taxonomy. **LANL HFV** can recover genetic sequences, aligning them using search interfaces, while the data are actually taken from GenBank. This HFV database is designed homologous to LANL HIV and LANL HCV databases. This database aims toward genetic information about HFV and the evolution and design of vaccines and drugs. One can get annotated sequences and other analytical tools (Geographic Search, Sequence Locator, HFV Align, PhyloPlace, Gapstreeze, N-Glycosite, Highlighter, Find Model) (Kuiken et al., 2012). **Flavitrack** is a database that holds annotated data on flavivirus sequences that is designed to identify conserved sequences, analyze mutational data and structural data, and track phenotypic evolution (Misra and Schein, 2007). Applications based on immunology and vaccine development by analytical tools are comprised in **FLAVIdb** along with antigenic data of flavivirus. It gets data from GenBank, GenPept, UniProt, IEDB, and PDB. Here, data and tools are integrated into a data mining system (Olsen et al., 2011).

In the **HVDB**, all the sequences obtained from INSDC are curated to the genome sequence of each virus. Phylogenetic relationships of each locus on the genome among each strain of a virus from a pool of HCV, HBV, and HEV are present (Shin-i et al., 2008). RNA virus database provides amino acid sequences for Open Reading Frames and complete translated genomes for all viruses present in the database (Belshaw et al., 2009). The **Subviral RNA database** is an online interface for research related to viroids, satellite RNAs, and related sequences of RNA of human hepatitis delta virus along with their analysis. It contains several RNA sequences, their RNA motifs, and analysis tools (Rocheleau and Pelchat, 2006).

PhISITE database holds detailed information about regulatory elements of several bacteriophages. Here the required information can be searched; all annotated genomes can be visualized with a graphical genome browser; Gene Regulatory Networks can be built, visualized, and simulated by BioTapestry tool (Klucar et al., 2010).

DPVweb holds information on viruses, viroids, fungi, and protozoa. This also contains detailed, curated information of sequences of completed or incomplete up to one complete gene. Viruses with RNA or ssDNA are also included that are fully sequenced (Adams and Antoniw, 2006). HESAS (HERVs Expression and Structure Analysis System) is a database holds information about human endogenous retroviruses (HERVs) and is used to understand their effects on the human functional gene expression, whereas HERVd enables one to find data on retroviral elements of the human genome with analysis (Kim et al., 2005; Pace et al., 2002).

12. Small RNA analysis tools

MicroRNAs (miRNAs) are small RNA molecules that can interfere in posttranscriptional level and thus regulate gene expression of the host as well as virus. The interlinked mechanism between viruses and host miRNAs is very important, and it is required to be studied. **ViTA** is a web-based database that performs computational relationship between a virus and host miRNA. It provides effective annotations that include host miRNA expression and virus-infected tissues. Also, through the graphical interface, it enables one to investigate the miRNA roles in viruses. Here the recreation and presentation of data include three main steps: data collection from different databases and literatures, information mining from collective data and sequence handling, and host miRNA target prediction by evaluating MFE. For predicting sites of miRNA target in viruses, miRanda and TargetScan are applied, and the TargetScan is quite reliable while considering humans, which can help in further studies. BLAST is used to obtain conserved regions in each species (Faiza et al., 2019; Hsu et al., 2007). **Vir-Mir database** provides an integrated interface on potential viral miRNA hairpins and provides modules to point out the potential target of the viral miRNA in selected host genomes using RNA hybrid program (Li et al., 2007).

Small interfering RNA (siRNA) and short hairpin RNA (shRNA) were found to be effective in inhibiting viruses. Information about each siRNA or shRNA is provided by **HIVsirDB**, which is a manually selected and organized HIV-inhibiting siRNAs database. It has several complementary siRNAs that differ in one to many bases with the target sites, and more than 100 escape mutant sequences are included in this database. This database contains many fields containing HIV strain, target region, efficiency and target sequence conservation, and siRNA sequence. It has many tools like siRNAmap for siRNAs mapping on target genome, HIVsirblast for BLAST against the database, and siRNAalign for siRNAs alignment (Tyagi et al., 2011). **VIRsiRNAdb** is a manually curated database containing siRNA/shRNA viral genome regions along with information on efficacies of many selected siRNAs retrieved from different assays. It also includes siRNA sequence, virus subtype, target genome region, cell type, target object, experimental assay, efficacy, off-target, and siRNA matching with viral sequences of reference. It has many siRNA analysis tools like siTarAlign that provides alignment of siRNA with user-defined sequences. It enables one to take the most suitable viral siRNA for antiviral therapy development with the best designing of siRNA tools (Thakur et al., 2012). **siVirus** is a software that provides siRNA constructions for antiviral RNA interference and helps in designing complex siRNAs for targeting highly divergent pathogens like HIV, HCV, influenza virus, and SARS coronavirus (Naito et al., 2006). Visitor and viRome softwares analyze viral siRNA sequence data sets (Antoniewski, 2011; Watson et al., 2013). Reconstruction of the entire viral genome using siRNA from a sample can be achieved by using Paparrazi. Paparazzi wipes out DI-explicit reads to improve the nature of the remade genome. Paparazzi comprises a promising option in contrast to Sanger sequencing in this specific situation and a powerful apparatus to consider antiviral RNAi systems by precisely evaluating vsiRNA along the reproducing viral genome (Vodovar et al., 2011).

13. 2019-nCoV and its databases

The new coronavirus, i.e., severe acute respiratory syndrome coronavirus 2 (SARS-CoV 2) or 2019- novel coronavirus (nCoV-2019), is an RNA stranded virus from *Betacoronavirus* genus that is responsible for the recent COVID-19 outbreak (Wu et al., 2020; https://www.who.int/emergencies/diseases/novel-coronavirus-2019/technical-guidance/naming-the-coronavirus-disease-(covid-2019)-and-the-virus-that-causes-it). It has spread all across the globe since its inception and has been declared a global pandemic by the World Health Organization. Effective vaccines are still under development, and a huge amount of biologic data related to the virus and disease that can be accessed worldwide is required for this.

CoronaVIR is a platform that helps in analysis of coronavirus genomic and proteomic data. It has different sections. Genomics contains data on whole genome, protein sequences, and nucleotide sequences. Diagnosis contains information about diagnostic primers and diagnostic tests. Immunotherapy contains information and provision for epitope mapping, peptide-based therapeutics, vaccine adjuvants, and siRNA-based therapeutics. Drug Designing helps in identifying potential drug targets and molecules, predicting cell penetrating peptides, and retrieving information on the 3D structure of SARS-CoV 22 proteins. Besides all these, it provides useful links for important information about the virus and the disease, and one can also submit data on this platform (https://webs.iiitd.edu.in/raghava/coronavir/f.php).

Semantic Scholar-CORD-19 is a search and discovery tool that is powered by artificial intelligence that uses machine learning techniques to curate information from different publications related to coronavirus to present them in comprehensive way to make it easy for researchers and to save time (https://www.semanticscholar.org/cord19).

2019 Novel Coronavirus Resource (2019nCoVR) is a database that presents comprehensive data about genomic and proteomic sequences and their metadata from NCBI, GISAID, NMDC, and CNBC/NGDC. It provides visualization functionalities for analysis of genomic variation that are based on data collected from 2019-nCoV strains. It has many online tools for genomic assembly for gathering raw NGS data and comparing them, variation identification for NGS data alignment and identification of genetic sequences, variation annotation for performing functional annotation on mutation site, genome annotation, BLAST, and AI diagnosis based on chest X-ray and CT imaging (https://bigd.big.ac.cn/ncov?lang=en).

14. Conclusion

The databases and resources mentioned here can prove to be a great help for progressing in virus-related researches. Not only it would make the data retrieval process less sophisticated, but also it would save both time and resources while enabling the researchers to develop new approaches to eliminate any kind of viral catastrophe in the future. Indeed, this new era of computational technology has changed the way of data retrieval and data analysis, and probably, this is the best option to take forward and make it more developed. As we know, contemporary virology has many drawbacks, so it cannot give results in determining a particular disease. Viroinformatics provides the opportunity to assemble the incomplete puzzle of contemporary virology to understand more on how viruses cause disease. However, a well-established validation of viroinformation using advance tools and technology with multidisciplinary approach in identifying diseases, diagnoses, and treatment using computational intelligence will upgrade the way of studying viroinformatics.

Acknowledgement

YDS is very much thankful to the Vice Chancellore of Central Agricultural University, Imphal, for providing the facilities.

References

Adams, M.J., Antoniw, J.F., 2006. DPVweb: a comprehensive database of plant and fungal virus genes and genomes. Nucleic Acids Res. 34 (Suppl. l_1), D382–D385.

Antoniewski, C., 2011. Visitor, an informatic pipeline for analysis of viral siRNA sequencing datasets. In: Antiviral RNAi. Humana Press, pp. 123–142.

Alcantara, L.C.J., Cassol, S., Libin, P., Deforche, K., Pybus, O.G., Van Ranst, M., Galvao-Castro, B., Vandamme, A.M., De Oliveira, T., 2009. A standardized framework for accurate, high-throughput genotyping of recombinant and non-recombinant viral sequences. Nucleic Acids Res. 37 (Suppl. l_2), W634–W642.

Awany, D., Allali, I., Dalvie, S., Hemmings, S., Mwaikono, K.S., Thomford, N.E., Gomez, A., Mulder, N., Chimusa, E.R., 2019. Host and microbiome genome-wide association studies: current state and challenges. Front. Genet. 9, 637.

Beerenwinkel, N., Daumer, M., Oette, M., Korn, K., Hoffmann, D., Kaiser, R., Lengauer, T., Selbig, J., Walter, H., 2003. Geno2pheno: estimating phenotypic drug resistance from HIV-1 genotypes. Nucleic Acids Res. 31 (13), 3850–3855.

Belshaw, R., de Oliveira, T., Markowitz, S., Rambaut, A., 2009. The RNA virus database. Nucleic Acids Res. 37 (Suppl. l_1), D431–D435.

Bonhoeffer, S., May, R.M., Shaw, G.M., Nowak, M.A., 1997. Virus dynamics and drug therapy. Proc. Natl. Acad. Sci. U. S. A. 94 (13), 6971–6976.

Calderwood, M.A., Venkatesan, K., Xing, L., Chase, M.R., Vazquez, A., Holthaus, A.M., Ewence, A.E., Li, N., Hirozane-Kishikawa, T., Hill, D.E., Vidal, M., 2007. Epstein–Barr virus and virus human protein interaction maps. Proc. Natl. Acad. Sci. U. S. A. 104 (18), 7606–7611.

Carette, J.E., Guimaraes, C.P., Varadarajan, M., Park, A.S., Wuethrich, I., Godarova, A., Kotecki, M., Cochran, B.H., Spooner, E., Ploegh, H.L., Brummelkamp, T.R., 2009. Haploid genetic screens in human cells identify host factors used by pathogens. Science 326 (5957), 1231–1235.

Chatr-Aryamontri, A., Ceol, A., Peluso, D., Nardozza, A., Panni, S., Sacco, F., Tinti, M., Smolyar, A., Castagnoli, L., Vidal, M., Cusick, M.E., 2009. VirusMINT: a viral protein interaction database. Nucleic Acids Res. 37 (Suppl. l_1), D669–D673.

Chaitanya, K.V., 2019. Structure and organization of virus genomes. In: Genome and Genomics. Springer, Singapore, pp. 1–30.

Cherry, S., 2009. What have RNAi screens taught us about viral–host interactions? Curr. Opin. Microbiol. 12 (4), 446–452.

Chowdhary, M., Rani, A., Parkash, J., Shahnaz, M., Dev, D., 2016. Bioinformatics: an overview for cancer research. J. Drug Deliv. Therapeut. 6 (4), 69–72.

Combet, C., Garnier, N., Charavay, C., Grando, D., Crisan, D., Lopez, J., Dehne-Garcia, A., Geourjon, C., Bettler, E., Hulo, C., Mercier, P.L., 2007. euHCVdb: the European hepatitis C virus database. Nucleic Acids Res. 35 (Suppl. l_1), D363–D366.

Cook, H.V., Doncheva, N.T., Szklarczyk, D., Von Mering, C., Jensen, L.J., 2018. Viruses. STRING: a virus-host protein-protein interaction database. Viruses 10 (10), 519.

Curlin, M.E., Iyer, S., Mittler, J.E., 2007. Optimal timing and duration of induction therapy for HIV-1 infection. PLoS Comput. Biol. 3 (7).

Depledge, D.P., Puthankalam, S.K., Sadaoka, T., Beady, D., Mori, Y., Placantonakis, D., Mohr, I., Wilson, A., 2018. Native RNA sequencing on nanopore arrays redefines the transcriptional complexity of a viral pathogen. bioRxiv 373522.

Duitama, J., Kumar, D.M., Hemphill, E., Khan, M., Măndoiu, I.I., Nelson, C.E., 2009. PrimerHunter: a primer design tool for PCR-based virus subtype identification. Nucleic Acids Res. 37 (8), 2483–2492.

Ertl, R., Klein, D., 2014. Transcriptional profiling of the host cell response to feline immunodeficiency virus infection. Virol. J. 11 (1), 52.

Faiza, M., Tanveer, K., Fatihi, S., Wang, Y., Raza, K., 2019. Comprehensive overview and assessment of microRNA target prediction tools in *Homo sapiens* and *Drosophila melanogaster*. Curr. Bioinf. 14 (5), 432–445.

Ferron, F., Rancurel, C., Longhi, S., Cambillau, C., Henrissat, B., Canard, B., 2005. VaZyMolO: a tool to define and classify modularity in viral proteins. J. Gen. Virol. 86 (3), 743–749.

Foley, B.T., Korber, B.T.M., Leitner, T.K., Apetrei, C., Hahn, B., Mizrachi, I., Mullins, J., Rambaut, A., Wolinsky, S., 2018. HIV Sequence Compendium 2018 (No. LA-UR-18-25673). Los Alamos National Lab.(LANL), Los Alamos, NM (United States).

Friedel, C.C., Haas, J., 2011. Virus–host interactomes and global models of virus-infected cells. Trends Microbiol. 19 (10), 501–508.

Fu, W., Sanders-Beer, B.E., Katz, K.S., Maglott, D.R., Pruitt, K.D., Ptak, R.G., 2009. Human immunodeficiency virus type 1, human protein interaction database at NCBI. Nucleic Acids Res. 37 (Suppl. 1), D417−D422.

Gnaneshan, S., Ijaz, S., Moran, J., Ramsay, M., Green, J., 2007. HepSEQ: international public health repository for hepatitis B. Nucleic Acids Res. 35 (Suppl. 1), D367−D370.

Goodacre, N., Aljanahi, A., Nandakumar, S., Mikailov, M., Khan, A.S., 2018. A reference viral database (RVDB) to enhance bioinformatics analysis of high-throughput sequencing for novel virus detection. mSphere 3 (2).

Guirimand, T., Delmotte, S., Navratil, V., 2015. VirHostNet 2.0: surfing on the web of virus/host molecular interactions data. Nucleic Acids Res. 43 (D1), D583−D587.

Guo, F.B., Zhang, C.T., 2006. ZCURVE_V: a new self-training system for recognizing protein-coding genes in viral and phage genomes. BMC Bioinf. 7 (1), 9.

Gupta, P.P., Kasmi, Y., Podlipnik, Č., 2020. Introduction to computational and bioinformatics tools in virology. In: Emerging and Reemerging Viral Pathogens. Academic Press, pp. 121−145.

Hayer, J., Jadeau, F., Deleage, G., Kay, A., Zoulim, F., Combet, C., 2013. HBVdb: a knowledge database for hepatitis B Virus. Nucleic Acids Res. 41 (D1), D566−D570.

Hong, J.J., Wu, T.Y., Chang, T.Y., Chen, C.Y., 2013. Viral IRES prediction system-a web server for prediction of the IRES secondary structure in silico. PloS One 8 (11).

Hsu, P.W.C., Lin, L.Z., Hsu, S.D., Hsu, J.B.K., Huang, H.D., 2007. ViTa: prediction of host microRNAs targets on viruses. Nucleic Acids Res. 35 (Suppl. 1), D381−D385.

Huang, Y., Li, Y., Burt, D.W., Chen, H., Zhang, Y., Qian, W., Kim, H., Gan, S., Zhao, Y., Li, J., Yi, K., 2013. The duck genome and transcriptome provide insight into an avian influenza virus reservoir species. Nat. Genet. 45 (7), 776−783.

Jabeen, A., Ahmad, N., Raza, K., 2018. Machine learning-based state-of-the-art methods for the classification of rna-seq data. In: Classification in BioApps. Springer, Cham, pp. 133−172.

Jones, M., Dry, I.R., Frampton, D., Singh, M., Kanda, R.K., 2014. RNA-seq analysis of host and viral gene expression highlights interaction between varicella zoster virus and keratinocyte differentiation. PloS Pathog. 10.

Khan, F.N., Qazi, S., Tanveer, K., Raza, K., 2017. A review on the antagonist ebola: a prophylactic approach. Biomed. Pharmacother. 96, 1513−1526.

Kim, T.H., Jeon, Y.J., Kim, W.Y., Kim, H.S., 2005. HESAS: HERVs expression and structure analysis system. Bioinformatics 21 (8), 1699−1700.

Klucar, L., Stano, M., Hajduk, M., 2010. phiSITE: database of gene regulation in bacteriophages. Nucleic Acids Res. 38 (Suppl. 1), D366−D370.

Kuiken, C., Thurmond, J., Dimitrijevic, M., Yoon, H., 2012. The LANL hemorrhagic fever virus database, a new platform for analyzing biothreat viruses. Nucleic Acids Res. 40 (D1), D587−D592.

Kuiken, C., Yusim, K., Boykin, L., Richardson, R., 2005. The Los Alamos hepatitis C sequence database. Bioinformatics 21 (3), 379−384.

Lawrence, J., 2002. DengueNet−WHO's internet based system for the global surveillance of dengue fever and dengue haemorrhagic fever. Wkly. Releases (1997−2007) 6 (39), 1883.

Li, S.C., Shiau, C.K., Lin, W.C., 2007. Vir-Mir db: prediction of viral microRNA candidate hairpins. Nucleic Acids Res. 36 (Suppl. 1), D184−D189.

Lim, H.C., Curlin, M.E., Mittler, J.E., 2011. HIV therapy simulator: a graphical user interface for comparing the effectiveness of novel therapy regimens. Bioinformatics 27 (21), 3065−3066.

Lin, F.K., Pan, C.L., Yang, J.M., Chuang, T.J., Chen, F.C., 2009. CAPIH: a web interface for comparative analyses and visualization of host-HIV protein-protein interactions. BMC Microbiol. 9 (1), 164.

Lockman, S., Shapiro, R.L., Smeaton, L.M., Wester, C., Thior, I., Stevens, L., Chand, F., Makhema, J., Moffat, C., Asmelash, A., Ndase, P., 2007. Response to antiretroviral therapy after a single, peripartum dose of nevirapine. N. Engl. J. Med. 356 (2), 135−147.

Mihara, T., Nishimura, Y., Shimizu, Y., Nishiyama, H., Yoshikawa, G., Uehara, H., Hingamp, P., Goto, S., Ogata, H., 2016. Linking virus genomes with host taxonomy. Viruses 8 (3), 66.

Misra, M., Schein, C.H., 2007. Flavitrack: an annotated database of flavivirus sequences. Bioinformatics 23 (19), 2645−2647.

Moldován, N., Tombácz, D., Szűcs, A., Csabai, Z., Snyder, M., Boldogkői, Z., 2018. Multi-platform sequencing approach reveals a novel transcriptome profile in pseudorabies virus. Front. Microbiol. 8, 2708.

Myers, R.E., Gale, C.V., Harrison, A., Takeuchi, Y., Kellam, P., 2005. A statistical model for HIV-1 sequence classification using the subtype analyser (STAR). *Bioinformatic*s 21 (17), 3535−3540.

Naito, Y., Ui-Tei, K., Nishikawa, T., Takebe, Y., Saigo, K., 2006. siVirus: web-based antiviral siRNA design software for highly divergent viral sequences. Nucleic Acids Res. 34 (Suppl. 2), W448−W450.

O'Grady, T., Wang, X., Höner zu Bentrup, K., Baddoo, M., Concha, M., Flemington, E.K., 2016. Global transcript structure resolution of high gene density genomes through multi-platform data integration. Nucleic Acids Res. 44 (18), e145.

Olsen, L.R., Zhang, G.L., Reinherz, E.L., Brusic, V., 2011. FLAVIdB: a data mining system for knowledge discovery in flaviviruses with direct applications in immunology and vaccinology. Immunome Res. 7 (3).

Onodera, K., Melcher, U., 2002. VirOligo: a database of virus-specific oligonucleotides. Nucleic Acids Res. 30 (1), 203−204.

Paces, J., Pavlícek, A., Paces, V., 2002. HERVd: database of human endogenous retroviruses. Nucleic Acids Res. 30 (1), 205−206.

Palmeira, L., Penel, S., Lotteau, V., Rabourdin-Combe, C., Gautier, C., 2011. PhEVER: a database for the global exploration of virus−host evolutionary relationships. Nucleic Acids Res. 39 (Suppl. 1), D569−D575.

Panjaworayan, N., Roessner, S.K., Firth, A.E., Brown, C.M., 2007. HBVRegDB: annotation, comparison, detection and visualization of regulatory elements in hepatitis B virus sequences. Virol. J. 4 (1), 136.

Pickett, B.E., Sadat, E.L., Zhang, Y., Noronha, J.M., Squires, R.B., Hunt, V., Liu, M., Kumar, S., Zaremba, S., Gu, Z., Zhou, L., 2012. ViPR: an open bioinformatics database and analysis resource for virology research. Nucleic Acids Res. 40 (D1), D593–D598.

Qureshi, A., Thakur, N., Tandon, H., Kumar, M., 2014. AVPdb: a database of experimentally validated antiviral peptides targeting medically important viruses. Nucleic Acids Res. 42 (D1), D1147–D1153.

Resch, W., Zaslavsky, L., Kiryutin, B., Rozanov, M., Bao, Y., Tatusova, T.A., 2009. Virus variation resources at the national center for biotechnology information: dengue virus. BMC Microbiol. 9 (1), 65.

Ribeiro, R.M., Bonhoeffer, S., 2000. Production of resistant HIV mutants during antiretroviral therapy. Proc. Natl. Acad. Sci. U. S. A. 97 (14), 7681–7686.

Rocheleau, L., Pelchat, M., 2006. The Subviral RNA Database: a toolbox for viroids, the hepatitis delta virus and satellite RNAs research. BMC Microbiol. 6 (1), 24.

Rozanov, M., Plikat, U., Chappey, C., Kochergin, A., Tatusova, T., 2004. A web-based genotyping resource for viral sequences. Nucleic Acids Res. 32, W654–W659.

Sharma, D., Priyadarshini, P., Vrati, S., 2015. Unraveling the web of viroinformatics: computational tools and databases in virus research. J. Virol. 89 (3), 1489–1501.

Shen, H.B., Chou, K.C., 2007. Virus-PLoc: a fusion classifier for predicting the subcellular localization of viral proteins within host and virus-infected cells. Biopolymers 85 (3), 233–240.

Shin-i, T., Tanaka, Y., Tateno, Y., Mizokami, M., 2008. Development and public release of a comprehensive hepatitis virus database. Hepatol. Res. 38 (3), 234–243.

Shu, Y., McCauley, J., 2017. GISAID: global initiative on sharing all influenza data–from vision to reality. Euro Surveill. 22 (13).

Singh, M., 2006. No vaccine against HIV yet-are we not perfectly equipped? Virol. J. 3 (1), 60.

Tcherepanov, V., Ehlers, A., Upton, C., 2006. Genome Annotation Transfer Utility (GATU): rapid annotation of viral genomes using a closely related reference genome. BMC Genomics 7 (1), 150.

Thakur, N., Qureshi, A., Kumar, M., 2012. VIRsiRNAdb: a curated database of experimentally validated viral siRNA/shRNA. Nucleic Acids Res. 40 (D1), D230–D236.

Tyagi, A., Ahmed, F., Thakur, N., Sharma, A., Raghava, G.P., Kumar, M., 2011. HIVsirDB: a database of HIV inhibiting siRNAs. PloS One 6 (10).

Upton, C., Hogg, D., Perrin, D., Boone, M., Harris, N.L., 2000. Viral genome organizer: a system for analyzing complete viral genomes. Virus Res. 70 (1–2), 55–64.

Van Doorslaer, K., Tan, Q., Xirasagar, S., Bandaru, S., Gopalan, V., Mohamoud, Y., Huyen, Y., McBride, A.A., 2012. The papillomavirus episteme: a central resource for papillomavirus sequence data and analysis. Nucleic Acids Res. 41 (D1), D571–D578.

Vodovar, N., Goic, B., Blanc, H., Saleh, M.C., 2011. In silico reconstruction of viral genomes from small RNAs improves virus-derived small interfering RNA profiling. J. Virol. 85 (21), 11016–11021.

Wang, S., Sundaram, J.P., Spiro, D., 2010. VIGOR, an annotation program for small viral genomes. BMC Bioinf. 11 (1), 451.

Wang, Y., Lupiani, B., Reddy, S.M., Lamont, S.J., Zhou, H., 2014. RNA-seq analysis revealed novel genes and signaling pathway associated with disease resistance to avian influenza virus infection in chickens. Poult. Sci. 93 (2), 485–493.

Wani, N., Raza, K., 2019. Raw sequence to target gene prediction: an integrated inference pipeline for ChIP-seq and RNA-seq datasets. In: Applications of Artificial Intelligence Techniques in Engineering. Springer, Singapore, pp. 557–568.

Watson, M., Schnettler, E., Kohl, A., 2013. viRome: an R package for the visualization and analysis of viral small RNA sequence datasets. Bioinformatics 29 (15), 1902–1903.

Wu, A., Peng, Y., Huang, B., Ding, X., Wang, X., Niu, P., Meng, J., Zhu, Z., Zhang, Z., Wang, J., Sheng, J., 2020. Genome composition and divergence of the novel coronavirus (2019-nCoV) originating in China. Cell Host Microbe 27 (3), 325–328.

Xiao, Y.L., Kash, J.C., Beres, S.B., Sheng, Z.M., Musser, J.M., Taubenberger, J.K., 2013. High-throughput RNA sequencing of a formalin-fixed, paraffin-embedded autopsy lung tissue sample from the 1918 influenza pandemic. J. Pathol. 229 (4), 535–545.

Yin, L., Yao, J., Gardner, B.P., Chang, K., Yu, F., Goodenow, M.M., 2012. HPV-QUEST: a highly customized system for automated HPV sequence analysis capable of processing next generation sequencing data set. Bioinformation 8 (8), 388.

Yuen, L.K., Ayres, A., Littlejohn, M., Colledge, D., Edgely, A., Maskill, W.J., Locarnini, S.A., Bartholomeusz, A., 2007. SeqHepB: a sequence analysis program and relational database system for chronic hepatitis B. Antivir. Res. 75 (1), 64–74.

Yusim, K., Richardson, R., Tao, N., Dalwani, A., Agrawal, A., Szinger, J., Funkhouser, R., Korber, B., Kuiken, C., 2005. Los alamos hepatitis C immunology database. Appl. Bioinf. 4 (4), 217–225.

Zhang, Y., Aevermann, B.D., Anderson, T.K., Burke, D.F., Dauphin, G., Gu, Z., He, S., Kumar, S., Larsen, C.N., Lee, A.J., Li, X., 2017. Influenza research database: an integrated bioinformatics resource for influenza virus research. Nucleic Acids Res. 45 (D1), D466–D474.

Zhang, X., Ma, X., Jing, S., Zhang, H., Zhang, Y., 2018. Non-coding RNAs and retroviruses. Retrovirology 15 (1), 20.

Zou, W., Chen, D., Xiong, M., Zhu, J., Lin, X., Wang, L., Zhang, J., Chen, L., Zhang, H., Chen, H., Chen, M., 2013. Insights into the increasing virulence of the swine-origin pandemic H1N1/2009 influenza virus. Sci. Rep. 3, 1601.

Zou, D., Ma, L., Yu, J., Zhang, Z., 2015. Biological databases for human research. Dev. Reprod. Biol. 13 (1), 55–63.

Chapter 14

Viroinformatics for viral diseases: tools and databases

Sarra Akermi[1], Sunil Jayant[1], Arabinda Ghosh[2], Ashwani Sharma[3], Subrata Sinha[4],*, and Surabhi Johari[5],*

[1]*Annotations Analytics Pvt Ltd., Gurgaon, Haryana, India;* [2]*Department of Botany, Guwahati University, Assam, Guwahati, India;* [3]*Computational Centre, Rennes, France;* [4]*Centre for Biotechnology and Bioinformatics Dibrugarh University, Assam, Dibrugarh, India;* [5]*School of Biosciences Institute of Management Studies Ghaziabad (University Courses), Uttar Pradesh, India*

Corresponding authors: E-mails: subratasinha@dibru.ac.in, surabhi.johari@imsuc.ac.in

Chapter outline

1. Introduction

Exponential growth of scientific work in the domain of virology has necessitated the implementation of bioinformatics to support the researcher. A huge amount of experimental genomic data has been generated due to progress in the field of molecular biology and bioinformatics. Several viroinformatics databases have been developed to collect big data from experiments and silico studies, evaluate the data and disseminate the available information that contains data regarding different viruses and provides tools for multiple sequence alignment, 3D visualization, homology modeling, and phylogenetic trees (Bianco et al., 2013). The necessity for computer-assisted technologies for genome structure, function, and evolution of viruses is growing exponentially to cater to various challenges in the field of virology. This chapter gives an overview of some of the important viral databases, tools and techniques that have developed during the last few years and have contributed to analyzing the viral genome. These viroinformatics resources have been developed that help to address the fundamental questions in virology, e.g., biodiversity of viruses, their classification as known and already discovered, viral protein plasticity and folding, and viral peptides identification (Hufsky et al., 2018). The databases and tools that have been recently developed and made available to virologists are discussed in the following sections.

2. Antiviral tools

Different viroinformatics tools have been developed to understand the function of and analyze the virus genome, analyzing genes, viral crossing over and recombination, and formation of different structures of the RNAs such as siRNA, shRNA, and miRNA. Other virus-based studies report on folding of RNA, interaction of one protein with another proteins (epitope-receptor interaction), structure prediction, and analysis of viral proteins, which will help the biologist for the annotation of viral genes, understanding their roles, and highly efficient antiviral drug discovery and vaccines. We list the following tools for viroinformatics for viral diseases.

2.1 Alvira

The Alvira tool is applicable for comparison of the targeted viral genome with other viral genomes. It involves multiple sequence alignment with the viral genome that is used for evaluating homology, gene annotation, and relationship between genomes of different viral strains. Alvira can perform the combination of nucleic and protein alignments from the coding sequences, and these alignments can be assigned to the corresponding genomes. The analysis can be carried out in two steps: removal of dissimilarities blocks with low homology and grouping highly matched blocks with higher percentage of homology. Further, based on these similarities, we can analyze and predict viral families and variation in their genomes. These variations can predict the difference in their genes, genetic mutation, and single nucleotide polymorphism to assign the impact of virulence. We can also predict complex information of gene characteristics and annotation of these genes with biologic properties that refer to dynamics of different virus populations (Enault et al., 2007). The Alvira server can be access by the website: http://bioinfo.genopole-toulouse.prd.fr/Alvira.

3. Antiviral databases

3.1 AVPdb

This provides information about antiviral peptides (AVPs) from 60 medically important viruses of great interest. This database is periodically manually curated and has experimentally checked information about 2683 AVPs including 624 updated AVPs. This database includes extensive details such as information about the viral sequence, Origin of the viral genes, information about the targeted virus, information about the cell line, different viral assays, prediction, and uses of several experiments and their efficacy (qualitative/quantitative) and association of different viruses with their respective diseases. The AVP production also provides details on the physicochemical properties of peptides and predicted structures. Several analytical tools such as basic local alignment search tool (BLAST) and MAP are also included to facilitate genome and gene-based information. AVPdb is intended to satisfy the scientific community's need to improve antiviral therapy (Qureshi et al., 2013a,b). The AVPdb can be accessed by http://crdd.osdd.net/servers/avpdb/ (Figs. 14.1 and 14.2).

3.2 AVP pred

It is designed for prediction of AVPs. The data has been collected from experiments with proven antiviral activity and assembled in the database by computational algorithm. Higher supercomputing simulations have been performed by high-performance computational machine learning techniques such as SVM, which includes descriptors from the peptide sequence, peptides blocks with antiviral properties, homolog sequence alignment, compositions of the amino acid, and physiochemical properties for antiviral peptide prediction with highly user-friendly web interface. The output of the AVP pred is provided in the form of numeric scoring as well as representation in the graphic form. The output incorporates a different variety of coloring schemes to represent the highly valuable score, which supports in selecting the highly effective AVPs. Therefore, it will support the experimental biologist who is working on peptide-based antiviral therapeutics development to predict the peptides of the research tool blast to scan related peptides in the CAMP, AMP, and Uniprot databases (Thakur et al., 2012). The database can be access by the link: http://crdd.osdd.net/servers/avppred/ (Fig. 14.3).

3.3 HIPdb

HIP database contains data collection of a manually curated database where information is collected and processed from experimentally validated human immunodeficiency virus (HIV) inhibitory peptides. These peptides are included by considering various pathways of the HIV virus having information of HIV infection signaling proteins, membrane fusion

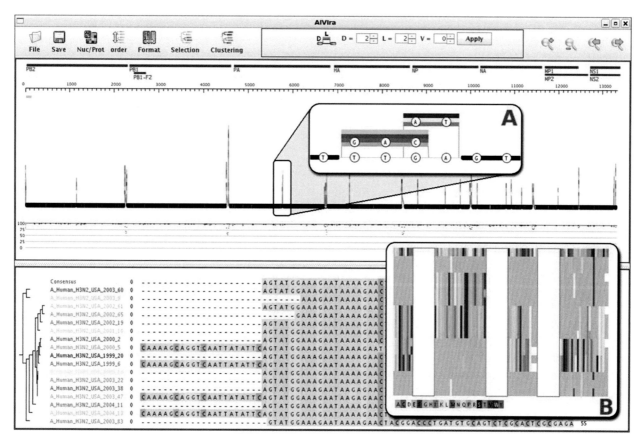

FIGURE 14.1 Graphics of Alvira server.

proteins, membrane receptors, proteins responsible for replication of the proteins, reverse transcription, etc. The nature of these peptides is chemical origin by peptide synthesis process or obtained from natural resources. The antiviral efficacy of these peptides is tested on different cell lines. This database contains information about sequence of the peptides, amino acid length of the peptides, obtaining source of the peptides, information about targeted proteins, tested on which cell lines, information about inhibition constant, which types of assays have been used, etc. It also has implemented online tools for performing homology prediction by BLAST and MAP for phylogenetic tree analysis. In addition, the peptides also have predicted structure and physicochemical properties. This database helps the experimental biologist to classify the best inhibitory peptides for the design of HIV-dependent peptide therapy (Qureshi et al., 2013a,b). HIPdb database can be accessed at the link: http://crdd.osdd.net/servers/hipdb (Fig. 14.4).

3.4 HIV-1 human interaction database

The HIV-1 database contains information about protein—protein interactions of the HIV proteins and details information of sites of knockdown human genes that are responsible for replication of the HIV virus and their pathogenecity and infectivity. Several data have been reported that have mentioned a number of proteins involved in the HIV virus interaction with the host cell receptors and viral protein interaction with the host cell proteins. However, it was difficult to understand until some simple database arrived with a clearer picture, and public access is still needed to those data. To provide more information about HIV virus, two entities, the Division of Acquired Immunodeficiency Syndrome and the National Institute of Allergy and Infectious Diseases, have taken the initiative to develop a comprehensive database. This database will contain collective information about interactions between HIV-1 and human cell proteins. This database has been

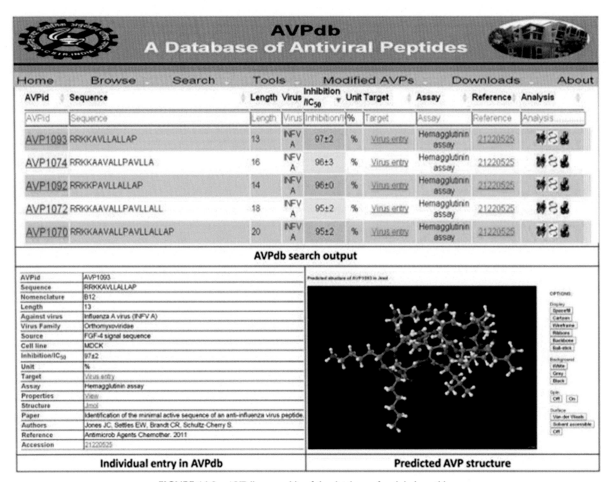

FIGURE 14.2 AVPdb: a graphic of the database of antiviral peptides.

developed with joint partnership between Southern Research Institute and the NCBI (Danso et al., 2015). The database is available at the link: https://www.ncbi.nlm.nih.gov/genome/viruses/retroviruses/hiv-1/interactions/ (Fig. 14.5).

3.5 The EuResist project

The EuResist provides detailed information to clinicians, scientists, and healthcare-associated people with digitally based prediction of potential antiviral therapy to HIV patients. It supports the clinician with the right way of using the antiviral therapy with combination of drugs, which is not possible to predict immediately by experimental approach. The EuResist undertaking proposed a novel technique to predicting the in vivo efficacy of antiretroviral drug regimens in opposition to a given HIV, based totally on the use of viral genotype statistics included with remedy reaction facts accrued in scientific practice (Zazzi et al., 2012). The EuResist server can be access by the link: http://engine.euresist.org/database/ (Fig. 14.6).

3.6 Stanford SARS-CoV-2 antiviral research database

COVID-19 is a global catastrophe affecting over 4.5 million people in 200 nations to date. There is a race against time to develop a drug or a vaccine against it, but none of the efforts have yielded a proven cure without potential risks yet. The modus operandi of treatment currently relies on drug repurposing. Antimalarial drugs chloroquine and hydroxychloroquine have garnered the most attention recently as a successful remedy for COVID-19. However, the use of these drugs is still questionable due to undetermined efficacy and side effects. The Coronavirus Antiviral Research Database is designed to

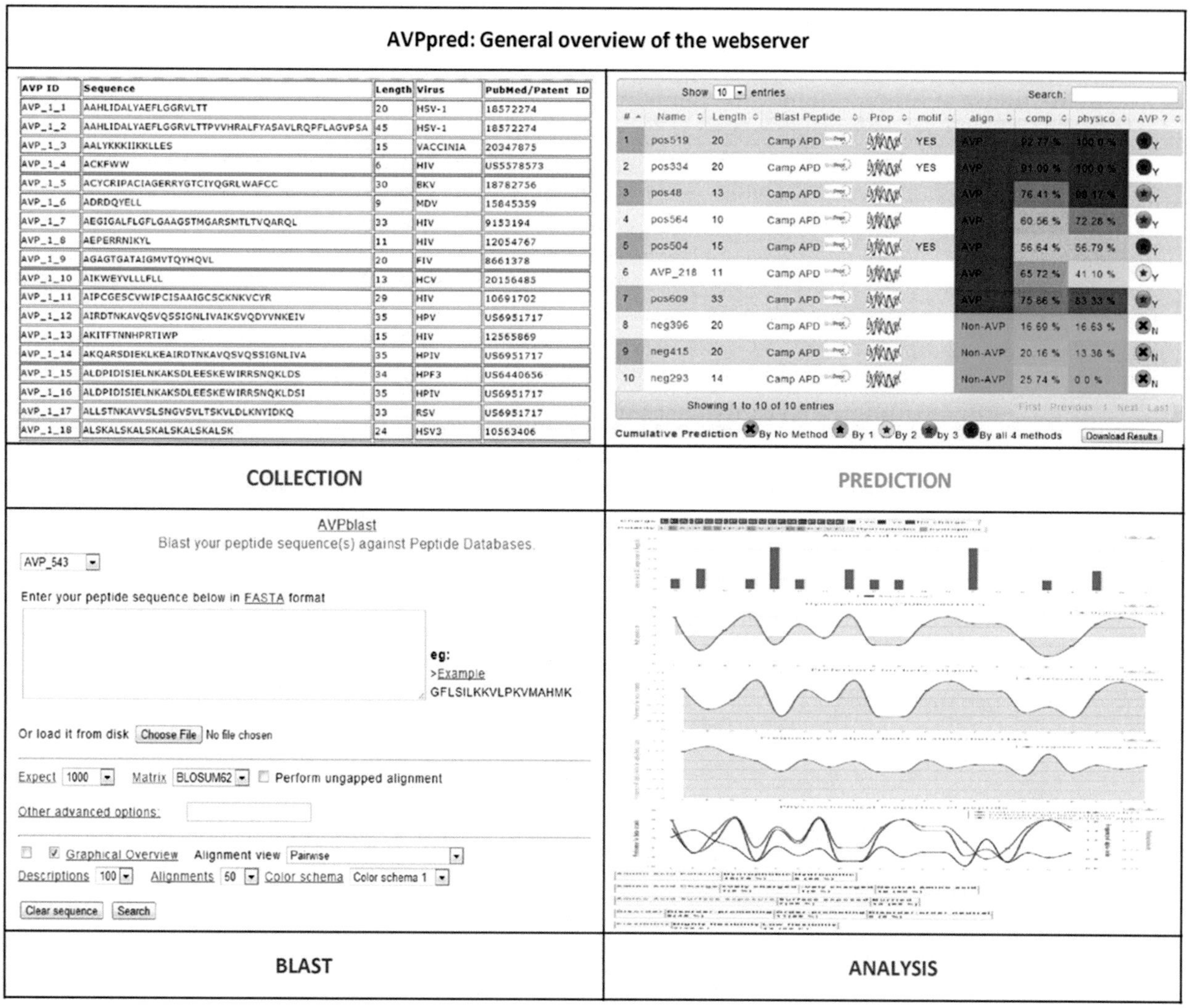

FIGURE 14.3 An overview of web servers. AVPpred web server outline and functionality.

expedite the development of SARS-CoV-2 antiviral therapy. This database supports drug development efforts by (1) using experimental effects to facilitate comparisons between extraordinary candidate antiviral compounds; (2) highlighting gaps in coronavirus antiviral drug improvement research; (3) assisting scientists, medical investigators, public health officials, and funding companies to prioritize the maximum promising compounds and repurposed drugs for additional improvement; (4) offering an objective, evidenced-based, source of statistics for the public; and (5) creating a hub for the exchange of thoughts among coronavirus researchers whose comments is sought and welcomed. The database can be access by the link: https://covdb.stanford.edu/ (Fig. 14.7 and Table 14.1).

4. Case study

4.1 Evaluating genome relationship between SARS-CoV-2 strains at different geolocations

Coronaviruses are identified by having crown-like spikes on their surface. Coronaviruses (CoVs) are part of the Coronaviridae family that create severe infection in the lungs of mammals (Cava et al., 2020). Earlier, three novel strains of coronaviruses infected the human population, which originated from different species such as bat and at last infected humans after crossing the species barrier, called a spillover event (Parrish et al., 2008). First, severe acute respiratory syndrome coronavirus (SARS-CoV) infected the Chinese population (2002) in the Guangdong province and claimed 774 lives (Poon et al., 2004). Further, in 2012, Middle East respiratory syndrome coronavirus (MERS-CoV) emerged in the

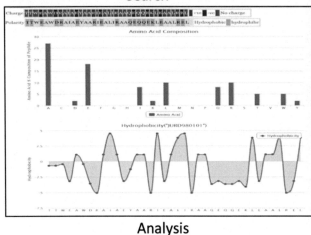

FIGURE 14.4   User interface in the HIPdb.

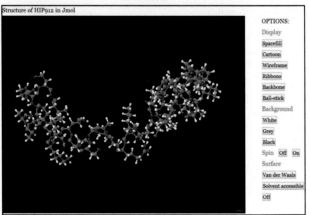

FIGURE 14.5   Searching human genes for HIV-1 genes.

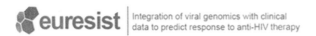

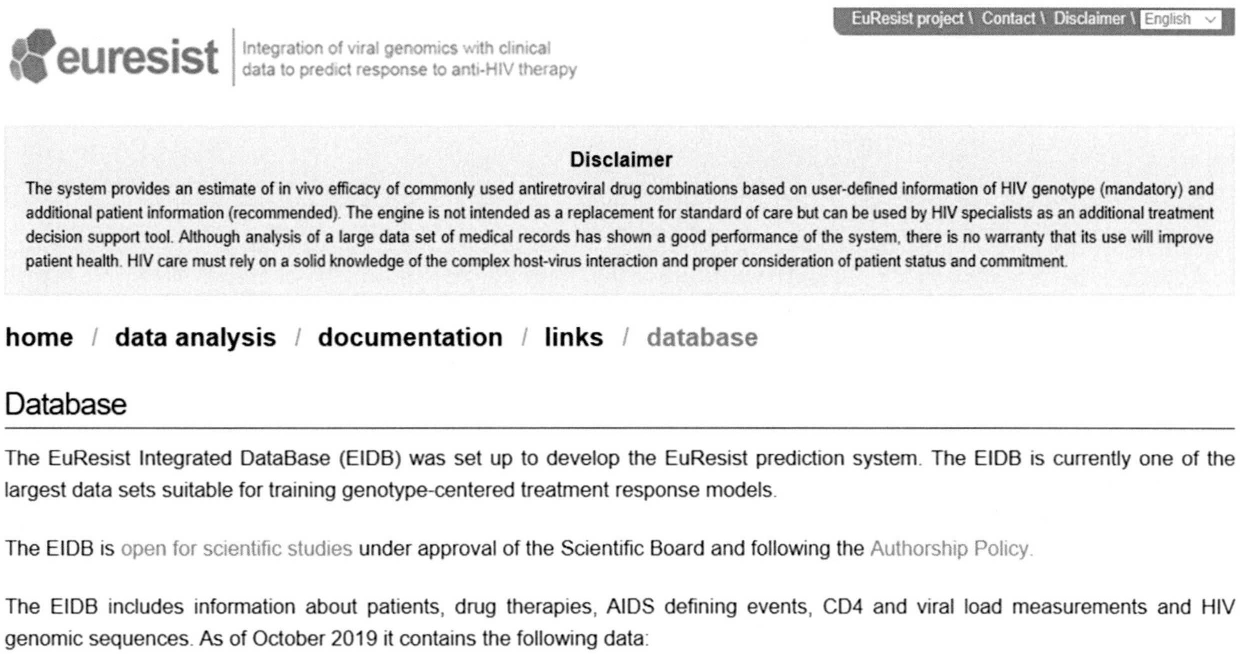

EuResist project \ Contact \ Disclaimer \ English
eurеsist
Integration of viral genomics with clinical data to predict response to anti-HIV therapy
Disclaimer
The system provides an estimate of in vivo efficacy of commonly used antiretroviral drug combinations based on user-defined information of HIV genotype (mandatory) and additional patient information (recommended). The engine is not intended as a replacement for standard of care but can be used by HIV specialists as an additional treatment decision support tool. Although analysis of a large data set of medical records has shown a good performance of the system, there is no warranty that its use will improve patient health. HIV care must rely on a solid knowledge of the complex host-virus interaction and proper consideration of patient status and commitment.
home / data analysis / documentation / links / database
Database
The EuResist Integrated DataBase (EIDB) was set up to develop the EuResist prediction system. The EIDB is currently one of the largest data sets suitable for training genotype-centered treatment response models.
The EIDB is open for scientific studies under approval of the Scientific Board and following the Authorship Policy.
The EIDB includes information about patients, drug therapies, AIDS defining events, CD4 and viral load measurements and HIV genomic sequences. As of October 2019 it contains the following data:

FIGURE 14.6 EuResist tools and database.

Arabian Peninsula and was spread to 27 countries through air travel routes claiming 858 lives (Zhou et al., 2020). Furthermore, in December 2019, the third novel coronavirus emerged called SARS-CoV-2 in Wuhan, Hubei province of China, and it is called COVID-19 (Wu et al., 2020). It spreads through close contact with an infected person through water droplets and nasal discharge (Repici et al., 2020; Wu et al., 2020). COVID-19 was declared a global pandemic by WHO on June 16, 2020, and it has infected 8,072,093 people and killed more than 4,37,478 worldwide.

Worldwide research groups have been endeavoring to develop antiviral vaccines, earlier (Khan et al., 2017) and in a recent outbreak, to counter the spread and for treatment of COVID-19 (Kolifarhood et al., 2020; Qazi et al., 2021). Recent studies have revealed different antivirals, antimalarials, and natural products for tentative treatment (Yan et al., 2020). Antivirals agents such as interferon α (IFN-α), phosphate, ribavirin, and arbidol have been showing promising results but lead to mild to moderate side effects (Dong et al., 2020). Lopinavir is another example of antiviral against HIV, which has shown promising results against SARS-CoV activity (Chu et al., 2004). Further, favipiravir against influenza is another drug that calls for attention (Delang et al., 2018). Recent studies involving 80 patients demonstrated that it had higher potent antiviral action than other antivirals and fewer side effects than lopinavir/ritonavir (Dong et al., 2020). Also, Zhang et al. investigated melatonin, which is a biomolecule, claiming that it may act as a potential adjuvant in COVID19 vaccines. Subsequently, remdesivir is another antiviral that has potential efficacy against both SARS-CoV and MERS-CoV (Sheahan et al., 2017) and may show promising results against COVID-19, but it is currently under clinical trials (Dong et al., 2020). However, it has efficacy against a range of pathogenic viruses, including both SARS-CoV and MERS-CoV in in vitro and in vivo models (Wang et al., 2020). We performed a genome-wise comparison case study of SARS-CoV-2 from different locations using the NCBI virus server (Fig. 14.8).

We selected SARS-CoV-2 genome from different geolocations of the world (USA, Germany, France, Spain, Italy, Brazil, India, China, Thailand).

Multiple sequence alignment confirmed that SARS-CoV-2 strains are found to be the same in the samples collected from different geographic locations (Fig. 14.9).

However, the phylogenetic analysis revealed that the samples collected from different geographic locations are not indicating the same genome sequences. These samples are matching with different locations based on the genome sequence relationship (Fig. 14.10).

TABLE 14.1 Web servers and virus analysis software repositories.

S.No.	Tool	Key features	Website
1	ALVIRA Databases	Application using multiple sequence alignment	http://bioinfo.genopole-toulouse.prd.fr/Alvira
2	AVPdb	Database of antiviral peptides	http://crdd.osdd.net/servers/avpdb
3	AVPpred	Antiviral peptide prediction algorithm	http://crdd.osdd.net/servers/avppred
4	HIPdb	Database of HIV-inhibiting peptides	http://crdd.osdd.net/servers/hipdb
5	AVP-IC$_{50}$Pred	Predictor of peptide antiviral activity in terms of half maximal inhibitory concentration (IC$_{50}$)	http://crdd.osdd.net/servers/ic50avp/
6	HIV-1 human interaction database	HIV-1 virus and host cell interaction	https://www.ncbi.nlm.nih.gov/genome/viruses/retroviruses/hiv-1/interactions/
7	EuResist project	Digitally based prediction of potential antiviral therapy to the HIV patients	https://www.euresist.org/
8	Korea influenza sequence and epitope database	Genetic information about influenza viruses	http://influenza.cdc.go.kr/search/na.mdr
9	Stanford SARS-CoV-2 antiviral research database	Understanding SARS-CoV-2 antiviral therapy	https://covdb.stanford.edu/
10	VirusSeq	For finding viral integration events	http://odin.mdacc.tmc.edu/_xsu1/VirusSeq.html
11	ZCURVE_V	Antiviral gene-finding tool	http://tubic.tju.edu.cn/Zcurve_V/
12	Virus-PLoc	Prediction of subcellular location of viral proteins	http://www.csbio.sjtu.edu.cn/bioinf/virus
13	VGO	Annotation of complete viral genomes	http://athena.bioc.uvic.ca/virology-ca-tools/vgo/
14	ViPR	Integrated repository of viral data	http://www.viprbrc.org
15	VIROME	Classification of viral metagenomic sequences	http://virome.dbi.udel.edu
16	Virus-host DB	Viruses and their hosts information	https://www.genome.jp/virushostdb/
17	GISAID	Collection of influenza data	https://www.gisaid.org/

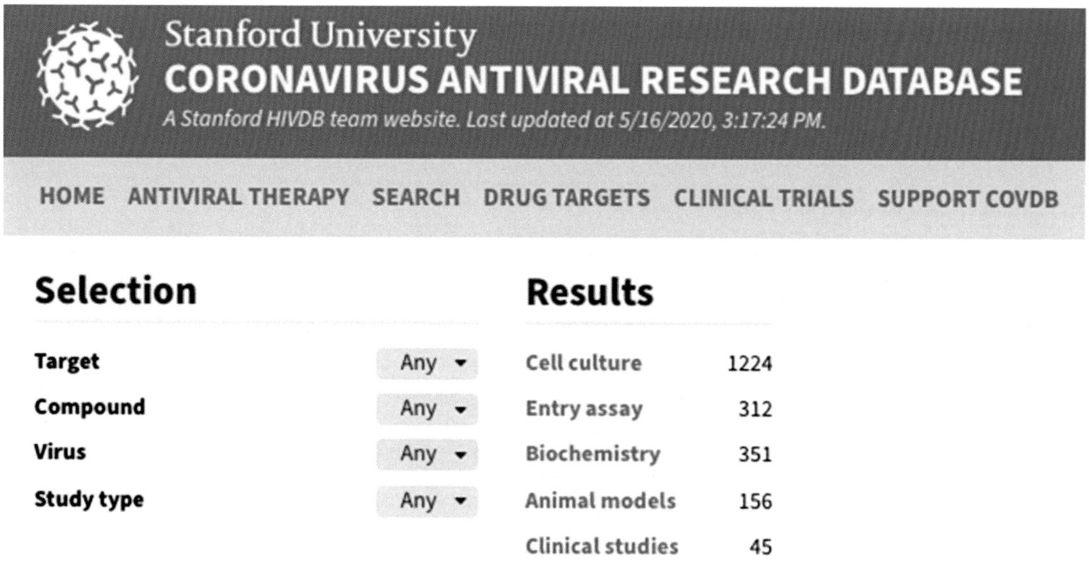

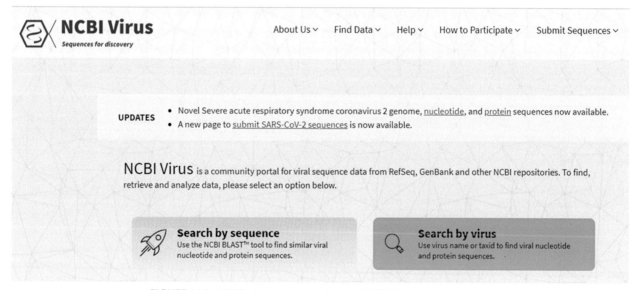

FIGURE 14.7   Stanford SARS-CoV-2 antiviral research database.

FIGURE 14.8   NCBI virus server to perform SARS-CoV-2 genome comparison.

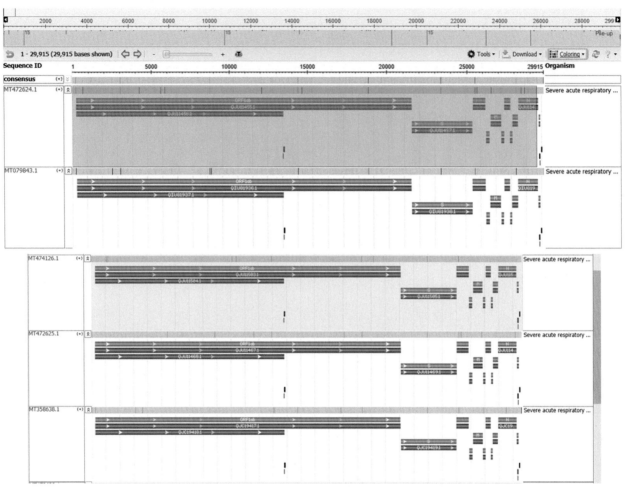

FIGURE 14.9 Multiple sequence alignment between genome of SARS-CoV-2 samples.

FIGURE 14.10 Phylogenetic analysis between SARS-CoV-2 genome.

5. Conclusion

The main contribution by the turn of this century has been the next-generation DNA sequence technology that enabled genomics and bioinformatics work on the characterization of viruses and bacteriophages. Numbers of reference viruses are added in the database on a daily basis to provide a comprehensive representation of various types of viruses, including the information of the viral genomes, irrespective of their size, to facilitate bioinformatics analysis using high-throughput sequencing and to classify them into known and new viruses. Thus recent developments in computational biology, database management systems, machine learning, and artificial intelligence significantly will deliver high throughput information gathering of viruses, their mode of action, pathogenesis, genomics, and proteomics for future drug and vaccine development. Our case study reveals that the current coronavirus strain may undergo some mutations in different populations from different geolocations. The phylogenetic analysis reveals that these strains show variation in their genomic signatures. However, still, we need to confirm by genetic-based experimental analysis, which is quite expensive and time consuming.

Acknowledgments

The authors wish to thank the DirectorCenter for Biotechnology and the Director of the Institute for Management Studies for providing their support in designing the paper. Authors also kindly acknowledge Indian Science and Technology Foundation (ISTF), Delhi for all support.
Conflicts of interest
The authors state that no conflict of interest has been found for our work.
Author's contributions
Sarra Akermi and Sunil Jayant helped to design the study and the writing of the manuscript. The concept and introduction were extensively prepared by Arabinda Ghosh and Ashwani Sharma. The analysis was drawn up by Surabhi Johari and Subrata Sinha, who contributed extensively to the design of the work. All contributors accepted the final version of the manuscript.

References

Bianco, A.M., Marcuzzi, A., Zanin, V., Girardelli, M., Crovella, J.V.S., 2013. Database tools in genetic diseases research. Genomics 101 (2), 75–85.

Cava, C., Bertoli, G., Castiglioni, I., 2020. In silico discovery of candidate drugs against Covid-19. Viruses 12, 404–416.

Chu, C.M., Cheng, V.C., Hung, I.F., Wong, M.M., Chan, K.H., Chan, K.S., Kao, R.Y., Poon, L.L., Wong, C.L., Guan, Y., Peiris, J.S., Yuen, K.Y., 2004. HKU/UCH SARS study group. Role of lopinavir/ritonavir in the treatment of SARS: initial virological and clinical findings. Thorax 59 (3), 252–256.

Danso, A.-A., Fu, W., Wallin, C., Katz, K.S., Song, G., Darji, D., Rodney Brister, J., Ptak, R.G., Pruitt, K.D., January 28, 2015. HIV-1, human interaction database: current status and new features. Nucleic Acids Res. 43 (D1), D566–D570. https://doi.org/10.1093/nar/gku1126.

Delang, L., Abdelnabi, R., Neyts, J., 2018. Favipiravir as a potential countermeasure against neglected and emerging RNA viruses. Antivir. Res. 153, 85–94.

Dong, L., Hu, S., Gao, J., 2020. Discovering drugs to treat coronavirus disease 2019 (COVID-19). Drug Discov. Ther. 14 (1), 58–60.

Enault, F., Fremez, R., Baranowski, E., Faraut, T., 2007. Alvira: comparative genomics of viral strains. Bioinformatics 23 (16), 2178–2179.

Hufsky, F., Ibrahim, B., Beer, M., Li, D., Le, M.P., McMahon, D.P., Manja, M., 2018. Virologists—heroes need weapons. PLoS Pathogens 14 (2), e1006771.

Khan, F.N., Qazi, S., Tanveer, K., Raza, K., 2017. A review on the antagonist ebola; a prophylactic approach. Biomed. Pharmacother. 96, 1513–1526. https://doi.org/10.1016/j.biopha.2017.11.103. Elsevier.

Kolifarhood, G., Aghaali, M., Saadati, H.M., Taherpour, N., Rahimi, S., Izadi, N., Nazari, S.S.H., 2020. Epidemiological and clinical aspects of COVID-19; a narrative review. Arch. Acad. Emerg. Med. 8 (1), e41.

Parrish, C.R., Holmes, E.C., Morens, D.M., Park, E.C., Burke, D.S., Calisher, C.H., Laughlin, C.A., Saif, L.J., Daszak, P., 2008. Cross-species virus transmission and the emergence of new epidemic diseases. Microbiol. Mol. Biol. Rev. 72 (3), 457–470.

Poon, L.L.M., Leung, C.S.W., Tashiro, M., Chan, K.H., Wong, B.Y.W., Yuen, K.Y., Guan, Y., Peiris, J.S.M., 2004. Rapid detection of the severe acute respiratory syndrome (sars) coronavirus by a loop-mediated isothermal amplification assay. Clin. Chem. 6 (1), 1050–1052.

Qazi, S., Sheikh, K., Faheem, M., Khan, A., Raza, K., 2021. A coadunation of biological and mathematical perspectives on the pandemic COVID-19: a review. Coronaviruses 2. https://doi.org/10.2174/2666796702666210114110013.

Qureshi, A., Thakur, N., Himani, T., Kumar, M., 2013a. AVPdb: a database of experimentally validated antiviral peptides targeting medically important viruses. Nucleic Acids Res. 42, 1147–1153.

Qureshi, A., Thakur, N., Kumar, M., 2013b. HIPdb: a database of experimentally validated HIV inhibiting peptides. PLoS One 8 (1), e54908.

Repici, A., Maselli, R., Colombo, M., Gabbiadini, R., Spadaccini, M., Anderloni, A., Silvia, C., Alessandro, F., Milena, D.L., Piera, A.G., Gaia, P., Elisa, C.F., Elena, A., Michele, L., 2020. Coronavirus (COVID-19) Outbreak: what the department of endoscopy should know. Gastrointest. Endosc. 5107 (20), 30245–30255.

Sheahan, T.P., Sims, A.C., Graham, R.L., Menachery, V.D., Gralinski, L.E., et al., 2017. Broad-spectrum Antiviral GS-5734 inhibits both epidemic and zoonotic coronaviruses. Sci. Transl. Med. 9 (396), eaal3653.

Thakur, N., Qureshi, A., Kumar, M., 2012. AVPpred: collection and prediction of highly effective antiviral peptides. Nucleic Acids Res. 40, 199—204.

Wang, M., Cao, R., Zhang, L., Yang, X., Liu, J., Xu, M., Shi, Z., Hu, Z., Zhong, W., Xia, G., 2020. Remdesivir and chloroquine effectively inhibit the recently emerged novel coronavirus (2019-nCoV) in vitro. Nat. Cell Res. 30, 269—271.

Wu, Y.C., Chen, C.S., Chan, Y.J., 2020. The outbreak of COVID-19: an overview. J. Chin. Med. Assoc. 83 (3), 217—220.

Yang, S.N.Y., Atkinsonb, S.C., Wang, C., Lee, A., Bogoyevitchc, M.A., Borgb, N.A., Jans, D.A., 2020. The broad spectrum antiviral ivermectin targets the host nuclear transport importin alpha/beta1 heterodimer. Antivir. Res. 177, 104760.

Zazzi, M., Incardona, F., Rosen-Zvi, M., Prosperi, M., Lengauer, T., Altmann, A., Sonnerborg, A., Lavee, T., Schulter, E., Kaiser, R., 2012. Predicting response to antiretroviral treatment by machine learning: the EuResist project. Intervirology 55, 123—127.

Zhou, Y., Hou, Y., Shen, J., Huang, Y., Martin, W., Cheng, F., 2020. Network-based drug repurposing for novel coronavirus 2019-nCoV/SARS-CoV-2. Nat. Cell Discov. 6 https://doi.org/10.1038/s41421-020-0153-3.

Further reading

Qureshi, A., Tandon, H., Kumar, M., 2015. AVP-IC50 Pred: multiple machine learning techniques based prediction of peptide antiviral activity in terms of half maximal inhibitory concentration (IC50). Biopolymers. https://doi.org/10.1002/bip.22703.

Chapter 15

Machine learning in translational bioinformatics

Nadia Ahmad[1,*], Piyus Mohanty[1,*], Narendra Kumar[1] and Ekta Gandotra[2]

[1]Department of Biotechnology and Bioinformatics, Jaypee University of Information Technology, Waknaghat, Himachal Pradesh, India; [2]Department of Computer Science & Engineering and Information Technology (CSE & IT), Jaypee University of Information Technology, Waknaghat, Himachal Pradesh, India

*Corresponding authors: E-mail: nadia.apetan@gmail.com, piyus22.pm@gmail.com

Chapter outline

1. Introduction

Translational bioinformatics (TBI) is an interdisciplinary field that is on the rise. TBI applications include aptly translating cellular, molecular, genetic, and clinical data collected into products for clinical purposes (Larrañaga et al., 2006). It can be used for diagnosis, evaluation of treatment, and forecasting future trends. It plays an important role in bridging clinical research and application for the welfare of human health (Dixit and Prajapati, 2015). TBI is a relatively new field, and it has a broader scope as it integrates various health-related topics and issues such as systems for cancers and rare human diseases to pharmacogenomics and biomarkers. One of the important applications of TBI includes precision medicine, which attempts to provide personalized solutions by taking into consideration the individual clinical profiles coupled with genomic and environmental data. This enhances the personalized analysis as the data diversity increases and hence the scope of treatment. In the long term, incorporating molecular data with clinical data will reap benefits that will further research and therapeutic developments. To do so the major hurdles are storage, analysis, dimensionality reduction, parameters tuning, and pattern identification, albeit there are several other problems (Sung, 2012). This is where machine learning (ML) comes into the picture as a boon for identification and reduction of parameters as well as integrating analysis with designing predictive measures using the dataset collected. ML has become the go-to tool for gaining enrichment information and hence has been used massively to a point wherein it has been employed to every subarea of health and clinical informatics (Havaei et al., 2016). With the increase in the influx of complex biologic and clinical data, it is imperative that the use of ML in TBI be highlighted. The objective of using ML is to identify the pattern and then accordingly design algorithms that have the ability to efficiently predict and also get better with time (Awad and ELseuofi, 2011).

TBI is an emerging discipline and has created its own niche even in the era wherein personalized medicine has taken over (Bonggun et al., 2019). With the advent of electronic records and high-throughput technologies, the time has come to develop novel approaches to deal with the increasing datasets to acquire knowledge and insights (Tenenbaum, 2016).

Modeling and monitoring biomedical, wellness, and healthcare data from individuals and converging data on a population scale have a massive potential to improve understanding of the transition to the healthy state of human physiology to disease setting. Wellness monitoring devices and companion software applications capable of generating alerts and sharing data with healthcare providers or social networks are now available (Yan, 2017).

With the increase in biologic data and computational processing power, computational methods have made a way to biomedical sciences and associated domains. The workflows and data resources involved in bioinformatics have steadily been employed. Services such as BioGPS and Cytoscape are being used for functional enrichment and data visualization. Workbenches like Taverna and Kepler have also been used (Shameer et al., 2017).

As high-throughput technologies are evolving at a fast pace, more and more data are being generated, be it biologic data in the form of DNA, RNA, or protein. Biologic networks are quite intricate and integrated, so it is important to study the essential functions as well as their involvement in disease development (Dai et al., 2015). Identifying systematically the genetic information comprising genetic mutations has become an integral part of gaining insights. Ultimately, biological pathways are important and are needed to be studied in detail to reveal the landscape of molecular interactions and mechanisms associated with complex diseases (Ahmad et al., 2020).

Cloud computing technology has been viewed as a key player in future genomic research and analysis. Through various studies, it has been found that it is an effective alternative for analysis when compared to conventional computational clusters carried out locally. This makes it an important technology in the future for analysis of translational research (Pastur-Romay et al., 2016).

Data generation has become comparatively easy with different technologies emerging, but the major hassle is data integration and analysis methodology, which is the main concern as it requires extensive research. This in turn will help in better dealing with clinical data and drawing inferences related to clinical practices. Novel algorithms are being developed to deal with patient data to better understand different mechanisms (Leung et al., 2016).

2. AI, ML, and DL background

Before getting into ML, we need to know about artificial intelligence (AI), as it is an umbrella term encompassing ML and deep learning (DL). It is a term coined by John McCarthy. It enables machines to think independently without any mediation from humans to make decisions (Bini, 2018). It has become a part of day-to-day activities with applications in digital assistants (Apple's Siri, Amazon's Alexa, etc.), proctoring examinations (Mercer's Mettl, ProctorU, and many more), transportation (Uber being a prime example employing AI, for detailed info https://eng.uber.com/machine-learning/), and conventional examples being robots (an example being Roomba 980 model vacuum). The goal of the application of AI in any research concerns itself with finding a way of learning from the data available and at the same time, to enhance the decision-making capabilities to predict inferences successfully (Poole et al., 1998). AI has enormous potential in the field of healthcare as it can handle complex data sets as well as incorporate complexities from compound systems, an example being tending to patients, which is a multistep process and has factors that are highly variable. It is important to note that this process not only involves people but also machines, hence increasing the complexity. It is critical that a control and a predictive system be employed that can learn continuously from the prior data and also optimize itself as it collects more data in the future. This might be difficult for human beings to pull off, so computational systems are used to ease the burden. It has been used to develop a scheduling tool for optimizing surgical schedules by UCH Colorado. The algorithm developed used the prior data available and predicted the future trend to create the seamless allocation of operating rooms (OR). This led to an increase in the OR revenue by 4%, as well as better coordination in the OR doctor allocation. Alongwith decreasing the patient waiting time by around 50% (=https://leantaas.com/?press-release=uchealth-improves-operating-room-efficiency-lowering-wait-times-and-improving-patient-experience-with-leantaas). Various healthcare facilities have employed modified and optimized AI-based algorithms for different purposes (Fig. 15.1).

Coming to **ML,** which is contemplated as a subset of AI, it concerns itself with improving the functionality as it learns continuously from the data. In the prior examples, it is quite evident that this field has shown promise in optimizing performance, which could be in the form of increased accuracy of predicted results. ML-based methods use statistical theories to build a computational model, as the main goal is to make accurate inferences from the data sample. This process comprises of two major steps: one being training and building the model over the large data set and the other being predicting inferences from the generated model efficiently. Apart from the accuracy, there are several other parameters such as time and space complexity, interpretability, and finally, the transparency these are also quite important measures to be considered (Larrañaga et al., 2006). As the data compiled is incomplete and nonuniform the following steps have to be followed to be analyzed efficiently (Fig. 15.2).

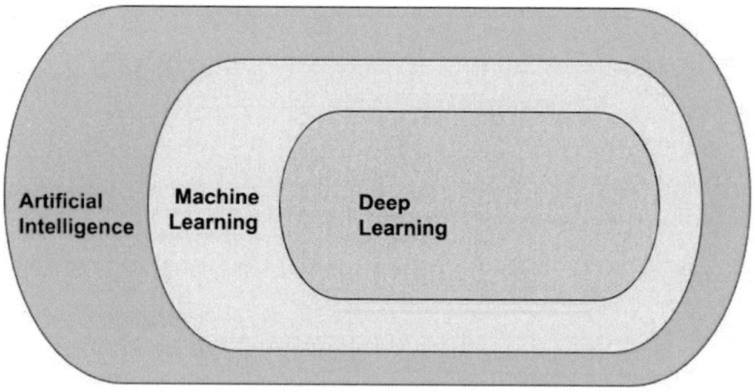

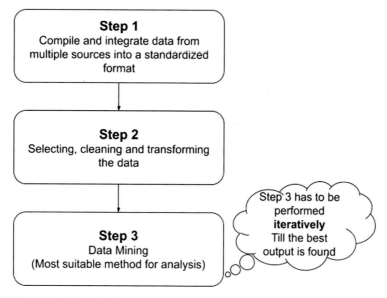

FIGURE 15.1 Explaining the relationship between AI, ML, and DL.

Apart from the aforementioned steps, there are several other minor steps involved, but this flowchart encompasses only the major steps. The most well-known example for ML-based application in healthcare is a software called Watson Health by IBM (https://www.ibm.com/in-en/watson-health/learn/healthcare-data-analytics). It recommends diagnostic and treatment measures for different cancers, by analyzing patient records and imaging reports, as well as the individual genome, to give a personalized touch to healthcare. It uses the state-of-the-art AI-based techniques to supplement the decision-making abilities of a physician and also aid in determining the possibility of a certain cancer that could have been missed by the naked eye (Jabeen et al., 2018). The application of AI as a supplementary measure is known as cognitive computing (Mitchell, 1997). There are several hurdles that are needed to be overcome before its seamless integration into the healthcare sector with reasons such as issues pertaining to migration of data across the electronic health records (EHRs), budget overrun possibilities, and many more other such hurdles.

As conventional ML-based algorithms require domain-specific knowledge to decipher the features of relevance while building a model, a new or rather a branch of ML has emerged known as **DL** that circumvents the knowledge and feature selection barrier; besides that, it also paves a way for parallel computation as well as the integration of several sophisticated algorithms in the mix (Raza, 2017). It has been extensively used in speech and image recognition. Every year, several new algorithms are made, and people compete on different platforms for better deciphering of image contents and classification, one famous example being the Kaggle image classification competition (https://www.kaggle.com/c/il18auc). DL has had quite an impact in transforming the healthcare system. One example of many is the application of DL-based algorithms for simulation of drug toxicity rather than the conventional method of animal testing. This method generates high accuracy results and has been encouraged by the FDA to pharmaceutical companies (Aliper et al., 2016). Some of the applications are going to be discussed in the application table in the application section.

FIGURE 15.2 Schematic diagram representing the major steps involved in ML-based analysis.

3. Text mining in TBI

Text mining is a subfield of TBI, and it has immense research scope. It is a subfield that concerns itself with associating biomedical research with clinical practices and the other way around as well. There are two basic methodologies (Dai et al., 2015).

One is rule-based, which is commonly called knowledge-based; the other method is machine learning-based, alternatively called statistical-based method. A lot of systems are composites of these methodologies (Yan, 2012). Mutual tasks have had a significant impact on the shaping of this field. Text mining softwares for TBI are considered quite important, and it is imperative that stringent measures be taken to ensure that the quality is of utmost standard along with carrying out proper software testing.

ML-based approaches in text mining are based on steps comprising of initial steps concerned with providing the system with a rightly labeled set of data, which is known as supervised learning. It could be the key parts of a speech in form of tokens or the position where a gene name has been used. The system has to then figure out the apt method for analysis by going through all the hints available and targeting the area of research it concerns itself with. An example is a document system whose main objective is to classify text that helps the researchers working in that field by correlating words with research areas. Let us consider murine as a keyword. Then, it must be associated with mice, so be of interest to researchers working in that specific area or its associated areas. There are several ML-based algorithms that can be used for the analysis, but the most important thing to build a successful system is the selection of set of features to be used for the classification, as this is the crux of the system. For example, a part of speech tagger may use the apparent parts of speech of the two preceding words as a feature for deciding the part of speech of a third word (Faro et al., 2012). It is widely believed that the systems built using ML-based methods are faster to make when compared to rule-based systems, as building rules manually takes time (Larrañaga et al., 2006). But a point to be noted is that constructing an extractor is quite time-consuming, and building a supervised model is even tougher than that. Hence, this must be kept in mind when we consider it as a quicker alternative to rule-based methods.

4. Biobanks using AI and ML

The fusing of the genomics data with EHRs unlocks the door for various research questions, one such question being the identification of genomic variants that play an important role in human health. ML and AI are at the center for solving this puzzle.

The predominant challenge that computational procedures are well-suited to is the definition of phenotypes that are more precise than those provided by disease diagnoses captured in billing codes. The major hurdle is the incorporation of appropriate mathematical functions for medication, and apart from that, the measures that are taken in the laboratory along with other such data that can aid in more accurate diagnosis have to be considered. ML-based methods are suitable for building models of phenotypes of diseases. After the phenotypes are extracted precisely, the following step comprises of relational analysis. Once phenotypes are derived accurately, afterwards, relational analysis are carried out. Genome-based association studies in epidemiologic research have concentrated mostly on statistical-based tests, taking into account all the genomic variants that have been removed from environmental and genomic contexts. This increases the speed of interpretation considerably, but in doing so, there is a loss of context-dependent information that the univariate model fails to take into consideration. ML-based methods provide seamless integration of statistical methods as well as other nonadditive factors. Furthermore, ML can comprehend the wide array of genetic effects induced on a normal basis. The advancement and the use of ML-based methods in biobanks is still ongoing, and it is in its early days of research. There are several issues that have to be resolved as research progresses such as ensuring that the right methods be used for cleaning the data as well as interpreting the data and results, and lastly, proper validation methods have to be selected, making it a viable moral option. Automated machine learning is an emerging application that can be used to resolve the issue of selecting the right method for a set of data. It itself finds the most suitable algorithm for better analysis and interpretation of data, and it is in the same vein of AI, where the objective of AI is to build methods that are able to perform as a human analyst without actual human intervention in the process. It is essential to note that the aim of ML-based methods is to discover results that would have been missed out by the conventional statistical-based methods, which in turn would make it a more comprehensive solution as the parameters are well-tuned and their influence on the end results being incorporated.

5. ML- and DL-based applications in health informatics

With the inflow of highly complex data, the significance of data analysis in health informatics has grown considerably and that too at a fast pace. This has led to the need for models that are data driven. Apart from that, the use of ML-based approaches in health informatics has also intensified. DL is a method that at core uses artificial neural networks for mimicking the way the human nervous system works. It is a powerful tool if used appropriately. It can be used to change the dynamics of the research in this field. It can open unexplored avenues as well as provide insights that may have been lacking in the earlier methods. As the computational powers are increasing rapidly with an increase in processing power, as well as fast and large storage capabilities coupled with parallelization, these have led to researchers being more inclined to DL- and ML-based approaches for analyzing and predicting data. It is important to go into detail to why it is so convenient in analyzing and predicting a data set. The reason for it is quite simple: the capacity to generate optimized features that are of high level followed by the ease in the interpretation of input data. The applications of DL in health informatics include medical imaging, pervasive sensing for monitoring health and well-being, and medical informatics, as well as in public health, among others.

5.1 Medical imaging

Medical image analysis plays an important role in modern medicine. Analyzing and diagnosing from a mere image is quite difficult, so computer-aided diagnostic approaches have been used to provide insights into the possible disease mechanism (Havaei et al., 2016).

To prepare a model based on the brain scan for diseases such as sclerosis, stroke, and Alzheimer requires a detailed understanding of the functioning of the brain as well as the entire layout of it. Convolutional networks (CNNs) have become an important tool in the research community when it comes to dealing with medical imaging, as they have been successfully used in the subfield of computer science, i.e., computer vision, along with their capability in terms of parallel processing with graphics processing unit (GPUs) demonstrated. This has made them a lucrative method to be used in the analysis of medical images. The interesting fact is that CNNs applied to medical imaging have had quite a success, demonstrated by a survey that highlights the CNN approaches used in segmentation of brain pathology as well as in an editorial that discusses the use of DL techniques for computer-aided detection along with segmentation and shape analysis (Xu et al., 2016).

DL equips the model to automate as well as extract relevant features along with the required classification procedure. It provides accessibility to object features by exploring the feature hierarchy, and to their interactions as well. It has a comparatively easy training process, and with some minor systemic tuning, it will make the model robust and hence the go-to method.

In medical image analysis, the application of DL methods is yet to be realized thoroughly, so there is a need for further research.

A large set of labeled data is required for the purpose of disease detection and classification to draw meaningful inferences using DL techniques (Xu et al., 2016). Another important aspect is that the images have to be annotated properly to reveal all the important features for identification purposes as well as for building a model (Wang et al., 2016). This in reality is quite tedious and costly as it involves doctors and computational analysts to work together.

5.2 Health and well-being assessment through pervasive sensing

Pervasive sensors consist of wearable, ambient sensors, as well as implantables, which facilitate continuous administration of health. An example is a sensor that can help in tackling obesity by measuring the food intake along with energy expended through various activities in a day. It provides the user and the health professionals with the required insights for necessary steps to be taken to prevent the aforesaid condition. It is even more important for elderly patients who are suffering from chronic diseases to be monitored regularly, which can be done by ambient wearable sensors. Furthermore, they lead to the improvement of the quality of the healthcare received as well as the ease with which it can be used, which is a very big merit. It can significantly improve the care received by patients with disabilities through constant monitoring via wearable and assistive implantable devices. Whereas, it is mandatory for critical patients to be monitored continuously; it is important to keep a track of blood pressure and body temperature as well as other important vital signs. The data generated from these devices can be used for improving treatment measures (Huang et al., 201).

5.2.1 Activity recognition and evaluating energy expenditure

The data generated from smartwatches and different types of sensor nodes are not reliable, which makes it quite tough to build a DL model using the data acquired from these sources.

Rav'ı et al. (2017), Ravi et al. (2016) proposed a technique for preprocessing that would circumvent the unreliability of the data generated because of differences in the placement along with orientation by standardizing the data through the use of the said technique.

5.2.2 Assistive devices recognition

Assistive devices have to recognize generic objects, for which they should be able to understand the different dynamics of the object such as its 3D structure, shape, and volume. This has to be taken into consideration as they play an important role in providing audio as well as tactile feedback. For an impaired patient, it is critical that the assistive device is able to alert them about the obstacles along their path or information about the surroundings. To demonstrate the application of CNN in assisting individuals to avoid obstacles was demonstrated by Poggi et al. (Poggi and Mattoccia, 2016), wherein they used this methodology to generate a robust system for obstacle detection for visually impaired individuals. Assistive devices have been proposed for identification of hand gestures, which can be used by disabled patients, and they can be used for the purpose of interpreting sign languages. This can also be used for touchless human–computer interaction in a surgical setting, showcasing the extent of its application. Practically, it is a very difficult task due to its sheer complexity as well as hand gesture variations. A deep neural network-based method was used by Huang et al. (Huang et al., 2015) for recognizing sign language through a model trained using the real-sense data.

5.2.3 Vital sign abnormalities detection

For patients in severe conditions, it is critical to monitor vital signs and check for abnormalities in them. The main issue with devices measuring vital signs is that they are prone to be affected by noise and other such issues.

ML-based approaches have been found useful in detecting abnormalities under various conditions. But they have not been used extensively in the clinical setting. A hurdle associated with continuous sensing is that a large amount of data is generated, an example being EEG, which generates a large amount of time-sequential data, which warrants the use of an online algorithm that can process different and varying data.

Wulsin et al. (Wulsin et al., 2010) proposed an approach to find the irregularity in EEG waveforms. It is very tough to interpret the EEG waveforms, as the input signal has high dimensionality, aside from the fact that there is a lack of knowledge pertaining to how the brain works. It is noted that DBNs (deep belief networks) surpass support vector machine (SVM) in their decision-making capacity along with giving results quicker, with an estimated time of about 10 s for more than 40,000 samples for DBN.

Jia et al. (Jia et al., 2014) proposed a DL method to identify perceptive states of EEG using a restrictive Boltzmann machine. Even though the training set is small and has a lot of noise, the approach still has high accuracy. DL has played an important role in extending the services of pervasive sensors for a wide array of application in the field of health informatics. The successful examples where the accuracy has considerably increased are sensors that measure calorie intake, detect anomalies in vital signs, interpret sign languages, among many others. DL has been used to further increase the efficiency as well as real-time processing for many other applications. But that being said, attention should also be paid to building hardware for better parallel processing using less power.

5.3 Medical informatics

It focuses mainly on analyzing large data sets that are compiled from different healthcare settings with the emphasis on enhancing support systems for clinical decisions or for accessing high-quality medical data and medical services. EHRs are records that store detailed information of a patient's records, be it medical history or allergies, and all the relevant information required for analyzing a patient's health (Andreu-Perez et al., 2015). Handling this big data efficiently will yield significant insights that can be used for disease management. This is easier said than done for the following reasons:

a) The data collected is quite complex because of irregularity in the formatting of the records as well as varying from patient to patient.
b) Apart from this, the records contain information from images, lab results, and other unstructured informative texts.
c) There are lots of parameters involved that are needed to be taken into consideration, such as the interval between onset and the time wherein the symptoms appear. So, a lot of variable factors creep in.
d) There is an inability of conventional methods to comprehend large and unstructured data.

ML-based approaches have been used to design and scale up big and complex datasets. The success lies in the fact that these approaches can be used for novel feature and pattern identification. They can deal with datasets by employing supervised and unsupervised learning to get the desired results. Hence, it is not surprising that it has become an integral part of health and medical research. An example of this case is an experiment carried out by Shin et al. (Shin et al., 2016), wherein they used DL to link radiology images and a typical report picture. Another example is where Liang et al. (Liang et al., 2014) used an upgraded version of CDBN for training datasets consisting of hypertension and the Chinese medical diagnosis from the EHR database. Putin et al. (Putin et al., 2016) used deep neural networks (DNNs) for identification of markers to predict human chronological age using blood samples. Futoma et al. (Futoma et al., 2015) compared different models to check their ability for prediction of hospital readmission based on data collected from the EHR database. ML-based methods generally have higher accuracy when compared to traditional approaches.

Apart from DNN, recurrent neural networks (RNNs) have also been used to memorize sequential events that could help in building a model that can better deal with the interval between onset and symptoms. It is important to discover novel patterns that can lead to a new hypothesis and broaden the scope of research (Yang and Leff, 2015), as the final goal is to discover important features and disease characteristics that will help in different phases of clinical research. Even though ML-based methods are superior, they still have some downfalls.

5.4 Public health

The main aim of public health is to prevent diseases and to analyze the factors such as social behaviors concerning environmental factors and most importantly promote healthcare. They mostly take into consideration different proportions of the population as and when the situation demands. The applications vary from surveillance during epidemics and monitoring as well as predicting air quality, etc. Existing computational methods are quite limited and face an issue in incorporating real-time information, so it could be difficult to predict the adverse effects of drugs being approved in haste. Some research reported that annually 60,000 people die due to poor air quality, which leads to pulmonary diseases. They proposed a model for prediction of air pollutants using sensor data collected from 52 cities of Japan. This model demonstrated that a DNN-based approach finds it difficult to deal with real-world data as it is evolving at a fast pace.

Nowadays, researchers have started showing interest in utilizing phone metadata for characterizing as well as tracking human behaviors. Metadata mostly comprises the location of the phone call or text, which can be used to determine demographic information (Zou et al., 2016). Generally, the metadata along with the EHRs, social media, and the mobile network have been extensively used as a means to inform people about public health (Huang et al., 2015). The models face issues due to data unavailability as EHRs and other records are not easily accessible due to privacy concerns (Ong et al., 2015). Hence, there is a need for data privacy and accessibility that will ensure the patient's records are not misused, which in turn would enable the researchers to access their records (Table 15.1).

6. Limitations and challenges

ML-based methods have not been able to completely provide a solution. Hence, researchers are quite skeptical about the use of ML.

Potential issues are as follows:

1) The DL model in its entirety is quite difficult to interpret (Erhan et al., 2009). Hence, explaining the results predicted through this methodology is difficult, so optimizing this model is also tough (Erhan et al., 2010).
2) For a good model, a large dataset is required. Even though there is an explosion of healthcare data, there are still a lot of issues, from privacy to conversion of paper records to electronic records (Srivastava et al., 2014). Aside from this, the specific disease data available are quite limited (Nguyen et al., 2015). But this is a double-edged sword. With an increase in the volume of data, the computational powers are tested in terms of speed, storage, processing, and validation.
3) With limited data, there is a chance of overfitting, as the training model memorizes the training set, so it is necessary to be cross-validated to prevent errors from creeping in (LeCun et al., 2015).
4) Another important hurdle is the input data. As input data does not have a fixed format, the raw data needs to be modified. Preprocessing of data and finding the important features are quite challenging (Szegedy et al., 2013). If we have a big dataset, then the model training time increases considerably, so dimensionality reduction is also important keeping in mind that still the important features are trained for better classification and prediction (Venter et al., 2001). Apart from this, if the features are exploited, the results might be biased, so nearly all ML-based models are susceptible to manipulations as such (Lander et al., 2001). The major challenge is the smooth integration of ML in healthcare and associated fields (Havaei et al., 2016).
5) Apart from the aforementioned issues, there are issues such as the knowledge available in the data mining domain being insufficient. With the increase in biological datasets, there is the introduction of new complex data objects accompanied by noise as well as chances of repetition increases, making it difficult to build and train a good model.
6) ML in TBI requires most importantly domain-specific experts who have the vision and means to accomplish knowledge extraction from available datasets. This is quite important as considerable knowledge is lost or not found as people or researchers employing ML in TBI lack knowledge and skill to curate knowledge.

7. Conclusion

ML has become a focal point in the research pertaining to health informatics, TBI, and other clinical research fields. It has considerably reduced human intervention, making the dataset less error prone as well as more structured. As ML is being extensively used, its scope has been increasing day by day. EHRs along with medical images are smoothly integrated for better and refined analysis. Up until now, ML-based approaches have been used for understanding data from unstructured sources. Information from medical images of cytological notes of patients suffering from tumor may contain information pertaining to its stage and where it is spreading along with the pace of it. This information is quite critical in improving the efficiency of predicted results. But there are several technical challenges such as securing data of patients and that their corresponding clinical data is quite costly. The dataset not only comprises of sick patients, but a large fraction of healthy individuals' records are also needed. It is important for any ML-based model that they are trained with large and less error prone datasets. Securing data with the assurance of privacy of data from the patients makes it quite tough to avail. Then

TABLE 15.1 Depicting various applications of ML-based methods in TBI.

Application	ML algorithm used	Description	References
Stroke prediction	SVM	Various physiologic parameters were used as the input data for an SVM-based prediction for stroke diagnosis, and the resultant model has 90% accuracy	Jeena and Kumar, 2016.
Clustering of cancer subtypes	DBN	Algorithm-contrastive divergence used over a DBN model, comprising different cancer subtypes	Liang et al., 2015.
Identification of novel lipocalins	SVM	Sequence-based analysis of protein sequences to predict whether the proteins are lipocalins http://bioinfo.icgeb.res.in/lipocalinpred/	Ramana and Gupta, 2009.
Prostate cancer prediction	Bayesian belief networks	10 different ML-based methods have been used to predict prostate cancer class. The best model used Bayesian belief networks with an accuracy of 94.11%	Raza and Hasan, 2015.
Metagenomic classification	RNN + DBN	Metagenomic classification using methods such as RNN and DBN as opposed to conventional multilayer perceptron method	Ditzler et al., 2015.
Prediction of protein-coding map	RNN	Multistep approach for predicting residue contact points for applications such as structure prediction for proteins http://scratch.proteomics.ics.uci.edu/cgi-bin/new_server/sql_predict.cgi	Di Lena et al., 2012.
Reconstruction of magnetic resonance imaging (MRI)	SDAE	The use of SDAE for faster reconstruction of MRI, making it a more dynamic alternative compared to existing solutions	Sümbül et al., 2009.
Quantitative Structure-activity relationship (QSAR) studies	DNN + DBN	DBN has been used over the Kaggle data, which comprises of around 70k molecules. The resultant model outperforms the prior methods	Ghasemi et al., 2017.
DeepLoc-protein subcellular prediction	RNN	Sequence information has been used for prediction of subcellular localization using RNN http://www.cbs.dtu.dk/services/DeepLoc/	José Juan Almagro Armenteros et al., 2017.

there is the need for equipment, for monitoring and diagnosis, and the data obtained from them can be used for further research. Many researchers have been using various ML-based methods to identify novel features/patterns in the field of health informatics, as a wide array of free packages are available that can support the research. ML has sparked quite an intrigue, as it has become the go-to approach, but caution should be taken in making sure that it should not be used as a silver bullet for every challenging situation that comes our way. There is still a lot of research to be done whether the large dataset used yields viable results. Therefore, we can comment that ML-based methods can be used to create a positive impact on the research spectra with the help of advancement in computational power. There is still a need for the development of new algorithms that will further the research and work on decreasing the existing limitations.

Abbreviations

AI Artificial intelligence
ANN Artificial neural network
CNN Convolutional neural network
DBM Deep Boltzmann machines
DBN Deep belief network
DL Deep learning
MI Medical imaging
ML Machine learning
MRI Magnetic resonance imaging
QSAR Quantitative structure activity relationship
RNN Recurrent neural network
SDAE Stacked denoising auto encoder
SVM Support vector machine
TBI Translational bioinformatics

References

Ahmad, N., Jabeen, N., Raza, K., 2020. Machine learning based outlook for the analysis of SNP-SNP interaction for biomedical big data. In: Lecture Notes in Electrical Engineering, vol. 601. Springer, pp. 13−22. https://doi.org/10.1007/978-981-15-1420-3_2.

Aliper, A., Plis, S., Artemov, A., Ulloa, A., Mamoshina, P., Zhavoronkov, A., 2016. Deep learning applications for predicting pharmacological properties of drugs and drug repurposing using transcriptomic data. Mol. Pharm. 13 (7), 2524−2530.

Andreu-Perez, J., Poon, C.C.Y., Merrifield, R.D., Wong, S.T.C., Yang, G.Z., 2015. Big data for health. IEEE J. Biomed. Health Inf. 19 (4), 1193−1208.

Awad, W.A., ELseuofi, S.M., 2011. Machine learning methods for spam E-mail classification. IJCSIT 3 (1).

Bini, S.A., 2018. Artificial intelligence, machine learning, deep learning, and cognitive computing: what do these terms mean and how will they impact health care? J. Arthroplasty 33 (8), 2358−2361.

Bonggun, S., Sungsoo, P., Hong, J.H., Ho, J.A., Chun, S.H., Kang, K., Ahn, Y.-H., Ko, Y.H., Kang, K., 2019. Current trends in translational bioinformatics. Front. Genet. https://doi.org/10.3389/fgene.2019.00662.

Dai, H.-J., Wei, C.-H., Kao 3, H.-Y., Liu, R.-L., Tsai, R.T.-H., Lu, Z., 2015. Text mining for translational bioinformatics. Biomed Res. Int. 2015, 368264. https://doi.org/10.1155/2015/368264. Epub 2015 Aug 25.

Di Lena, Nagata, K., Baldi, P., 2012. Deep architectures for protein contact map prediction. Bioinformatics 28 (19), 2449−2457. https://doi.org/10.1093/bioinformatics/bts475.

Ditzler, G., Polikar, R., Rosen, G., September. 2015. Multilayer and recursive neural networks for metagenomic classification. IEEE Transactions on NanoBioscience 14 (6), 608−616. https://doi.org/10.1109/TNB.2015.2461219.

Dixit, P., Prajapati, G.I., 2015. Machine learning in bioinformatics: a novel approach for DNA sequencing. In: 2015 Fifth International Conference on Advanced Computing & Communication Technologies, Haryana, pp. 41−47. https://doi.org/10.1109/ACCT.2015.73.

Erhan, D., Bengio, Y., Courville, A., Vincent, P., 2009. Visualizing Higher-Layer Features of a Deep Network (limit).

Erhan, D., Courville, A., Bengio, Y., 2010. Understanding Representations Learned in Deep Architectures.

Faro, A., Giordano, D., Spampinato, C., 2012. Combining literature text mining with microarray data: advances for system biology modeling. Briefings Bioinf. 13 (1), 61−82. https://doi.org/10.1093/bib/bbr018.

Futoma, J., Morris, J., Lucas, J., 2015. A comparison of models for predicting early hospital readmissions. J. Biomed. Inf. 56, 229−238.

Ghasemi, Fahimeh, Mehridehnavi, A.R., Fassihi, Afshin, Pérez-Sánchez, Horacio, 2017. Deep neural network in biologic activity prediction using deep belief network. Appl. Soft Comput. 62. https://doi.org/10.1016/j.asoc.2017.09.040.

Havaei, M., Guizard, N., Larochelle, H., Jodoin, P., 2016. Deep Learning Trends for Focal Brain Pathology Segmentation in MRI. CoRR, vol. abs/1607.05258.

Huang, T., Lan, L., Fang, X., An, P., Min, J., Wang, F., 2015. Promises and challenges of big data computing in health sciences. Big Data Res. 2 (1), 2−11.

Huang, J., Zhou, W., Li, H., Li, W., 2015. Sign language recognition using real-sense. In: Proc. IEEE China SIP, pp. 166−170.

Jabeen, A., Ahmad, N., Raza, K., 2018. Machine learning-based state-of-the-art methods for the classification of RNA-seq data. In: Dey, N., Ashour, A., Borra, S. (Eds.), Classification in BioApps. Lecture Notes in Computational Vision and Biomechanics, vol. 26. Springer, pp. 133−172. https://doi.org/10.1007/978- 3-319-65981-7_6.

Jeena, R.S., Kumar, S., 2016. Stroke prediction using SVM. 2016 International Conference on Control, Instrumentation, Communication and Computational Technologies (ICCICCT), Kumaracoil. pp. 600–602. https://doi.org/10.1109/ICCICCT.2016.7988020.

Jia, X., Li, K., Li, X., Zhang, A., 2014. A novel semi-supervised deep learning framework for affective state recognition on eeg signals. In: Proc. Int. Conf. Bioinformat. Bioeng., pp. 30–37.

José Juan Almagro Armenteros, Casper KaaeSønderby, SørenKaaeSønderby, Henrik Nielsen, Ole Winther, 2017. DeepLoc: prediction of protein subcellular localization using deep learning. Bioinformatics 33 (21), 3387–3395. https://doi.org/10.1093/bioinformatics/btx431.

Lander, E.S., et al., 2001. Initial sequencing and analysis of the human genome. Nature 409 (6822), 860–921.

Larrañaga, P., Calvo, B., Santana, R., Bielza, C., JosuGaldiano, I.I., Lozano, J.A., Armañanzas, R., Santafé, G., Pérez, A., Robles, V., March 2006. Machine learning in bioinformatics. Briefings Bioinf. 7 (1), 86–112.

LeCun, Y., Bengio, Y., Hinton, G., 2015. Deep learning. Nature 521 (7553), 436–444.

Leung, M.K., Delong, A., Alipanahi, B., Frey, B.J., 2016. Machine learning in genomic medicine: a review of computational problems and data sets. Proc. IEEE 104 (1), 176–197.

Liang, M., Li, Z., Chen, T., Zeng, J., 2015. Integrative data analysis of multi-platform cancer data with a multimodal deep learning approach. IEEE/ACM Trans. Comput. Biol. Bioinf. 12 (4), 928–937. https://doi.org/10.1109/TCBB.2014.2377729.

Liang, Z., Zhang, G., Huang, J.X., Hu, Q.V., 2014. Deep learning for healthcare decision making with emrs. In: Proc. Int. Conf. Bioinformat. Biomed., pp. 556–559.

Mitchell, T.M., 1997. Machine Learning. McGraw-Hill.

Nguyen, A., Yosinski, J., Clune, J., 2015. Deep neural networks are easily fooled: high confidence predictions for unrecognizable images. In: Proc. IEEE Conf. Comput. Vis. Pattern Recognit., pp. 427–436.

Ong, B.T., Sugiura, K., Zettsu, K., 2015. Dynamically pre-trained deep recurrent neural networks using environmental monitoring data for predicting pm2. 5. Neural Comput. Appl. 27, 1–14.

Pastur-Romay, L.A., Cedrón, F., Pazos, A., Porto-Pazos, A.B., 2016. Deep artificial neural networks and neuromorphic chips for big data analysis: pharmaceutical and bioinformatics applications. Int. J. Mol. Sci. 17 (8).

Poggi, M., Mattoccia, S., 2016. A wearable mobility aid for the visually impaired based on embedded 3d vision and deep learning. In: Proc. IEEE Symp. Comput. Commun., pp. 208–213.

Poole, D.L., Mackworth, A., Goebel, R.G., 1998. Computational Intelligence and Knowledge. Computational Intelligence: A Logical Approach, pp. 1–22.

Putin, E., et al., 2016. Deep biomarkers of human aging: application of deep neural networks to biomarker development. Aging 8 (5), 1–021.

Ravi, D., Wong, C., Lo, B., Yang, G.Z., June 2016. Deep learning for human activity recognition: a resource efficient implementation on low-power devices. In: Proc. 13th Int. Conf. Wearable Implantable Body Sens. Netw., pp. 71–76.

Ramana, J., Gupta, D., 2009. LipocalinPred: An SVM-based method for prediction of lipocalins. BMC Bioinf 10, 445. https://doi.org/10.1186/1471-2105-10-445.

Rav`ı, D., Wong, C., Deligianni, F., Berthelot, M., Andreu-Perez, J., Lo, B., Yang, G.-Z., 2017. IEEE J. Biomed. Health Inf. 21 (1).

Raza, K., 2017. Protein features identification for machine learning-based prediction of protein-protein interactions. In: Proc. of Communications in Computer and Information Science, vol. 750. Springer, pp. 305–317. https://doi.org/10.1007/978-981-10-6544-6_28.

Raza, K., Hasan, A.N., 2015. A comprehensive evaluation of machineLearning techniques for cancer class prediction based on microarray data.Int. J. Bioinf. Res. Appl.Inderscience 11 (5), 397–416. http://doi.org/10.1504/IJBRA.2015.071940.

Shameer, K., Badgeley, M.A., Miotto, R., Glicksberg, B.S., Morgan, J.W., Dudley, J.T., 2017. Translational bioinformatics in the era of real-time biomedical, health care and wellness data streams. Briefings Bioinf. 18 (1), 105-124. https://doi.org/10.1093/bib/bbv118.

Shin, H.-C., et al., May 2016. Deep convolutional neural networks for computer-aided detection: CNN architectures dataset characteristics and transfer learning. IEEE Trans. Med. Imag. 35 (5), 1285–1298.

Srivastava, N., Hinton, G.E., Krizhevsky, A., Sutskever, I., Salakhutdinov, R., 2014. Dropout: a simple way to prevent neural networks from overfitting. J. Mach. Learn. Res. 15 (1), 1929–1958.

Sümbül, U., Santos, J.M., Pauly, J.M., 2009. A practical acceleration algorithm for real-time imaging. IEEE Trans. Med. Imag. 28, 2042–2051.

Sung, W.-K., 2012. Bioinformatics applications in genomics. IEEE 45 (6).

Szegedy, C., et al., 2013. Intriguing Properties of Neural Networks. CoRR, vol. abs/1312.6199. Available: http://dblp.uni-trier.de/db/journals/corr/corr1312.html#SzegedyZSBEGF13.

Tenenbaum, J.D., 2016. Translational bioinformatics: past, present, and future. Genom. Proteom. Bioinf. 14 (1), 31–41. https://doi.org/10.1016/j.gpb.2016.01.003.

Venter, J.C., et al., 2001. The sequence of the human genome. Science 291 (5507), 1304–1351.

Wang, J., MacKenzie, J.D., Ramachandran, R., Chen, D.Z., 2016. A deep learning approach for semantic segmentation in histology tissue images. Proc. MICCAI 176–184.

Wulsin, D., Blanco, J., Mani, R., Litt, B., December 2010. Semi-supervised anomaly detection for eeg waveforms using deep belief nets. In: Proc. 9th Int. Conf. Mach. Learn. Appl., pp. 436–441.

Xu, T., Zhang, H., Huang, X., Zhang, S., Metaxas, D.N., 2016. Multimodal deep learning for cervical dysplasia diagnosis. Proc. MICCAI 115–123.

Yan, Q., 2017. Applying Translational Bioinformatics for Biomarker Discovery: Translational Bioinformatics and Systems Biology Methods for Personalized Medicine, pp. 55–65.

Yan, Q., 2012. Translational bioinformatics in psychoneuroimmunology: methods and applications. Methods Mol. Biol. 934, 383-400. https://doi.org/10.1007/978-1-62703-071-7_20.

Yang, G.-Z., Leff, D.R., 2015. Big data for precision medicine. Engineering 1 (3).

Zou, B., Lampos, V., Gorton, R., Cox, I.J., 2016. On infectious intestinal disease surveillance using social media content. In: Proc. 6th Int. Conf. Digit. Health Conf., pp. 157–161.

Chapter 16

An enhanced feature selection and cancer classification for microarray data using relaxed Lasso and support vector machine

Aina Umairah Mazlan[1], Noor Azida Sahabudin[1,*], Muhammad Akmal Remli[2,3], Nor Syahidatul Nadiah Ismail[1] and Kayode I. Adenuga[4]

[1]*Faculty of Computing, Universiti Malaysia Pahang, Pekan, Pahang, Malaysia;* [2]*Institute for Artificial Intelligence and Big Data, Universiti Malaysia Kelantan, Kota Bharu, Kelantan, Malaysia;* [3]*Data Science Department, Universiti Malaysia Kelantan, Kota Bharu, Kelantan, Malaysia;* [4]*Faculty of Enterprise, Creative and Professional Studies, Farnborough College of Technology, Hampshire, United Kingdom*

Corresponding author: E-mail: azida@ump.edu.my

Chapter outline

1. Introduction

Cancer, also known as malignant tumors in medical terms, is the biggest killer disease in a number of countries. The number of deaths and new cancer cases is arising year by year. It is estimated that the cancer burden worldwide will increase by an approximate 22.2 million by 2030 (Mahdavifar et al., 2016). This deadly disease may affect everyone at all ages, but the risk increases with age (Lin et al., 2019). According to the Yu et al., (2018), cancer is the term for diseases triggered by the unregulated production of irregular body cells. Cancer cells may also invade other tissues via the blood and lymph systems to certain areas of the body.

Cancer can be classified into diverse types that are generally named based on the type of cell where the cancer originates (Yu et al., 2018). Lung cancer, breast cancer, prostate cancer, and ovary cancer are some examples of the common cancer types. Lung cancer and breast cancer had the highest mortality rates in men and women, respectively (Bray et al., 2018; Lin et al., 2019). The high morbidity and mortality of cancer mostly is caused from diagnosed disease at a late stage (Dogan, 2019).

As discussed in this section, it is proven that cancer is a serious burden disease in health problems. Therefore, much research has been done to find out better ways to prevent, diagnose, and treat this disease to reduce number of deaths. This research also studies detection and classification of cancer using the microarray data. Microarray-based gene expression has emerged as a capable technique for classification and prediction of cancer (Pyingkodi and Thangarajan, 2018).

There are several limitations in microarray gene expression data. Expression data for multiple genes are huge and also include expression of nonessential genes (Raza, 2014). However, this can be solved by applying feature selection before proceeding to the classification. In this research, some technique of feature selection will be studied before choosing the most appropriate method.

The techniques may be divided into three types: filter, wrapper, and embedded methods (Pyingkodi and Thangarajan, 2018). The work is proposed to apply embedded techniques to obtain the best method of selecting the feature. Feature selection is very significant especially for dimensionality reduction to improve classification accuracy (Huo et al., 2020; Li et al., 2018; Nair and Bhagat, 2019).

Through this study, the best feature selection method will be chosen and applied to microarray data before it will be classified. Finally, the microarray cancer data will be classified to determine different cancer subtypes using the support vector machine (SVM) classifier. The radial basis function kernel is used in SVM to improve the prediction accuracy of the classification (Huo et al., 2020).

To validate the efficacy of the proposed method, three datasets of cancer microarray were chosen for the experiment. This study uses 10-fold cross-validation to test a prediction model's performance. Then we use the accuracy, AUC, and Kappa statistics to evaluate the prediction system's results. The outcome of the study will be discussed to provide knowledge for the future research in this area.

2. Related work

Cancer is a common and chronic disease with numerous genetic and environmental risks. The death rate from cancer is the same as its incidence rate, and both rates are significantly rising every year, causing serious public health problem all around the world. In 2018, there were nearly 18.1 million new diagnoses of cancer and 9.6 million deaths worldwide (Bray et al., 2018). The number of cancer patients in 2014 reached about 14.5 million and is predicted to increase to nearly 19 million by 2024 (Pan et al., 2016). Over 60% of new cancer cases worldwide emerge in Asia, Africa, and Central and South America (Guo et al., 2020). Approximately 70% of cancer-related mortality globally also emerges in these regions. Lung cancer is the most common of both sexes with the highest incidence and death rates, followed by breast cancer in females, prostate and colorectal cancer for incidence, and colorectal, stomach, and liver cancer for mortality.

Cancer is defined as a disease that is caused by uncontrolled cell growth within the body (Neekhra et al., 2017). Cancer cells can also invade or spread to other body parts through the blood and lymph systems (Angahar, 2017). Most cancers form a lump or mass called a tumor (Yu et al., 2018). Benign is another term for noncancerous tumors, while malignant is a term for cancerous tumors. However, there are some cancers like leukemia that do not often form tumors (Beevi and Remya, 2013). These cancer cells instead grow in the body's blood cells or other cells. Biopsy is needed to determine whether a tumor is benign or cancerous (Sinha, 2018). Then the biopsy is examined under a microscope by a pathologist.

Cancer is not only one disease but a group of diseases. According to the National Cancer Institute, there are more than 100 distinct types of cancer. Most cancers are named based on the type of cell where the cancer began (Yu et al., 2018). Cancer is classified according to the following groups: carcinoma, sarcoma, lymphoma, and leukemia (Neekhra et al., 2017). Carcinoma, which includes over 90% of human cancers, originates from epithelial cells (Chang and Ketter, 2001). These include the most common cancers such as breast, colon, stomach, skin, and lung cancer. A sarcoma is a rare cancer that starts in the connective tissue (Jain et al., 2010). Leukemia and lymphoma are cancers that originate in the blood and lymph system.

Microarray technology has become an essential tool for several scientists to investigate the expression of different genes in a particular organism (Remli et al., 2017; Whitworth, 2010). This technology is important in the area of genetics because the micro dimension of the chips used can have numerous genes needed for wide gene expression analysis (Hasanali and Howe, 2019). However, microarray technology has grown more mature in medical research and application for more than 30 years of development (Huo et al., 2020). The application of microarray technology is therefore still important for cancer classification study. Instead of cancer classification, microarray application can also be applied for cancer diagnosis and treatment (Wang et al., 2018).

Gene expression profiling by microarray technology has emerged as an effective technique for classification and prediction of cancer (Pyingkodi and Thangarajan, 2018). The data on gene expression may be used to train a classifier to identify a disease (Raza, 2019). Gene expression data typically has a dimensional disaster with thousands of genes and a limited number of samples (Kang et al., 2019). Thousands of genes in data on gene expression make the data enormous and difficult for any machine learning technique to learn (Raza and Hasan, 2015). To avoid the dimensionality disasters, it is important to select effective characteristics genes from high-dimensional data for cancer classification (Singh and Vyas, 2014). In recent years, creating an efficient model of cancer diagnosis focused on the gene expression study, becoming a popular subject in bioinformatics research (Lu et al., 2017).

The emergence and advances in bioinformatics led to an increased use of gene expression data for medical research. These data has been widely used to understand the function of genes and the relationship between genes (Tarek et al., 2017) and assist in diagnosis and treatment of cancer (Raut et al., 2010). Advancement in biologic computational approaches has sparked analysis of gene expression data and further study on cancer classification (Sharma and Rani, 2017). Recently, there have been various classification techniques proposed using these data. For cancer classification, these methods differ from statistical approaches to machine learning algorithms (Ragunthar and Selvakumar, 2019). High dimensionality of gene expression data makes classification a difficult task, so genes selection is a preliminary step in most of the classifiers (Huo et al., 2020; Kang et al., 2019).

Feature selection is a main step in machine learning as this would assist in enhancing the performance of the learning algorithm (Kotsiantis, 2011). The most effective feature that truly contributes to the model training can be easily extract from an extremely huge dataset (Huo et al., 2020). The pros of feature selection include reduced overfitting, improving accuracy, reduced training time, and reduced model complexity (Ragunthar and Selvakumar, 2019). Three selection techniques are available, namely, filter, wrapper, and embedded methods (Venkatesh and Anuradha, 2019). The features selected in a filter method use statistical measures, while the selected subset of features in the wrapper method depends on the classifier. Embedded methods are a combination between the filter and wrapper algorithms, which include selection methods such as LASSO. Hence the methods need to be applied to the gene expression dataset for reducing dimensionality, thereby improving accuracy and model performance.

Classification is a vital part of the processing and analysis of microarray data, focused primarily on the classification significance of gene expression data (Kang et al., 2019). Numerous forms of machine learning have been commonly used in work in cancer classification issues. Cancer classification commonly uses unsupervised and supervised classification methods (Huo et al., 2020). Methods of unsupervised classification find the sample structure focused on sample similarities, such as K-means (Sinaga and Yang, 2020). The weakness of unsupervised methods is ignorance of information about the sample type. Supervised classification includes SVM, neural networks, decision tree, and random forests etc (Singh et al., 2016). The benefit is to know the sample information to reduce predictive error. SVM is one of the most well-known classifiers for cancer classification. For classification, it has less computation time and the best performance. SVM was effectively employed to identify cancer (Wang et al., 2017).

Recently, a gene expression study provided a reference in cancer diagnosis at the molecular level (Kang et al., 2019). It is a tough challenge to determine the relevance of characteristic genes for classification and successfully classify the different subgroups of cancer. In this study, we propose an enhanced method for cancer classification called rL-SVM (relaxed Lasso and SVM). The dataset of cancer is first normalized by z-score. Secondly, there is the use of a relaxed Lasso in selecting genes, and finally, SVM acts as a classifier. For the experiment and 10-fold cross-validation testing, we select a dataset of two-class and two multiclass datasets. To verify the effectiveness of the suggested approach, we evaluate the accuracy of classification and the number of features in other articles. The experimental findings reveal that the rL--SVM method performs better and selects fewer features.

This chapter contain five sections. Section 2 discusses the related work. Section 3 includes cancer dataset description, feature selection methods, evaluation indicator, and model development. Section 4 reports the proposed method experimental findings. Lastly, Section 5 presents the conclusion.

3. Materials and methods

3.1 Datasets

This chapter will use three datasets of cancer microarray, namely, DLBCL, MLL, and lymphoma. All datasets are on the website: https://github.com/QUST-AIBBDRC/rL-GenSVM/. DLBCL dataset contains 77 samples of 7129 genes and two classes, MLL dataset contains 72 samples of 12,582 genes and three classes, and lymphoma dataset contains 62 samples of 4026 genes and three classes (Kang et al., 2019). The cancer datasets are described in Table 16.1.

TABLE 16.1 Microarray datasets information.

Datasets	No. of sample	No. of genes	No. of class	No. of instances per class
DLBCL	77	7,129	2	19/58
MLL	72	12,582	3	24/20/28
Lymphoma	62	4,026	3	42/9/11

3.2 Methods

3.2.1 Relaxed Lasso (rL)

rL is proposed as a soft- and hard-thresholding generalization method (Meinshausen, 2007). The selection of variable and reduction of coefficients are regulated by two different parameters: λ and ϕ. rL uses a set of features selected by ordinary Lasso to estimate parameter and select the variable for the second time. Meinshausen has also stated that the number of features does not affect the relaxed Lasso convergence rate.

3.2.2 Kruskal–Wallis rank sum test (KW)

KW is one of the statistical methods used extensively in the datasets for gene expression (Maniruzzaman et al., 2019). It is a nonparametric test, so it does not assume the data to be normally distributed. Such a method can check if the distribution of many populations is substantially different (Kang et al., 2019). Most nonparametric tests use a method of variable ranking (Harrar and Bathke, 2008). The feature subset can be selected either manually or by setting a threshold from the ranking list. This statistical approach would seem to be less optimal, but it can be highly efficient as it does not involve any search strategy (Nnamoko et al., 2014).

3.2.3 Sparse group Lasso (SGL)

The method proposed of group Lasso has no sparseness within a group (Huo et al., 2020). For problems with grouped covariates, which are assumed to have both sparsity of groups and within groups, they proposed a regularized linear regression model with the penalties L_1 and L_2. The parameter for the convex combination of the Lasso and group Lasso penalties is $\alpha \in [1, 0]$ (Simon et al., 2013). In SGL, gene variables are assumed to act in groups; thus, the method may be used to classify especially relevant genes in pathways of interest by using grouping knowledge of the gene features (Vangimalla et al., 2016).

3.2.4 Support vector machine

Cortes and Vapnik (1995) proposed a supervised SVM method. It has numerous uses in study of classification and regression. This has benefits in solving small samples, recognizing high-dimensional and nonlinear patterns, and can be extended to machine learning problems like function fitting (Huo et al., 2020). This method finds an optimal hyperplane that maximizes the separating of training data between classes. In addition, the kernel function used in the training of SVM is able to overcome the dimensionality catastrophe problem (Xie et al., 2019). The right kernel function will significantly increase the classification model's accuracy. Many widely used kernel functions are linear, radial basis, and sigmoid (Kancherla et al., 2019).

3.2.5 Generalized multiclass SVM (GenSVM)

GenSVM was proposed by Van and Groenen (2016). This approach uses simplex encoding to formulate the problem of multiclass SVM. When $K = 2$, it reduces the problem of multiclass SVM to a binary SVM. The loss function of GenSVM incorporates and extends three current multiclass SVMs that use the sum of hinge errors by implementing adjustable hinge function and the l_p error norm.

3.3 Evaluation indicator and model development

This chapter utilizes k-fold cross-validation to test a predictive model's performance. And we are using the accuracy, AUC, and Kappa statistics to evaluate the prediction system's results. The different performance metrics are as follows:

True positives (TP) is the number of correctly classified positive samples. True negatives (TN) is the number of correctly classified negative samples. False negatives (FN) is the number of misclassified negative samples. False positives (FP) is the number of misclassified positive samples.

$$ACC = \frac{TP + TN}{TP + TN + FP + FN} \tag{16.1}$$

The classification performance is evaluated for two-class datasets using AUC, which is insensitive to sample class balance; Kappa is used for multiclass datasets to evaluate classifier output, which represents the consistency of actual and predicted values (Kang et al., 2019).

The proposed system cancer classification is called rL-SVM for convenience. The basic framework is illustrated in Fig. 16.1. The method proposed has been implemented in R version 3.6.2 on Windows 10 operating on a laptop with Intel (R) Core (TM) i7-4710HQ CPU @ 2.50 GHz with 8.00 GB of RAM.

The steps of the rL-SVM method of cancer classification are defined as follows:

(1) Carry out cancer dataset z-score normalization.
(2) Using the Lars algorithm, obtain $\lambda_1 > \ldots > \lambda_s = 0$ penalty term sequence and $\omega_1, \ldots, \omega_s$ variable set to each dataset.
(3) Use rL to estimate the parameter using variables in ω_k and obtain a set of feature genes from reducing the coefficient with λ_k penalty term, producing matrix $X_{N \times k}$ with N samples and k variables.
(4) SVM with a kernel function of radial basis acts as a classifier.
(5) Calculate 10-fold cross-validation of the ACC, AUC, and Kappa for classification method evaluation.

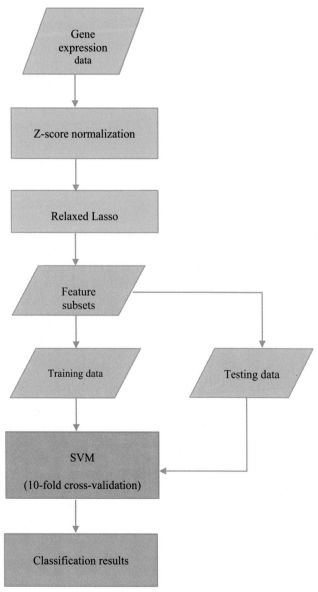

FIGURE 16.1 Flowchart of the selection and classification process of the feature gene.

TABLE 16.2 Comparison method proposed in two-class datasets with several other feature selection methods.

	SGL-SVM		rL-GenSVM		rL-SVM (proposed)	
Datasets	NF	ACC (AUC)	NF	ACC (AUC)	NF	ACC (AUC)
DLBCL	7	99.43% (1.000)	9	98.16% (0.97)	8	97.68% (1.000)

TABLE 16.3 Comparison method proposed in multiclass datasets with several other feature selection methods.

	SGL-SVM		rL-GenSVM		rL-SVM (proposed)	
Datasets	NF	ACC (Kappa)	NF	ACC (Kappa)	NF	ACC (Kappa)
MLL	15	98.31% (0.9831)	13	98.04% (0.9697)	14	98.59% (0.9818)
Lymphoma	8	99.67% (0.992)	9	99.36% (0.9874)	8	99.71% (0.9922)

4. Results and discussion

To show the proposed method's validity, we compare accuracy and number of features with other methods. Tables 16.2 and 16.3 show the accuracy, AUC, Kappa, and number of feature genes (NF) for each dataset. The accuracy was measured by 10-fold cross-validation of all samples on each dataset, and feature genes were selected by optimal accuracy. Tables 16.2 and 16.3 demonstrate the comparison of ACC and NF for the method proposed and other existing methods.

The following methods are described as follows: SGL-SVM combines KW with regularization method SGL for feature selection and SVM for cancer classification (Huo et al., 2020). Kang et al. (2019) proposed to use rL to select feature genes and generalized multiclass SVM (GenSVM) as a classifier for predicting classification accuracy. Whereas, this chapter uses rL-SVM as a method for selecting features and classifying cancer.

Table 16.2 reveals that Huo et al. (2020) selected seven genes for the DLBCL dataset to achieve 99.43% ACC using SGL-SVM. Kang et al. (2019) selected nine genes utilizing rL-GenSVM and received 98.16% ACC. Our method selected eight genes and reaches the ACC 97.68%.

Table 16.3 shows that for MLL datasets, Huo et al. (2020) selected 15 genes using KW&SGL and received 98.31% ACC from SVM. Kang et al. (2019) selected only 13 genes using rL-GenSVM and the ACC reaches 98.04%, while this chapter selected 14 genes and obtained classification accuracy to 98.59%. Among them, for lymphoma dataset, eight genes were selected, and the classification accuracy was 99.67%, 99.36%, and 99.71%, respectively. The results show a highly competitive accuracy between those methods.

In summary, the comparison of these methods indicated that rL-SVM is dependent on the regularization term l_1 to reduce NF. The classification model may improve the accuracy of the DLBCL, MLL, and lymphoma datasets considerably. The classification accuracies are 97.68%, 98.59%, and 99.71%, respectively. The result of a satisfactory classification of cancer is given.

5. Conclusion

The emergence of big data makes gene expression-based cancer classification a popular topic in bioinformatics. This chapter proposed an enhanced cancer classification method, called rL-SVM. The dataset of cancer is first normalized by z-score. Secondly, there is the use of a relaxed Lasso in selecting genes, and finally, SVM acts as a classifier. For the experiment and 10-fold cross-validation testing, we select a dataset of two-class and two multiclass datasets. To verify the effectiveness of the suggested approach, we evaluated the accuracy of classification and the number of features in other articles. The experimental findings show that the method proposed has better performance and achieves better accuracy for classification with fewer selected feature genes. rL-SVM can be used in large, high dimension, and small sample cancer classification. In addition, the research identified several limitations and contributions that can be made in future work. In this research, by utilizing the Lasso function, there are possibilities for the exclusion of informative features from gene expression data and the inclusion of noninformative features affecting the output of a classifier. Besides, for huge datasets, these methods can be time consuming and require high computational cost. In future work, therefore, statistical method may be applied with an improved solution of feature selection to apply it on other cancer datasets. A combination of different methods may be implemented to further reduce the number of feature genes and increase classification accuracy.

Acknowledgment

This work was supported by the Universiti Malaysia Pahang under RDU scheme (Grant number: RDU190396) and Ministry of Higher Education under Fundamental Research Grant Scheme-RACER (Grant number: RACER/1/2019/ICT02/UMP//3 and RACER/1/2019/ICT02/UMP//1.

References

Angahar, L.T., 2017. An overview of breast cancer epidemiology, risk factors, pathophysiology, and cancer risks reduction. MOJ Biol. Med. 1, 92−96. https://doi.org/10.15406/mojbm.2017.01.00019.

Beevi, S.A., Remya, R.S., 2013. An overview on acute lymphocytic leukemia detection using cell image segmentation. J. Comput. Eng. 14, 22−29.

Bray, F., Ferlay, J., Soerjomataram, I., Siegel, R.L., Torre, L.A., Jemal, A., 2018. Global cancer statistics 2018: GLOBOCAN estimates of incidence and mortality worldwide for 36 cancers in 185 countries. CA Cancer J. Clin. 68, 394−424. https://doi.org/10.3322/caac.21492.

Chang, K.D., Ketter, T.A., 2001. Special issues in the treatment of paediatric bipolar disorder. Expert Opin. Pharmacother. 2 (4), 613−622. https://doi.org/10.1517/14656566.2.4.613.

Cortes, C., Vapnik, V., 1995. Support-vector networks. Mach. Learn. 20, 273−297.

Dogan, N., 2019. Global patterns of incidence and mortality in lung cancer. Eurasian J. Med. Oncol. 3, 28−32. https://doi.org/10.14744/ejmo.2018.0025.

Guo, W., Tan, H.Y., Chen, F., Wang, N., Feng, Y., 2020. Targeting cancer metabolism to resensitize chemotherapy: potential development of cancer chemosensitizers from traditional Chinese medicines. Cancers 12. https://doi.org/10.3390/cancers12020404.

Harrar, S.W., Bathke, A.C., 2008. Nonparametric methods for unbalanced multivariate data and many factor levels. J. Multivariate Anal. 99, 1635−1664. https://doi.org/10.1016/j.jmva.2008.01.005.

Hasanali, M., Howe, C.W., 2019. An examination of machine learning algorithms for missing values imputation. Int. J. Innovative Technol. Explor. Eng. 8, 415−420. https://doi.org/10.35940/ijitee.l1081.10812s219.

Huo, Y., Xin, L., Kang, C., Wang, M., Ma, Q., Yu, B., 2020. SGL-SVM : a novel method for tumor classification via support vector machine with sparse group Lasso 486. J. Theor. Biol. https://doi.org/10.1016/j.jtbi.2019.110098.

Jain, S., Xu, R., Prieto, V.G., Lee, P., 2010. Molecular classification of soft tissue sarcomas and its clinical applications. Int. J. Clin. Exp. Pathol. 3, 416−429.

Kancherla, D., Bodapati, J.D., Veeranjaneyulu, N., 2019. Effect of different kernels on the performance of an SVM based classification 1−6. Int. J. Recent Technol. & Eng.

Kang, C., Huo, Y., Xin, L., Tian, B., Yu, B., 2019. Feature selection and tumor classification for microarray data using relaxed Lasso and generalized multi-class support vector machine. J. Theor. Biol. 463, 77−91. https://doi.org/10.1016/j.jtbi.2018.12.010.

Kotsiantis, S.B., 2011. Feature selection for machine learning classification problems: a recent overview. Artif. Intell. Rev. 42, 157. https://doi.org/10.1007/s10462-011-9230-1.

Li, Z., Xie, W., Liu, T., 2018. Efficient feature selection and classification for microarray data. PLoS One 13, 1−21. https://doi.org/10.1371/journal.pone.0202167.

Lin, L., Yan, L., Liu, Y., Yuan, F., Li, H., Ni, J., 2019. Incidence and death in 29 cancer groups in 2017 and trend analysis from 1990 to 2017 from the Global Burden of Disease Study. J. Hematol. Oncol. 12, 1−21. https://doi.org/10.1186/s13045-019-0783-9.

Lu, H., Chen, J., Yan, K., Jin, Q., Xue, Y., Gao, Z., 2017. A hybrid feature selection algorithm for gene expression data classification. Neurocomputing 256, 56−62. https://doi.org/10.1016/j.neucom.2016.07.080.

Mahdavifar, N., Ghoncheh, M., Pakzad, R., Momenimovahed, Z., Salehiniya, H., 2016. Epidemiology, incidence and mortality of bladder cancer and their relationship with the development index in the world. Asian Pac. J. Cancer Prev. APJCP 17, 381−386. https://doi.org/10.7314/APJCP.2016.17.1.381.

Maniruzzaman, M., Jahanur Rahman, M., Ahammed, B., Abedin, M.M., Suri, H.S., Biswas, M., El-Baz, A., Bangeas, P., Tsoulfas, G., Suri, J.S., 2019. Statistical characterization and classification of colon microarray gene expression data using multiple machine learning paradigms. Comput. Methods Progr. Biomed. 176, 173−193. https://doi.org/10.1016/j.cmpb.2019.04.008.

Meinshausen, N., 2007. Relaxed lasso. Comput. Stat. Data Anal. 52, 374−393. https://doi.org/10.1016/j.csda.2006.12.019.

Nair, R., Bhagat, A., 2019. Feature selection method to improve the accuracy of classification algorithm. Int. J. Innovative Technol. Explor. Eng. 8, 124−127.

Neekhra, S., Awasthi, H., Singh, D.C.P., 2017. Cancer: An Overview, 6, pp. 2845−2849.

Nnamoko, N., Arshad, F., England, D., Vora, J., Norman, J., 2014. Evaluation of filter and wrapper methods for feature selection in supervised machine learning. 15th Annu. Postgrad. Symp. Converg. Telecommun. Netw. Broadcast. 63−67.

Pan, S.T., Li, Z.L., He, Z.X., Qiu, J.X., Zhou, S.F., 2016. Molecular mechanisms for tumour resistance to chemotherapy. Clin. Exp. Pharmacol. Physiol. 43, 723−737. https://doi.org/10.1111/1440-1681.12581.

Pyingkodi, M., Thangarajan, R., 2018. Informative gene selection for cancer classification with microarray data using a metaheuristic framework. Asian Pac. J. Cancer Prev. APJCP 19, 561−564. https://doi.org/10.22034/APJCP.2018.19.2.561.

Ragunthar, T., Selvakumar, S., 2019. Classification of gene expression data with optimized feature selection. Int. J. Recent Technol. Eng. 8, 4763−4769. https://doi.org/10.35940/ijrte.B1845.078219.

Raut, S.A., Sathe, S.R., Raut, A.P., 2010. Gene expression analysis-a review for large datasets. J. Comput. Sci. & Eng.

Raza, K., 2014. Clustering analysis of cancerous microarray data. J. Chem. & Pharm. Res. 6, 488−493.

Raza, K., 2019. Analysis of microarray data using artificial intelligence based techniques. Biotechnol. Con. Methodol. Tool. App. IGI Global.

Raza, K., Hasan, A.N., 2015. A comprehensive evaluation of machine learning techniques for cancer class prediction based on microarray data. Int. J. Bioinform. Res. Appl. https://doi.org/10.1504/IJBRA.2015.071940.

Remli, M.A., Daud, K.M., Nies, H.W., 2017. K-Means Clustering with Infinite Feature Selection for Classification Tasks in Gene Expression Data. https://doi.org/10.1007/978-3-319-60816-7.

Sharma, A., Rani, R., 2017. An optimized framework for cancer classification using deep learning and genetic algorithm. J. Med. Imaging Heal. Inform. 7, 1851−1856. https://doi.org/10.1166/jmihi.2017.2266.

Simon, N., Friedman, J., Hastie, T., Tibshirani, R., 2013. A sparse-group lasso. J. Comput. Graph Stat. 22, 231−245. https://doi.org/10.1080/10618600.2012.681250.

Sinaga, K.P., Yang, M.-S., 2020. Unsupervised K-means clustering algorithm. IEEE Access 8, 80716−80727. 1−1. https://doi.org/10.1109/access.2020.2988796.

Singh, A., Thakur, N., Sharma, A., 2016. A review of supervised machine learning algorithms. In: Proc. 10th INDIACom; 2016 3rd Int. Conf. Comput. Sustain. Glob. Dev. INDIACom, 2016, pp. 1310−1315.

Singh, B., Vyas, O.P., 2014. A meta-heuristic regression-based feature selection for predictive analytics. Data Sci. J. 13, 106−118. https://doi.org/10.2481/dsj.14-032.

Sinha, T., 2018. Tumors: benign and malignant. Cancer Ther. Oncol. Int. J. 10, 1−3. https://doi.org/10.19080/ctoij.2018.10.555790.

Tarek, S., Abd Elwahab, R., Shoman, M., 2017. Gene expression based cancer classification. Egypt. Informatics J 18, 151−159. https://doi.org/10.1016/j.eij.2016.12.001.

Van, G.J.J., Groenen, P.J.F., 2016. GEN: a generalized multiclass support vector machine. J. Mach. Learn. Res. 17, 1−42.

Vangimalla, R.R., Jeong, H.H., Sohn, K.A., 2016. Integrative regression network for genomic association study. BMC Med. Genom. 9 https://doi.org/10.1186/s12920-016-0192-7.

Venkatesh, B., Anuradha, J., 2019. A review of feature selection and its methods. Cybern. Inf. Technol. 19, 3−26. https://doi.org/10.2478/CAIT-2019-0001.

Wang, A., An, N., Chen, G., Liu, L., Alterovitz, G., 2018. Subtype dependent biomarker identification and tumor classification from gene expression profiles. Knowl. Base Syst. 146, 104−117. https://doi.org/10.1016/j.knosys.2018.01.025.

Wang, H., Zheng, B., Yoon, S.W., Ko, H.S., 2017. A support vector machine-based ensemble algorithm for breast cancer diagnosis. Eur. J. Oper. Res. 267, 687−699. https://doi.org/10.1016/j.ejor.2017.12.001.

Whitworth, G.B., 2010. An introduction to microarray data analysis. Methods Enzymol. 470, 19−50. https://doi.org/10.1016/S0076-6879(10)70002-1.

Xie, T., Yao, J., Zhou, Z., 2019. DA-Based Parameter Optimization of Combined.

Yu, C., Chen, R., Li, J.J., Li, J.J., Drahansky, M., Paridah, M., Moradbak, A., Mohamed, A., Owolabi, F.L., Abdulwahab taiwo, H., Asniza, M., Abdul Khalid, S.H., Sharma, T., Dohare, N., Kumari, M., Singh, U.K., Khan, A.B., Borse, M.S., Patel, R., Paez, A., Howe, A., Goldschmidt, D., Corporation, C., Coates, J., Reading, F., 2018. An Overview of Cancer Treatment Modalities. Intech 13. https://doi.org/10.1016/j.colsurfa.2011.12.014.

Chapter 17

Fuzzy rule-driven data mining framework for knowledge acquisition for expert system

L.J. Muhammad[1,*], E.J. Garba[2], N.D. Oye[2], G.M. Wajiga[2] and A.B. Garko[3]

[1]*Mathematics and Computer Science Department, Federal University of Kashere, Gombe State, Nigeria;* [2]*Computer Science Department, Modibbo Adama University of Technology, Yola, Adamawa State, Nigeria;* [3]*Computer Science Department Federal University Dutse, Jigawa State, Nigeria*
Corresponding author: E-mail: lawan.jibril@fukashere.edu.ng

Chapter outline

1. Introduction

An expert system (ES) is a system that nearly earns the ability of the human experts in decision-making (Turban and Ja, 2001; Idris et al., 2013). The goal of every ES is to solve complex problems by reasoning with knowledge rather than conventional procedural codes like other computer systems (Ji et al., 2012; Muhammad et al., 2018). ES is the computer application software that manipulates symbolic descriptions of heuristics and facts to emulate the reasoning processes of a human expert (Spangler et al., 1989). ES is built in the process, which is termed knowledge engineering, in the course of which knowledge about the domain to model is drawn from human experts and other sources by software engineers or knowledge engineers (Muhammad et al., 2019a,b; Benfer et al., 2012; Hussain et al., 2019). Replication of human knowledge and expertise to the knowledge base of an ES then to end users involves three activities, including knowledge acquisition, knowledge inference (knowledge reasoning), and knowledge representation (Turban and Ja, 2001; Idris et al., 2013; Benfer et al., 2012).

Replication or transfer of human knowledge and expertise to the knowledge base of an ES is one of the problematic activities in the development and implementation of every ES (Idris et al., 2013). According to (Feigenbaum, 1982), knowledge acquisition is the problematic bottleneck in the construction of an application-oriented ES. Knowledge acquisition has been known as a troublesome phase in the development and implementation of every ES especially for modeling medical tasks (Pandey and Mishra, 2009; Boose, 1989; Muhammad et al., 2018). Various techniques have been used for knowledge acquisition including interview, questionnaire, and machine learning techniques, among others (Boose, 1989; Vlaanderen, 1990; Muhammad et al., 2020).

Knowledge reasoning activity involves application of logical rules to the knowledge base to deduce or infer new information or knowledge (Muhammad et al., 2019a,b; Idris et al., 2013). The inference engine is the hallmark of every ES and infers its conclusion with reasoning from the replicated human knowledge and expertise in the knowledge base of an ES (Boose, 1989; Idris et al., 2013; Muhammad et al., 2015, 2020). However, this activity is not as problematic as knowledge acquisition activity (Turban and Ja, 2001).

Knowledge representation involves the activity of encoding the replicated human knowledge and expertise in the knowledge base of an ES into an appropriate readable format to end users of the system (Goodall, 1985). Knowledge representation implies a systematic means of encoding what an expert knows about a knowledge domain in an appropriate medium (Yahaya et al., 2019; Muhammad et al., 2019a,b). Therefore, it is one of the critical activities in the course of the development and implementation of every ES (Pandey and Mishra, 2009; Turban and Ja, 2001; Idris et al., 2013). Various techniques including semantic networks, frame-based technique, rule-based technique, case-based technique, fuzzy logic technique, database technique, scripts technique, object-oriented technique, and hybrid technique have been used for knowledge presentation (Vlaanderen, 1990). Fuzzy logic-based technique is the mostly used technique for knowledge presentation in the course of the ES development because of its ability to handle the uncertainty and complexity that usually is involved in decision-making (Pratihar, 2013; Ji et al., 2012; Muhammad et al., 2018, 2019a,b).

However, the success of any ES mainly depends on the quality, completeness, and accuracy of the information stored in the knowledge base (Muhammad et al., 2019a,b; Oladipupo, 2012). In this study, a new approach has been proposed, which is termed "fuzzy rule-driven data mining framework to knowledge acquisition for expert system," that addresses the issue of the problematic bottleneck often associated with the transfer of knowledge from a human domain expert to the knowledge base of an ES, which is called "knowledge acquisition."

2. Knowledge acquisition

Knowledge acquisition can be defined as the processes of extracting knowledge from various sources of human experts to the knowledge base of an ES (Pandey and Mishra, 2009; Muhammad et al., 2019a,b). It is also defined as a process of replicating new human knowledge or modifying existing human knowledge in the knowledge base of an ES (Hart, 1986; Pathak and Arul, 2020; Pandey and Mishra, 2009). Therefore, knowledge acquisition facilities the assimilation of the knowledge and even past experience of different human experts, for example, an agricultural diagnostic ES that requires many human experts from different fields such as nutrition, pathology, breeding, plant production, and entomology (Pandey and Mishra, 2009; Vlaanderen, 1990; Singh, 2013; Li and Fu, 2007). There are many conventional techniques employed by scholars to replicate the human knowledge and expertise to the knowledge base of an ES that include interview, verbal protocol, machine learning induction, observational studies, conceptual sorting, and multidimensional scaling. However, the knowledge acquisition remains the most difficult task in the development of the ES. According to (Oladipupo, 2012), knowledge acquisition has been known as bottleneck, especially for modeling medical tasks. Knowledge acquisition had been known for a very long time as a troublesome phase in the development of the ES (Muhammad et al., 2018, 2019a,b; Haruna et al., 2019). According to (Okafor and Osuagwu, 2007), the fundamental challenges for development of an ES are the acquisition of knowledge from human experts to the knowledge base of an ES. According to (Feigenbaum, 1982), knowledge acquisition is a problematic bottleneck in the construction of the application-oriented ES. This study addresses the issue of the problematic bottleneck often associated with the transfer of knowledge and expertise from a human domain expert to the knowledge base of an ES, which is called "knowledge acquisition."

3. Related work

Knowledge acquisition is one of the critical phases or activities in the development and implementation of every ES (Pandey and Mishra, 2009; Muhammad et al., 2019a,b). It was reported in the literature that knowledge acquisition is the most difficult and precarious stage in the knowledge engineering process, especially in the medical field, because of the large amount of data that has potentially life-threatening consequences of incorrect conclusion as well as imprecise causal knowledge (Muhammad et al., 2019a,b; Oladipupo, 2012). There are many scholarly works done to address the issue of knowledge transfer between human domain experts to the knowledge base of an ES. In (Hoi-Kau and Richards, 1993), a new technique of knowledge acquisition was presented in the work based on the grounded theory methodology, but it is capable of dealing with unstructured interview data only. However, the study only introduced the theoretical foundation of the new technique, and it has not been implemented nor evaluated. In (Crowther and Hartnett, 1996), a deeper knowledge technique where human knowledge can be elicited using repertory grid techniques, which get domain experts to rank objects against concepts, was proposed. However, the knowledge can only be represented by a series of satellite images. In (Evsukoff et al., 1997), a new knowledge acquisition approach to minimize the intrinsic difficulties of the knowledge acquisition process was proposed. However, the approach only minimizes the intrinsic difficulties of the knowledge acquisition process with no emphasis to generate accurate knowledge. A knowledge acquisition technique in which knowledge is acquired on the degree of the maturity of the human expert know-how to generate the accurate knowledge was introduced in (Hongmei et al., 2002). However, the technique is only a viable solution to build and grow a medical ES through the internet. The approach to acquire the knowledge based on demographics, experience, business value, and behavioral attributes was proposed (Shah et al., 2006). However, the approach can only be applied to acquire the knowledge for the ES of a customer contact center. In (Qingzhang et al., 2007), a novel knowledge acquisition approach that is able to elicit explicit knowledge as well as implicit knowledge was proposed. However, the approach is only to help the knowledge engineers to select appropriate data mining algorithms to discover useful knowledge. An interactive knowledge acquisition approach having dynamic knowledge conversion and creation process for the explicit and tacit knowledge was proposed (Yan and Zetian, 2007). However, the process to generate knowledge with the approach is not well defined. An automatic approach of acquiring knowledge from a human expert to knowledge based on the system was proposed (Tsipouras et al., 2008). However, the human expert is not well involved in every stage of acquiring the knowledge to the knowledge base of the ES. A new method of knowledge acquisition based on relational database was introduced and adopted in the development of an ES for dam safety monitoring (Xiaosheng and Bo, 2008). The conventional data collection techniques were used to transfer the knowledge to the knowledge base of an ES. In the study of (Lianxiang et al., 2009), an attribute reduction algorithm based on a discernibility matrix to do attribute reduction and then extract productive rules using the rule extraction algorithm was employed. However, the conventional data collection techniques were used to transfer the knowledge to the knowledge based of an ES. In the work of the (Oladipupo, 2012), association rule data mining was used to address the long-time concern of knowledge engineers in developing an ES, where a new approach termed "fuzzy association rule mining expert-driven approach to knowledge acquisition" was proposed. The approach is an expert-driven knowledge discovery concept where Apriori association rule data mining algorithm is used to uncover the knowledge from a historical dataset (Oladipupo, 2012). The knowledge was transferred from a human domain expert to the knowledge base of the expert system to avoid sharp boundary problems (Oladipupo, 2012). The study used Long Beach V.A. Medical Center as a Cleveland Clinic Foundation database as a source of knowledge to the system without ascertaining its relevance and validity using a data mining algorithm (Oladipupo, 2012). A hybrid data mining model used to extract classification knowledge for an ES was proposed by (Sneha et al., 2012). However, the study used a basic data mining algorithm to extract the knowledge without ascertaining its validity. In the study of (Debabrata et al., 2012), a structured interview was adopted for knowledge acquisition for development of an ES for diagnosis of coronary artery diseases (CADs). In the work, multiple phases of interviews with a human domain expert were carried out by the knowledge engineers. A well-defined questionnaire was also developed with the advice of the human expert of the domain to collect sample data from the patients. In the study of (Lei et al., 2012), the new knowledge acquisition method was based on graphic techniques, which effectively simplified the difficulty and was easy to maintain and understand the knowledge acquired. However, the method of knowledge acquisition is based on graphic representation. In the work of (Idris et al., 2013), a fuzzy relational database management system based on C4.5 algorithm in which the algorithm was applied to transfer the human knowledge and expertise to the knowledge base of an ES was developed. However, the study concentrates only on the interpretability of the output of the system rather than accuracy of the generated rules. An ES framework with an integrated knowledge base that combined the knowledge fed by multiple experts was presented (Devraj and Vikas, 2015). However, the technique and methodology of the study are not well articulated. The study of (Rybina and Danyakin, 2017) proposed an automatic temporal knowledge acquisition technique based on AT-TECHNOLOGY work bench and problem-oriented methodology for building the knowledge base of an ES. The study only addressed the issue of knowledge transfer for temporal data. A hybrid fuzzy machine learning approach for knowledge transfer was proposed in the study of (Jirawit et al., 2017) for development of an ES. But the study was aimed to provide appropriate interpretations of the knowledge not to provide comprehensive and accurate knowledge in the knowledge base of an ES. An easy-to-use data-driven knowledge acquisition was proposed (Spangler et al., 1989). The overall user experience of the proposed technique was efficient in terms of attractiveness, as well as its pragmatisms, but the accuracy of the technique was not determined in the study.

4. Fuzzy rule-driven data mining framework

Fuzzy rule-driven data mining (FRDDM) is a framework that addressed the problematic bottleneck often associated with the knowledge transfer between human experts to the knowledge base of an ES. The framework adopted the data mining knowledge discovery process model developed by (Fayyad et al., 1996) for extracting or discovering hidden patterns or useful and novel knowledge from a dataset. The framework focuses on extracting interesting knowledge from a dataset or uncovering hidden patterns from historical data using an improved C4.5 decision tree classification algorithm proposed by (Yahaya et al., 2018) in form of a crisp set of rules for subsequent transformation into a fuzzy set of rules or values. The data are captured or collected by reviewing related documents, interview, and observation of the problem domain. Human experts are involved and consulted to capture their opinion about the data of the problem domain. The interval boundaries, membership functions, and the rules of consequences are defined and set based on the perception and consultation of the human experts to solve or minimize the problem of having incorrect knowledge in the knowledge base of an ES. The conceptual architecture of the FRDDM framework is shown in Fig. 17.1. The major components of the framework are discussed as follows.

i. **Historical data**: Historical data is one of the most important components of the framework because it is from this phase that knowledge is transfered to the knowledge base of an ES using past data (past experience of the human expert). The data must be structured instead of unstructured because the framework does not support unstructured data. There must be a set of input variables and output variables in the dataset (labeled data).

ii. **Human domain expert**: The human domain expert is a person who is familiar with the problem domain to model in addition to knowledge and expertise of the domain. The system engineer will work closely with the human domain expert to understand the problem domain to determine and come up with solution goals of the problem. The system engineer must learn, understand, and be acquainted with some domain-specific terminologies of the problem domain to model.

iii. **Fuzzy rule-driven data mining process model**: In this component, data preprocessing activities are involved in which data cleaning, integration, transformation, reduction, selection, and analysis are carried out. Insightful useful and novel knowledge from the dataset using the classification data mining algorithm is also carried out. Decision tree rules generation, rule elicitation, rule evaluation, and rule selection are also done in this stage. The phases of this component are discussed in the following subsection.

   a. **Data preprocessing and cleaning**: In this stage the data collected would undergo preprocessing and cleaning scrutiny. Missing data would also be dealt with. The framework adopted K-nearest neighbor (K-nn) method to impute the missing or supply values for missing data, thus completing the data set proposed by (Batista and Monard, 2003). The main benefit of K-nn method is predicting both qualitative and quantitative attributes.

   b. **Data mining algorithm**: The data mining classification algorithm for uncovering useful and novel knowledge from the dataset is determined in this phase. FRDDM framework adopted improved C4.5 algorithm proposed by (Yahaya et al., 2018) for finding hidden patterns or knowledge.

   c. **Data mining**: In this phase, decision tree algorithm is to be used to analyze the data, recognizes similarities among data objects, and to create a model that predicts the value of a target variable based on several input variables.

   d. **Interpretation of mined pattern**: The visualization of the decision tree generated from the dataset with the data mining algorithm is done and corresponding decision tree rules or production rules are also generated.

   e. **Rule selection and consolidation of discovered knowledge**: This is the final stage where the set of the production rules or crisp rules generated from the decision tree would be selected because there might be too many rules or irrelevant rules. There are many rules selection or rule filtering methods, but FRDDM framework adopted hybrid rule selection technique (RST) proposed by (Noor et al., 2009).

   f. **Transformation of crisp set rules into fuzzy set of rules**: In this phase, the crisp set of rules selected using RST are to be converted into fuzzy set rules. Therefore, the linguistic variable of each attribute is determined, and the membership function of each linguistic variable for both input and output is determined, calculated, and visualized using MATLAB. The crisp set of rules is transformed or converted into a corresponding fuzzy set of rules value.

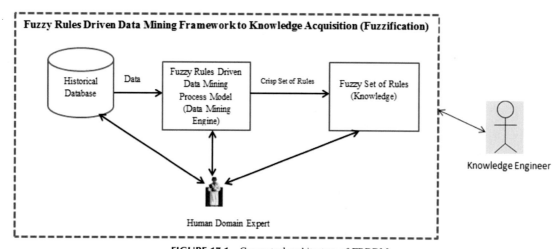

FIGURE 17.1 Conceptual architecture of FRDDM.

5. Practical application of fuzzy rule-driven data mining framework

The real-life usage or application of the proposed framework is very important because it would be used as a benchmark to validate and evaluate the efficiency of the proposed framework. The medical field was chosen because of the problematic bottleneck often associated with knowledge transfer from human domain experts to the knowledge base of an ES. Moreover, there are many uncertainties and complexities associated with diagnostic decision-making of diseases. An ES for diagnosis of CADs was developed with the proposed framework. Therefore, knowledge acquisition of an ES for diagnosis of CADs using FRDDM framework was adopted and applied. Historical diagnostic data of CAD patients were collected from two hospitals in Kano State, Nigeria, which are Murtala Mohammed and Abdullahi Wase General Hospitals. The data was collected with the approval of the Ministry of Health, Kano State, Nigeria. Five hundred and six (506) data instances of diagnostic cases of CAD patients between 2003 and 2017 in both hospitals were captured. Age, chest pain, blood pressure, low density lipoprotein (LDL), glucose, creatinine, high density lipoprotein (HDL), triglyceride, body mass index (BMI), and diagnostic status of the patients were the attributes considered and recorded. Table 17.1 shows the description of unit and ranges of each attribute of the CAD dataset.

The cardiologists and biochemists worked closely in both hospitals in defining and understanding the risk factors and symptoms for diagnosis of CADs and other medical terminologies related to the problem domain. The dataset of CADs was preprocessed, cleaned, and built into a desired weka file format called Attribute-Relation File Format. A weka is machine learning software used for data mining and machine learning tasks such as classification and regression among other tasks.

An improved C4.5 classification algorithm was chosen and used for finding hidden patterns or useful knowledge in the CADs dataset. The algorithm was proposed by (Yahaya et al., 2018) in which L's hospital rule was used, and the algorithm uses an average of information gain and information gain ratio instead of information gain ratio used by conventional C4.5 algorithm (Yahaya et al., 2018). The algorithm has also less time complexity and a higher level of prediction accuracy compared to traditional C4.5 algorithm. Hence, it has $O(n)$ time complexity, which is much smaller compared to C4.5 algorithm that has $O(n(\log_2 n)^2)$ (Yahaya et al., 2018). The improved C4.5 data mining algorithm was encoded into weka and ran simultaneously with C4.5 and random tree algorithms. The performance result of the algorithms is shown in Table 17.2.

The decision tree generated by using improved C4.5 was converted or transformed into crisp rules. Next are some of the corresponding crisp rules generated from the decision tree:

a) IF (Heart Rate < 99.5 bpm & BP < 152.5 mm Hg & Triglyceride < 315.5 mg/dL & Creatinine < 0.15 mg/dL & Age - < 47 yr) THEN Negative

b) IF (Heart Rate < 99.5 bpm & BP < 152.5 mm Hg & Triglyceride < 315.5 mg/dL & Creatinine < 0.15 mg/dL & Age - > 47 yr) THEN Positive

TABLE 17.1 Description of units and ranges of the attributes of CAD dataset.

SN	Attribute	Units	Range
1	Age	yr	1–150
2	Blood pressure	mmHg	90–190
3	Glucose	mg/dL	37–295
4	Cholesterol	mg/dL	128–575
5	Triglyceride	mg/dL	40–690
6	HDL	mg/dL	10.6–73
7	LDL	mg/dL	10–220
8	Creatinine	mg/dL	0.6–3.3
9	Body mass	kg/m^2	20.28–40.25
10	Heart rate	bpm	42–124
11	Chest pain	Typical angina (4), atypical angina (3), nonanginal pain (2), asymptomatic (1)	1–4
12	Diagnosis of CAD	Positive (1), negative (2)	0,1

TABLE 17.2 Performance evaluation results.

SN	Algorithm (data mining classifier)	Accuracy (%)
1	C4.5	83.99
2	Random tree	82.81
3	Improved C4.5	86.56

c) IF (Heart Rate < 99.5 bpm & BP < 152.5 mm Hg & Triglyceride ≥ 152.2 mg/dL & Creatinine < 2.85 mg/dL) THEN Negative

d) IF (Heart Rate < 99.5 bpm & BP < 152.5 mm Hg & Triglyceride ≥ 152.2 mg/dL & Creatinine => 1.52 mg/dL & Chest pain = non_anginal) THEN Negative

e) IF (Heart Rate < 99.5 bpm & BP < 152.5 mm Hg & Triglyceride ≥ 152.2 mg/dL & Creatinine =>2.2 mg/dL & Chest pain = asymt & BMI ≥ 19 kg/m^2) THEN Negative

f) IF (Heart Rate < 99.5 bpm & BP < 152.5 mm Hg & Triglyceride ≥ 152.2 mg/dL & Creatinine => 2.2 mg/dL & Chest pain = asymt & BMI ≥ 19 & age < 65 yr) THEN Positive

g) IF (Heart Rate < 99.5 bpm & BP < 152.5 mm Hg & Triglyceride ≥ 152.2 mg/dL & Creatinine => 2.2 mg/dL & Chest pain = atyp_angina & Glucose < 69.5 mg/dL) THEN Positive

h) IF (Heart Rate < 99.5 bpm & BP < 152.5 mm Hg & Triglyceride ≥ 152.2 mg/dL & Creatinine => 2.1 mg/dL & Chest pain = atyp_angina & Glucose ≥ 69.5 mg/dL) THEN Positive

i) IF (Heart Rate ≤ 99.5 bpm & BP < 152.5 mm Hg & Triglyceride ≥ 152.2 mg/dL & Creatinine < 2.1 mg/dL & Chest pain = atyp_angina & Glucose ≥ 69.5 mg/dL) THEN Negative

j) IF (Heart Rate ≤ 99.5 bpm & BP < 152.5 mm Hg & Triglyceride ≥152.2 mg/dL & Creatinine < 2.1 mg/dL & Chest pain = typ_angina) THEN Positive

RST proposed by Ref (Noor et al., 2009) was adopted for rules selection of the crisp rules of that generated using improved C4.5. Therefore, the crisp set of rules selected using RST are converted into fuzzy set rules. The linguistic variable of each attribute is determined, and membership function of each linguistic variable of both input and output variables are also determined, calculated, and visualized using MATLAB. All the crisp rules generated using improved C4.5 decision tree algorithm were transformed into the corresponding fuzzy set of rules. Table 17.3 shows all the variables of the system with their respective range and linguistic terms.

Trapezoid membership function is adopted for all input variables, while triangular membership is adopted for output variables. Next is the sample of the fuzzy set of rules.

a) IF (HR = Normal & BP = Normal & Triglyceride = Low & Creatinine = Low & Age = Young) THEN Healthy

b) IF (HR = Normal & BP = Low & Triglyceride = Normal = High & Creatinine = Low & Age = Adult) THEN Mild

c) IF (HR = Low & BP = Normal & Triglyceride = Normal & Creatinine = Low & Age = Adult) THEN Moderate

d) IF (HR = Low & BP = Low & Triglyceride = Low & Creatinine = Low & Age = Old) THEN Severe

e) IF (HR = Normal & BP = Normal & Triglyceride = High & Creatinine = Low) THEN Healthy

f) IF (HR = Low & BP = Low & Triglyceride = High & Creatinine = Normal) THEN Mild

g) IF (HR = Normal & BP = Normal & Triglyceride = High & Creatinine = High & Chest pain = non_anginal) THEN Healthy

h) IF (HR = Low & BP = Low & Triglyceride = High & Creatinine = High & Chest pain = non_anginal) THEN Mild

i) IF (HR = Low & BP = Normal & Triglyceride = High & Creatinine = High & Chest pain = asymt & BMI = Normal) THEN Healthy

j) IF (HR = Normal & BP = Low & Triglyceride = High & Creatinine = High & Chest pain = asymt & BMI = High) THEN Mild

k) IF (HR = Low & BP = Normal & Triglyceride = High & Creatinine = High & Chest pain = asymt & BMI = Normal & Age = Young) THEN Moderate.

TABLE 17.3 Input and output variables with linguistic terms and ranges.

Input (variable)	Range	Linguistic term
Age	< 40 yr 35–70 yr > 60 yr	Young Adult Old
Blood pressure (BP)	< 134 mm Hg 128–154 mm Hg >147 mm Hg	Low (hypotension) Normal (nomotension) High (hypertension)
Glucose	< 108 mg/dL 100–126 mg/dL > 120 mg/dL	Low (normal) Normal (prediabetes) High (diabetes)
Cholesterol	< 197 mg/dL 188–225 mg/dL > 217 mg/dL	Low Normal High (hypercholesterolemia)
Triglyceride	< 50 mg/dL 45–150 mg/dL > 142 mg/dL	Low Normal High
High density of lipoprotein (HDL)	< 40 mg/dL 35–59 mg/dL > 55 mg/dL	Low Normal High
Low density of lipoprotein (LDL)	< 130 mg/dL 120–160 mg/dL > 150 mg/dL	Low Normal High
Creatinine	< 0.7 mg/dL 0.5–1.3 mg/dL > 1.1 mg/dL	Low Normal High
Body mass index (BMI)	< 10 kg/m^2 8–25 kg/m^2 > 22 kg/m^2	Underweight Normal Obese
Heart rate (HR)	< 50 bpm 45–75 bpm > 70 bpm	Low Normal Fast
Chest pain	1 2 3 4	Typical angina Atypical angina Nonangina Asymptomatic
Diagnosis result	< 4 2–6 4–8 > 6	Healthy Mild Moderate Severe

6. Fuzzy rule-driven data mining-based expert system

FRDDM framework to knowledge acquisition is an integrated standard fuzzy-based ES architecture. The general framework of a fuzzy system has three components, which include fuzzifier for fuzzification, inference mechanism for reasoning, and defuzzifier for defuzzification, as shown in Fig. 17.2.

The ES that adopted the framework for its knowledge acquisition is termed "fuzzy rule-driven data mining-based expert system." FRDDM framework to knowledge acquisition is an integrated standard fuzzy-based ES architecture, and Fig. 17.3 shows the concept of the architecture.

The fuzzy rule-driven data mining expert system (FRDDM-ES) has three phases, which include the following:

i. **Fuzzification**: In this phase, the crisp set of rules generated using improved C4.5 algorithm has been transformed into a fuzzy set of rules. However, the membership function of the linguistic variables of the input attributes and the output

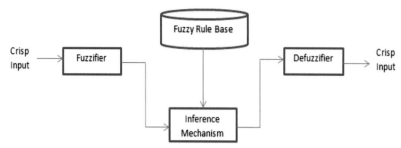

FIGURE 17.2 General framework of a fuzzy system.

attribute of the CAD dataset are determined. The membership functions of all linguistic variables are calculated and visualized using MATLAB. Trapezoid membership function is adopted for all input attributes, while triangular membership is adopted for the output attribute. Following are the linguistic terms defined for each attribute with their respective membership functions. Fig. 17.4 shows the membership functions of the linguistic variables of age.

However, the chest pain input attribute has four linguistic variables, which are typical angina, atypical angina, nonangina, and asymptomatic. One patient can have only one type of chest pain at a time. To represent chest pain, 1 = typical angina, 2 = atypical angina, 3 = nonanginal, and 4 = asymptomatic. Hence, there is no fuzziness or overlap for this input attribute because the patient has just one chest pain at a time. The membership functions of each pain are shown in Fig. 17.5.

The result of diagnosis output variable has four linguistic variables, which are healthy, mild, moderate, and severe. The membership function of each linguistic variable is defined as shown in Fig. 17.6.

Therefore, our proposed framework called fuzzy rule-driven data mining framework to knowledge acquisition is used for fuzzification. MATLAB is used for implementation. The system has 87 rules.

ii. **Knowledge inference or knowledge reasoning:** This involves application of logical rules to the knowledge to deduce new information. The inference engine draws conclusions from the replicated human knowledge and expertise in the knowledge base of the ES, which is the hallmark of the ES (Turban and Ja, 2001; Ishaq et al., 2020). Mamdani

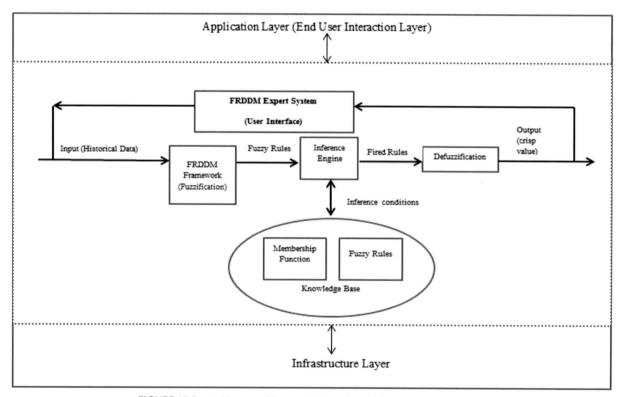

FIGURE 17.3 Architecture of fuzzy rule-driven data mining-based expert system.

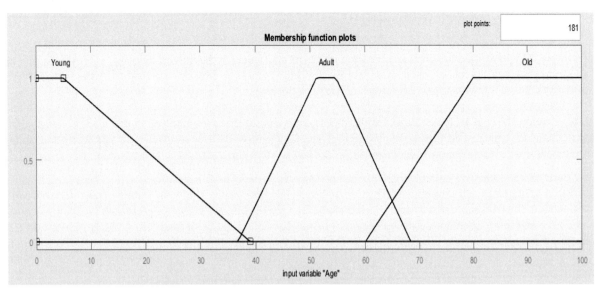

FIGURE 17.4 Membership functions of the linguistic variables of age.

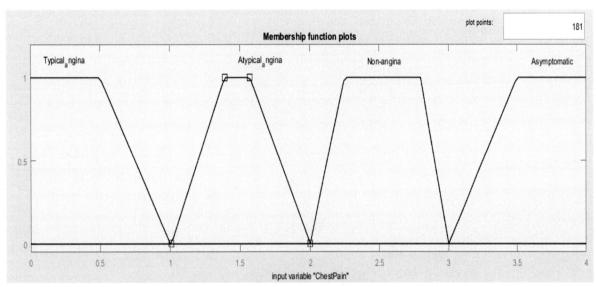

FIGURE 17.5 Membership functions of the linguistic variables of chest pain.

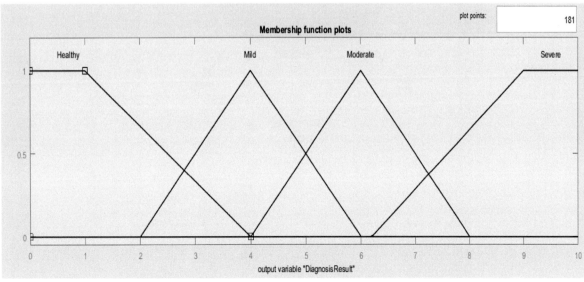

FIGURE 17.6 Membership functions of the linguistic variables of diagnosis.

inference technique is used to stimulate reasoning of expert physicians in the field of diagnosis of CADs in this work. The Mamdani fuzzy inference system is widely used mostly because it provides reasonable results with a relatively simple structure with intuitive and interpretable nature of the rule.

iii. Defuzzification: In this phase, the fuzzy set of rules is converted into a crisp set of rules. This is the opposite operation of fuzzification (Reza et al., 2018; Raza, 2019a,b). The defuzzifier technique employed in this work is called centroid, and it returns the center of the area under the curve (Debasis). Centroid defuzzifier is the most physically appealing and prevalent among defuzzification techniques (Raza, 2019a,b).

Like other fuzzy inference systems, FRDDM-ES implemented in MATLAB has five primary graphical user interfaces (GUIs) that can all interact and exchange information with each other, as shown in Fig. 4.21. Any of the interfaces can read and write both to the workspace and to the disk (the read-only viewers can still exchange plots with the workspace and/or the disk). Like any fuzzy inference system, any or all of these five GUIs can be opened. These GUIs of FRDDM-ES are Membership Editor Viewer, Rule Editor Viewer, Rule Viewer, and Surface Viewer. The GUIs of FRDDM-ES are shown in Fig. 17.7.

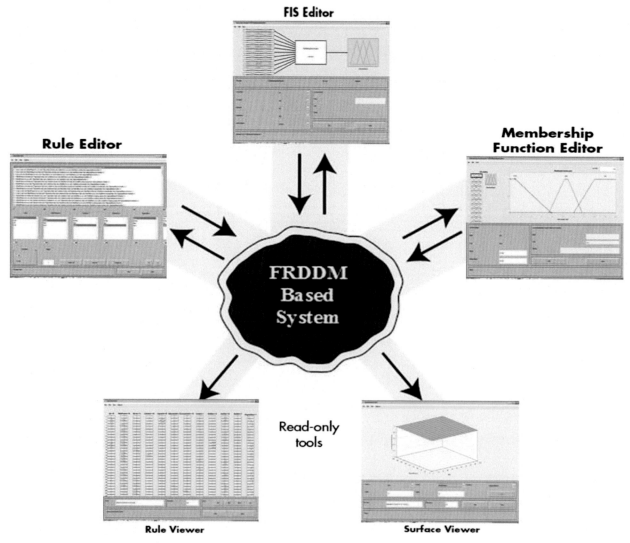

FIGURE 17.7 GUIs of fuzzy rule-driven data mining-based expert system.

7. Evaluation of the fuzzy rule-driven data mining framework-based expert system

There are four classes of linguistic variables of the system output in FRDDM-ES, which are healthy, mild, moderate, and severe. Patients that are considered normal patients are those whose conditions are healthy or mild, while patients that are considered abnormal patients are those whose conditions are moderate or severe. The following techniques were considered for performance evaluation of the system:

i. True positive (TP) is used to show the number of patients who are abnormal and correctly identified by the system.

ii. True negative (TN) is used to show the number of patients who are normal and correctly identified by the system.

iii. False positive (FP) is used to show the number of patients who are abnormal and incorrectly identified by the system.

iv. False negative (FN) is used to show the number of patients who are abnormal and incorrectly identified by the system.

v. Specificity is used to show the percentage of patients who are normal and correctly identified by the system. It is determined as follows:

$$\text{Specificity} = \frac{tn}{tn + fp} \tag{17.1}$$

vi. Sensitivity is used to show the percentage of patients who are abnormal and correctly identified by the system. It is determined as shown next:

$$\text{Sensitivity} = \frac{tp}{tp + fn} \tag{17.2}$$

vii. Accuracy is used to show the percentage of patients correctly identified by the system. In the present work (four-class problem), it is determined as follows:

$$\text{Accuracy} = \frac{h + i\, j + k}{N} \tag{17.3}$$

where h is the number of rules correctly classified with healthy condition of the patients, i is the number of rules correctly classified with mild condition of the patients, j is the number of rules correctly classified with moderate condition of the patients, j is the number of rules correctly classified with severe condition of the patients, and N is the total number of rules in the knowledge base of the system.

The knowledge base of the FRDDM-ES has 87 rules with four classes. These rules were validated against the human expert-driven data collected from Murtala Mohammed and Abdullah Wase General Hospitals, Kano. There were 22 rules classified as healthy and 24 rules classified as mild, which were considered for normal or healthy patients. So, the total number of rules classified for healthy patients is 46. While for abnormal patients, 21 rules are classified as moderate and 20 rules as severe. So, the total number of rules classified for abnormal patients is 41. Table 17.4 shows the statistics of the general classes of patients.

Out of 22 rules classified as healthy, 20 rules were correctly in conformity with the data-driven human expert, so only two rules were not in conformity with the data. Out of 24 rules classified as mild, 23 rules were correctly in conformity with data-driven human expert, so only one rule was not in conformity with the data. Therefore, the system correctly classified 43 normal rules; however, three rules were wrongly classified as normal.

Out of 21 rules classified as moderate, 18 rules were correctly in conformity with data-driven human expert, so only three rules were not in conformity with the data. Out of 20 rules classified as severe, 19 rules were correctly in conformity

TABLE 17.4 General classes of patients.

Class	Total number of rules	No. of rules correctly classified	No. of rules wrongly classified
Healthy	22	20	2
Mild	24	23	1
Moderate	21	18	3
Severe	20	19	1
Grand total	**87**	**80**	**7**

with data-driven human expertise, so only one rule was not in conformity with the data. Therefore, the system correctly classified 37 abnormal rules; however, four rules were wrongly classified as abnormal. The validation results of FRDDM-ES are as follows:

a. True positive (TP) = 37
b. True negative (TN) = 43
c. False positive (FP) = 3
d. False negative (FN) = 4
e. Specificity $= \frac{43}{46} = 93.50\%$
f. Sensitivity $= \frac{37}{41} = 90.20\%$
g. Accuracy $= \frac{80}{87} = 91.95\%$

Therefore, the system has 91.95% overall accuracy, which is excellent, so the accuracy determines the proportion of the total number of predictions that were correct. At the same time, the system has 93.50% accuracy to classify normal patients correctly by adopting the proposed framework (specificity) and 90.20% accuracy to classify abnormal patients correctly by adopting the proposed framework (sensitivity). This showed that the system performed excellently by adopting the proposed framework termed "fuzzy rule-driven data mining framework to knowledge acquisition for expert system." Fig. 17.8 shows the system performance.

8. Conclusion

The success of every ES lies in the correctness of the knowledge available in its knowledge base. However, knowledge acquisition has been a problem activity in the development and implementation of ESs, and it is one of the principal challenges for the system engineer. This work proposed a new theoretical and application-oriented framework termed FRDDM to address the issue of the problematic bottleneck often associated with the transfer of knowledge from a human domain expert to a knowledge-based ES, which is called "knowledge acquisition." The framework has been proven to be a very efficient approach for modeling diagnosis of disease, and it can be further applied in other domains such as manufacturing, engineering, and management, among others.

9. Limitations and future direction

The framework proposed in this study was applied to develop a fuzzy ES for diagnosis of CADs to efficiently determine its accuracy. Therefore, the framework needs to be further applied in other domains such as agriculture, mining, education, and learning. In the future, the framework can be applied by levering fuzzy type 2 instead of type 1 because fizzy type 2 handles uncertainty and complexity more appropriately than fuzzy type 1. Adaptive network-based fuzzy inference technique can be used to further improve the framework in future work because the technique integrates both fuzzy logic and neutral network, and this will further improve the framework.

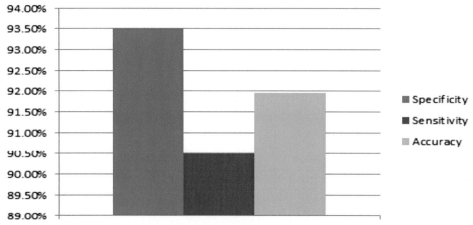

FIGURE 17.8 System performance.

References

Batista, G., Monard, M.C., 2003. Experimental Comparison of K-Nearest Neighbour and Mean or Mode Imputation Methods With the Internal Strategies Used by C4.5 and CN2 to Treat Missing Data. Tech. Rep. University of Sao Paulo.

Benfer, R., Brent, E., Furbee, L., 2012. Knowledge Acquisitio in Expert Systems. SAGE Publications, Inc., pp. 36−52

Boose, J.H., 1989. A survey of knowledge acquisition techniques and tools. Knowl. Acquis. 1 (1), 3−37.

Crowther, P., Hartnett, J., 1996. Using repertory grids for knowledge acquisition for spatial expert systems. In: Proceeding of IEEE, Australian New Zealand Conference on Intelligent Information Systems.

Debabrata, P., Mandana, K.M., Sarbajit, P., Debranjan, S., Chandan, C., 2012. Fuzzy expert system approach for coronary artery disease screening using clinical parameters. J. Knowl. Based Syst. 36, 162−174.

Debasis, S., 2018. Defuzzification Techniques. Retrieved from. http://cse.iitkgp.ac.in/∼dsamanta/courses/sca/resources/slides/FL-03%20Defuzzification.pdf. (Accessed 29 January 2020).

Devraj, R.J., Vikas, D., 2015. Expert system for the management of insect-pests in pulse crops. In: Proceedings of IEEE, 2nd International Conference on Computing for Sustainable Global Development (INDIACom).

Evsukoff, A., Gentil, S., Branco, A.C.S., 1997. A knowledge acquisition method for fuzzy expert systems in diagnosis problems. In: Proceedings of IEE 6th International Fuzzy Systems Conference.

Fayyad, U., Piatesky-Shapiro, G., Smyth, P., Uthurusamy, R. (Eds.), 1996. Advances in Knowledge Discovery and Data Mining. AAAI Press, Cambridge.

Feigenbaum, E.A., 1982. Knowledge Engineering. Department of Computer Science, Stanford University, Stanford, CA.

Goodall, A., 1985. Expert Systems (Computer Science). Learned Information, University of California.

Hart, A., 1986. Knowledge Acquisition for Expert Systems. McGraw-Hill, New York.

Haruna, A.A., Muhammad, L.J., Yahaya, B.Z., et al., 2019. An improved C4.5 data mining driven algorithm for the diagnosis of coronary artery disease. In: 2019 International Conference on Digitization (ICD), Sharjah, United Arab Emirates, pp. 48−52.

Hoi-Kau, Y., Richards, T.J., 1993. GTKAT: a grounded theory based knowledge acquisition tool for expert systems. In: Proceedings of IEEE, First New Zealand International Two-Stream Conference on Artificial Neural Networks and Expert Systems.

Hongmei, Y., Yingtao, J., Jun, Z., Bingmei, F., 2002. Internet-based knowledge acquisition and management method to build large-scale medical expert systems. In: Proceeding of IEEE, Second Joint 24th Annual Conference and the Annual Fall Meeting of the Biomedical Engineering Society] [Engineering in Medicine and Biology].

Hussain, S., Muhammad, L.J., Ishaq, F.S., Yakubu, A., Mohammed, I.A., 2019. Performance evaluation of various data mining algorithms on road traffic accident dataset. In: Satapathy, S., Joshi, A. (Eds.), Information and Communication Technology for Intelligent Systems. Smart Innovation, Systems and Technologies, vol. 106. Springer, Singapore.

Idris, M., Pervez, A., Tariq, J.A., Syed, S.Z., 2013. Fuzzy rule based classification for heart dataset using fuzzy decision tree algorithm based on fuzzy RDBMS world. Appl. Sci. J. 28 (9), 1331−1335.

Ishaq, F.S., Muhammad, L.J., Yahaya, B.Z., Abubakar, A., 2020. Fuzzy based expert system for diagnosis of diabetes mellitus. Int. J. Adv. Sci. Technol. 136, 39−50.

Ji, J., Pang, W., Zhou, C., Han, X., Wang, Z., 2012. A fuzzy k-prototype clustering algorithm for mixed numeric and categorical data. Knowl. Based Syst. 30, 129−135.

Jirawit, Y., Thepparit, S., Keshav, D., 2017. STEM learning concept with fuzzy inference for organic rice farming knowledge acquisition. In: Proceeding of IEEE, 11th International Conference on Software, Knowledge, Information Management and Applications (SKIMA).

Lei, D., Qingdong, L., Xingyue, S., Chen, B., 2012. Graphical representation technology for knowledge acquisition of fault diagnosis system. In: Proceeding of IEEE International Conference on Computer Science and Service System.

Li, Y., Fu, Z., 2007. A framework of knowledge transfer process in expert system development. In: 2007 International Conference on Wireless Communications, Networking and Mobile Computing, Shanghai, pp. 5597−5600.

Lianxiang, J., Huawang, L., Genqing, Y., Qinrong, Y., 2009. Knowledge acquisition model for satellite fault diagnosis expert system. In: Proceeding of IEEE International Conference on Computational Intelligence and Software Engineering.

Muhammad, L.J., Garba, A., Abba, G., 2015. Security challenges for building knowledge based economy in Nigeria. Int. J. Secur. Appl. 9, 1.

Muhammad, L.J., Garba, E.J., Oye, N.D., Wajiga, G.M., 2018. On the problems of knowledge acquisition and representation of expert system for diagnosis of coronary artery disease (CAD). Int. J. u- e- Serv. Sci. Technol. 11 (3), 49−58.

Muhammad, L.J., Ahmad, A.H., Ibrahim, A.M., et al., 2019a. Performance evaluation of classification data mining algorithms on coronary artery disease dataset. In: IEEE 9th International Conference on Computer and Knowledge Engineering (ICCKE 2019). IEEE. Ferdowsi University of Mashhad 978-1-7281-5075-8/19/$31.00 ©.

Muhammad, L.J., Garba, E.J., Oye, N.D., Wajiga, G.M., 2019b. Modelling techniques for knowledge representation of expert system: A survey. J. Appl. Comput. Sci. Math. 13 (28).

Muhammad, L.J., Islam, M.M., Usman, S.S., et al., 2020. Predictive data mining models for novel coronavirus (COVID-19) infected patients' recovery. SN Comput. Sci. 1, 206.

Muhammad, L.J., Algehyne, E.A., Usman, S.S., 2020. Predictive supervised machine learning models for diabetes mellitus. Nat. Comput. Sci. 1, 240. https://doi.org/10.1007/s42979-020-00250-8.

Noor, A.S., Venkatachalam, P.A., Ahmad, F.H., 2009. Diagnosis of coronary artery disease using artificial intelligence based decision support system. In: Proceedings of the International Conference on Man-Machine Systems (ICoMMS).

Okafor, E.C., Osuagwu, C.C., 2007. Issues in structuring the knowledge-base of expert systems. Electron. J. Knowl. Manag. 5 (3), 313−322.

Oladipupo, O.O., 2012. A Fuzzy Association Rule Mining Expert-Driven Approach to Knowledge Acquisition (Ph.D. thesis). Covenant University.

Pandey, B., Mishra, R.B., 2009. Knowledge and intelligent computing system in medicine. Comput. Biol. Med. https://doi.org/10.1016/j.compbiomed.2008.12.008.

Pathak, A.K., Arul, V.J., 2020. A predictive model for heart disease diagnosis using fuzzy logic and decision tree. In: Elçi, A., Sa, P., Modi, C., Olague, G., Sahoo, M., Bakshi, S. (Eds.), Smart Computing Paradigms: New Progresses and Challenges. Advances in Intelligent Systems and Computing, vol. 767. Springer, Singapore.

Pratihar, D.K., 2013. Soft Computing: Fundamentals and Applications.

Qingzhang, C., Chao, C., Xiaoying, C., 2007. An intelligent knowledge discovery system with a novel knowledge acquisition methodology. In: Proceeding of EEE, Fourth International Conference on Fuzzy Systems and Knowledge Discovery.

Raza, K., 2019a. Improving the prediction accuracy of heart disease with ensemble learning and majority voting rule. In: Advances in Ubiquitous Sensing Applications for Healthcare, U-Healthcare Monitoring Systems: Design and Applications. Academic Press, Elsevier, pp. 179−196. https://doi.org/10.1016/B978-0-12-815370-3.00008-6.

Raza, K., 2019b. Fuzzy logic based approaches for gene regulatory network inference. Artif. Intell. Med. 97, 189−203. https://doi.org/10.1016/j.artmed.2018.12.004.

Reza, S., Hadi, K.A., Mostafa, L., Marjan, G., Hossein, D., Kazem, Z., 2018. Design a fuzzy rule-based expert system to aid earlier diagnosis of gastric cancer. Acta Inform. Med. 26 (1), 19−23.

Rybina, G.V., Danyakin, I.D., 2017. Combined method of automated temporal information acquisition for development of knowledge bases of intelligent systems. In: 2017 2nd International Conference on Knowledge Engineering and Applications (ICKEA), London, pp. 123−127.

Shah, S., Roy, R., Tiwari, A., 2006. Development of fuzzy expert system for customer and service advisor categorization within contact center environment. In: Applications of Soft Computing: Recent Trends. Springer Berlin Heidelberg, New York, pp. 197−206.

Singh, R., 2013. JESS Based Expert System for Rice Plant Disease Diagnosis (Ph.D. thesis). Department of Computer Science, Gauhati University, pp. 133−154.

Sneha, L.V., Swetha, P.Y.L., Bhavya, M., Geetha, G., Suhasini, D.K., 2012. Combined methodology of the classification rules for medical data-sets. Int. J. Eng. Trends Technol. 3 (1), 32−36.

Spangler, A.M., Ray, C.D., Hamaker, K., 1989. Knowledge acquisition for expert system development. Comput. Electron. Agric. 4, 23−32.

Tsipouras, M.G., Exarchos, T.P., Fotiadis, D.I., Kotsia, A., Naka, A., Michalis, L.K., 2008. A decision support system for the diagnosis of coronary artery disease. In: Proceedings of the IEEE Symposium on Computer-Based Medical Systems.

Turban, E., Ja, E., 2001. Decision Support Systems and Expert Systems. Copyright, sixth ed. Prentice Hall, Upper Saddle River, NJ.

Vlaanderen, M.J., 1990. Automated Knowledge Acquisition for Expert Systems: An Overview. Faculty of Philosophy. Erarmus University Rotterdam.

Xiaosheng, L., Bo, Z., 2008. Research on knowledge base of dam safety monitoring expert system based on relational database. In: Proceeding of IEEE International Symposium on Knowledge Acquisition and Modeling Workshop.

Yahaya, B.Z., Muhammad, L.J., Abdulganiyyu, N., Ishaq, F.S., 2018. An improved C4.5 algorithm using L' hospital rule for large dataset. Indian J. Sci. Technol. 11 (47), 1−8.

Yahaya, B.Z., Muhammad, L.J., Abdulganiyyu, N., Ishaq, F.S., Atomsa, Y., 2019. Arithmetic mean of information gain and correlation ratio based decision tree algorithm for accident dataset mining: a case study of accident dataset of Gombe − Numan −Yola high way. Niger. Int. J. Adv. Sci. Technol. 127, 51−58.

Yan, L., Zetian, F., 2007. A framework of knowledge transfer process in expert system development. In: IEEE, International Conference on Wireless Communications, Networking and Mobile Computing.

Further reading

Maqbool, A., Rahman, A., Wajahat, A.K., Soyeon, C.H., Jaehun, B., Taeho, H., Dohyeong, K., Sungyoung, L., Byeong, H.K., 2018. A data-driven knowledge acquisition system: an end-to-end knowledge engineering process for generating production rules. Special section on recent computational methods in knowledge engineering and intelligence computation. IEEE J. Access 6, 15587−15605.

Chapter 18

An efficient bioinformatics algorithm for healthcare: Detection and counting of leukocytes, blasts, and erythrocytes

Ana Carolina Borges Monteiro[1,*], Yuzo Iano[1], Reinaldo Padilha França[1] and Rangel Arthur[2]

[1]*School of Electrical Engineering and Computing (FEEC), State University of Campinas (UNICAMP), Campinas, São Paulo, Brazil;* [2]*Faculty of Technology (FT), State University of Campinas (UNICAMP), Limeira, São Paulo, Brazil*

Corresponding authors: E-mail: monteiro@decom.fee.unicamp.br, padilha@decom.fee.unicamp.br

Chapter outline

1. Introduction

Translational research is understood as research that ranges from basic science to the practical application of that knowledge. In the case of medicine, research groups are usually divided into basic research groups and clinical research groups, leaving a gap between these two types of research, so sometimes the knowledge produced by basic research is not well used (Mitchell, 2016).

Translational medicine adds advantages to the development of research today, respecting all the precepts of research ethics, allowing the reduction of the doctor's need to delve into less relevant details of basic research and to be able to focus on treatment goals; simultaneously, the basic researcher avoids the need for specialized theoretical knowledge, often irrelevant to him, since interdisciplinarity is one of his guidelines. This area has specific objectives related to the generation and dissemination of scientific knowledge in the area, inserting the program's graduates in teaching and research institutions as researchers, who are also committed to developing teaching strategies aimed at basic education, disseminating science, and disseminating extramural knowledge (Guo and Liu, 2018; Malley, 2018).

Through it, areas at different stages of development are approached, which in many cases are situations in which bench research is extremely advanced compared to clinical studies, and it is through translational medicine that it is possible to bring together its extensions of research. Still, technologies under development can be applied more quickly in surgical and diagnostic procedures, for example (Mediouni et al., 2018).

Translational medicine integrates basic research groups with clinical research groups, closing the gap between these two types of research, coupled with its primary guideline to bring up the most relevant findings, quickly and reliably. Since it is possible to efficiently know the pathophysiology of diseases, favoring the development of new drugs and their clinical

Translational Bioinformatics in Healthcare and Medicine. https://doi.org/10.1016/B978-0-323-89824-9.00018-5

application, there is an acceleration of the transmission of knowledge and the creation of therapeutic protocols (Barile et al., 2017; Lamb and Curtin, 2019).

With the application of joint efforts through multidisciplinary teams, it becomes faster to obtain practical results, whether for clinical, surgical treatments, or technology development in the medical field. Just as the necessary structure for the application of translational medicine must meet this new concept of faster transfer of information from the laboratory to clinical practice, it also involves changes in teaching concepts, implying greater collaboration between different disciplines of knowledge such as chemistry, physics, engineering, and transdisciplinary research, among others (Lamb and Curtin, 2019; Soldner and Jaenisch, 2018).

Therefore, this chapter presents a bioinformatics algorithm with the objective of reaching all these points, highlighting at lower computational cost and less processing time, correlated with the high precision and accuracy in the identification, detection, counting, and classification of erythrocytes (RBC) and leukocytes present in digital sample images of blood smear fields stained, as well as related to better execution performance. The focus is on the horizon of bioinformatics and translational medicine guidelines, with the purpose of developing a low-cost methodology, without the need for specific equipment, which is accessible to disadvantaged populations.

2. Vision computational and health informatics from a historical perspective

Vision is the most advanced human sense acting directly on human perception. Since humans are restricted to the visual range of the electromagnetic spectrum, devices/equipment designed to display images cover almost every electromagnetic spectrum. In this way, devices/equipment can act on imaging from sources that humans are familiar with to associate with imaging, such as computer-generated digital images, electron microscopy, or even ultrasound. Thus, digital image processing (science understood as the manipulation of an image) fits the broad and vast area of applicability (Reisman et al., 2018; Sliney, 2016).

An image contains $f(x, y)$, being delimited as a two-dimensional continuous function, having x and y as the coordinates of the spatial plane, together with the amplitude of f in whatever duo of coordinates (x, y) that is known the grayscale intensity. The amplitude values as well as x and y, of f, are all finite, and are called digital imaging. The digital image is made up of a finite number of elements, with each element having its own value as well as location, which are called pixels (Shih and Frank, 2017; Russ, 2016).

Thus, the attention in digital image processing techniques comes from two main areas of application: (1) pictorial information improvement for human understanding and (2) image data processing for autonomous machine storage, representation for perception, and transmission. However, there is no general agreement in the literature as to at what point does image processing end and several other reports of related areas appear as computer vision and image analysis. This differentiation is often carried out to determine image processing as a study discipline where both process inputs are images (Dubey et al., 2018; Bajaj et al., 2018).

The first application of digital imaging was carried out by the newspaper industry by sending images via a submarine cable going from New York to London, and vice versa. It was introduced in the mid-1920s, by the Bartlane cable image transmission system, which had the advantage of reducing the time from more than a week to just 3 h. After crossing the Atlantic, the images were received by specialized equipment, which was responsible for the reconstruction and printing of the image (Campbell-Kelly, 2018; Haigh et al., 2016).

However, some initial problems in the visual quality of the digital image related to printing procedures and color level intensity distribution have been reported. For this reason, the printing method used was terminated in the early 1920s and was replaced by a technique based on reproducing photographs taken on punched tapes at the telegraph terminal reception. In 1929, the Bartlene system was improved to encode images in 15 distinct gray levels. During this period, the system was introduced for the development of a film plate via light beams, which was modulated by encoded imaging tape. This fact considerably improved the process (Seeram, 2015).

The examples referred to involved only digital images and do not consider digital image processing because computers had not yet been invented. Thus, it can be seen that the history of digital image processing has a direct dependence on the evolution of digital computers, devices, equipment, and technologies that support the inclusion of data storage, presentation, and transmission. Through the invention of abacus over 500 years ago in Asia Minor was the foundation for the invention of today's computers, which began to be developed in the last 200 years. The word "computer" comes from the verb "compute" which, in turn, means "calculate" In the 17th century, Scottish mathematician John Napier was responsible for the invention of the "slide rule" It was the first analog counting instrument capable of performing logarithmic calculations. This invention was considered the mother of modern calculators (Nicholls, 2019; Collen and Ball, 2015).

However, only in 1940, the two main concepts for the development of the modern digital computer were created: (1) computational branch and (2) memory that stores a program and its data. Such concepts are the establishment of the main hardware item of a computer, also known as processor or CPU (central processing unit). Started with von Neumann, it was a series of major advances that have made today's computers capable of digital image processing (Seeram, 2015; Nicholls, 2019).

In the 1950s, first-generation computers operated by electronic circuits and valves were created. They had restricted use, besides being huge and consuming a lot of energy. An example is the first electronic digital computer, known as the Electronic Numerical Integrator and Computer (ENIAC), which consumed about 200 kW and had 19,000 valves. For the next decade, still very large, second-generation computers operated employing transistors, which replaced the larger and slower valves. In this period, they were already being sold commercially (Nicholls, 2019; Collen and Ball, 2015).

These early computers were capable of performing significant image processing tasks. A work used computational techniques for the enhancement of images acquired by a space probe that began in Pasadena, California, in the mid-1964s, where Ranger 7, designed by the Jet Propulsion Laboratory, stood close to the moon and captured images of the lunar surface and transmitted them. Later, this was performed by a computer processor that corrected several types of image distortion inherent at the edge of television and camera (Baxevanis et al., 2020). In parallel with these space applications, the potential of digital image processing started to be used in remote observation, medical imaging, astronomy, and terrestrial resources (Seeram, 2015; Nicholls, 2019; Collen and Ball, 2015).

During the 1970s, axial computed tomography (CAT) was also invented, also denominated computed tomography, which for application of medical diagnostic image processing is one of the most significant milestones. CAT is a procedure in which a detector ring surrounds the patient (or even object) and an X-ray source connected to the detector ring is rotated over the object. X-rays, in turn, cross the object and are collected by the ring detectors. Tomography constitutes algorithms using the data obtained to construct an image representing the relative portion through the 3D object (Nelson and Staggers, 2016).

Tomography was created by Allan M. Cormack and Godfrey N. Hounsfield, winning Nobel Prize for medicine in 1979. Importantly, in 1895, the X-ray was discovered by Wilhelm Conrad Roentgen, winning in 1910 the Nobel Prize in physics. From inventions like these, a century later, they were leading and stimulating the image processing areas to the most active application of the day. Another example is from the main uses of gamma-ray imaging used in nuclear medicine. The procedure consists of injecting radioactive isotope emitting gamma rays on the patient and observing its decay. The images are produced by collecting the gamma-ray emission from the detectors. The principle is the same as tomography and X-ray (Seeram, 2015; Nelson and Staggers, 2016; Figueiredo et al., 2017).

Along with the creation of new imaging diagnostic methodologies, the first difficulties in acquiring medical images arose, many of them due to the presence of noise in the images. Thus, around the early 1970s came the area entitled medical informatics. This branch of knowledge can be seen as an interdisciplinary area that links problems from medical areas with engineering solving techniques. Health informatics studies develop computer systems supporting medical activities, which is a specialization that links communications and healthcare IT (information technology) with a focus on improving patient care. It deals with the analysis and digital processing of bioelectric signals, digital processing of medical images, acquiring, studying, and managing health data, and applying medical concepts in conjunction with health IT systems to help clinicians provide better care of health. It directly refers to tools, development of monitoring systems, technologies and tactics, diagnostic and decision support, and intelligent systems assisted by computer used by physicians in the provision of care, referring to the use of information science, from electronic medical records to diagnostic tools for pathology (Watts, 2016; Silberstein and John, 2017).

3. The importance of blood medical analysis

Nowadays, the medical areas are facing a challenge: to make quality healthcare possible for underprivileged populations and/or those not assisted by the government. The United States, for example, is a country with great economic power, but its population does not have free access to health. For governance, health is the commitment of each resident individual. On the other hand, we can see Brazil, a developing country that faces some recession in its economy, but nonetheless it provides free health to its entire population from medical care, surgery, and high-cost medicines. However, the Brazilian population that wants this type of free care, called the Unified Health System, faces long queues to reach these benefits. Unfortunately, for health, the time taken to diagnose and start treatment is paramount (Keohane et al., 2019; McPherson and Pincus, 2017).

In this context, we must consider that the first medical examination that points to some type of health problem is the blood count. Complete blood count is a laboratory test value requested in the laboratory medical routine, as it directly offers the analysis and diagnosis of pathologies or is used as an indicator for the detection of various diseases. This exam is formed by leukogram and platelet, as well as erythrogram, evaluating the amount and morphology of these cell types (Monteiro et al., 2017; Borges Monteiro et al., 2019; Wei et al., 2017).

Red blood cells, erythrocytes or RBC, are visualized as biconcave disc-shaped cells that are anucleated and responsible for transporting oxygen through four iron molecules, constituted by a tetramer (two α chains, and two β chains). The most striking feature of cell maturation is the reticulocyte exit from the bone marrow into the bloodstream, where within 72 h is the expulsion of its cell nucleus, resulting in erythrocytes (Monteiro et al., 2017; Borges Monteiro et al., 2019; Wei et al., 2017).

Leukocytes are the body's defense cells, composing the adaptive immune response, and also the innate immune response. They are also known as white blood cells or WBCs and are related to two distinct classes, being agranulocyte and granulocyte. Granulocyte has antimicrobial and antiinflammatory action, i.e., they are the defense cells that disperse granules in the cytoplasm; with the presence of cytoplasmic granules, it is characteristic that these cells have a variable amount of lobes, known as polymorphonuclear cells, more specifically, eosinophils, basophils, and neutrophils. Agranulocyte has only one lobe, not having granules visible under optical microscopy, and it is called a monomorphonuclear cell, which in more detail are monocytes and lymphocytes (Monteiro et al., 2017; Borges Monteiro et al., 2019; Wei et al., 2017).

In the course of hematopoiesis, the cells tend to integrate the granulocytic series, synthesizing granules and cytoplasmic proteins, resulting in neutrophils, eosinophils, and basophils. The azurophilic in the color characteristic is relative to primary granules, in charge of the conversion of precursor cells known as myeloblasts (immature blood cells) into promyelocytes (granulocyte precursor). Subsequently, the emergence of specific granules occurs, being incumbent for the progression to neutrophil, eosinophil, and basophil myelocytes (Monteiro et al., 2017).

Platelets are also called thrombocytes, and they are blood cells responsible for blood clotting. They are 2−3 μm in diameter and round in shape. Thrombopoietin drives the bone marrow to produce megakaryocytes, which are large cells, usually manufactured in the liver, where from their cytoplasm, platelets are made. Platelets not used in clots circulate for 7 to 10 days and are then destroyed (Monteiro et al., 2017; Borges Monteiro et al., 2019).

4. Translational medicine

The concept of translational research has gained prominence within the scientific community, where the aim of translational research is to promote integration between producers and users of scientific research, and it is associated with the transfer of biomedical knowledge generated in basic research to different areas of clinical research. It is considered the fastest way for scientific information to be transmitted both for clinical research and for healthcare practice, especially concerning the diagnosis, treatment, and prevention of diseases, since these investigations contribute to a better understanding and perception of pathophysiologic mechanisms and complex interactions that occur in biologic systems (Mitchell, 2016; Lamb and Curtin, 2019).

Translational research means an effective transfer of new knowledge, mechanisms, and techniques for the health of the population, collaborating, unequivocally, for medical decision-making. It seeks to design and study, as soon as possible, new diagnostic and/or therapeutic approaches, based on the most recent advances in basic science and/or technology. However, it is necessary to have a work team made up of different professionals with different expertise able to identify and prioritize needs and situations of greater complexity to effectively use the results obtained to solve clinical or public health problems (Guo and Liu, 2018; Mediouni et al., 2018).

It is characterized as a biphasic process, since new knowledge moves from basic science to clinical science, i.e., from the laboratory to the bedside, and from clinical science to the health of patients and public health, i.e., at the bedside health care, and bidirectional, as the flow of information migrates from the laboratory to the clinic and from the clinic back to the laboratory, i.e., bench to bedside and back again. Within the scope of clinical analysis, this transfer of knowledge between the basic and clinical sciences, based on translational investigations, has had an impact on the areas of immunology, endocrinology, oncology, neurology, neuroscience, and human reproduction (Barile et al., 2017; Wei et al., 2017; Hsu and Hwang, 2019).

Of the same importance that translational clinical analysis provides greater scientific support for medical interventions, informing in which context these interventions will be most effective, translational research in the clinical laboratory demonstrates how a group of biochemical and molecular variables contributes to the choice of the best pharmacologic and/or clinical or surgical intervention (Meyers, 2018).

However, one of the main challenges within the medical and educational environment today is translational research, in the sense of reducing the gaps between scientific knowledge and effective strategies in healthcare that improve patient outcomes. The concept of translational medicine encompasses three aspects related to the acceleration of transmission of knowledge from basic research to the clinical application, respective to the deepening of clinical observations, in search of a better pathophysiologic understanding through interaction with basic science and, consequently, application to professionals of basic knowledge and concepts from clinical research (Albani and Prakken, 2009; Piccini et al., 2009).

Translational medicine seeks to accelerate the transmission of knowledge generated in research, transforming this knowledge into practical instruments for diagnostic investigation and/or treatments, in the same way as the transfer of knowledge obtained in other areas of science or even from bench experiences to clinical practice of the doctor, with a special emphasis on accelerating the application of what we know for the benefit of patients, thus creating a new paradigm in medical research called "bench to bed" (Mitchell, 2016; McCarthy et al., 2013).

Thus, translational medicine seeks to offer patients in the health system better quality in terms of treatment and outcome of results. It is a new paradigm that allows the transference of knowledge constructed on the bench to clinical practice and correlates and associates with the field of public health. One of the goals of translational medicine, in reality, is broader and more complex, consisting of naturally developing the idea in the use of knowledge originated not only in biomedical laboratories but also from other disciplines—engineering, chemistry, physics, biology, informatics, among other areas knowledge—to test its validity in clinical pathophysiology research, tests, and clinical trials among others, aiming to discover and/or verify the pharmacodynamic, pharmacologic, clinical and/or other effects of medication and/or identify adverse reactions, as well as the development of new methodologies for greater agility in the diagnosis of diseases (Matthews et al., 2006; Felfly and Haddad, 2014).

Thus, researchers in the field of healthcare and managers, as well as workers in the exact areas of knowledge, have been directing research with this focus and objectivity, based on the knowledge conceived in biomedical laboratories or even not, relating that learning produced in basic and applied sciences, with a focus improving health services. Notwithstanding, there is the need to transfer the knowledge obtained in clinical research to medical practice and the improvement of health services, scheduling research on events, effectiveness, and cost-effectiveness, comparing procedures already tested (Littman et al., 2007; Plebani, 2008).

Translational medicine is a study that is optimizing the potential of the scientific method and the multidisciplinary nature of science, thus accelerating the transfer of knowledge for the application and improvement of health services. It contributes to the development of innovative approaches, accelerating the transfer of knowledge. It also encourages the training of interdisciplinary researchers, who can establish a network of information exchanges and partnerships required for the development of translational medicine and contributions to public health (Kurpinski et al., 2014).

Such contributions to public health maximize health decision-making, which is fundamental for maintaining the health of the population, whether with disease prevention, as in the case of immunizations and vaccines, or with health promotion actions, as in the case of new diagnostic methods, aiming at improving the quality of life of the population affected or not by health problems (Terzic and Waldman, 2010).

5. Bioinformatics

Bioinformatics aggregates knowledge from biosciences, informatics, and exact sciences for the acquisition, management, analysis, and prognosis of medical and biologic data, which consists of data or measures collected from biologic sources such as DNA, RNA, proteins, enzymes, biologic images, among others. It is the marriage between computer science and biology, since computers are able to store more and more information, to process it more and more quickly, at an ever lower cost (Lesk, 2019).

It is a conjunction of IT, computer science, and genetics to not only ascertain and assay genetic information, but all biologic data that requires analysis and processing. It works in hospitals, clinics, pharmaceutical, agricultural, medical, and biomedical industries, in biotechnology, microbiology, clinical, and image analysis laboratories, and in applications in several areas, such as health, environment, and agriculture. Through the use of informatics and computation together, analysis tools capture and interpret biologic data, integrating mathematical, computational methods, and statistics to assay biologic, biophysical, and biochemical data. This is through technology and science on digital learning, management, processing, treatment, and manipulation of biologic information (Baxevanis et al., 2020).

Currently, the emphasis of bioinformatics is progressively shifting from the accumulation of data to its interpretation. Through the genetic sequencing performed, for example, a large volume of data has been generated over the past few years. These data need to be analyzed, and considering that laboratory analysis is difficult and expensive, sophisticated computational tools are necessary for the analysis of the data obtained (Min et al., 2017).

Bioinformatics is a science that arises as a result of new technologies, mixing concepts from the health field with aspects of the exact sciences to present precise results in molecular analyses. For example, in the health area, in the case of a cancer prognosis, through the analysis of the DNA or RNA sequencing data extracted from the biopsy, it is possible to verify possible significant genetic alterations. As well as through analysis and digital image processing, it is possible to diagnose the disease. Also from the analysis of large databases, related to tumor information, clinical studies, and other information on the subject, using the knowledge built on big data, and using artificial intelligence, it is possible to create and implement algorithms that help in choosing the best treatments for patients (Min et al., 2017; Sehgal et al., 2018; Xia, 2018).

Another context of visualization of bioinformatics is in the pharmaceutical industry, through the supervision and selection of substances and molecules, where from these analyses, it is possible to guide the manipulation of components for the development of medicines (Wooller et al., 2017).

Bioinformatics is an interdisciplinary field, which can be seen as a science that fits within the guidelines of translational medicine, which uses concepts from computing, information science, mathematics, statistics, physics, and chemistry, having a great impact in areas such as medicine. Since the increase in the quantity and complexity of biologic information, it is necessary to gather knowledge of biosciences, informatics, and exact sciences of a multi- and interdisciplinary character to analyze diseases, indicate treatments, and increase the quality of new products and medicines. Since it is necessary to be able to interpret data and transform it into information, it is then possible to recognize patterns that will be used in the analysis (Min et al., 2017; Sehgal et al., 2018; Xia, 2018).

This multi- and interdisciplinary approach applied to biotechnology and health allows the transposition of biologic processes to bioinformatics to understand the applicability in the processes of biosciences, ranging from basic cellular and anatomic knowledge to the generation of trajectories, modeling, simulation, and control of genetic manipulators, fundamentals in molecular biology, and modeling of biomolecule systems (Baxevanis et al., 2020).

Biology today is not only based on laboratory experiments, but also information, in fact, a lot of information. DNA, RNA, and protein sequences, even other biologic data, which is human information, collected from scientific experiments, are generated all the time. This must be stored in databases, each time bigger, and all the information generated must be accessed and "prepared" to be able to be interpreted, which can lead to conclusions that are very relevant to the advancement of science. Bioinformatics is an area of research that requires a multidisciplinary approach, necessarily implying the ease of relating to different areas of knowledge, which requires a capacity for abstraction because the problems are not clear and the solutions need to be further refined (Pucker et al., 2019).

6. Hemogram

The traditional blood count is performed by collecting 4 mL of the patient's venous blood, with or without fasting, in a tube with anticoagulant EDTA (ethylenediaminetetraacetic acid) or even heparin, another natural anticoagulant substance. One should be careful with these samples, avoiding the presence of hemolysis, i.e., broken RBCs that cause the minor counting concerning the utter amount of these cells, or even lipemia that is the presence of triglyceride fat, making it arduous to read by colorimetric methods, or even clots that are relative to lower blood cell counts platelets. It is not advised to use antiinflammatories, antibiotics, or antiallergics hours before the exam, as this may diminish the number of WBCs and may hide allergic or infectious states. Smoking is not advisable at least 2 h before the exam, as this factor results in a change in hematocrit, hemoglobin, and hematimetric indexes (Ciesla, 2018).

Quantitative and qualitative analysis of blood cells leads to precise indications and diagnoses of a wide range of diseases, whether they are hematologic or not. Some of the diseases detected by blood count are genetic anemia (sickle cell anemia, spherocytosis anemia, thalassemia), deficient anemia (iron deficiency anemia, megaloblastic anemia), leukemias, parasitic infections, viruses, allergic reactions, coagulation disorders, hemorrhages, polycythemias, infections, acute infections, and bacterial infections, among others (Ciesla, 2018).

The manual blood count is directly linked to the use of nonautomated equipment along with human performance. This is more time consuming and is less reliable, but it does make the exam cheaper. Due to calculations and counts, it is related to execution by health professionals. In a scenario of small laboratories, it is considered a good alternative as long as the request for exams is low, where in return the cost for the acquirement of reagents and hematologic equipment does not satisfy the cost benefit of the method (Green and Wachsmann-Hogiu, 2015).

Automating the blood count causes greater agility in the performance related to performing these exams as well as releasing the reports. In turn, it will become a more costly procedure taking into account the manual procedure. In the mid-1950s, impedance principle for cell counts was introduced by Coulter Electronics, Inc, based on the factor that in an electrically conductive solution, bad conductor cells are diluted. Through a hole with a diameter around 100 µm, an electric current is passed, causing cell suspension to be weighed. This electrical current comes from two electrodes, one placed on the outside of the hole, negatively charged, and another placed on the inner side of the hole, and positively charged. Every time the cell passes through the hole, it will cause an interruption in the electric current generating a change in conductance. As a result, it will be counted as a particle of each of these interruptions (Monteiro et al., 2019).

The impedance principle, over the years, has been qualified with counters that are able to measure cell volume. It is the outcome of the correlation (similarity or relationship) of the proportionality of the cell volume with the magnitude of the interruption of the electric current, i.e., pulses. It was noted that large pulses increased from larger volumes, just as small pulses corresponded to small volumes. A new idea known as the threshold conception was created, which means a correlation between the magnitude of the cell volume and electric current. This conception corresponds to the classification of these cells concerning their volume, allowing the detection of globular volume, referring to the hematocrit to comply with manual blood counting, because this process complies without the necessity for microcentrifugation. Both the impedance principle and threshold conception are charged for the insertion of multiparameter devices in the market, using separate channels for counting, sufficient for concomitant realization of cellular counts (Ciesla, 2018; Green and Wachsmann-Hogiu, 2015).

In the mid-1960s, it was built up by the conductivity technique that was considered high-frequency electromagnetic current, being accountable for supply information at par cell volume, cytoplasmic content, and nucleus size of granulations. Later, in mid-1970s, hydrodynamic fluid techniques and laser light scatters were inserted, where they preserved the granulations and nuclei of leukocytes (white cells), repressing only the cytoplasmic membrane. These techniques are grounded in the principles of reflection and refraction, and even diffraction of emitted light. However, with respect to these techniques, RBCs are not detected or identified, so one must quantify erythrocytes (RBC) by hydrodynamic focus and flow cytometry to solve this problem, where through a very thin capillary, the erythrocytes are counted one by one. By laser beam, with light scattering analyzing at different angles of deviation, the RBCs are then subjected, where cell size is indicated at zero degrees, and at 10 degrees, there is an indication of the internal structure, and at 90 degrees, it is possible to identify leukocytes and their granulation content as well as their lobularity characteristics (Green and Wachsmann-Hogiu, 2015; Xu et al., 2016; Qiu et al., 2018).

In present times, there is a vast scenario of multiparameter devices using conductivity, impedance, and light scattering techniques, which may also be associated with the use of reagents performing analysis of cytochemical characteristics of cells and even specific cell types, as myeloperoxidase (abundant in neutrophilic granulocytes) (Green and Wachsmann-Hogiu, 2015).

7. Blood counting and digital image processing

In recent years, many imaging techniques have been used for medical purposes, including blood cell detections and counts in digital blood smear images.

Through a review of the literature, it is possible to note that in 2011, Kareem and colleagues developed a new methodology that avails the basic knowledge concerning the brightness and structure of the elements. The Giemsa dye has properties where staining a certain sample assists in identification by segment, and it identifies the exact location of cells present in the digital image with respect to the total quantity of erythrocytes as well as their exact position on Giemsa-stained slides (Kareem et al., 2011).

Arivu et al., in mid-2012, carried out a blood cell count by converting to grayscale, performing segmentation, then noise removal, and so removed border elements, and finally counted RBCs. For WBCs, they followed a digital image conversion to binary approach, performing noise reduction, then space-filling, and finally removing cells with weakly determine borders (Arivu Selvan and Moorthy, 2012). In the same year, Nasrul Humaimi developed a computer vision system capable of detecting together with estimating the amount of RBCs and WBCs in a digital image sample (Mahmood and Mansor, 2012a,b).

The following year, Mahmood and colleagues using blood smear images automatically counted 10 cells. For this, the Hough transform methodology was used, where the results were compared with the conventional manual methodology (Mahmood and Mansor, 2012a,b). Still, in 2013, Mohammed conducted research with 140 digital images of blood cells related to ALL (acute lymphocytic leukemia). The images were converted to grayscale, and the cell nucleus segmentation was performed using the Otsu method, which is a grayscale delimitation method. Thus, through the dark coloration of the nucleus, its detection was possible compared to the surrounding components (Mohammed et al., 2013).

In 2014, G. Usha Rani and Sumeet Chourasiya, using the techniques of Hough and watershed transforms, managed to improve an image by reducing noise. Thus, it was concluded that the accuracy of the proposed algorithm used is dependent on the camera (optical instrument) used and the size of the objects to be captured (Chourasiya and Rani, 2014). At the beginning of 2015, Nasreen and researchers employed in RGB format digital images containing blood cells. Image segmentation was performed in grayscale using the "Graytresh" function in Matlab. The Otsu method was used in this function, choosing the threshold minimizing the classes between black and white pixel variance. Blood cell detection was made by the Hough transform finding circles in images (Nasreen et al., 2015).

The following year, Sahastrabuddhe and colleagues conducted a study of five patients in which digital images of RBCs and WBCs present in blood smears were captured. Digital image processing in RGB format was performed, and the image segmentation was made through the Hough circular transform, for what was responsible for the erythrocytes count, with the result expressed through the highest count found. Leukocytes were counted through morphologic operations (Sahastrabuddhe and Ajij, 2016).

In 2017, Ghane and colleagues segmented leukocytes by grouping the modified k-means and watershed techniques. The study has three stages: (1) leukocyte segmentation from a microscopic image, (2) cell image nucleus extraction, and (3) overlapping cell and nucleus separation (Ghane et al., 2017).

8. Leukemia

Leukemia is a malignant disease of WBCs. Its main feature is the increase and the concentration of diseased cells in the bone marrow replacing normal and healthy blood cells. Bone marrow (or just marrow) is located inside long bones and is responsible for the synthesis of new blood cells. Leukemia can be understood as the process where a blood cell that has not yet reached maturity (blasts) undergoes a genetic mutation that turns it into a cancer cell. This abnormal cell does not function properly, multiplies faster, and has changed apoptosis rates. In this way, healthy bone marrow blood cells are replaced by abnormal cancer cells. The causes of leukemia are not yet defined, but it is suspected that certain factors are related with a high risk of developing several specific types of the disease, such as smoking, family history, and exposure to benzene, formaldehyde, pesticides, and ionizing radiation, among others (Silberstein and John, 2017; Jaffe et al., 2016; Xu, 2019).

Decreased erythrocytes cause anemia, the symptoms of which include fatigue, shortness of breath, palpitation, and headache, among others. Reduction in WBCs causes low immunity, leaving the body more prone to often severe or recurrent infections. Decreased platelets cause bleeding, the most common being gums and nose, and bruising and/or petechiae on the skin (Silberstein and John, 2017; Jaffe et al., 2016).

The patient may develop swollen but painless lymph nodes, particularly in the armpits and neck; fever or night sweats; abdominal discomfort that is caused by swelling of the liver or spleen; weight loss for no apparent reason; and bone and joint pain. If the disease affects the central nervous system, headaches, disorientation, vomiting, nausea, and double vision may develop. Once the disease has set in, the disease progresses rapidly, requiring treatment to be started soon after diagnosis and classification (Silberstein and John, 2017).

There are over 12 types of leukemia, the four primary ones being CML (chronic myeloid leukemia), which in general affects mainly adults, AML (acute myeloid leukemia), which in general, affects both adults and children, CLL (chronic lymphocytic leukemia), which usually does not show symptoms (it is more frequent after 55 years), and ALL, which is the most common type of leukemia in children, though it also affects adults. Many studies have examined the role of risk factors in AML and ALL. Leukemias can be divided into two large groups: chronic leukemias and acute leukemias. Chronic leukemias are characterized by the fact that early in the disease, leukemic cells are still able to do some work on normal WBCs. Doctors usually discover the disease during a routine blood test. Slowly, chronic leukemia becomes worse. As the amount of leukemic cells is increasing, lymph node swelling (infections) or infections appear. When they appear, the symptoms are mild, but they gradually get worse. In turn, in acute, leukemic cells cannot do any work of normal blood cells. The number of leukemic cells grows rapidly, and the disease gets worse in a short time (Bernard et al., 2017).

Leukemias can also be grouped based on the types of WBCs they affect lymphoid or myeloid. Those that afflict lymphoid cells are known as lymphoid, lymphoblastic, or lymphocytic cells. Leukemia that afflicts myeloid cells is known as myeloid or myeloblastic (Jaffe et al., 2016; Hiddemann, 2016).

Chronic lymphoid leukemia develops slowly, affecting lymphoid cells. Most people over 55 years old are diagnosed with this type. It is rare to find cases in children. The CML harms myeloid cells, developing slowly at first. It particularly affects adults. The ALL afflicts lymphoid cells and gets worse rapidly. It is commonly found in cases in young children, but it also occurs in adults. The AML afflicts the myeloid cells and advances rapidly. It afflicts both adults and children, but the incidence increases with increasing age (Bernard et al., 2017; Schramm et al., 2018).

Treatment is based on chemotherapy, which focuses on destroying leukemia cells, so the bone marrow has the possibility of producing normal cells naturally again. According to the National Cancer Institute (INCA), there are 257,000 new cases of leukemia per year worldwide, of which about 56% occurs in men. The highest occurrence rates are found in New Zealand, Australia, and North America. The number of new cases of leukemia has been increasing especially in older people. Childhood cancer is the most common leukemia, ranging from 25% to 35% of cases. However, early diagnosis of this condition may increase the patient's chances of cure by up to 80% (Jaffe et al., 2016; Xu, 2019).

In the face of all these aspects, the present study proposes to develop a low-cost methodology for recognition and detection of RBCs, leukocytes, platelets, and blasts in digital blood smear images. This methodology is based on digital image processing techniques. By reducing the cost of methodology, disadvantaged populations may have an early diagnosis of several diseases, including leukemia.

9. Methodology

In the Matlab 2014a simulation software environment, a hybrid digital blood smear segmentation algorithm was developed. Matlab is short for "matrix laboratory" While other computational languages work mainly as numbers one at a time, Matlab is able to operate on all arrays and commands. All Matlab variables are multidirectional commands, regardless of the data type under analysis. An array is a two-dimensional command often used for linear algebra (Moore, 2017; Higham and Higham, 2016).

Matlab's applicability in the applicable area of digital image processing is an extensive configuration of multidimensional array processing functions of each image (two-dimensional numeric arrangements), with easy-to-use functions coupled with an expressive programming language, and it produces easy image processing processes for compact and clear writing, thus providing optimal software prototyping for image processing problems (Higham and Higham, 2016; Kwon and Bang, 2018).

This developed algorithm is based on ideas from the watershed transform, Hough transform, and morphologic operations methodologies. Thus, it was named WHT-MO. First, 12 open access database images respective to blood smear images involving nonpathologic RBCs are used, and leukocytes and platelets are selected on open access platforms. Subsequently, these images are sent to the Matlab Integrated Development Environment software, where they undergo a preprocessing process, aiming to correct problems related to brightness, contrast, and sharpness.

This image then goes through the process of morphologic operations, constituting a vast join of digital image processing procedures concerning the shape of binary images, consisting of the consecutive steps of opening, erosion, closure, dilation, and reconstruction. Dilatation adds pixels with relation to the edges of objects present in a digital image, repairing breaks or likely intrusive elements. Erosion respective to the removal of pixels from the edges of the digital image is used to split linked objects or even remove extrusions. Erosion and dilation are responsible for replacing the image value f in one pixel $(x; y)$ with the very smallest (supreme) value relative to f in relation to structuring element B (B', which is a reflection of its own B around the origin), resulting in "expansion" of the image. The opening is applied for eliminating protrusions. The closure is used to blend long, thin spaces, fill in contour spaces, eliminate small holes, and smooth outlines. The reconstruction is tasked with extracting significant information related to existing shapes in the image. Thus, morphologic operations are responsible for creating a mask over the original image and removing all morphologically resembling pixels with leukocytes, in full maturation state. Counts results were released separately. The leukocytes quantified in this step include both normal and blast cells, which are leukemia indicative cells.

This image goes through the action of the transformed watershed. This technique was inspired by nature, being introduced to digital imaging science by Digabel and Lantuéjoul, and later called watershed transform, where it was used by Beucher and Lantuéjoul with the same objective of identifying regions on a surface, detecting their contours. These introductory proposals, along with work on morphologic segmentation by Meyer and Beucher, established the use of the watershed transform. The main advantages of watershed transform segmentation are (1) the results are regions connected as closed boundaries of a single-pixel type, (2) the boundary regions adhere well to the actual object boundaries, and (3) the combination of regions produced by the watershed segmentation is equal to the whole image (Russ, 2016; Cousty, 2018). In this context, transform watershed was employed in digital blood smear images with the task of detecting erythrocytes, being responsible for recognizing sets of pixels that have similar aspects to the staining and size of erythrocytes. After detection, each red-colored cell is labeled with a number according to the counting order.

Finally, the same image is segmented by the Hough transform. This methodology recognizes if a specific shape is located in the digital image. It is necessary to be grouped around the parameter values that correspond to that shape, so the mapping of every point in the parameter space is done, where parametric shapes of the digital image are identified through accumulated points in the relative parameter space, performed by scattered approach maps and respective disjoint elements to this image locating point agglomeration, initiated by P.V.C. Hough in 1962 (Monteiro et al., 2018; Wani and Raza, 2018). Thus, the platelet detection is done by Hough transform, which detects the border points in each cell by drawing the circle with relation to radius and origin, as well as using the three-dimensional matrix, having the initial two dimensions employed representing the coordinates of the matrix. This increases following the ratio in which every instant the circle is drawn around the radii on each edge point it has together an appropriate accumulator.

Finally, erythrocytes, leukocyte, and platelet counts have their counting results released separately. The logic of the WHT-MO algorithm can be seen in Fig. 18.1.

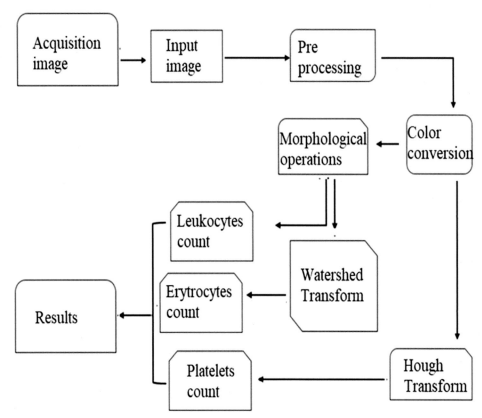

FIGURE 18.1 Algorithm WHT-MO logical representation.

10. Results and discussion

After image processing by the WHT-MO algorithm, numeric results are released as well as images of the cell counting processes, as shown in Figs. 18.2—18.5. These images, besides demonstrating the methodology functioning, can be used as a parameter data veracity analysis.

As stated earlier, 12 digital images (samples) of blood smear fields were used. These images have 1836 erythrocytes (RBC), 20 leukocytes (WBC), and 145 platelets per field. Open access platform images were manually counted with platelets, erythrocytes, and leukocytes by a biomedical professional (Fig. 18.6). Subsequently, to verify the accuracy of the WTH-MO algorithm, the obtained values were counted by the proposed methodology (Fig. 18.7). The same process was performed for the detection, identification, and count of immature leukocytes, as shown in Fig. 18.8.

The comparison of the results showed an accuracy of 100% for erythrocytes, 90% for mature leukocytes and platelets, and 91.7% for immature leukocytes (blasts) in the WHT-MO methodology. Platelet accuracy is justified by the presence of macro- and microplatelets present in the images. Chips tend to measure less than 1.5 μm, and macroplatelets have a diameter greater than 3 μm in diameter. Therefore, they do not fit the normal parameters stipulated in the WHT-MO algorithm. The accuracy of 91.7% is due to the fact that blasts naturally have very distinct morphologic characteristics per se depending on the lineage they represent. Such characteristics can be seen in variations in color, chromatin presentation, shape, and nucleus—cytoplasm relationship.

It can be observed that the research by Arivu Selvan and Moorthy (2012) and Sahastrabuddhe and Ajij (2016) presented accuracy values of 75% and 87%, respectively. Thus, the WHT-MO algorithm has a higher accuracy of 16.7% and 4.7%, respectively. The accuracy of a methodology is a key factor in clinical analysis, as it ensures that reports are issued correctly. Wrong reports can subject patients to inadequate treatment or neglect treatment they need. This performs harm to the health of patients and laboratories, which may be held liable for their errors.

Another very important factor for medical examinations is the time. In this context, the time taken for the simultaneous counting of RBCs, leukocytes, and platelets was accounted for by the *cputime* function. This function is in charge of measuring the processing time of each sample, i.e., determining how many seconds it takes for the variables to be allocated at the time of the first simulation. Fig. 18.9 shows the processing times of the WHT-MO methodology for the recognition and detection of mature blood cells, while the processing time measurement of immature leukocyte images is shown in Fig. 18.10.

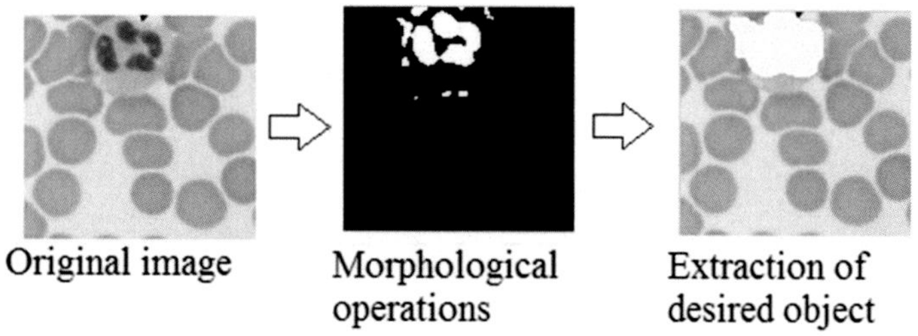

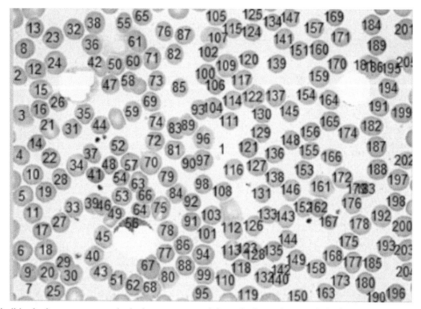

FIGURE 18.2 Leukocyte detection by morphologic operations.

FIGURE 18.3 The "holes" in the image represent the leukocytes removed from the image by morphologic operations. Erythrocytes are labeled by the watershed transform.

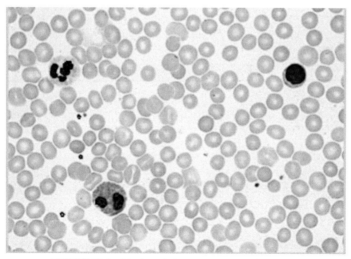

FIGURE 18.4 Platelets circled by the transformed Hough.

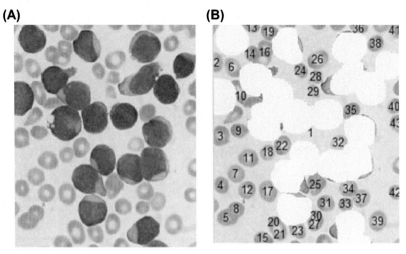

FIGURE 18.5 Segmentation by the WT-MO algorithm: (A) original image and (B) segmented image.

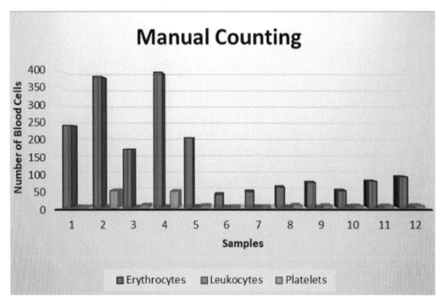

FIGURE 18.6 Manual counting in blood smear images by a biomedical professional.

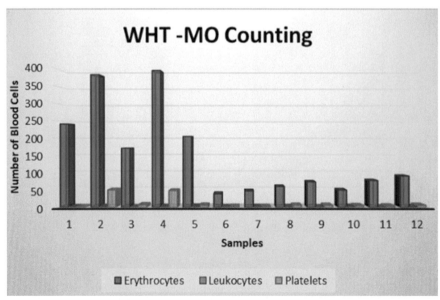

FIGURE 18.7 Blood cell count by the WHT-MO algorithm.

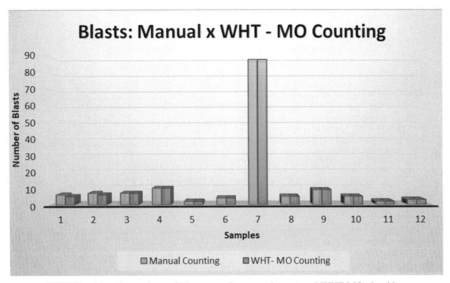

FIGURE 18.8 Comparison of blast count by manual count and WHT-MO algorithm.

The WHT-MO algorithm had an average processing time equivalent to 7.35 s on an Intel Core i3 computer with 4 GB RAM. This hardware was chosen because it is one of the most available on the market and most affordable. The shorter the processing time of an image is, the greater is the number of exams per hour, the greater the number of people per day, and the faster the referral to appropriate treatments.

In addition, the faster a diagnosis of leukemia is made, the soonest the patient can be related to more specific hematologic exams that help classify the leukemia subtype as well as the most appropriate type of treatment. Speed in pathology detection, as well as early initiation of treatment, directly impacts cure rate success.

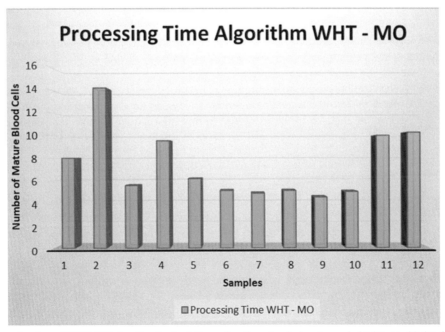

FIGURE 18.9 Processing time of WHT-MO algorithm in simulations of erythrocytes, leukocytes, and platelets considering full maturation phase.

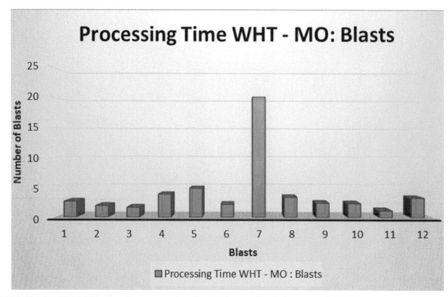

FIGURE 18.10 WHT-MO algorithm processing time in image simulations containing immature leukocytes (blasts).

11. Research and future development

As a future development, aiming at the application of this algorithm on large scale, the identification of the handled samples will be done sequentially through the entry of data in a database, with the logic of correspondence between the sample and the patient's data.

Since in a sequential file the items are organized in such a way to access a particular record, they are stored according to the order of insertion, which is important due to the time taken for the exam for control purposes and medical monitoring. In this sense, the sequence of the file can be based on the ordering through some key, i.e., a field or a combination of fields, still relating the simplicity of the respective application to implementations of basic operations, i.e., low programming complexity.

For the purpose of preventing a mismatch with other patient data, in the same way, it will be possible to search for all the results achieved by a given patient, stimulating e-health (digital health), which is a more comprehensive concept that deals with several digital solutions that aim to improve people's health and quality of life from the perspective of using digital patient data.

As well as encouraging the development of mHealth (mobile health), these are health practices carried out using mobile devices such as smartphones, digital assistants, and monitoring devices, as the most common means that connect doctors and patients. From the perspective that the patient can receive this information through text messages, e-mails, secure portals, instant messages, or chat, it eliminates the need to schedule follow-up visits or consultations in the office.

12. Conclusions

The purpose of translational medicine is, therefore, to accelerate this long road that aims at structuring interdisciplinary and multidisciplinary medical research groups, in which naturally there is a collaboration between the basic area and the professional, clinical, surgical, or epidemiologic areas, all with a focus on the development of new technologies applied to health.

Translational medicine seeks to promote interdisciplinarity and accelerate the bidirectional exchange between basic science and clinical science to translocate basic laboratory research findings to employed environments encompassing patients and populations.

Bioinformatics, unlike traditional biology studies, uses quantitative measures, which have allowed mathematics, computing, and engineering to build models that help explain molecular phenomena, for example. It is a branch of science that aims at grouping, interpreting, and elucidating biologic events through the organization and understanding of data and information based on the use of tools from biology, computing, mathematics, and related areas.

The performance of bioinformatics is an interdisciplinary sphere arising from the amount of biologic data obtained, organization of that information, and the extraction and abstraction of knowledge from this mass of data, making it possible to distinguish, classify, and segment data, as in the case of this research.

Applying engineering techniques to medical fields has shown increasingly promising results. An example of this is the WHT-MO methodology that meets the main requirements necessary for the realization and implementation of a medical methodology: accuracy and time. Thus, this technique can be used in laboratories in underdeveloped as well as in developed countries. For underprivileged populations, WHT-MO can replace high-cost equipment, while in developed countries, it can be used as a confirmatory tool for hematologic reports released by conventional hematologic equipment. This will have a positive impact on both the detection of easily treated diseases and leukemias. Thus, it is expected that patients with access to a low-cost quality medical examination will have faster and more accurate diagnoses, which will have a positive impact on their lives. After all, early diagnosis has a greater chance of cure as well as impacts on reducing adult and child mortality.

Future work will involve the detection of pathologic aspects related to erythrocytes, leukocytes, and platelets through deep learning tinctures, as well as the development of a graphical and independent Matlab software interface, which will facilitate the use of the methodology by medical professionals.

References

Albani, S., Prakken, B., 2009. The advancement of translational medicine—from regional challenges to global solutions. Nat. Med. 15 (9), 1006—1009.

Arivu Selvan, K., Moorthy, S., 2012. Analyzing blood cell images to differentiate WBC and counting of linear & non-linear overlapping RBC based on morphological features. Elixir Comp. Sci. & Engg. 48, 9410—9413.

Bajaj, L., Gupta, K., Hasija, Y., 2018. Image processing in biomedical science. In: Advances in Soft Computing and Machine Learning in Image Processing. Springer, Cham, pp. 185—211.

Barile, S., Polese, F., Saviano, M., Carrubbo, L., 2017. Service innovation in translational medicine. In: Innovating in Practice. Springer, Cham, pp. 417—438.

Baxevanis, A.D., Bader, G.D., Wishart, D.S. (Eds.), 2020. Bioinformatics. John Wiley & Sons.

Bernard, S.C., et al., 2017. Pediatric leukemia: diagnosis to treatment—a review. J. Cancer Clin. Trials 2 (2), 1.

Borges Monteiro, A.C., Iano, Y., França, R.P., Arthur, R., 2019. Medical-laboratory algorithm WTH-MO for segmentation of digital images of blood cells: a new methodology for making hemograms. Int. J. Simul. Syst. 20. Science & Technology.

Campbell-Kelly, M., 2018. Computer, Student Economy Edition: A History of the Information Machine. Routledge.

Chourasiya, S., Rani, U., 2014. Automatic red blood cell counting using watershed segmentation. (IJCSIT) Int. J. Comput. Sci. & Inf. Technol. 5 (4), 4834—4838.

Ciesla, B., 2018. Hematology in Practice. FA Davis.

Collen, M.F., Ball, M.J., 2015. In: The History of Medical Informatics in the United States. Springer.

Cousty, J., 2018. Segmentation, Hierarchy, Mathematical Morphology Filtering, and Application to Image Analysis. Diss.

Dubey, A., et al., 2018. A detailed study of digital image processing. IIOAB J. 9 (2), 33—42.

Felfly, H., Haddad, G.G., 2014. Hematopoietic stem cells: potential new applications for translational medicine. J. Stem Cell. 9 (3), 163.

Figueiredo, G.L.A., et al., 2017. Right to the city, right to health: what are the interconnections? Ciên. Saúde Colet. 22 (12), 3821—3830.

Ghane, N., Vard, A., Talebi, A., Nematollahy, P., 2017. Segmentation of white blood cells from microscopic images using a novel combination of K-means clustering and modified watershed algorithm. J. Med. Sign. & Sens. 7 (2), 92—101.

Green, R., Wachsmann-Hogiu, S., 2015. Development, history, and future of automated cell counters. Clin. Lab. Med. 35 (1), 1—10.

Guo, X., Liu, J., 2018. Basic concept of translational medicine. In: Atlantoaxial Fixation Techniques. Springer, Singapore, pp. 33—36.

Haigh, T., et al., 2016. ENIAC in Action: Making and Remaking the Modern Computer. MIT Press.

Hiddemann, W., 2016. Handbook of Acute Leukemia. Springer International Publishing.

Higham, D.J., Higham, N.J., 2016. MATLAB Guide, vol. 150. Siam.

Hsu, H.Y., Hwang, P.A., 2019. Clinical applications of fucoidan in translational medicine for adjuvant cancer therapy. Clin. Transl. Med. 8 (1), 15.

Jaffe, E.S., et al., 2016. Hematopathology E-Book. Elsevier Health Sciences.

Kareem, S., Morling, R.C.S., Kale, I., 2011. A Novel Method to Count the Red Blood Cells in Thin Blood Films, 978 -1-4244- 9474-3/11©2011 IEEE.

Keohane, E.M., Otto, C.N., Walenga, J.M., 2019. Rodak's Hematology-E-Book: Clinical Principles and Applications. Elsevier Health Sciences.

Kurpinski, K., Johnson, T., Kumar, S., Desai, T., Li, S., 2014. Mastering translational medicine: interdisciplinary education for a new generation. Sci. Transl. Med. 6 (218), 218fs2.

Kwon, Y.W., Bang, H., 2018. The Finite Element Method Using MATLAB. CRC Press.

Lamb, J.A., Curtin, J.A., 2019. Translational medicine: insights from interdisciplinary graduate research training. Trends Biotechnol. 37 (3), 227—230.

Lesk, A., 2019. Introduction to Bioinformatics. Oxford university press.

Littman, B.H., Di Mario, L., Plebani, M., Marincola, F.M., 2007. What's next in translational medicine? Clin. Sci. 112 (4), 217—227.

Mahmood, N.H., Mansor, M.A., 2012a. Red blood cells estimation using hough transform technique. Int. J. 3 (2).

Mahmood, N.H., Mansor, M.A., April 2012b. Red blood cells estimation using hough transform technique. Sign. & Image Proc. Int. J. 3 (2).

Malley, R., 2018. Introduction of new journal section—translational medicine. Pediatr. Infect. Dis. J. 37 (11), 1175.

Matthews, P.M., Honey, G.D., Bullmore, E.T., 2006. Applications of fMRI in translational medicine and clinical practice. Nat. Rev. Neurosci. 7 (9), 732—744.

McCarthy, J.J., McLeod, H.L., Ginsburg, G.S., 2013. Genomic medicine: a decade of successes, challenges, and opportunities. Sci. Transl. Med. 5 (189), 189sr4-189sr4.

McPherson, R.A., Pincus, M.R., 2017. Henry's Clinical Diagnosis and Management by Laboratory Methods E-Book. Elsevier Health Sciences.

Mediouni, M., Schlatterer, D.R., Madry, H., Cucchiarini, M., Rai, B., 2018. A review of translational medicine. The future paradigm: how can we connect the orthopedic dots better? Curr. Med. Res. Opin. 34 (7), 1217—1229.

Meyers, R.A. (Ed.), 2018. Translational Medicine: Molecular Pharmacology and Drug Discovery. John Wiley & Sons.

Min, S., Lee, B., Yoon, S., 2017. Deep learning in bioinformatics. Briefings Bioinf. 18 (5), 851—869.

Mitchell, P., 2016. From Concept to Classroom: What Is Translational Research?.

Mohammed, E.A., et al., 2013. Chronic lymphocytic leukemia cell segmentation from microscopic blood images using watershed algorithm and optimal thresholding. In: 26th IEEE Canadian Conference of Electrical and Computer Engineering (CCECE).

Monteiro, A.C.B., et al., 2018. A comparative study between methodologies based on the hough transform and watershed transform on the blood cell count. In: Brazilian Technology Symposium. Springer, Cham.

Monteiro, A.C.B., et al., 2019. WT-MO algorithm: automated hematological software based on the watershed transform for blood cell count. In: Applications of Image Processing and Soft Computing Systems in Agriculture. IGI Global, pp. 39—79.

Monteiro, A.C.B., Iano, Y., França, R.P., December 2017. Detecting and counting of blood cells using watershed transform: an improved methodology. In: Brazilian Technology Symposium. Springer, Cham, pp. 301—310.

Moore, H., 2017. MATLAB for Engineers. Pearson.

Nasreen, N., Kumar, C., Nabeel, A.P., 2015. Counting of RBC using circular hough transform with median filtering. The Third National Conference on Emerging Trends in Engineering (NET 2015). Bonfring, GEC Kozhikode, pp. 150—153. ISBN 978-93-85477-33-1.

Nelson, R., Staggers, N., 2016. Health Informatics-E-Book: An Interprofessional Approach. Elsevier Health Sciences.

Nicholls, M., 2019. Sir Godfrey Newbold Hounsfield and Allan M. Cormack., pp. 2101—2103.

Piccini, J.P., Whellan, D.J., Berridge, B.R., Finkle, J.K., Pettit, S.D., Stockbridge, N., et al., 2009. Current challenges in the evaluation of cardiac safety during drug development: translational medicine meets the critical path initiative. Am. Heart J. 158 (3), 317—326.

Plebani, M., 2008. The changing scenario in laboratory medicine and the role of laboratory professionals in translational medicine. Clin. Chim. Acta 393 (1), 23—26.

Pucker, B., Schilbert, H.M., Schumacher, S.F., 2019. Integrating molecular biology and bioinformatics education. J. Integr. Bioinform. 16 (3).

Qiu, X., et al., 2018. Microfluidic channel optimization to improve hydrodynamic dissociation of cell aggregates and tissue. Sci. Rep. 8 (1), 2774.

Reisman, S., et al., 2018. Biomedical Engineering Principles. CRC Press.

Russ, J.C., 2016. The Image Processing Handbook. CRC Press.

Sahastrabuddhe, A.P., Ajij, S.D., October 2016. Blood group detection and RBC, WBC counting: an image processing approach. Int. J. Eng. and Comput. Sci. ISSN: 2319-7242 5 (10), 18635—18639.

Schramm, M., et al., 2018. Infant acute leukemia—clinical, imunophenotypic and molecular profile of patients treated at instituto nacional de Câncer—INCA, a single center in Brazil. Clin. Lymphoma Myeloma & Leukemia 18.

Seeram, E., 2015. Computed Tomography-E-Book: Physical Principles, Clinical Applications, and Quality Control. Elsevier Health Sciences.

Sehgal, S.A., Tahir, R.A., Mirza, A.H., Mir, A., 2018. Introduction to Structural Bioinformatics.

Shih, Frank, Y., 2017. Image Processing and Mathematical Morphology: Fundamentals and Applications. CRC Press.

Silberstein, L.E., John, A., 2017. Hematology: Basic Principles and Practice E-Book: Basic Principles and Practice. Elsevier Health Sciences.

Sliney, D.H., 2016. What is light? The visible spectrum and beyond. Eye 30 (2), 222.

Soldner, F., Jaenisch, R., 2018. Stem cells, genome editing, and the path to translational medicine. Cell 175 (3), 615—632.

Terzic, A., Waldman, S.A., 2010. Translational medicine: path to personalized and public health. Biomarkers Med. 4 (6), 787—790.

Wani, N., Raza, K., 2018. Multiple kernel learning approach for medical image analysis. In: Soft Computing Based Medical Image Analysis. Elsevier, pp. 31—47. https://doi.org/10.1016/B978-0-12-813087-2.00002-6.

Watts, J., 2016. Brazil's health system woes worsen in economic crisis. Lancet 387 (10028), 1603—1604.

Wei, D.Q., Ma, Y., Cho, W.C., Xu, Q., Zhou, F. (Eds.), 2017. Translational Bioinformatics and its Application. Springer.

Wooller, S.K., Benstead-Hume, G., Chen, X., Ali, Y., Pearl, F.M., 2017. Bioinformatics in translational drug discovery. Biosci. Rep. 37 (4).

Xia, X., 2018. Bioinformatics and the Cell: Modern Computational Approaches in Genomics, Proteomics and Transcriptomics. Springer.

Xu, Y., et al., 2016. A review of impedance measurements of whole cells. Biosens. Bioelectron. 77, 824—836.

Xu, M.L. (Ed.), 2019. Hematopathology E-Book, Vol. 12. Elsevier Health Sciences. No. 3.

Index

Printed in the United States
by Baker & Taylor Publisher Services